India in the World since 1947

Andreas Hilger / Corinna R. Unger
(eds.)

India in the World since 1947

National and Transnational Perspectives

PETER LANG
Frankfurt am Main · Berlin · Bern · Bruxelles · New York · Oxford · Wien

Bibliographic Information published by the Deutsche Nationalbibliothek
The Deutsche Nationalbibliothek lists this publication in the Deutsche Nationalbibliografie; detailed bibliographic data is available in the internet at http://dnb.d-nb.de.

Cover Design:
© Olaf Gloeckler, Atelier Platen, Friedberg

ISBN 978-3-631-61178-4

www.peterlang.de

We would like to express our gratitude to several colleagues who have supported this project. Christopher Shaw, Craig Taylor, and Valentina Ramona de Jesus Uribe provided much-appreciated help with language editing, copy editing, and formatting. Arnold Kegebein offered invaluable technical support. We would also like to thank the Hamburg office of Peter Lang Publishers for their attentive and reliable cooperation in putting this volume into print.

Table of Contents

Introduction: India in the World since 1947

Andreas Hilger – Corinna R. Unger

In recent years, "India" has become a favorite metaphor to describe developments and phenomena considered characteristic of "globalization." Rapid economic and population growth, environmental degradation, geostrategic rivalries, megacities, global cultural production: India has it all. Accordingly, India receives much coverage in the media, and comparisons and contrasts with China abound. Yet the excitement about contemporary and future developments in India has produced surprisingly little interest in the historical background of the processes we are observing today. Historians of independent India – both in India and elsewhere – have continued either to focus on diplomatic problems or to situate their studies squarely in the nation state. The transnational turn does not seem to have caught the attention of many historians of contemporary India. We believe, however, that a transnational perspective on the 65 years of India's independence has much to offer and some to add to existing studies. Our argument is based on the observation that India has a rich history of transnational connections and exchanges, and that it is important to contextualize India's current developments in its transnational history. Much of what has been happening in the past twenty years has roots which reach back much farther. Only if we study India in the world since 1947 can we understand India in the world today and tomorrow.

Obviously, starting our account with 1947 is based on a pragmatic decision. South Asia and, in later years, the Indian Raj, had a long history of transnational connections and exchanges. Trade, scholarly, religious, and artistic exchanges, and colonialism had contributed to a specific mixture of regionalisms and cosmopolitanism in India. When India became independent in 1947, it did not suddenly become a full-fledged, well-defined, uncontested or unambiguous nation state. In its twisted transformation into a nation state, many of India's transnational ties and interdependencies stayed alive, others were replaced by new ones, some of them diplomatic, others economic, cultural, or religious. Diplomatically, the Cold War situation demanded that India position itself in the world; its representatives, led by Nehru, chose non-alignment and established close relations with countries belonging to the Global South. India also secured a visible position in international forums like the United Nations. Within Asia, India played an important strategic and political role, especially vis-à-vis the People's Republic of China. On the economic level, independent India tried to overcome its economic dependence on Great Britain and the other industrialized nations through a policy of import-substitution industrialization. Yet to close the largest gaps in food, money, and technology, India had to ask for and accept economic and technical aid from the First and the Second Worlds; hence, new forms of economic dependence evolved. Socially, independent India had to come to terms with the co-existence of multiple ethnic, religious and linguistic groups, many of which felt (more) loyal to groups outside India's national borders than to New Delhi. For centuries, Indians had migrated to other parts of the world; in the second half of the twentieth century, new, faster communication technologies fostered multidirectional flows of cultural goods and ideas, religious practices, and other exchanges.

The emphasis on India's transnational entanglements is not to suggest that the Indian nation state did not matter in the years after 1947. Undoubtedly, the new leadership wanted the state to play a decisive role in most aspects of Indian life in the post-independence period: In the view of the ruling elites under Nehru and his successors, the majestic tasks independent India faced since 1947 – creating a national identity, providing for a comprehensive and broadly accepted national vision, promoting India's economic and social development, and securing its national independence – could not be realized without a strong nation state. Hence, one could argue that India's post-independence history was characterized by the simultaneity of national and transnational processes, some of which fueled each other while others produced tensions.

To study the interplay between national and transnational trends and developments, we propose to rely on four analytical, interdependent categories: Identities, ideas, resources, and power. In our understanding, those categories can be useful in trying to gain insight into the complex and multifaceted spheres of negotiations, interactions, and competitive situations which characterized India since 1947, and which have contributed to shaping India as we observe it today.

The question of what kind of national, regional, and cultural identity would be possible and appropriate for as complex and heterogeneous a society as India's has occupied scholars and politicians for decades. Holding together the newly created Indian state became one of the central challenges for the Nehru government in the post-1947 years. Should, and could, India decide on a national religion, a national language, a national identity? Was it possible, under the impact of the violent partition of the Indian subcontinent, to create a sense of commonality that bridged the divisions between Hindus and Muslims, between regional cultures, between castes and languages? *William Gould's* discussion of Indian secularism and the positions and strategies of Muslims in India before and after independence highlights the relevance of religious divisions in Indian politics and the imprints left on Indian society by the colonial era. Under these circumstances, did minority policies have the potential to overcome differences within the new nation? Who was going to be left out by these policies, and what kind of consequences would the Indian state be faced with as a result? The linguistic secessionism India experienced in the years and decades following independence, and the measures the Indian government used to prevent a break-up of the union, which *Nicolas Blarel* describes in his essay, provide insight into both the possibilities and the limitations of the Indian state in tackling problems arising from cultural diversity and political competition. Similarly, radical political ideas and groups worked to undermine the hegemony of Nehru's Congress Party. In the eyes of Delhi, the presence and demands of the Communist Party, which held close ties to Moscow, challenged India's political sovereignty, most famously in the cases of Telengana and Kerala, as the contribution by *Vijay Singh* illustrates.

While heavily occupied with a range of domestic problems, India at the same time had to position itself within Asia and define its role as an Asian nation. As *Manjeet Pardesi* demonstrates, the tense relationship with China and Pakistan shaped India's foreign and security policies to a remarkable degree. Under the conditions defined by Sino-Indian rivalry, the build-up of the Indian military presented an attempt to overcome the structural limitations imposed on Indian foreign policy and to anchor and expand India's influence on the continent. India also tried to establish itself as an international player. Its leading role in the non-aligned movement, and Nehru's prominence in many Third World nations, served this goal well. In fact, *Jennifer Bussell* argues that India's democratic strength was due in large part to Nehru's successful foreign policy based on the strategy of non-alignment. Yet even a self-confident, proudly non-aligned India could not escape the Cold War struggle and the influence of the United States. *Robert McMahon* provides an overview of this complicated relationship. It is complemented by *Srinath Raghavan's* exploration of the Indo-Soviet Treaty of 1971, which reflected Indira Gandhi's attempt to secure and stabilize India's regional interests and identity at a time when South and Southeast Asia were in turmoil. In those years, Europe might have seemed far away, but, as *Amit Das Gupta* shows with his analysis of diplomatic relations between New Delhi, East Berlin, and Bonn, Indian politicians closely followed European developments and tried to identify situations which could serve India's interests in building a reputation as a serious and reliable actor.

Yet it would be shortsighted to look only at India in trying to understand how Indian identities evolved in the years after 1947. Indian diasporas in different parts of the world participated in and contributed to the process, while at the same time rendering the question of what "being Indian" meant ever more complex, as *Sunil Bhatia* and *Anjali Ram* investigate in their essay. The media played an important role in this context. Whereas Bollywood movies are often considered an effort in Indian self-marketing abroad, the role those productions play for Indian diasporas in keeping a sense of commonality and ties to India alive should not be underestimated. Generally, the role and the presence of the media shaped Indian society and mirrored its political and cultural development at the same time. *Nadja-Christina Schneider*, in discussing the "medialization" of Indian society, argues that the pedagogical role the media played in Indian public life in the 1950s and 1960s, particularly their support of the national goal of "development," slowly but surely made way for more market-oriented media practices and for programs (especially on television) which promoted an image of Indian "modernity" intimately tied to consumerism.

The construction of the Delhi Metro and the building of the city of Chandigarh are perhaps the most famous and most visible expressions of the effort to create and present – to Indians and to the world – a "modern India." As we learn from *Michael Mann's* history of the Delhi Metro, the roots of independent India's infrastructure policies and programs reach back far into the colonial era. Urbanization, while largely unplanned by the British, became a priority of the new India. By drawing on the prestige of the French architect Le Corbusier and the ideas discussed by the Congrès Internationaux d'Architecture Moderne (CIAM) in the interwar period, Chandigarh, described here by *Boris Niclas-Tölle*, presented a distinct example of the transnational transfer and adaptation of ideas and practices in a postcolonial situation. Similarly, economists from a variety of countries traveled to India in the postwar years to study the Indian economy – a singular opportunity to test new methods – and offer advice to the Delhi government on economic policy issues. Many members of the Indian administration were not very eager to receive advice, but Indian chief planner Mahalanobis used the presence of international experts to gain legitimacy for his development strategy of rapid industrialization, *David Engerman* argues. In highlighting the nexus between Indian economic development and international prestige, one can draw a parallel to India's eagerness to become a nuclear power, which *Hans-Joachim Bieber* portrays in his essay. Producing sufficient amounts of cheap energy was a precondition for India to industrialize, while proving that Indian scientists, with the support of know-how from abroad, were able to master nuclear technology would, Indian politicians hoped, end once and for all debates about India being "backward."

Generally, economic problems loomed large over India in the post-1947 years and, in the perception of many Indians, seriously inhibited their country's aspirations. Resource scarcity was one problem. Another was the predominance of agriculture and the question of how to provide employment for millions of formally unskilled laborers in an industrializing economy. In this situation, India's high population growth rate caused increasing concern among politicians, economists, and public health administrators in India and abroad. Conceptual continuities reaching back to the colonial period, as well as transnational actors, influenced independent India's family planning policies, according to *Mohan Rao*, whose contribution closes with a critical discussion of the privatization of Indian health services in the context of globalization. *Dietmar Rothermund's* essay probes deeper into the effects of globalization on the Indian economy by providing a detailed picture of India's past and present efforts to promote employment and curb unemployment.

Under the notably difficult circumstances characterizing the situation of India since 1947, many observers were, and are, honestly surprised that the Indian democracy has been able survive and grow stronger. The opening and liberalization of the Indian economy since the early 1990s have placed new pressure on Indian society, but also created possibilities for new developments. While we know, thanks to the essays contained in this volume, some about India's past, India's future appears wide open.

I. Identities

India in Asia: India's relations with Southeast Asia and China, 1962-1991

Manjeet S. Pardesi

Introduction

This paper aims to understand India's relations with China and its Southeast Asian neighbors in the period between the 1962 Sino-Indian War and the end of the Cold War in 1991. It will be argued that India's "tilt" towards the former Soviet Union, the closed nature of the Indian economy, and India's military interventions in its South Asian neighborhood led many (pro-Western) Southeast Asian states to view India as a threatening state for much of the Cold War period. Furthermore, the emergence of the China-Pakistan entente followed by a Chinese-Pakistani-American alignment meant that India's relations with China continued to remain limited but conflict-ridden during this period. It was not until 1988 that the stalemate in Sino-Indian relations was broken by Prime Minister Rajiv Gandhi's landmark trip to China, which took place at the time of Sino-Soviet rapprochement and the erosion of the Indo-Soviet partnership. This period also coincided with the growth of Indian military power. India's relations with Southeast Asia began to improve only after the end of the Cold War (and the Indo-Soviet partnership) and the opening up of the Indian economy in 1991.

India in Asia, 1947-1962

Jawaharlal Nehru, the first Prime Minister of India and the "founding architect"[1] of its foreign policy, vigorously opposed global military blocs and chose to safeguard the strategic autonomy of his newly independent state by pursuing a policy of non-alignment.[2] At the same time, an inchoate India-centered pan-Asianism was central to Nehru's approach to Asia. He was convinced that as a consequence of its actual and latent (potential) material power and due to its geostrategic location, India was bound to play a central role in Asian affairs. "It is well-recognized today all over the world that the future of Asia will be power-

1 Dixit, Makers of India's Foreign Policy; Raja Ram Mohun Roy, Letter to Yashwant Sinha, 77.

2 On India's policy of nonalignment, see Thomas, "Nonalignment and Indian Security: Nehru's Rationale and Legacy," 153-171.

fully determined by the future of India. India becomes more and more the *pivot of Asia*."[3]

In order to position itself at the center of Asian geopolitics, India undertook some very important foreign policy initiatives. Even before independence, Nehru authorized the Indian Council of World Affairs to organize an "unofficial" Asian Relations Conference (ARC) – the first gathering of Asian countries and colonial territories organized by an Asian state – in New Delhi.[4] India also played a leading diplomatic role in supporting the independence of Indonesia in the late 1940s. New Delhi even organized the Conference on Indonesia in New Delhi – the first conference led by an Asian government to deal with a specific issue in Asia – to promote the cause of Indonesia's independence.[5] Newly independent Burma, which was plagued with numerous insurgencies in the late 1940s, was the first foreign state to receive arms, ammunition, and transport planes from India as early as 1949.[6] India also played a very active diplomatic role in the decolonization of Indo-China in the early 1950s. The Geneva accord on Indo-China had established three International Commissions of Supervision and Control (ICSC) for Vietnam, Cambodia, and Laos. Each of these commissions was headed by an Indian chairman.[7]

On the eve of India's independence, Nehru had articulated an "Asian Monroe Doctrine," that was the complete disappearance of Western militaries from Asia, and for which cooperation with China was deemed essential.[8] Nehru believed that recognition of Tibetan independence would earn India permanent hostility from China, which would also have meant the end for Asia's recrudescence in world affairs, for which Sino-Indian cooperation was essential in Nehru's view. Consequently, Nehru's India discontinued its diplomatic relations with the Nationalist regime of Jiang Jieshi, and became one of the first non-

---

3 Nehru's address to India's Chief Ministers on 2 October 1949. Quoted in Gopal, Jawaharlal Nehru: A Biography, 59.

4 The ARC ran from 23 March 1947 through 12 April 1947. It was a gathering of over 200 delegates from 30 countries and colonial territories. See Appadorai, "The Asian Relations Conference in Perspective," 275-285.

5 This conference was attended by delegates from a total of 15 countries. Thien, India and South East Asia, 92-102.

6 On the Indian government's military and financial help to Burma, see Ton, India and South East Asia, 169-172.

7 For details, see Sardesai, Indian Foreign Policy in Cambodia, Laos, and Vietnam.

8 Nehru, "A Monroe Doctrine for Asia," August 9, 1947. For the full text, see Selected Works of Jawaharlal Nehru, Second Series, Volume III, 133-5.

communist states to recognize the People's Republic of China in late 1949.[9] Nehru accepted the "One China" policy and did not raise the issue of China's military annexation of Tibet in 1950-51 at the United Nations. In 1954, India and China signed the *Panchshila* agreement, in which India explicitly recognized Chinese sovereignty in Tibet.[10] Nehru's India also acted as mediator between China and the world during the Korean War (1950-53). After the Korean armistice was signed, India took over the task of chairing the commission for the repatriation of prisoners and agreed that Indian troops would be in charge of that process.[11] In 1955, with the complete backing of Nehru, Indonesia organized the Bandung Conference, an event during which Nehru's India introduced China and its Premier Zhou Enlai to the countries of Africa and Asia (and indeed the world).[12]

However, Sino-Indian relations deteriorated rapidly after China's brutal repression of the Tibetan uprising in 1959 and the escape of the Dalai Lama into exile in India on 30 March 1959, where he was granted refuge by the Nehru government. By this time, the Sino/Tibetan-Indian border issue had further soured relations.[13] China feared Indian expansionism (New Delhi's "forward policy" along their ill-defined borders) and believed that India wanted to restore Tibet's "buffer state" status between the two countries. The rising tension led to a short but bitter war between China and India in 1962, which India, whose forces were ill-prepared, lost.[14] China declared a unilateral ceasefire after restoring the *status quo ante* (pre-1959).[15] The meeting of the non-aligned states of Asia and Africa generated no public support for India during the 1962 Sino-Indian War.[16]

---

9 For details, see Panikkar, In Two Chinas: Memoirs of a Diplomat. Panikkar was India's last ambassador to Nationalist China and the first ambassador to Communist China.

10 Goldstein, A History of Modern Tibet, Volume 2, 464-477.

11 Heimsath, India's Role in the Korean War.

12 Mukherji, "Appraising the Legacy of Bandung: A View from India." Quoted in Tan and Acharya, Bandung Revisited: The Legacy of the 1955 Asian-African Conference for International Order, 160-179.

13 Ganguly, Sumit. "India and China: Border Issues, Domestic Integration, and International Security." Quoted in Frankel and Harding, The India-China Relationship: What the United States Needs to Know, 103-133.

14 Garver, John. "China's Decision for War with India in 1962." Quoted in Johnston and Ross, New Directions in the Study of China's Foreign Policy, 86-130.

15 While China came to decisively control the disputed Aksai Chin region in the western sector, the PLA unilaterally withdrew from the eastern sector.

16 Heimsath and Mansingh, A Diplomatic History of Modern India, 79.

India's disastrous military defeat, which came at a time when the Cold War was becoming entrenched in Southeast Asia, showed that India would not be able to offer traditional military security to the newly emergent states of Southeast Asia. However, this was deemed essential by the Southeast Asian states, which were facing numerous security issues related to the maintenance of their territorial integrity, insurgencies (often with external support), and the development of viable national identities. "It was evident even before [the] Geneva [accords on Indo-China] that recognition as a major power was a primary political aim of Chinese diplomacy, in pursuit of which India – then pre-eminent in Asia – had to be first befriended and then humbled."[17] Following India's loss at the hands of the Chinese, India became a relatively marginal player in Southeast Asia for the rest of the Cold War.

India in Asia, 1962-1991

Overhauling India's Security Policy

The Sino-Indian War had come as a huge shock to the Indian political and strategic communities. India's military defeat reduced its status in the developing world. Nehru's hope for Asian solidarity, predicated on peaceful relations with China, was shattered. The Sino-Indian War also had a major impact on Indian defense and foreign policy. India began a program of massive military modernization and trained ten new mountain divisions for high-altitude warfare. New Delhi also decided to build a forty-five squadron air force, and raised its defense production base while upgrading its operational infrastructure.[18] More importantly, the "issue of military reverses at the hands of China went beyond military preparedness to India's conceptual approach to international affairs."[19]

The war with China proved that India needed military help from external powers to meet the Chinese military challenge. India sought and received military assistance from the United States and the United Kingdom. These Western powers provided India with its first modern air defense systems.[20] India and the United States also engaged in limited cooperation with regard to the Chinese occupation of Tibet after the war.[21] In October 1962, the Indian Ministry of Home Affairs set up an Indo-Tibetan Border Police Force (ITBF) to guard India's bor-

---

17 Stargardt, "The Emergence of the Asian System of Powers," 594.

18 Kavic, India's Quest for Security: Defense Policies: 1947-1965, 192-207.

19 Nayar and Paul, India in the World Order: Searching for Major-Power Status, 150.

20 Anthony, The Arms Trade and Medium Powers: Case Studies of India and Pakistan 1947-1990, 50.

21 Kohli and Conboy, Spies in the Himalayas: Secret Missions and Perilous Climbs.

ders with China/Tibet. The ITBF force included ethnic Tibetans in its ranks.[22] However, Indo-American military co-operation proved to be of a limited and short-lived nature.

Pakistan, India's subcontinental rival, and a staunch military ally of the United States by this time, had profound misgivings about the American-India military relationship. India itself was uncertain about close military cooperation with Washington, whose representatives demanded that India must commit to opposing communism globally prior to the establishment of substantive military cooperation between the two countries.[23] Finally, the outbreak of India's second war with Pakistan over Kashmir in 1965 led to an arms embargo by the United States against the subcontinent that ended the nascent American-Indian military cooperation. Consequently, India came to view the United States as an unreliable military-strategic partner – a sentiment that persisted in New Delhi for the rest of the Cold War.

India's Security Perceptions vis-à-vis China

In the aftermath of the 1962 war, the militarization of Tibet had a strong impact on India's perception of China. The 17-Point Agreement of 1951 between Tibet and China, which had legitimized the Chinese military annexation of Tibet, had granted a substantial degree of autonomy to Tibet.[24] However, by the time of the Chinese military crackdown of Tibet in 1959, any semblance of Tibetan autonomy as promised in the Agreement and implemented in the early 1950s "was destroyed".[25] As a consequence of the 1959 Lhasa revolt and the 1962 war, the presence of the People's Liberation Army (PLA) in Tibet increased dramatically, which was perceived in New Delhi as a significant deterioration of India's security situation.[26]

Sino-Indian relations became further strained after China conducted its first nuclear test on 16 October 1964 in Lop Nur with Soviet assistance.[27] The Chinese nuclear test became the basis for a vigorous debate in the Indian Parliament and the media on whether or not India should pursue a nuclear weapons program. India sought but was unable to obtain a nuclear umbrella from the United

---

22 McGranahan, "Tibet's Cold War: The CIA and the Chushi Gangdrug Resistance, 1956-1974."

23 Barnds, India, Pakistan, and the Great Powers, 195.

24 For a text of this agreement, see Shakya, The Dragon in the Land of the Snows: A History of Modern Tibet since 1947, 449-452.

25 Garver, Protracted Contest, 56.

26 Fravel, Strong Borders, Secure Nation: Cooperation and Conflict in China's Territorial Disputes, 78.

27 Lewis and Xue, China Builds the Bomb.

States, the Soviet Union, and other great powers.[28] While the nuclear option was never discarded, the failure to obtain a nuclear guarantee led India to continue, albeit slowly, its Subterranean Nuclear Explosions Project (SNEP), which had begun in 1964.[29] India's scientific establishment also played an important role in their country's nuclear quest.[30]

At the same time, China dramatically improved its relations with India's other rival, Pakistan. In May 1962, even before the Sino-Indian war, China and Pakistan agreed to demarcate their boundaries.[31] China's Xinjiang province shares a border with Pakistan in the Northern Areas (Hunza and Baltistan in Jammu and Kashmir) – a disputed territory between India and Pakistan.[32] In fact, while the Sino-Indian war was underway, China and Pakistan were negotiating the exact location of their boundaries. The agreement was announced in May 1963. China received 1,050 square miles from Pakistan in exchange for 750 square miles of its own territory.[33] India was particularly irked that Pakistan had ceded parts of a region that was a disputed territory between India and Pakistan. Article 6 of the Sino-Pakistani border agreement allows India to re-open negotiations with China should its claim over all of Kashmir be recognized.[34] In order to avoid such an outcome, and as a consequence of its own geopolitical rationale, China began supporting Pakistan's position on Kashmir.[35]

The logic of the China-Pakistan entente became apparent to India's security planners when China threatened to open a second front against India during the 1965 India-Pakistan War.[36] China is believed to have helped Pakistan plan and implement Operation Gibraltar, an anti-India uprising in Kashmir.[37] Later, during the conventional war between India and Pakistan, the People's Liberation

---

28 Noorani, "India's Quest for a Nuclear Guarantee," 490-502.

29 This ultimately resulted in India's first nuclear test in 1974. See Ganguly, "Why India Joined the Nuclear Club," 30-3.

30 Abraham, The Making of the Indian Atomic Bomb: Science, Secrecy, and the Postcolonial State. Also see the contribution by Hans-Joachim Bieber in this volume. On the influence of India's scientific community on foreign policy in this period, see Harper and Doel, "Environmental Diplomacy in the Cold War: Weather Control, the United States, and India, 1966-1967," 115-138.

31 On the details of the Sino-Pakistani border demarcation, see Dobell, "Ramifications of the China-Pakistan Border Treaty," 283-295.

32 On the Kashmir dispute, see Ganguly, The Crisis in Kashmir: Portents of War, Hopes of Peace.

33 Ganguly, "Border Issues, Domestic Integration, and International Security," 118.

34 See Dobell, "Ramifications of the China-Pakistan Border Treaty," 288.

35 Garver, "China's Kashmir Policies," 1-24.

36 Garver, Protracted Contest, 194-204.

37 Ganguly, Conflict Unending: India-Pakistan Tensions since 1947, 31-50.

Army's troop movements in Tibet suggested that China considered opening a second front against India.[38] While the war came to an end before China's overt intervention, Indian strategists had to consider the possibility of a two-front war involving China and Pakistan from 1965 onwards.

India and Southeast Asia in the 1960s

While India and Indonesia had enjoyed close relations in the 1950s, their differences grew more pronounced in the 1960s due to a number of related factors, particularly India's low-key support for Indonesia's territorial claims over West Irian/Papua, and the two countries' different positions in the non-alignment movement.[39] Indonesia received support from China for its revolutionary ideology during this period and maintained strict neutrality during the 1962 Sino-Indian war. Later, during the 1965 India-Pakistan War, Indonesia threatened to open another front against India by attacking the Andaman and Nicobar Islands.[40] An important reason for Indonesia's hostility in this situation was that India was critical of Indonesia's policy of *Konfrontasi* towards Malaysia. In fact, a mob related to Indonesian communist groups sacked the Indian embassy in Jakarta in 1965.[41]

Meanwhile, the United States became increasingly embroiled in the Vietnam War. India was "opposed to the Western cause in Vietnam", calculating that it could thereby undermine the Cold War system of rival military blocs in its neighborhood.[42] India's vociferous opposition to American involvement in Vietnam created difficulties in its relations with a number of pro-Western states in Southeast Asia that had formed a regional grouping, the Association of Southeast Asian Nations (ASEAN), in 1967.[43] Notably, India did not receive an invitation to join ASEAN (contrary to the widely held but erroneous belief that

38 Garver, Protracted Contest, 203.

39 Ramachandran, "India-Indonesia Relations - 1947-1975." Quoted in Subrahmanyam, Self-Reliance and National Reliance, 147-158.

40 Ayoob, India and Southeast Asia: Indian Perceptions and Policies, 41.

41 Ramachandran, "India-Indonesia Relations," 164.

42 Thakur, "India's Vietnam Policy, 1946-1979," 957-976; Lawrence, "The Limits of Peacemaking: India and the Vietnam War, 1962-67."

43 ASEAN's initial members included Indonesia, Malaysia, Singapore, Thailand, and the Philippines. Of these, Thailand and the Philippines were close allies of the United States while Malaysia and Singapore had a western orientation, first through the 1957 Anglo-Malaya Defence Agreement that eventually gave way to the Five Power Defence Agreement in 1971. (The five powers included Britain, Australia and New Zealand in addition to Malaysia and Singapore). See Leifer, "Conflict and Regional Order in Southeast Asia."

India was invited to join but had declined to do so)[44] and was disappointed about this lack of integration.[45] However, to a significant extent it was New Delhi's fault for sending mixed (or at least unclear) messages to the ASEAN states. In the late 1960s, Prime Minister Indira Gandhi suggested the establishment of a regional grouping in Asia, a suggestion which sounded remarkably similar to the Asian collective security system proposed by the former Soviet Union.[46] India's Minister of External Affairs, Mohammedali Chagla, had propagated the idea of such a "Council of Asia" during his Southeast Asian tour in 1967, too. Gandhi presented the idea to Kuala Lumpur during her 1968 visit to Malaysia. Understandably, many Southeast Asians thought that India was undermining ASEAN by promoting an alternative.[47] Given India's problems with Indonesia, it seems quite possible that Indonesia wanted to keep India away from the grouping in Southeast Asia.

However, Singapore was (and continues to remain) a champion of India's involvement in the strategic architecture of this region. In the immediate aftermath of China's first nuclear test, Lee Kuan Yew, the first Prime Minister of Singapore, urged India to conduct a nuclear test to counter-balance Chinese power in the region.[48] In the second half of the 1960s, Lee had asked India to train and equip the military of his new city-state, which had been born in 1965.[49] Lee added that he would welcome an Indian naval presence in Southeast Asia.[50] Furthermore, prior to his first official visit to India, Lee is reported to have urged India to adopt an "Asian Monroe Doctrine" in order to prevent "poaching" in Asia.[51] However, after suffering a military debacle at the hands of China in 1962 and having fought a major war with Pakistan in 1965, New Delhi did not respond to Singapore's request for military assistance. India was neither economically strong nor militarily powerful enough to implement its own version of the Monroe Doctrine in Asia of which Nehru had spoken at the dawn of India's independence.

---

44 For example, see Kaul, "ASEAN-India Relations during the Cold War," 55.

45 Ayoob, India and Southeast Asia, 11.

46 Sridharan, The ASEAN Region in India's Foreign Policy, 69-76.

47 Kaul, "ASEAN-India Relations During the Cold War." Quoted in Grare and Mattoo, India and ASEAN: The Politics of India's Look East Policy, 55.

48 Ghoshal, "India and Southeast Asia: Prospects and Problems." Quoted in Ghoshal, India and Southeast Asia: Challenges and Opportunities, 96.

49 Huxley, Defending the Lion City: The Armed Forces of Singapore, 11. Also see Suryanarayan, "Looking Ahead: India and Southeast Asia in the 1990s, New Perspectives, New Challenges," quoted in Ghoshal, India and Southeast Asia, 16.

50 Ghoshal, "India and Southeast Asia," 96.

51 Quoted in Dutt, India's Foreign Policy, 277-278.

Changing Geopolitical Alignments

As noted earlier, Western military assistance to India came to an end with the onset of the 1965 India-Pakistan War. However, India needed military assistance from the great powers in the face of the Chinese challenge, especially given the possibility of a two-front scenario involving China and Pakistan. It was under these conditions that India turned to the Soviet Union. This decision was taken in spite of the fact that Indian military hardware was primarily of Western (European) origin heretofore, and that its military doctrine was influenced by the West due to the British colonial legacy. The Sino-Soviet split that had become apparent by this time paved the way for New Delhi's partnership with Moscow.[52]

The Soviet Union offered India advanced technology under favorable terms to New Delhi. It offered India technology through licensed production, agreed to payments under barter arrangements (principally through commodities), provided New Delhi with cheap long-term credit agreements to pay for these systems, and entered into rupee-based trade arrangements, manipulating the rupee-ruble exchange rate to allow favorable trade balances for India.[53] Soviet-Indian cooperation culminated in the 1971 Treaty of Peace, Friendship, and Cooperation, which was signed on the eve of the Bangladesh War.[54]

In the meantime, in an effort to take advantage of the Sino-Soviet split, US Secretary of State Henry Kissinger made a secret trip to China in 1971, having used Pakistan as a conduit to (tacitly) ally with Beijing in an attempt to shift the balance of power in the world.[55] During the 1971 Bangladesh War, the United States also gave China its consent to attack India if New Delhi escalated the war in West Pakistan.[56] The United States also dispatched a US Navy battle group, the *USS Enterprise* (which strategists in New Delhi believed to carry nuclear arms) to the Bay of Bengal to warn India against escalating the war in the west. The dispatch of the *USS Enterprise* was also meant as a signal to the Soviet Union to desist from taking military action against China in the event of a Chinese attack on India.[57] While China provided limited economic and military assistance to Pakistan, its level of involvement in 1971 was much lower than in 1965. India succeeded in the vivisection of Pakistan (and the creation of Bangladesh), and emerged as the predominant military power in South Asia. This pattern of

52 Lüthi, The Sino-Soviet Split, 1956-1966: Cold War in the Communist World.

53 Mehrotra, India and the Soviet Union: Trade and Technology Transfer.

54 See Racioppi, Soviet Policy Towards South Asia since 1970.

55 Goh, Constructing the US Rapprochement with China, 1961-1974: From 'Red Menace' to 'Tacit Ally.'

56 Garver, Protracted Contest, 207-215.

57 Garver, Protracted Contest, 322.

American and Chinese alignment (together with Pakistan) against Indian (and Soviet) interests continued through the 1970s and the early 1980s.

In the meantime, Britain had announced its decision to withdraw its naval power from "east of the Suez" in 1967.[58] The Indian Navy announced its intention to assume the functions of the British Navy after the latter's withdrawal from the region.[59] At the time, India neither had the resources nor the vision to fill such a role. Nevertheless, New Delhi's announcement created suspicions about India's policy towards Southeast Asia in Indonesia.[60] Along with the withdrawal of the British forces came the enunciation of the so-called Guam Doctrine by US President Richard Nixon. While the doctrine lacked a precise definition, the United States was announcing its intention to not get militarily involved on the Asian mainland.[61]

Even before Southeast Asia could come to terms with the meaning of Western disengagement from the region, India signed the 1971 treaty with the former Soviet Union. India had emerged as the pre-eminent power in South Asia with the dismemberment of Pakistan, and to some extent also regained its status as a military power that it had lost after 1962. However, the Southeast Asian states again became suspicious of India's designs for the region, as they saw Soviet power lurking behind India's new status at a time when the Western powers were disengaging from the region.[62] The strategic environment in Southeast Asia became more complicated with Sino-American rapprochement in the early 1970s.

The Strengthening of the Sino-Pakistani Strategic Nexus

The 1971 war between India and Pakistan and the Indian military's dismemberment of the eastern wing of Pakistan through the creation of Bangladesh only heightened Pakistan's threat perception vis-à-vis India. In March 1972, Pakistan's President, Zulfikar Ali Bhutto, initiated the country's nuclear weapons program in order to meet what Pakistan perceived as an existential security threat from India.[63] It was under these conditions that Bhutto sought help from China. While the genesis of the Sino-Pakistani nuclear relationship remains un-

58 By 1974, all of Britain's deployments east of the Suez (with the exception of Hong Kong) were withdrawn.

59 This decision was announced in 1969. See Thomas, "The Indian Navy in the Seventies," 500-518.

60 Dipoyudo, "Indonesia-India Bilateral Relations," 509-523.

61 See Girling, "The Guam Doctrine," 48-62.

62 Gupta, "Waiting for India: India's Role as a Regional Power," 171-184.

63 Ahmed, "Pakistan's Nuclear Weapons Program: Turning Points and Nuclear Choices," 183.

known, it is widely believed that it began in the 1970s – perhaps after India's 1974 nuclear test – during the tenure of Bhutto.[64] China had tried to build up Pakistan to militarily balance India's power soon after the 1962 Sino-Indian war.

Similarly, China's proliferation of strategic technologies to Pakistan was a part of a larger strategy to contain India in South Asia by practicing balance of power politics.[65] It has been shown that arguments based on bureaucratic politics or commercial gains cannot explain the persistence with which a centralized political system like China has transferred these technologies to Pakistan over a long period of time.[66] China is believed to have not only sent missile technologies and components to Pakistan but also fissile material and tested nuclear warhead designs.[67]

The Sino-Pakistani nuclear and strategic relationship remained strong until the end of the Cold War. In the midst of the 1990 India-Pakistan nuclear crisis, Chinese Defense Minister Qin Qiwei led a delegation to Pakistan and assured Islamabad that the Chinese government would "never" change its policy of "supporting the Pakistani government, people, and armed forces in safeguarding their state sovereignty and territorial integrity, no matter how the international situation changes."[68] While it is true that China has become more cautious in its nuclear and missile assistance to Pakistan since the mid-1990s, especially after signing the nuclear Nonproliferation Treaty (NPT) in 1992, it should be noted that China completely transformed the strategic balance in the subcontinent by that time as a result of the proliferation of its strategic technologies to Pakistan.[69]

Moreover, China had begun to construct a road through the Karakoram mountain range, a direct land-route which connected China's Xinjiang province with Pakistan's Northern Areas, soon after the 1962 Sino-Indian war and the 1963 Sino-Pakistani border agreement. In 1978, China and Pakistan formally announced the opening of the Karakoram Highway linking the two countries

---

64 Paul, "The Enduring Sino-Pakistani Nuclear/Missile Relationship and the Balance of Power Logic," 4.

65 Paul, "Chinese-Pakistani Nuclear/Missile Ties and the Balance of Power." Similarly, Bernier has argued that China's proliferation of strategic technologies to states such as North Korea, Iran, Libya, Syria, and Pakistan is a part of China's strategy to use these states as "strategic proxies" in order to further its "geopolitical goals." See Bernier, "Asia's Shifting Strategic Landscape: China's Strategic Proxies," 629-643.

66 Paul, "Chinese-Pakistani Nuclear/Missile Ties and the Balance of Power."

67 Malik, "Nuclear Proliferation in Asia: The China Factor," 31-41.

68 Quoted in Garver, "China's Kashmir Policies," 9.

69 According to many analysts, Pakistan is believed to have had at least one unassembled nuclear weapon by June 1989. See Perkovich, India's Nuclear Bomb: The Impact on Global Proliferation, 303.

across their Himalayan borderlands. This highway was of great strategic value. First, it allowed China "to give military aid to Pakistan", as Li Xiannian, Deputy Premier of China stated when the highway was completed.[70] Second, by providing China with access to the Gilgit region in Pakistan's Northern Areas, it allowed China to monitor Indian attempts to cut the lines of communication between Xinjiang and Tibet through the Aksai Chin region.[71] The Aksai Chin region (approximately 38,000 square kilometers), an extension of the Tibetan plateau, is a disputed region between India and China. The Chinese had started building a road via this region to connect Tibet with Xinjiang soon after the emergence of the People's Republic in 1949. Given the poor connection between Tibet and China, control over this road and the Aksai Chin region was very important for China to consolidate its rule in Tibet.[72] Third, the Karakoram Highway helped integrate the Northern Areas with the rest of Pakistan. When Pakistan (and India) became independent in 1947, the Northern Areas were physically, economically, and politically cut off from the rest of Pakistan.[73] More importantly, India considered the Northern Areas to be a part of Jammu and Kashmir, a state disputed between the two South Asian rivals. By building the highway, China demonstrated its support for Pakistan on the Kashmir dispute between India and Pakistan. Finally, China had an interest in ensuring that the Northern Areas remained part of Pakistan because the only land borders Pakistan shared with China ran between the Northern Areas and Xinjiang. Even today, the highway possesses strategic importance. According to several reports, a large number of Chinese soldiers are believed to be stationed in the Northern Areas on a long-term basis. Furthermore, there are plans to link the Karakorum Highway to the port of Gwadar at the mouth of the Persian Gulf, thereby giving China an alternative route to access energy resources from the Middle East.[74]

The Slow Road to Sino-Indian Rapprochement

Sino-Indian relations remained tense throughout the 1960s. The militaries of the two countries briefly clashed near the Nathu La and Cho La passes in the central sector of their disputed border in 1967, a conflict during which several dozen

70 Quoted in Isphani, Roads and Rivals: The Political Uses of Access in the Borderlands of Asia, 200.

71 Isphani, Roads and Rivals, 205-6.

72 Garver, Protracted Contest, 80-88.

73 Isphani, "Roads and Rivals," 194.

74 Harrision, "China's Discreet Hold on Pakistan's Northern Borderlands." Also see Gupta, "Army passes intel to Govt: PLA men at pass linking PoK to China."

soldiers on both sides were killed.[75] Soon thereafter, China initiated the first step to improve relations between the two countries in 1970: Mao Zedong approached Brajesh Mishra, the Indian charge d'affairs, in Beijing, and greeted him warmly at a reception. The reason for China's interest in improving relations with India was the bitter border war China had fought with the Soviet Union a year earlier.[76] Beijing wanted to avoid the hostility of two large powers on both its northern and southern borders. However, the Sino-US rapprochement (via Pakistan), the 1971 Indo-Soviet treaty, and the 1971 Bangladesh War prevented any improvement in bilateral relations.

In 1974, India demonstrated its nuclear abilities by conducting a nuclear test which was dubbed a "peaceful nuclear explosion". As noted earlier, India had genuine security concerns including China's nuclear capabilities, the emerging Sino-Pakistani entente, and even a perceived nuclear threat from the United States. The Chinese, who had begun to covertly assist the Pakistani nuclear program in the 1970s, were critical of India's nuclear test and accused New Delhi of trying to scare its neighboring countries. The Chinese also believed (erroneously) that India had become nuclear with Soviet help.[77]

Relations between India and China further deteriorated after India absorbed Sikkim into the Indian Union in 1975.[78] Sandwiched between India and Tibet, Sikkim had been a protectorate of India since the country's independence in 1947. In an attempt to reduce political tensions with Beijing, Prime Minister Indira Gandhi restored full diplomatic relations with China in 1976. India and China had withdrawn their ambassadors after the 1962 war, but diplomatic relations were never fully severed.

When Mao passed away in 1976 and Indira Gandhi was ousted in the 1977 general elections, the situation was open to change. Atal Bihari Vajpayee, the Foreign Minister of the new Janata Party coalition government, visited China in 1979 in an attempt to improve ties. Vajpayee was the most senior Indian dignitary to visit China since Vice-President Sarvepalli Radhakrishnan's visit to Beijing in 1958. However, during Vajpayee's visit, China attacked Vietnam, which was India's communist friend in Southeast Asia. Furthermore, the Chinese leader Deng Xiaoping spoke of teaching Vietnam a "lesson" just as China had done to India in 1962. As a consequence, Vajpayee cut short his visit and returned to India.

---

75 See Fravel, Strong Borders, Secure Nation: Cooperation and Conflict in China's Territorial Disputes, 197-9.

76 Ganguly, "Border Issues, Domestic Integration, and International Security," 120.

77 On the reactions of the Chinese vice-premier Deng Xiaoping to India's 1974 nuclear test, see Sharma, India-China Relations, 1972-1991, Part II, 128-9.

78 Garver, Protracted Contest, 170-175.

In 1980, Deng reiterated Zhou Enlai's 1960 proposal of an east-west swap to settle the territorial dispute between the two countries.[79] China was eager to overcome its border disputes in order to focus on its domestic economic development. However, just as in 1960, China's offer for a swap was informal. Moreover, India was again not interested in the Chinese proposal to swap territories.[80] The Chinese proposal was therefore withdrawn in 1985. Yet there were signs of improvement nonetheless. China's foreign minister Huang Hua paid a return visit to India in 1981. The Chinese agreed to open two ancient Hindu pilgrimage sites in Tibet – Kailash and Mansarovar – to win public support with the Indian public. After Huang's visit, the two sides began border talks in December 1981. China agreed to discuss the border issue sector by sector, which New Delhi preferred (as opposed to a package deal favored by Beijing). In turn, India agreed to begin negotiations without demanding the Chinese vacate all territory claimed by India.[81]

Yet a number of developments in the 1980s complicated Sino-Indian relations once again. In 1984, Indian soldiers seized key positions in the Siachen Glacier, a disputed region between India and Pakistan, which worried Chinese strategists.[82] It was noted earlier that the Karakoram Highway had strengthened China's military position vis-à-vis India in the western sector. However, the Indian position in Siachen now gave India the ability to isolate Pakistan from mainland China "within a few hours, with little or no warning."[83] Thus, by 1984, India was able to reverse some of the negative strategic fallout from the Karakoram Highway for its own security.

Two years later, in December 1986, India granted full statehood to Arunachal Pradesh (the region in the eastern sector that was claimed by China). Although this step was simply a "logical evolution of [Indian] administrative proc-

---

79 The basic premise was that the territorial dispute could be settled if India dropped its claim to the Aksai Chin region in the western sector which was under Chinese control. In return, the Chinese would drop their claim on the region now known as Arunachal Pradesh which was under Indian administration.

80 For an explanation of India and Chinese positions on this issue, see Garver, Protracted Contest, 100-6.

81 Ganguly, "The Sino-Indian Border Talks, 1981-1989: A View from New Delhi," Asian Survey Volume 29, Number 12 (December 1989), 1126. Eight rounds of talks were held between 1981 and 1988 with the two sides discussing the "basic principles" to settle their border dispute as well as the "situation on the ground."

82 On the Chinese dimension in Siachen, see Raghavan, Conflict without End, 19-28.

83 Tan Eng Bok, "How Does the PLA Cope with 'Regional Conflict' and 'Local War'?." Quoted in Yang, China's Military: The PLA in 1990/91, 151.

ess," the Chinese saw it as a "possible legal erosion to their claim."[84] Soon thereafter, Sino-Indian forces clashed briefly in 1986 in the Sumdorong Chu Valley of Arunachal Pradesh. The mobilization of forces by both sides over the next one year or so sparked "fears of a second China-India war."[85]

In 1986-87, under the leadership of the maverick Indian General K Sundarji, India launched an exercise in armed diplomacy that combined air and land-based operations along the disputed eastern border with China. Code-named Operation Chequerboard, its mission was to test China's response as well as that of the United States and the Soviet Union. The mock exercise, which simulated a limited war in the McMahon Line area, heightened tensions along the Sino-Indian border, with close to 400,000 troops of both the sides stationed along this border at its peak.[86] However, the exercise was quickly terminated under mounting international pressure.[87] By then, the Indian air force had estimated that its killing ratio in a conflict with China in this region was ten to one in India's favor.[88] The overall results of this exercise convinced the Indian government "of its capability to successfully decide any regional confrontation" with China.[89]

While India clearly had robust military capabilities by the late 1980s (especially when compared to 1962) and could withstand a Chinese military attack, India had no clear political and military objectives as far as the offensive use of force against China was concerned. It was clear to India's decision makers that India could not unilaterally use its armed forces to settle the boundary issue with China or to guarantee Tibetan autonomy.[90] However, India's strong military capabilities meant that India extended a warm hand to China from what it perceived to be a position of military strength. The late 1980s further saw the emergence of India as a regional power with military interventions in Sri Lanka and the Maldives.[91]

At the same time, Operation Brasstacks had caused a serious war scare with Pakistan. India's military resources were seriously stretched and it made sense

---

84 Ganguly, "The Sino-Indian Border Talks, 1981-1989: A View from New Delhi," 1130-1.

85 Fravel, Strong Borders, Secure Nation, 199.

86 Hazarika, "India and China cite each other for massing troops in the Himalayas."

87 Cohen, India: Emerging Power, 148.

88 Tan Eng Bok, "How Does the PLA Cope with 'Regional Conflict' and 'Local War'?," 150.

89 Tan Eng Bok, "How Does the PLA Cope with 'Regional Conflict' and 'Local War'?," 151.

90 Hussain, "India's China Policy: Putting Politics in Command." Quoted in Kumar, Yearbook on India's Foreign Policy, 1989.

91 Hagerty, "India's Regional Security Doctrine."

to de-escalate the Sino-Indian rivalry, especially since it did not offer a military solution. Another important reason why India decided to de-escalate its rivalry with China seems to have been a consequence of the loss of unqualified Soviet support that it had received in its relations with China. The loss of Soviet support became apparent during the 1986 Sumdorong Chu incident mentioned above, about which the Soviet press made absolutely no statement.[92] Later, when Soviet leader Mikhail Gorbachev travelled to India in 1986, he refused to side with India in its conflict with China.[93] Finally, during his visit to Delhi a month before Rajiv Gandhi's trip to China in 1988, Gorbachev stressed the common interests of the three states.[94] This was the clearest sign that India was losing the strong diplomatic and military support that it had received from the Soviets since 1971 in New Delhi's competition with Beijing.

Those years were also the period of Sino-Soviet rapprochement. Soviet force reductions along the Sino-Soviet and Sino-Mongolian frontiers, the acceptance by the Soviets of the main channel of the Amur and Ussuri rivers as the demarcation line for the Sino-Soviet boundary, and the Soviet withdrawal from Afghanistan in the late 1980s led to a major thaw in Sino-Soviet relations. China was also concerned with other security threats in the late 1980s. China had engaged in some naval clashes with the Vietnamese over the Spratly Islands in 1988.[95] Furthermore, the democratization of Taiwan from 1987 onwards was a serious concern for the Chinese. Taiwan democratized under a tacit security guarantee by Washington in an attempt to make itself a more attractive partner of the United States (and the Western world).[96] Finally, India did not intervene in the crisis in Tibet which began in late 1987.[97] Given China's other preoccupations, the Chinese side decided in favor of de-escalation as well.

The most visible symbol of Sino-Indian rapprochement was Prime Minister Rajiv Gandhi's trip to China in December 1988, the first such visit made by either side in more than three decades. Gandhi's trip broke the impasse that had been plaguing their relations since the 1962 Sino-Indian War, and led the top leadership of the two sides to come to an understanding that Sino-Indian trade and commercial relations could be improved before their border issue was resolved.[98]

---

92 Garver, "The Indian Factor in Recent Sino-Soviet Relations," 80.
93 Garver, "The Indian Factor in Recent Sino-Soviet Relations," 81.
94 Mansingh and Levine, "China and India: Moving Beyond Confrontation," 40.
95 Kivimäki, "'Reason' and 'Power' in Territorial Disputes: The South China Sea."
96 Cheng, "Democratizing the Quasi-Leninist Regime in Taiwan."
97 Pardesi, "Instability in Tibet and the Sino-Indian Strategic Rivalry: Do Domestic Politics Matter?"
98 Ghosh, "Dynamics of India-China Normalisation."

The visit also led to the creation of the Joint Working Group (JWG) that was to develop a resolution of the border dispute. Headed by the Indian Foreign Secretary and the Chinese Foreign Vice Minister, the JWG was supposed to alternately meet in Beijing and New Delhi every six months.[99] Although the meetings did not lead to any breakthrough on the vexed Sino-Indian border issue, they helped to maintain a steady and positive momentum in China's and India's bilateral relations. They also provided the framework for the 1993 Agreement on the Maintenance of Peace and Tranquility and the 1996 Agreement on Confidence Building Measures (CBMs). As per these agreements, the two sides have agreed not to use force against each other to settle their border dispute. They have also established hotlines between border troop commanders and agreed to limit and reduce the size of their forces along specific regions along their border. Finally, India and China have agreed to avoid large-scale military exercises involving more than one division (15,000 troops) along their border, while providing prior notification of exercises involving more than one brigade (5,000 troops).[100]

Strategic Divergence between India and Southeast Asia

In the aftermath of the 1971 Bangladesh War, India, the pre-eminent regional power in the subcontinent, was unable to "look east" towards Southeast Asia. The "oil shocks" of the 1970s and the economic boom in the Gulf that followed it caused India to "look west" towards the oil-rich countries of West Asia (or the Middle East).[101] India was also concerned about the efforts of Iran to play the role of a regional power in South Asia. In 1972, the Shah of Iran had declared that any attack on Pakistan would be tantamount to an attack on Iran, and that Tehran was committed to the territorial integrity of Pakistan.[102] These international developments together with India's position on the Vietnam War prevented New Delhi from engaging Southeast Asia in any meaningful sense throughout the 1970s.

India's muted response to the Soviet invasion of Afghanistan in 1979, and the recognition by New Delhi of the Heng Samrin government in Kampuchea (Cambodia) after Vietnam invaded that country further alienated India from Southeast Asia. The Kampuchean case in particular was a more serious concern for ASEAN countries which were then worried about Vietnam's military power

---

99 On the formation of the JWG, see Mansingh, "India-China Relations in the Post-Cold War Era," 289-293. The JWG met fourteen times between 1989 and 2002.

100 Sidhu and Yuan, China and India: Cooperation or Conflict?, 124-6.

101 Thomas, "Energy Politics and Indian Security."

102 On Iran's efforts to position itself as a South Asian power, see Gupta, "Waiting for India," 178-180.

(and its links with the former Soviet Union).[103] However, India sought to play an active diplomatic role between the Indo-Chinese countries and ASEAN during the Kampuchean crisis. Vietnam's invasion of Kampuchea was followed by China's invasion of Vietnam in 1979.[104] "Gandhi realized that if India were to become the paramount power in South Asia it would have to prevent a Chinese advance into Southeast Asia."[105] Consequently, Gandhi recognized the Heng Samrin government in opposition to Beijing's preference for its Khmer Rouge clients.

After Rajiv Gandhi became Indian Prime Minister, New Delhi sought to play the role of an "honest broker" between Vietnam and ASEAN.[106] In January 1987, Vietnam's position was comprehensively formulated for the first time and then communicated to the Indian Minister of External Affairs, Natwar Singh, for transmission to ASEAN. In March, April and July 1987, Singh visited all six ASEAN states and the three Indo-Chinese countries. India also made it clear that it would like to be one of the guarantors of an international agreement on Kampuchea.[107] India became a member of the 1989 Paris Accords on Cambodia.

While India was trying to raise its diplomatic profile in Southeast Asia, the rapid build-up of India's naval and military power in the 1980s, and its development of a naval (and a possible air base) in the Andaman and Nicobar Islands at the mouth of the Straits of Malacca, emerged as a major cause of concern for the Southeast Asian states.[108] India had received an offer for a second aircraft

---

103 Vietnam had launched an invasion of Kampuchea in December 1978 and had ousted the government of the Khmer Rouge. The Heng Samrin regime installed by Vietnam was recognized by Indira Gandhi's government in India in 1980. For details, see Ayoob, India and Southeast Asia, 53-71.

104 See Buszynski, "Vietnam Confronts China," 829-843. Also see Zhang, "China's 1979 War with Vietnam: A Reassessment."

105 Ayoob, India and Southeast Asia, 56.

106 Ayoob, India and Southeast Asia, 59.

107 Thakur, The Politics and Economics of India's Foreign Policy, 252. India sent military contingents to Cambodia in 1991 as a part of both the United Nations Advance Mission in Cambodia (UNAMIC) as well as the United Nations Transitional Authority in Cambodia (UNTAC). In addition to these, India also sent a medical battalion to Cambodia as a part of UNTAC. Finally, India was chosen to be the co-chair of the Control Commission to assist UNTAC in implementing the peace accords.

108 See Naidu, "The Indian Navy and Southeast Asia," 72-85. India had been planning to upgrade its military facilities in the Andaman and Nicobar Islands since 1972. The 1980s witnessed significant infrastructure building on what was then known as FORTAN or Fortress Andaman and Nicobar. See Gordon, India's Rise to Power in the Twentieth Century and Beyond, 293-295.

carrier from Britain in 1985.[109] From 1988 to 1991, India leased a nuclear powered cruise missile submarine from the Soviet Union.[110] The late 1980s further saw the emergence of India as a regional power with military interventions in Sri Lanka and the Maldives.[111] There were concerns in many Southeast Asian states with significant Indian minorities that India might engage in gunboat diplomacy if ethnic Indians in that region were to be harmed or mistreated.[112] It was widely believed towards the end of the 1980s that India was transforming into "a regional superpower" and would emerge as "a global military power."[113]

Yet on the whole, India was at best a marginal player in Southeast Asia throughout this period. At worst, India created geopolitical tensions in Southeast Asia as a consequence of its alignment with the former Soviet Union. At times, Southeast Asian states perceived military threats from India. The Cold War was a period of "missed opportunities, mistrust, misperceptions, and bungling diplomacy"[114] in Indo-ASEAN relations, as India lacked an overall policy towards ASEAN as a grouping or towards the Southeast Asian region on the whole. The only notable success of Indian policy towards Southeast Asia was a result of the diplomatic role that New Delhi played during the Kampuchean crisis. India's relations with Southeast Asia began to improve only after the end of the Cold War (and the implosion of the former Soviet Union) and with India's economic reforms, which set in almost simultaneously. India immediately launched a formal "look east" policy to engage this economically dynamic region.[115]

Conclusion

India's defeat in the 1962 Sino-Indian war made it a marginal player in Asia's strategic affairs for the rest of the Cold War. The Sino-Pakistani entente which emerged soon after 1962 ensured that India remained merely a South Asian player even as Nehru had tried to position India as the leading Asian power soon after independence in 1947. India's subsequent focus on its northwestern border

---

109 Prakash, "India's Quest for an Indigenous Aircraft Carrier," 50-52.

110 "Submarine Proliferation: India, Current Capabilities," Nuclear Threat Initiative, Accessed on June 14, 2008. http://www.nti.org/db/submarines/india/index.html.

111 On India's military intervention in Sri Lanka and Maldives with an emphasis on the role of the navy, see Roy-Chaudhury, Sea Power and Indian Security, 134-146.

112 However, India's helplessness in responding to the mistreatment of Indians in Fiji in 1987 reassured Southeast Asian states to some extent. Naidu, "The Indian Navy and Southeast Asia," 82.

113 Munro, "India: The Awakening of an Asian Power."

114 Kaul, "ASEAN-India Relations during the Cold War," 62.

115 Pardesi, "Southeast Asia in Indian Foreign Policy: Positioning India as a Major Power in Asia." Quoted in India's Foreign Policy: Retrospect and Prospect.

with Pakistan and its northern and northeastern borders with China meant that India was unable to "look east" even after the rapid take off of the East Asian "tiger economies" from the 1970s onwards. Military defeat at the hands of China also reduced the perception of India as a regional balance to Chinese power in Southeast Asia. India's lackluster economic performance and its autarkic policies further widened the gap between India and Southeast Asia. New Delhi's criticism of the United States in Vietnam and its 1971 treaty with the former Soviet Union raised suspicions about India's intentions in Asia. Finally, India's rapid military build-up with Soviet assistance alarmed the Southeast Asian states in the 1980s. However, it was India's growing military capabilities which gave New Delhi the self-confidence to mend ties with Beijing at the time of the Sino-Soviet rapprochement just before the end of the Cold War. Finally, the end of the Cold War and the opening up of the Indian economy paved the way for India to reach out to Southeast Asia again.

Muslims in India: Secularism and its International Preconditions

William Gould

Introduction

One of the greatest debates within the Islamic world from the late 19th century to the present, has been how Muslims might navigate the line between the promotion of their communities' own vision of traditional values and culture, and 'modernity'. The crucial context to this debate has been the influence of 'Western' ideas in Islamic societies, principally around the organization of the state and its relationship to established religion. And it is precisely in those areas of the world in which European states historically exercised forms of influence, either formally as imperial powers, or more informally via trade and commercial dominance, that the debate has been most vigorously pursued. Some of the most significant 'foreign imports' for such societies were governmental and societal structures, particularly those which allowed colonial powers to operate most effectively in multi-ethnic contexts: principally, the concept of the secular state as a governmental form, and secularism as a political ideology. Even more forcefully, secularism was championed by movements directly opposing colonial powers, as a form of 'modern' political organization that allowed for the mobilization of 'national' institutions.

Discussions about modernity and secularism in Islamic societies therefore developed from attempts to define society in relation to a (sometimes colonial) foreign other: they related to the self-perception of communities in relation to external ideas about political organization, and in the context of a global Islamic *umma* (community). Such discussions also took place within the context of European imperial networks. Fundamental in the case of India was the figure of Sayed Ahmed Khan, the great founder of the Aligarh Anglo-Oriental College in the late nineteenth century, which later became the centre of subsequent Muslim religio-political mobilization. Sayed Ahmed Khan argued (before the term 'secularism' had any currency) that education in Persian or Arabic for most Muslims should not be focussed solely on the acquisition of religious texts, but be a means to qualify for official employment, as provided by the colonial state in India. For him, Islamic theological education could be transformed by bringing more Muslims into contact with western institutions and by squaring the scriptural authorities of Islam with what he saw as the strengths of 'western' rationalism. This was about the fulfilment of Islamic society at the forefront of world civilisation: to claim for Islam the advances of science.[1] A later, clearer attempt to promote secularism directly, not just as a principle within education, but as an ideal of governance within a Muslimn society, in this case Eqypt, was that of Shaykh Ali Abd al-Raziq, in his al-Islam wa 'Usul al-Hukm, published in 1925. This stated that Islam was a religion, not a state, or a spiritual edifice rather than a political institution.[2]

This thesis led Abd al-Raziq to be defrocked by the Azharite Committee of Ulema. And sadly, the reigniting of his discussion in modern times has led to the polarization of debate on secularism in some parts of the Islamic world, in which Islamists have turned the term into a form of opprobrium, championing instead a 'return to Islam', against an equally vociferous secularist position.[3] However, this essay will argue that the specific development of secularism in other parts of the Islamic world was quite different and did not divide along such binaries. In India, where Muslims were in a powerful minority, highly creative and integrative forms of secularism developed. These were both fragile, but also potentially effective in protecting freedom of religion for minorities in India. In more theoretical ways though, what happened to secularism in India can be generalized to other Islamic contexts. Tracing the histories of these forms of secularism potentially shifts our notion of what secularism and the secular state are: Abd al-Raziq's arguments highlighted a particular trend in the development of the idea of the secular state, where such ideas took root in a late colonial or postcolonial context. In British occupied Egypt, religion and politics were not easily separated, yet somehow secularism as a concept could still exist. As one scholar of contemporary Egypt has suggested, the precariousness of secularism's categories were at the root of secular power in these states.[4] As we will see below, some of these same features of fragility and uncertainty, working as fundamental features, characterized secularism and the secular state in India.

At the broadest level, the establishment of a secular state in India appeared to be the outcome of a straightforward ideological battle. Crucial for India was the nature of its transition to independence, involving the creation of a separate 'Muslim' state (Pakistan), and a long-standing political conflict between advocates of unitary nationalism and Muslim separatism. But this division and separation between 'Muslim' Pakistan and 'secular', Congress dominated India obscured more complex realities. To trace the roots of discussions about the quality of Indian secularism we need to go back to the late nineteenth century. In In-

1 Lelyveld, "Disenchantment at Aligarh," 85-102.
2 Najjar, "The Debate on Islam and Secularism in Egypt."
3 Najjar, "The Debate on Islam and Secularism in Egypt," 1-2.
4 Agrama, "Secularism, Sovereignty, Indeterminacy," 495-523.

dia too, politics was infused with religion, not only because of the existence of a highly heterogeneous Muslim minority, but also because of the ideological and political debates that revolved around 'Hinduism' from that time. Hand in hand with the growth of institutional and mass anti-colonial nationalism went public pronouncements about the inter-relationship between religious community and national community. From the 1880s and 1890s, via the movements driven by the likes of B.G. Tilak, Aurobindo, Madan Mohan Malaviya and later in the *swadeshi* movement of 1905-8, large numbers were mobilized around religious community themes, or during festivals. In contrast, via different institutions and importantly with a global outlook, a powerful Muslim minority (which formed majorities in the north east and north west) discussed how their religion related to political activity. And this was a Muslim population of global importance both then and today. According to the 2001 census, the Muslim population in India numbered around 160 million, or around 13.4% of the total population, which makes India's the third largest Muslim population after Indonesia and Pakistan.

Late colonial debates about whether or not the Indian state should be secular were certainly very different to the experience of secularization in Europe which accompanied the gradual separation of church and state. Indian secularism was never conceptualized along European lines and never could be, not least because there is not (and never was) an 'established' religious tradition in the subcontinent. In practical terms too, it is extremely difficult to separate out the 'religious' from 'non religious' practices of politics, and so in India, the secularism of particular institutions or political and constitutional structures did not necessarily (or even very commonly) mean that society too, would be 'secularized'.[5] In this sense, from its very earliest articulations in Indian politics in the late colonial period, and in its implied effect within the Constitution of India, secularism in India could only ever imply the selected separation of religion from politics within specific institutions. Most importantly, it promoted the idea that the state would maintain equal distance from all traditions and that all would be equally tolerated.

This immediately threw up problems for the working of India's Constitution, and of its juridical and political systems. In the 1950 Constitution's fundamental rights of citizenship, all citizens are required to be treated equally, without reference to birth, gender or religious affinity. Yet, the Constitution does require the state, in articles 15 and 17, to recognize and promote the special interests of particular 'schedules' of disadvantaged castes.[6] And since these sched-

5 Bhargava, "What is Secularism For?," 488-91.

6 Bayly, Caste, Society and Politics in India, 268.

ules are based on older colonial notions of caste, which brought into consideration religious notions of purity and pollution, the state is effectively distinguishing between citizens on religious lines. For example, the state is empowered to grant Dalits full access to Hindu religious institutions.[7] Indian law, too, allows the application of different bodies of family law on the basis of religious communities, and in particular permits the working of Muslim Personal Law. This is despite the creation of a 'Hindu Code Bill' that made the variety of regional systems of personal law for 'Hindus', relating to marriage, divorce, succession and maintenance more uniform.

However, this does not mean that secularism did not have a powerful purpose in India, or was ultimately unworkable in Indian conditions. In fact, this paper will argue that Indian secularism's most important role has been in its intermittent, yet powerful symbolic (and sometimes real) protection of Indo-Islamic culture and society, and those of other minorities. Key to the working of the Indian secular state as far as the principal Muslim organizations were concerned was the continued recognition of the separate interests and rights of religious minorities, but within the existing constitutional and political framework of the democratic state. It has allowed India's Muslims, despite the history of religious community separatism implicit in the creation of Pakistan, to theoretically maintain their status as citizens, with all the constitutional rights and duties that entailed, while continuing to protect their own religious cultures and practices.

The problems then were not in the model of Indian secularism, or its institutional implications, but in the matter of its political and everyday application. Indian secularism emerged out of particularly unusual circumstances. It was first debated and defined at a time when a range of movements were building 'national' institutions and promoting ideas of national belonging, in a struggle to replace a foreign (itself secular) colonial power. In this sense, the debates about secularism were always wrapped up in larger political agendas of mobilizing (and in the same instance defining) Indian society. This was a practice which, in the face of the colonial state's focus on religious and caste identities as a fundamental facet of Indian society, often led to the more forceful articulation of religious community. Because anti-colonial struggle took place at a popular level, and involved mass mobilization, secularism could also mean a range of different things to different political ideologues. It was also highly differentiated in its application, being dependent on forms of mobilization and spatial levels of governance.

---

7 For some case studies of how this worked, see Gallanter, "Hinduism, Secularism, and the Indian Judiciary," 268-96.

There were, however, dominant voices in the debates about how far the state should interfere in the religious lives of India's subject-citizens. And quite common in the Congress in north India in the 1930s – the pre-eminent institution of anti-colonial nationalism – was the idea that secularism was anticipated by Hindu philosophy and social organization.[8] These kinds of suggestions had a number of damaging implications. Firstly, they created ambiguities around the application of secularism within state institutions, which meant that there were often important dichotomies between the statement of state policy at a broad level, and its implementation on the ground.[9] Some late twentieth century critiques of secularism as a product of western Enlightenment thinking, and therefore inapplicable to India, have tended to reinforce this ambiguity.[10] Secondly, they tended to play into the hands of ideologues of the Hindu right, who naturally identify 'Hinduism' as the most 'catholic' religious tradition, containing within it principles of toleration. By extension, the Muslim community and Islam became the key agents of communal antagonism, leading one ideologue of the Hindu right to suggest that "Muslim communalism has now acquired a constitutional dignity by the term 'minority rights'".[11]

In order to understand how and why, since the 1980s, scholars have written about a 'crisis of Indian secularism', we therefore need to consider the period of state transition between the 1930s and 1960s, and principally the political adjustments following partition. This will form section I) which follows. In section II) we will examine how, in fact, there was a great deal of potential within the somewhat ambiguous secularism established in India, for the protection of Muslim minorities. The success of India's Muslim communities in promoting Indo-Islamic culture as a core feature of India's national identity, is partly testament to the idea that, although fragile, secularism is not exclusively of value to western states. However, from the 1980s, the security of Muslim communities and organizations in India was disrupted as a result of internal and global changes. In theory, minorities' civic rights remained as they always had been. Yet public intellectuals and the media began to discuss the decline of secularism as a core Indian value – a mood that was essentially driven by the rise of the Hindu right. Section III) will explore this latter phenomenon and its effects on Muslims in India, with specific reference to the destruction of the Babri Masjid in Ayodhya and its longer term implications.

---

8 Gould, Hindu nationalism and the Language of Politics in Late Colonial India, 6-7.

9 Gould, "Contesting 'Secularism' in Colonial and Postcolonial North India," 481-494.

10 Madan, "Secularism in its Place," 747-59.

11 Sankhdher, Secularism in India: Dilemmas and Challenges, 146; Seshadari was at that time General Secretary of the Rashtriya Swayamsevak Sangh See also in the same volume the contributions of Balraj Madhok, President of the Bharatiya Jana Sangh.

I. The Congress and Muslims before 1947

The history of the Indian National Congress's relationship with Muslim communities and institutions is one of the great subjects of historical enquiry, and it forms a crucial point of departure for exploring post-colonial Muslim politics in India. In most accounts, this is a history of gradual alienation, culminating in intense political conflict between Congress and Muslim League, and the latter's apparent demand for a separate sovereign state or states, first articulated (somewhat unclearly) in the Lahore resolution in March 1940. In most accounts, the Congress, although highly variable across India, and only barely representative of either anti-colonial nationalism, or the aspirations of the bulk of the Indian polity, worked on the basis of its secular ideology to recruit Muslims to its cause. To this end, the Congress, particularly in north India, attempted to overcome its associations, both symbolic and real, with organizations and ideologies of Hindu revivalism, through such movements as the 'Muslim Mass Contacts' campaign.[12] For the dominant historical analyses, it was the 'failure' of the naturally secularist approach of institutions like the Congress which ultimately generated Muslim 'alienation'.[13]

In order to explore this narrative of apparent Muslim alienation more fully however, it is necessary to explore the very variable and fluctuating nature of Muslim mobilization in India from the beginning of the century. One of the foundational strategies of the Muslim League, formed in 1906, was to petition the Government of India to implement separate electorates for Muslims. And as the civil services and police 'Indianised', communal representation dominated government discussions about how power might be distributed. For example, in the early 1930s, local governments considered the more careful fixing of communal proportions within the services. This was based on a longer tradition of fixing communal proportions: For example, the UP Board of Revenue had recruited at a rate of between 2 and 4 Muslims for every 5 Hindu appointments.[14] However, this was not a process entirely driven by the state itself. British policy in civil service and police recruitment, although guided to some extent by Orientalist notions of *esprit de corps* which identified ideal 'types' of government servant, was also influenced by community lobbying and preference.[15] After all, the colonial state, particularly at its everyday levels, could ill afford to depart

---

12 One of the fullest accounts of this movement can be found in Hasan, "The Muslim Mass Contacts Campaign," 2273-80.

13 See, for example, Pandey, The Ascendancy of the Congress in Uttar Pradesh.

14 Note by J.M. Clay, "Communal Representation," February 6, 1934 Appointments, United Provinces State Archives, Lucknow, Box 181, File 777/1931.

15 Gould, Bureaucracy, Community and Influence in India, 56-7.

from reliance on significant patterns of local dominance and influence, especially when it was run on a financial shoestring.

The most obvious examples of this were in the lobbying and appeals made in relation to colonial demography. For example, both the Hindu Mahasabha, (founded in 1915, but reformed in 1923), and the Muslim League in the same period, were engaged in pamphlet and newspaper debates about community decline and threats to the 'population', particularly in relation to census figures.[16] This was a politics which 'equated representation with recognition' at one level, in which political support for the Raj was promised in return for guaranteed representation.[17] However, there was certainly nothing fixed about these strategies, and they were not unique to Islamic ideas about *qaum*. There could be a range of positions within any one community grouping, with similar competition occurring within the Muslim community too. Following the extension of separate electorates for Muslims under the 1919 Government of India Act, Shi'a political organisations in UP, for example, claimed that they had been muscled out of legislative assembly seats reserved for Muslims by Sunni candidates. And it was against this background that the All India Shi'a Political Conference was formed in 1925, eventually with its own newspaper *Sarfaraz,* largely in opposition to the perceived Sunni dominance of the Muslim League.[18]

This tendency of the late colonial state to encourage representation by ethnic/religious group (described by one scholar as 'consociationalism')[19] changed over time. This meant that the strategies of Muslim organisations also had to adapt quickly. For example, the principle of separate electorates was the subject of rapidly changing negotiation, agreement, disagreement and redefinition – from the initial phase of Muslim League lobbying in 1906-7, to the Lucknow Pact negotiations of 1916, when Congress and League agreed for a time on separate electorates and one-third reservation for Muslims in a central government. The terms of these agreements shifted again, around a new set of international anti-colonial protests and alliances made between Hindu Congress leaders and Khilafatists in 1918-19. Following the All Parties conferences in 1928, which resulted in the Nehru report, the Muslim League was forced onto the defensive as separate electorates were rejected by the Congress, leading to the articulation of Jinnah's '14 Points'. The latter reinforced the idea that there should be adequate representation for minorities on all elected bodies. Then, by the early 1930s, the Communal Award proposals set the agenda for communal representa-

---

16 See, The Leader, (Allahabad), July 29, August 17-22, 1923.

17 Shaikh, Community and Consensus in Islam, 211.

18 Jones, "The Shi'a Muslims of the United Provinces of India," 210-11.

19 Wilkinson, "India, Consociational Theory and Ethnic Violence," 767-91.

tion in the new planned constitutional reforms of the mid 1930s. Both anti-colonial mobilisation (in the shape of the khilafat movement) and political loyalism (in the shape of the early Muslim League) could shape these demands. However, it was clear that the main institutions promoting 'Muslim' institutional representation worked in the interests of urban and landed elites: the Muslim League was criticised by leftists across the political agenda, and particularly in the Congress and Congress Socialist Party (CSP) as a party whose 'separatism' held no meaning for low status Muslim communities.[20]

It was not the case, however, that poorer Muslims were disinterested in community identity assertion. Other organisations, particularly in the cities and towns of northern India were explicitly religio-political in nature – such as the *tanzeem* and *tabligh* movements of the 1920 and 1930s in UP, especially those of the Shi'a community, which through the 1910s, 20s and 30s, increasingly distanced Shi'a politics from Sunni.[21] The recruitment methods for industrial workers in some of north India's larger cities, such as Kanpur took place through the employment of *mistris* whose approach reinforced community ties. Workers were appointed via community organisations and networks, and were often brought together around rituals and festivals. This had a demographic effect too: Muslims were concentrated, in some urban centres, in particular mohallas or neighbourhoods. These divisions were also reinforced following incidents of 'communal' conflict. For example, in Kanpur following the riot of March 1931, Muslim and Hindu mohallas of the city reportedly became more homogenous.[22] The nature of factory work could divide workers along caste and community lines, particularly where work involved animal products or activities defined as 'unclean' to caste Hindus. Workers were also not unaffected then by revivalist activity, especially as, in cities like Kanpur and Bombay, industrial employment tended to increase worker sectionalism.[23] Other opportunities for community mobilisation appeared in the shape of volunteer movements. Some, for example, the Khaksars, under the leadership of Allama Mashriqi, placed a stress on national service, or evolved in response to the growth of militarism during the 1940s, and in many respects promoted secular agendas.[24] Similar community based volunteer movements engaged in activities that reflected the heightened

20 This was in fact one of the main rationales for the Congress's decision to launch a 'Muslim Mass Contacts' campaign in the late 1930s, as a means of winning over popular Muslim support in opposition to the Muslim League. See Gould, Hindu nationalism, 223-232.

21 See Jones, "The Shi'a Muslims of the United Provinces of India," 180-185.

22 Barrier, The Roots of Communal Politics.

23 Joshi, "Bonds of Community, Ties of Religion," 397-8.

24 Gould, Hindu nationalism, Chapter 7.

political conflicts of the war years, including the Muslim National Guards – an organisation directly related to the Muslim League and the Congress-related Ahrars.[25]

Ultimately however, most of these movements served the interests of particular, regionally located communities for whom demands about weightage in the civil services, or legislative assemblies were related to the political circumstances of the locality. The interests of UP Muslims, who had traditionally dominated the police in that province, and some cadres of the civil services, were quite different to those of Muslim majority provinces, such as Punjab and Bengal. In the latter, politics revolved much more around cross-communal alliances, epitomized in the late 1930s and early 1940s by the leadership of Fazlul Huq, Chief Minister of Bengal between 1937 and 1943, who presented a radically different notion of 'community' to that of M.A. Jinnah. Huq challenged the ideas implicit in the Lahore Resolution and Jinnah's statements thereafter, that the Muslims as a whole constituted a 'separate nation', being for the most part more in favour of a cross-communal, independent Bengali state: a 'regional loyalty that cut across the religious divide'.[26] Typical of this kind of political stance was Huq's involvement in a cross-communal monster meeting in the town hall of Calcutta on the 9 March 1941, in relation to the 1941 census operations. The meeting saw the uniting of Muslim leaders in Bengal with representatives of a range of low caste and 'Scheduled Caste' associations. Huq and other Muslim League leaders made speeches championing the Scheduled Caste groups' and tribals' struggles against caste thraldom and promoting their minority interests.[27] Similarly in the Punjab, the Muslim League did not have sufficient influence before 1946 to form a ministry. The politics of the likes of Fazlul Huq then, exposed the highly fragile nature of what became the 'Pakistan demand', and illustrated the fact that Muslim political opinion was culturally, socially, linguistically and regionally divided.

The idea that 'Pakistan' was, at one level, Jinnah's bargaining tool to win Muslims power at the centre of a future Indian government then,[28] is perhaps suggested by these problems of representing Muslims as a united community in India. Muslims were divided by region, class and sect. However one element

---

25 Gould, Hindu nationalism, 198.

26 Aiyar, "Fazlul Huq, Region and Religion in Bengal," 1215.

27 Memorial of the Calcutta District Muslim League, 5.3.41 to Sir Reginald Maxwell, on Tribal Religion in Census, in "Complaints or representations from organisations representing different communities about matters of communal interest arising in regard to the census enumeration", National Archives of India (NAI), Home Dept. File No. 45/11/41 – Public.

28 Ayesha Jalal effectively presents this argument in The Sole Spokesman.

that did unite all Muslims was their constitutional and political position as 'minorities' within a colonial system that organized political and bureaucratic representation along ethnic lines. The position of Muslims and Muslim organizations therefore underwent a dramatic shift following Indian independence and the creation of Pakistan in 1947, and not only because of the international conflict and ideological dichotomy between these two largest of South Asian states. The very nature of Indian secularism, as we will see in the following section, created a very different context for community mobilization, when compared to the last decades of British India.

II. Muslims and the post-colonial state

The final negotiations between the leaders of the Congress, Muslim League and the last Viceroy in 1947 were, on the surface at least, about an ideological division between the champions of a future secular Indian state, and a minority of 'separatists' for whom nationality would be based around religious community. Yet, this was socially, institutionally and regionally complicated in such a way that Jinnah's demands for separate statehood could only ever have been highly theoretical. Nevertheless, most historical accounts of India's independence and partition reflect this dominant narrative, in which the main parties struggled over the working of the principle of communal parity in any future Indian government at the centre: the Congress accepting parity, but wanting to represent its own Muslims, and the League, under the leadership of M.A. Jinnah, claiming to be the sole representative of any future Muslim representation.[29] The historical memory of these negotiations, in which the Congress ultimately achieved its goal of governing a unitary India with a strong centre, with the League left with 'moth-eaten' scraps of Pakistan, has tended to reinforce a powerful discourse surrounding Indian secularism. Most of the new Indian regimes leaders are depicted as decrying the 'chaos' and mindlessness of partition, or as declaring (in the case of Acharya Kripalani and M.K. Gandhi) that they would continue to move across the new border, or to live in Pakistan. The new, Congress dominated, soon to be Nehruvian India was therefore to be a model democratic, developmental and most importantly, secular state, the crucible of reasonable liberal democratic values and of a shared national culture.

From the perspective of Muslim minorities in India, matters weren't quite so straightforward. Although the Constitution that was eventually established in 1950 contained till then the world's most elaborate and extensive provisions for

29 The debate over parity comes into most of the mainstream historical accounts, such as Wolpert, Jinnah of Pakistan; Jalal, The Sole Spokesman; Singh, The Origins of the Partition of India.

the protection of human rights, including freedom of religious expression; and although Muslim personal law was protected despite the passage of a Hindu Code Bill, constitutional and legal realities were not matched on the ground. Just as in the colonial period, the Raj had ostensibly created the image of a state committed to progressive self government, permeated by western liberal values but undergirded by state repression, so too was there a gulf between the statement and the application of state intentions after 1947. That this should be the case, was not only the result of colonial inheritance however. The specific circumstances of partition, the violence between communities brought in its wake, the confusions of citizenship rights and rehabilitation, the rapid empowerment of political leaders, had created a situation in which state and national security were, for most, not assured. And where such fears were most strongly expressed, so too were attempts made to draw out a unitary sense of national belonging.

For this reason, the government's anti-RSS (and anti-communist) drive, ostensibly in reaction to the assassination of M.K. Gandhi in January 1948, was more than simply a means of shoring up the authority of the new regime.[30] These actions were also used as a pretext for a more complex 'efficiency drive' in which the rooting out of old style 'colonial corruption' in the civil services and local government became a means of targeting 'suspect' Muslims in positions of authority. In the immediate aftermath of partition, executive officers were granted additional powers, not easily questioned or over-turned through the courts, which allowed for the summary arrest of those suspected of subversive activities.[31] Within the civil services itself, new powers given to heads of departments to 'root out useless officers' had also effectively given authorities the opportunity to remove those considered to be 'potential evacuees'. Similarly, rent controllers and those involved in the administration of evacuee property had a great deal of local autonomy. For example, the UP Custodian of evacuee property argued internally that it was often better to seize the property of Muslims, without recourse to 'lengthy' legal proceedings, if the officer in charge of such an action was 'morally convinced' that the Muslim in question was an evacuee.[32] This meant that Muslims who had been caught up in the communal violence of partition and its aftermath, like their Hindu counterparts on the other side of the

30 For a detailed analysis of the implications of Gandhi's assassination and funeral, see Khan, "Performing Peace," 57-80.

31 F.K. Roberts, "Muslims in the Indian Union," May 13, 1949, National Archives Kew (NAK), DO 133/105.

32 V.D. Dantyagi to Bhagwan Sahay, "Administration of Evacuee Property in UP – Method and Tracing out," Relief and Rehabilitation, August 27, 1949, UP State Archives, Box 41, File 552/49.

border, were placed under a special kind of scrutiny, particularly if their families had been divided. In November 1948, the UP government for example, decreed that Muslim government servants who had family members who had migrated to Pakistan should be required to bring them back within a month.[33]

A range of Hindu and Sikh evacuee communities which had passed over the borders of the north east and north west, had experienced the precarious conditions of government sponsored relief and rehabilitation, and themselves tended to turn towards informal mechanisms of self help.[34] In many cases, this involved quite aggressive forms of community assertion and the sponsorship of leaders associated with Hindu communal mobiliisation. P.D. Tandon, the Congress right-wing leader, and founder of the Hindu nationalist *Hind Rakshak Dal,*[35] received with sympathy complaints from Sindhi refugee organisations about the maladministration of Muslim officers and policemen in India.[36] The implications of conflict, following the movement of refugees and the specific targeting of Muslims in India (and minorities on the Pakistan side of the border), continued well into the 1950s. The 'Bengal disturbances' of February to March 1950 for example, involved police instigated attacks on Hindus in Khulna and Rajshaha districts of East Pakistan and led to the flight of around 30,000 people. In reaction, attacks took places against Muslims in Calcutta and surrounding areas (often sponsored by parties of the Hindu right) leading to extensive casualties and damage to Muslim properties. Following violence in some of the main cities of Bengal, a renewed form of propaganda warfare was reignited in newspapers on both sides of the border.[37] Refugee movement on the ground affected the broader politics of both refugee rehabilitation and the management of 'communalism' as it was defined by each state. One report from February 1950, described the effects of atrocity stories being brought by Hindus from East Bengal into Calcutta,

---

33 B.N. Jha to all Heads of Departments and other Principal Heads of Offices, "List of persons in government service who have gone or who intend to go to Pakistan," Police Dept, Box 392, f. 899/47 Uttar Pradesh State Archives (UPSA).

34 See for example, Chatterji, The Spoils of Partition.

35 This organisation is explored in Gould, Hindu Nationalism, Chapter 5, 7.

36 From refugees at Saharanpur, Mangal Sen, Chimman Lal Sharma, Bhagwan Das, Vali Ram, Divan Chand – Punjabis to PD Tandon, 9 November 1947 No. 184, NAI, Tandon Papers, File 301. The representative of the Sindhi Hindu Refugee Panchayat, Jaipur, Durgapur Camp, Gopaldas H Ladhani, Congress Social Worker to PD Tandon January 29,1950, Tandon Papers, File 301, NAI.

37 Inward Telegram to Commonwealth Relations Office, From UK High Commissioner in Pakistan, February 24, 1950, in Bengal Disturbances, February-March 1950, NAK, FO 371/84246, 18, and 21-3; Inward Telegram to Commonwealth Relations Office, From UK High Commissioner in Pakistan to UK High Commissioner in India, 27 February 1950, 30-32.

raising both security concerns in that city, but also igniting tougher attitudes towards Pakistan in the assemblies.[38]

In this context, it was relatively easy for high profile critiques of the new regime in India to highlight (as had happened from the 1930s, via League propaganda), the shallowness of Congress secularism. One A.R. Siddiqi, who had been mayor of Calcutta and MLA in Bengal before independence, publicly complained that Muslims were increasingly becoming 'a servant community' in India. According to Siddiqi, payments to Islamia Hospital in West Bengal were being held up; the salt import and distribution trade in Calcutta which had for many years been dominated by Muslims was now in the hands of Hindu traders, and the distribution of licenses in the hides and skin trades was discriminating against Muslims.[39] Certainly, external observers of the predicament of minorities in India, noticed that despite the installation of an ostensibly secular Congress regime, Muslims were bring treated with suspicion at a day to day level. One UK Foreign Office report of 14 October 1949 suggested that permits granted to Muslims in Bombay had fallen over the course of a year from around 6,000 to 1,500, and that the Evacuee Property Ordinance had hit wealthy Muslims hard, who 'privately [said] that they fear undertaking transactions for fear of being labelled intending evacuees'.[40] Another report noted Liaquat Ali Khan's view, that the Evacuee Property Ordinance was being 'applied with ferocity' in UP, to the extent that where one brother had gone to Pakistan and the other remained (even if the first had departed temporarily), half the house was seized.[41] These kinds of claims and feelings of insecurity provided fodder for the press in Pakistan.[42]

Historians have tended to suggest that the period between 1947 and 1951 was one of adjustment in which it was inevitable that the scars of partition would be inflamed for a time. Once Congress had established itself electorally, the institutional basis for secularism did seem, on the surface, to be set. The ultimate victory of a Nehruvian consensus in the Congress after the first general elections of 1951, involved the defeat of a challenge from the Hindu right within the party, in the person of P.D. Tandon, who won the Congress presidentship in 1950. This seemed to suggest that Congress's natural ideological position was one of unequivocal secular modernism. Yet there was an array of evidence that the dominance of Nehru within the party concealed a more complex and poten-

38 Inward Telegram to Commonwealth Relations Office. UK High Commission in India to UK High Commissioner in Pakistan, February 24, 1950, NAK, FO 371/84246, 9-11.

39 Note of a conversation with Mr. A. R. Siddiqi, NAK, FO 371/84246, 8-10.

40 Note of October 14, 1949, NAK, FO 371/84246, 12-13.

41 J.S.H. Shattock, 1 September 1949, Secret Report 02815/MIN/5, NAK, FO 371/84246, 32.

42 J.S.H. Shattock to Addison, August 20, 1949, NAK, FO 371/84246, 36.

tially more problematic relationship between the principal party of government and Indian Muslims. The Congress, as the dominant voice of the political mainstream and as one of the only coherent organizations at a national level (albeit quickly challenged by an array of regional parties), was the party of choice for most Muslims in key areas the early 1950s.[43] But in some crucial areas, sympathies were revealed within the party for the kinds of political positions held by the Bharatiya Janata Sangh (BJS), which had grown out of the Hindu Mahasabha. One such area surrounded the Hindu Code Bill, passed in a series of acts between 1955 and 1956, and which standardized systems of personal law for Hindus. In the assembly debates on these bills, which were ultimately watered down in their provisions, some of the key Hindu traditionalists within the Congress exerted their influence.[44] In the definition of a national language too, the long standing proponents of Hindi over Urdu (a language championed by key north Indian Muslim organizations) raised more questions about Congress's commitment to unequivocal secularism.[45]

Constitutionally too, Indian secularism possessed a potential fragility which reflected some of these ambiguities surrounding the post-colonial regime. And these too were to affect the position of Muslim communities and organizations after 1947. Significant here were the somewhat ambiguous 'directive principles' of the 1950 Constitution which allowed for a ban on cow slaughter. The closure or control of slaughter houses and the issue of cow protection generally, had been one of the central rallying calls of a range of Hindu nationalist organizations since the late 19th Century. In 1966, when a large anti-cow slaughter rally took place across north India, a number of Hindu Congress leaders showed sympathy for the cause, and in states such as UP and Bihar, a ban was put into effect. Yet the slaughter of cows had demonstrably become in the late colonial period an activity of both occupational and religious significance, particularly for poorer Muslim communities in north India.[46]

Understandably then, Muslim organizations adapted slowly and uncertainly to the context of Indian secularism. Whereas before independence, traditions of political separatism and communal representation had been a natural part of Muslim political organisation, it was more difficult to adjust to the new political climate, at least at first. The main religious seminaries of Dar-ul-Ulum at Deoband, UP and the Nadwat-ul-Ulama in Lucknow, and indeed the Jamaat-i-Islami recognized this discomfort at first, with the latter officially stating in 1952 that

---

43 For material on the voting patterns of Muslims, see Reeves et al., A handbook to elections in Uttar Pradesh.

44 For details on this process, see Som, "Jawaharlal Nehru and the Hindu Code."

45 Hasan, Legacies of a Divided Nation.

46 For a short case study of this situation, see Gould, "Contesting Secularism."

the modern secular state 'rests on the denial of God...' – a position which it changed, welcoming the idea of Indian secularism, in 1970.[47] This shift over the late 1950s and early 1960s was partly the result of the Muslim polity in India supporting the incumbent regimes of the Congress through the first three general elections of 1952, 1957 and 1962. It was also the result of the complete rejection of 'communal' organizations in the post-colonial period. But this spirit of accommodation with the party of the regime was relatively short-lived. Disenchantment with the Congress began to resurface from the mid 1960s, as a result of Congress's failure to alleviate Muslim under-representation in the Indian Administrative Service, police and army, and their inability to control an upsurge in anti-Muslim communal violence.[48]

In 1964, the Majlis-I Mushawarat was formed to express these Muslim grievances, and as an immediate reaction to riots in Calcutta, Jamshedpur and Jabalpur in the summer of that year. This organization did not, like the Muslim League, seek to enter politics directly, but aimed instead to influence policy making indirectly. In this sense, unlike the pre-1947 Muslim organizations, which aimed to reshape the notion of political representation by forwarding, in some cases, ideologies of separatism, the Majlis promoted Muslim interests within India's existing political system and constitutional structures. Its *People's Manifesto* of July 1966 therefore argued that Muslims should not attempt to see themselves as a politically separate entity, but should work within India's pluralistic system. It also promoted the idea of 'national integration', the promotion of inter-communal harmony in education, Urdu as a medium of education and expression, proportional representation, and social welfare. However, it did also call for the protection of Muslim personal law, even though reforms and changes were progressing in Pakistan, UAR, and Tunisia.[49] Although a range of parties supported it, there is evidence that the Congress's relative loss of Muslim support in the elections 1967 was partly explained by the Majlis's influence. Certainly in UP, quite a bit of thought went into the implications of opposing the Congress, when the main threat to the latter was the Hindu right wing BSP, which might benefit from such a shift in electoral loyalty.[50] Involved in supporting international policies of the Indian government, such as support for Palestine during the Arab-Israeli 6 day war of June 1967, the Majlis nevertheless was weakened when it split in 1968.[51]

---

47 Hasan, "Indian Muslims since Independence," 818-821.

48 Hasan, "Indian Muslims since Independence," 823.

49 Quraishi, "Emergence and Eclipse of Muslim Majlis-e-Mushawarat," 1229-1234.

50 Quraishi, "Electoral Strategy of a Minority Pressure Group," 980-981.

51 Quraishi, "Emergence and Eclipse," 1233-1234.

Another important shift from the mid to late 1960s was two further developments that had international dynamics. Firstly, the temporary growth in influence of the RSS and the BJS in 1964-1965 was related to the jingoism connected to the Indo-Pakistan war. This situation was, in turn, partly the result of changing Indian policy towards Kashmir, whereby the Indian government attempted to gradually integrate Kashmir's regime to India by engineering a more acceptable administration in 1964.[52] Secondly, there was also in this period a resurgence in communal violence. Recorded 'incidents' increased from 26 in 1960, to 92 in 1961 and 1,170 in 1964. In December 1963, a holy relic disappeared from Kashmir's Hazratbal mosque, which had international implications in terms of religious conflict: clashes immediately occurred in Jabbalpur in MP, and in Khulna and Jessore in East Pakistan, as a result of the Pakistani government's deliberate anti-Indian propaganda following the incident. Rumours of Hindu atrocities against Muslims in East Pakistan, resulted in the pulling down of some Muslim stalls in Calcutta by Hindu groups and a deputation to the High Commission of East Pakistan to demand the protection of Hindu minorities in the other state. Further incidents led to a mass march to the High Commissioner's office on 10 January 1964, and a large-scale riot on 11-13 January, in which Muslims were targeted. Cries of 'Pakistan zindabad' ('long live Pakistan') were reportedly heard in some of the Muslim slums and rumours spread of arms being provided to Indian Muslims by Pakistan.[53]

Despite these events, for the most part, the period of the 1960s and 1970s was not marked by anything like the level of ethnic conflict or tension of the years immediately leading up to independence, or to the period from the 1980s, which will be discussed more in the section which follows. This might be explained too, by the status of some of the principal Muslim organizations. Despite its gradual acquiesce to the Indian secular state in 1970, having previously followed Maududi's powerful stance against secularism, the Jamaat-i-Islami, as one of the principle organizations of fundamentalist revivalism, was subject to the close scrutiny of the Indian state over the 1960s and 1970s. This was particularly the case during Indira Gandhi's Emergency. Between 1975 and 1977, the organization was banned and many of its leaders were imprisoned. However the Jamaat-i-Islami's long-standing resistance to the idea of the secular state could not last, not least because the system of democratic secularism had effectively allowed the organization to have so much influence across a range of Muslim educational and political institutions: the Jamaat was involved in the formation

52 Visit of Mr. Z. A. Bhutto, March 1964, Brief for the Secretary of State, 11 March 1964, in 'Indo/Pakistan Kashmir Dispute', NAK, FO 371/175896.

53 Das, "The 1992 Calcutta Riot," 287-91.

of the Majlis-I Mushawarat, and it carried a lot of influence in the Aligarh Muslim University and other educational centres.[54] In this sense, India's political climate in this period effectively meant that the retrograde ideologies of the movement were diffused. Indeed, it had become apparent to some of the Jamaat's leaders by the 1970s that its anti-secular stance was also behind the times in relation to debates in countries like Indonesia and Egypt.[55]

Of greater significance to most Indian Muslims, as with other communities, were the day-to-day matters of everyday life, access to education, housing, markets, jobs and matters relating to the welfare of the family. In this last area, perhaps the most conservative and seemingly anti-secular position of some Muslim organizations has been their reaction to the demands for a uniform civil code. These include the Tablighi Jamaat, the Jamaat-i-Islami and the Jamiyat al-ulema. Importantly, the last of these organizations directly links the rights of Muslims to maintain their own personal law to the fundamental principles of Indian secularism: the potential abandonment of personal law has been likened to a breaking of the 'covenant' of composite nationalism, implicit in the alliance between Hindus and Muslims in pre-independence days.[56] Key to the working of Indian secularism as far as these organizations were concerned then, was the continued recognition of the separate interests and rights of religious minorities, but within the existing constitutional and political framework of the democratic state. As we will see in the next section too, changes in the mid 1980s led to the strengthening of this defensive position, in the setting up of an All India Personal Law Board.

Muslim responses to the postcolonial state after 1947 were characterized by three periods of political change and accommodation: firstly in the immediate aftermath of partition and independence, up to the first general elections, Muslim organizations had to rapidly adjust to a situation in which the ostensibly secular Indian state showed signs of fragility and inconsistency. The Congress's traditional role as the ostensible protector of minorities was thwarted at the level of everyday politics, and by the very complexities of how constitutional directives were implemented. Muslims experienced this situation in very variable ways, depending on region and culture. However, through the 1950s, most accommodated themselves to the pluralism of India's secular political system – a shift illustrated in the Muslim support for the Congress in the first three elections. A second shift occurred in the mid to late 1960s, as the Congress weakened electorally, as new upwardly mobile agricultural communities became po-

54 Hasan, Legacy of a Divided Nation, 206-8.

55 Agrama, "Secularism, Sovereignty, Indeterminacy," 518-523.

56 Hasan, "Indian Muslims since Independence," 840.

litically significant, and following a temporary rise in the popularity of the Hindu right. Also significant were the gradual changes in Indian government policy towards Kashmir, with the subordination of the National Conference there to the Congress.[57] Finally there was a third period of rapid transformation for Muslims in India in the early to mid 1980s, which again involved a resurgence in communal violence and a new range of controversies surrounding the nature of the secular state in India. This crucial period will be explored in the final section.

III. Muslims, secularism and the rise of the Sangh Parivar

Historians have traditionally attempted to explain the apparent resurgence in communal violence against Muslims in India in the 1980s, with reference to the rise of the Hindu right and the declining authority of the Congress in India.[58] There were approximately four times as many conflicts in that decade compared to the 1970s, with a particular peak from after early 1986 – a form of violence that was to increase still further in the early 1990s. The growth in 'communal' movements and parties over the same period has also been noted, increasing reportedly from less than a dozen in 1951, to over 500 by 1988.[59] The Congress lost more of its traditional Muslim following and the Bharatiya Janata Party or BJP (reformed from the BJS in 1981), stepped into the national and regional political spaces of relative Congress decline. Over the same period of the early to mid 1980s, historians have shown how the Congress increasingly embraced ideologies of Hindu 'majoritarianism', for example, adopting a typical Hindu right strategy of denouncing political opposition movements as 'anti national'.[60] This was not just about the increasing popularity of the institutions of the Hindu right but also the indifference and neglect of the principle of state secularism itself and the flirtation with communal mobilisation by a range of parties. For some writers, the apparently increasing popularity of religious fundamentalism, revivalism or communal mobilisation could be generalised to include other states, notably Pakistan in the 1980s.[61] However, the changes of the 1980s were also related to contingent political events in India and the peculiar quality (and limitations) of secularism and the secular state.

Connected to these new tensions facing the stability of Indian secularism, were some significant international changes and influences, which need to be

57 Balraj Puri, "Indian Muslims since Partition," 2143.

58 For example, Zoya Hasan, "Changing Orientation of the State," 27- 37.

59 Hasan, "Indian Muslims since Independence," 830.

60 Zoya Hasan, "Changing Orientation of the State," 30.

61 See for example, Mark Juergensmeyer, The New Cold War? Religious Nationalism Confronts the State.

taken into account, especially in their bearing on the self (and external) perception of Muslim organizations. During the 1980s, international events affected communal conflicts in new ways. For example, between September and October 1982, a series of riots broke out in Meerut, Uttar Pradesh, in which the Sangh Parivar organizations of the Hindu right attempted to mobilize Dalits as part of a broader campaign to pre-empt supposed Muslim conversions. In its propaganda against Muslims the Hindu right represented India as a unitary, pre-1947 entity, and paraded in processions with maps of Pakistan and Bangladesh depicted in the colour saffron. It popularised the idea of the rise of 'Islamic fundamentalism' in the Arab world, and the India-wide debates about a uniform civil code.[62] The 'threat' of Pakistan was a constant point of reference, with remarks and debates on the need to 'bring it back' to India or destroy it. In one such procession at Sholapur in 1982, the slogans heard repeated at a VHP rally included 'jalado, jalado Pakistan jalado' ('burn, burn Pakistan'), 'Ek dhakka aur do, Pakistan tor do' ('give one more push and break Pakistan'). Perhaps most interesting here were slogans about the specific fortunes of migrant Muslims and their properties: 'Ye desh Hinduon ka, nahin kisi ke bap ka' ('this country belongs to the Hindus and is not of somebody's father's property').[63]

Of significance in such events were developments in other parts of South Asia, which provided these kinds of slogans with extra currency. In Pakistan, the regime of Zia-ul-Huq had initiated what some described as a process of 'Islamicization'. Zia decreed that all aspects of social and political life, all offices of the state, politics and administration, would be 'regulated in accordance with Islamic Principles'.[64] Islamization also affected development policies targeted at women, reinforcing patrilinear conceptions of law and the legal process.[65] Madrasah foundation increased over the decade, especially those sponsored by the Jama'at-i-Islami.[66] In the early 1980s, Gulf state financial support was also linked to a desire to provide an Islamic bulwark against the invaders of Afghanistan, with some of the madrasahs' activitists being trained up to fight against the USSR. Many of the graduates of the new madrasahs were therefore keen to promote jihad in relation to events in Afghanistan, and some of the ulama modelled themselves on the example of the Taliban, and competed for funding from the Gulf states. But the apparently growing pertinence of ethnic and religious conflict was not confined to Islamic groups. In Sri Lanka, ethnic conflict be-

62 Engineer, "Behind the Communal Fury," 356-357.

63 Engineer, "Behind the Communal Fury," 357.

64 Speech of Zia-ul-Huq, August 14, 1977. Quoted in Noman, Pakistan: A Political and Economic History since 1947, 145.

65 See Weiss, "Women's Position in Pakistan," 863-80.

66 Keddie, "Pakistan's Movement against Islamization," 40-41.

tween the Sinhalese majority and Tamil minorities had, by 1984, grown into a full scale civil war and separatist movement. Within India itself, regional separatist movements in the Punjab and Assam were making fresh demands on the central government. The Congress regimes of the mid 1980s under the leadership of Rajiv Gandhi were not prepared either, however, to re-assert Congress's core secular ideologies, in the face of these challenges.

Clearly then, one of the concomitant weaknesses of Indian secularism was that while it provided space for the articulation of, and protection of Muslim minority rights, it also tended to let regimes off the hook when it came to the combating communal parties. And its coexistence with the continued use of religious motifs in political mobilization meant that events in other states involving the assertion of religious ideologies, could lead to direct political reactions in India. In fact, the argument should be taken further: that since the Congress had always sought to represent the broadest national constituencies possible, it was part of its own ideological logic that (as had been the case historically), it might appeal to religious sentiments and parties. This seemed to happen at moments when the Congress, as an organization, had less reason to outwardly promote a secular agenda (as in the 1920s-30s), or when it faced growing party political opposition and instability. In the mid 1980s, Rajiv's Gandhi's regime played to the two main communities: on the one hand, state affairs now involved Hindu symbolism and ritual, and the government sponsored television network (Doordarshan) sponsored the serialization of the two Hindu epics – the Mahabharata and Ramayana.[67] The government also pandered to Muslim orthodoxy in passing the Muslim Women (Protection on Rights of Divorce) Act of 1986, in response to the Supreme Court's upholding of a maintenance order against the erstwhile husband of one Shah Bano. The 'Shah Bano Affair' as it came to be known, in which the husband claimed he only had to pay maintenance for three months under the *Shariat* became a cause célèbre for organizations of Muslim revivalism attempting to combat what they viewed as the Indian state's interference in religious affairs. It was clear that the government had capitulated to the Muslim Personal Law Board on the issue, and there were large-scale demonstrations by Muslim organizations in cities such as Lucknow, rejecting the idea of a Uniform Civil Code.[68]

The affair was also, however, significant in the promotion of the agendas of the Hindu right in India, especially in the lead up to what became perhaps the most contentious religious conflict since independence. In February 1986, a Congress administration in UP had agreed to the re-opening (for Hindu worship)

---

67 For a detailed survey of this, see Rajagopal, Politics after Television.

68 Hasan, Legacy of a Divided Nation, 263-264.

of a site of long term dispute between Hindus and Muslims in Ayodhya. Under the leadership of L.K. Advani, and following a long-term VHP campaign on the issue, the BJP led a movement to rebuild a temple to Ram on the site of the Babri Masjid (built in 1528) in Ayodhya – the supposedly birthplace of Lord Ram. The Sangh Parivar claimed that the mosque had been built on the ruins of an ancient temple site and in 1990 Advani launched a *yatra* to the disputed site, reinforcing what came to be known as the Ram Janmabhoomi movement. The BJP reaped electoral dividends. But more seriously, on 6 December 1992, the Babri Masjid was attacked and largely destroyed by *kar sevaks,* leading to riots across north India and south west to Mumbai, which resulted in around 2000 deaths.[69] The political benefits for the BJP and associated movements continued through most of the 1990s, culminating in BJP power at the centre within the National Democratic Alliance. Muslims in general, even in north India, reacted to these events with some caution. The Babri Masjid Action Committee had, in February 1987, organised an anti-government demonstration against the re-opening of the Babri Masjid, which resulted in a mass meeting of around 300,000 in New Delhi. But after the mosque's demolition, the organisation collapsed.[70] The demolition of the Babri Masjid, like many other issues of long-standing religious significance in India has had political and international reverberations that continue right up to the present day. In 2002 a pogrom against Muslims in Gujarat was carried out by organizations of the Hindu right, with the apparent acquiescence of the state administration, after the setting on fire of a train carriage of Ayodhya pilgrims on 27 February. The legal wrangles also continue. In 2010, the Allahabad High Court ruled that the disputed site should be partitioned between two Hindu (Nirmohi Akhada, and Ram Lalla deity) and a Muslim organization (the Sunni Waqf Board). But this too has recently been stayed by a Supreme Court ruling.

The response of the Jamiyat-ul-ulama and of the ulama in general to the demolition was more forthright, and the Muslim Personal Law Board moved to set up Islamic courts, in a campaign to resolve issues on the basis of the Quran. This signaled a reaction on the part of the orthodox to promote still more conservative approaches to the resolution of issues relating to women. The reaction outside India was of a different order. The demolition of the Babri Masjid in India resulted in retributive violence against Hindus and temples in Pakistan. Its media reacted to these events by expressing doubts about the integrity of Indian secularism, and the extent to which Indian regimes were either able or willing to

---

69 For a detailed account of Ram Janmabhoomi see Van Der Veer, Religious Nationalism.

70 Hasan, Legacy of a Divided Nation, 312.

validate its legal principles.[71] In Bangladesh too, violence broke out in Dhaka as news filtered through about the demolition of the mosque in Ayodhya. The Indian Airlines office, the Indian Cultural Centre and the Bangladeshi Communist Party offices were all targeted and attacked and a number of temples were demolished.[72] The impact of events in India affecting Muslims globally was of course not at all new, as the Khilafat movement itself demonstrated. However, the 1980s was a period in which such global communications were enhanced and given new urgency.

What emerges from these incidents is the highly contingent ways in which the principles of Indian secularism have been applied on the ground in political practice –something which has made the political strategies of Muslim organisations both difficult to formulate and precarious, especially since the 1980s. On the one hand, the actions of local organisations, parties and movements combined with the political motivations of regimes that seek popular legitimacy, has created a range of loop-holes for the continued promotion of religious agendas by political parties. The Gujarat violence of 2002 provides a good example of this. The evidence collected on the violence was mostly unreliable.[73] Nevertheless, the Gujarat police invoked the Prevention of Terrorism Act to arrest 123 alleged conspirators, including Deobandis and alleged Islamic militants. Subsequent independent enquiries suggested that during the worst violence in Ahmedabad, the police had stood by or actively participated as the violence progressed. And India's National Human Rights Commission reported that much of the violence was premeditated by the Sangh Parivar and associated organisations, and that its implications reached to the top of the BJP-led Gujarat administration. The two principal commissions of enquiry - the Nanavati and the Banerjee commissions – were also politically motivated, representing different sides of the debate on the causes of the violence. On the other hand, state agencies in India continue to identify 'communalism' using the methods of colonial regimes and ethnographies, which presuppose the 'essential' characteristics of different ethnic groups. The Godhra Muslims were associated with the Ghanchi community who, in the manner of old colonial ethnographies, were described by previous studies of communal violence as 'backward' and 'aggressive'.[74] Similarly, the controversies surrounding Ayodhya date back at least to the mid 19th Century, and they show no signs of entirely dissipating today. But they are a con-

71 Monshipouri, "Backlash to the Destruction at Ayodhya," 711-721.

72 Ghosh, "Bangladesh at the Crossroads," 697-710.

73 "The truth about Godhra," The Hindu, Online Edition, January 29, 2005, last accessed on 20 March 2010, http://www.hindu.com/2005/01/23/stories/2005012303901400.htm.

74 Engineer, "Communal Riots in Godhra," 1638-1640.

stant reminder of how powerless ostensibly secular regimes have been in the protection of some of the oft-stated principles of Indian secularism.

Conclusion

Secularism has become one of the main political battlegrounds of the modern day state and political system. Yet in any context it is rarely adequately defined and certainly never applied consistently. Its parameters are, by the very nature of the complex societies in which it commonly appears, often in doubt, and vulnerable to change. This encourages rather than hinders discussion about secularism and such debates have certainly been common since the early 1990s. Secularism in India was, in certain phases of the country's democratic existence, clearly a powerful context in which Muslim communities, like other religious minorities, were able to protect and promote their civic and political rights, while worshiping freely. But as the global influence of India changed, and as the events of other states affected the internal politics of India in new ways, some of the inherent weaknesses of state secularism began to tell. Equally, when these global changes, particularly the relationship between India and other South Asian states (principally Pakistan), coincided with significant social and political changes in India, opportunities appeared for parties to test the malleability of secularism as the separation of religion from politics. Of great significance in this sense (although not discussed at length here), has been the rise of Dalit, 'Backward Caste' and 'Other Backward Caste' political movements since the early 1990s, partly as a result of social and political changes dating back to the late 1960s. As politics continues to revolve around sectional interests defined by ethnicity - the latent practices of communal mobilization are reignited. At one level this is the result of a gulf between the principles and the realities of state power, and the difficulty of applying the ideological frameworks of a highly centralized state machinery to India's many regions and local situations. But more importantly, it is about the continued power of historical modes of political mobilization, that take us back to the colonial era, especially when we consider the predicament of religious minorities.

Colonialism in India introduced a system that promoted at one and the same time, both ethnic/religious representation for political purposes, but also modern secular ideologies in the operation of the state. This clearly was crucial, and continues to mark the domestic policies of postcolonial states such as the UK and France in their policies towards minorities, immigration and community representation. However, the importance of India's colonial past, in defining the nature of post-colonial secularism, has also been in the kinds of regimes that emerged from the struggle against foreign power. The Congress was a movement that had to attempt to represent all Indian political interests, but in doing so it tended to contain within it, albeit sometimes obscured, a powerful ideological commitment (via its membership) to majoritarian representations of Indian national culture. These, at certain moments, privileged forms of religious mobilization, particularly around modern 'Hindu' motifs, whose ideologues in the late colonial period naturally embraced some of the 'modernising' trends of the period. This has meant that, from the beginning and even in the Nehruvian phase, the successor regime to the Raj was always capable of mobilizing communities on the basis of their religious affiliation. But at the same time, in terms of state institution building the same regimes were committed to the idea of a 'secular state'. Herein lies another of the ambiguities, or the ill defined sets of parameters of Indian secularism.

For the most part, this chapter has argued that this loosely defined secularism has often benefitted Muslim minorities in states such as India in unexpected ways. Clearly, during the 1950s and early 1960s, a range of Muslim institutions in India were able to develop and thrive and in general Muslim populations continued to coexist peacefully with other communities in most of the country. Even during the violence of the 1990s and early 2000s, when the Hindu right was seemingly on the ascendant, India's constitutional structures, and most importantly, her political system, have provided some protection for the free articulation of minority identities. This is perhaps most aptly demonstrated in the results of the 2004 election, which saw the return to power of the Congress at the centre, following a phase of BJP power. Politically, the Hindu right (rather like the Congress) cannot afford to pursue any hard line policies towards religious communities, or unravel the secular state, if it wishes to remain electable in what is a highly complex multi-ethnic, federal system.

Equally, the intermittent working of secularism in India has also been made possible by the heterogeneous nature of the Muslim community there. Movements of Muslim separatism in India in any period, have never been able to capture more than a minority, even though in some cases such minorities have been politically influential. This variation has also meant that attempts to promote fundamentalism, or religious radicalism in India as a whole have rarely been successful for very long. Neither have the vast majority of India's Muslims taken a serious interest in existence of Pakistan. In this sense, we need to be careful in thinking about the predicament of Muslims as the largest minority in India, to not, as was suggested in section i), examine the community as if it were a homogenous mass, and dominated by north Indian traditions. Here again, the different global experiences and perceptions of India's Muslim communities is significant. Certainly, the Urdu speaking Muslims of Uttar Pradesh suffered as a result of the departure of some of its key intellectual champions to Pakistan, and as a by-product of state governments in the region who have done little to protect it in relation to Hindi. However, Malayi, Tamil, Gujarati and Marathi Muslims have, since the 1980s, maintained a higher standard of living than their co-religionists in the north, partly as a result of higher levels of education, and partly as a result of economic ties with Hong Kong, Singapore and the Gulf states, via work migration.[75] Equally, most of the causes of the Urdu speaking north Indian Muslim organizations in the post 1947 period have not held much appeal for Muslims in other states of India. Indian secularism then, was perhaps not an ideological principle deliberately determined by different regimes of the twentieth century. It was perhaps more, a logical precondition of India's very political existence as a highly heterogeneous, yet unitary state.

75 Aiyar, Mani Shankar, Confessions of a Secular Fundamentalist, 180.

Linguistic Movements, Secessionism and State-Building in India

Nicolas Blarel

> *"In these matters of language one has to be very careful. One has to be as liberal as possible and not try to suppress a language. We should not try to coerce anybody into using a language, as far as possible. Whenever an attempt has been made to suppress a popular language or coerce the people into using some other language, there has been trouble." Jawaharlal Nehru*[1]

Introduction

Why do some ethnic conflicts escalate and end in territorial dismemberment while others are settled through negotiations? Why do some ethnic groups move from initial claims over cultural rights (such as public use of minority languages and cultural symbols in education and dealings with the state) with relatively low territorial implications to more radical demands for territorial autonomy?[2]

Ethnic mobilization among certain minority populations in multi-ethnic states like India has often led to varying demands ranging from greater participation in the decisions taken by the central state to self-rule (territorial autonomy), and even sometimes demand for complete secession. After independence, India had to manage its exceptional diversity in terms of languages, religions, castes and tribes while building its new institutions.[3] Unlike most Western states, India faced the problem of ethnic heterogeneity under conditions of a modern state-building project. Given these conditions, India's record on integrating and reassuring separate ethnic groups is mixed. The existing literature on Indian ethnic movements has highlighted factors such as inherited colonial insti-

---

1 Jawaharlal Nehru, The Official Languages, 16-32.

2 In this chapter, I shall refer to ethnic groups' demands or claims as calls made by legitimate representatives of an ethnically defined community against the state or central government for goods that may be collectively enjoyed by the community. This is a simplification as there is almost always a range of interests advocated by members of a group, as well as competition among actors within the groups over questions of means and goals. The concept 'ethnic groups' suggests that under certain circumstances individuals will unite even if divisions subsist at the subgroup level.

3 This chapter will use a broad definition of ethnicity advanced by Horowitz in his book Ethnic Groups in Conflict, 41-54. Horowitz argues that conflicts based on ascribed group identities such as race, language, religion, tribe, or caste can be called 'ethnic.'

tutions,[4] post-colonial institutional design,[5] elite and instrumental theories,[6] and degree of democratization[7] to explain the existence or absence of secessionist demands. These explanations, while introducing important variables, have neither managed to define the reasons for the onset of secessionist conflicts nor to explain the disparity of reactions by ethnic movements to state policies across the Indian Union. The existing studies have mostly ignored the dynamic process of ethnic groups interacting with the government over a longer period of time, and they have paid too little attention to how this process influenced separatist demands and the early Indian state-making process.

This chapter will address these questions with more specific reference to linguistic conflicts in post-independence India. In doing so, it will explore the link between the nature of the state's interaction with linguistic groups and the existence of secessionist claims. After independence, Indian national leaders had to cope with several language problems. The boundaries of British India did not conform to linguistic divisions, and demands for stronger minority linguistic rights emerged almost immediately after independence. Many observers agree that language policy has been one of India's main success stories in its state-making process. However, it is difficult to discern a linear and coherent state-making process in New Delhi's reactions to language-related secessionist demands. Fearing the possible 'balkanization' of India, the central government practiced a case-by-case approach to settle the different linguistic disputes.

This chapter proposes to explain different trajectories of movements for secession and autonomy by comparing two Indian regions in the post-independence years: Tamil Nadu and the Punjab. What the two regions had in common was the presence of a substantial minority community and the potential that the language conflicts would escalate into a secessionist struggle. Yet their relations with and the reaction of the central government towards their claims were very different. For example, in 1956 the Indian state decided to accommodate some linguistic and territorial autonomy demands from the Tamil movement but rejected other claims from the Punjabi Suba movement.[8] Why was

---

4 Chadda. "Integration through Internal Reorganization"; Adeney, Federalism and Ethnic Conflict Regulation; Wilkinson, Votes and Violence.

5 Lijphart, "The Puzzle of Indian Democracy"; Wilkinson, Votes and Violence; Stepan, Linz and Yadav, Crafting State-Nations.

6 Brass, Language, Religion, and Politics.

7 Kohli, "Can Democracies Accommodate Ethnic Nationalism?"; Gurpahal Singh, Ethnic Conflict in India.

8 Punjabi Suba which means Punjabi-speaking state was the proposed state reorganization by the Akali Dal (the political organization of the religious Sikh movement) in the

there state accommodation in the Tamil case and not in Punjab? Why were Punjabi territorial demands accommodated in 1966 and not in 1956?

Evidence from the two cases seems to prove that demands for secession are neither innate nor calculated in anticipation of state reaction but the outcome of reiterated interaction and growing trust or frustration with state authorities. Similarly, the Indian state's evolving and multifaceted strategy to manage and contain ethnic tensions was not premeditated; it was decisively shaped by its interactions with the various ethnic groups. It is my impression that previous studies have overlooked the dynamic nature of state-group interactions over a longer period of time and how it can impact capabilities and strategies of the involved actors.

Insights from and limitations of the existing literature on secession

Until recently, the literature on ethnic wars and secession focused almost exclusively on the political, economic, and social conditions that can provide the motive and opportunity for groups to rebel and secede. For example, some scholars have argued that ethnic conflict is more likely to happen when certain groups feel materially disadvantaged relative to other groups in a country, and when they fail to achieve their desired economic goals.[9] Other studies have analyzed how existing restrictions on cultural, linguistic and religious practices can lead to ethnic rebellions.[10] If ethnic minorities do not believe that central governments (often controlled by ethnic majorities) can guarantee their protection, secession might appear as the only alternative.[11] Building on similar arguments, some South Asia scholars have therefore considered that linguistically diverse regions were therefore considered to be latent bases of secessionist movements that could lead to the balkanization of the Indian Union.[12] These approaches tend to over-predict conflict.[13] They neglect dynamic factors like repeated interactions between the state authorities and ethnic groups and how the responding po-

---

1950s and 1960s which would result in the trifurcation of the former East Punjab province into three states: Punjab (India), Himachal Pradesh and Haryana.

9 Horowitz, Ethnic Groups in Conflict; Gurr, People Versus States; Collier and Hoeffler, "Greed and Grievance in Civil War"; Fearon, "Why Do Some Civil Wars Last So Much Longer Than Others?"; and Besancon, "Relative Resources."

10 Walker Connor, Ethnonationalism; Bartkus, The Dynamic of Secession; Barry Posen, "The Security Dilemma and Ethnic Conflict."

11 Fearon. "Commitment Problems and the Spread of Ethnic Conflict"; Toft, The Geography of Ethnic Violence.

12 Harrison for example predicted in the late 1950s a disintegration of the Indian state in The Most Dangerous Decades.

13 Ibid.

litical and institutional arrangements can satisfy the demands of regional, religious, ethnic, or other groups with secessionist potential.[14]

In recent years, new studies have developed more dynamic models to study patterns of interaction between states and ethnic groups.[15] Influenced by bargaining theory, this new scholarship mostly insists on the key role private information plays in the outbreak and resolution of conflict.[16] This literature identifies an uncertain strategic environment in which both the state and the ethnic groups evaluate their respective capabilities and intentions.[17] These studies have demonstrated that collective ethno-nationalist action requires not just structural opportunities but also strategic willingness to challenge the state. However, the limits of such approaches are especially visible in new emerging states like post-independence India, where new leaders and evolving institutions often gave mixed signals about their ethnic policies.[18] Hence, the studies do not capture the degree of variation in strategies of accommodation and violence that the state can use, and they do not pay adequate attention to how this variation influences groups' demands and strategies. For example, how can we explain that some groups like the Tamils in India felt more confident that they would obtain concessions within the institutional framework than the Sikhs in Punjab, who escalated their demands? Where did these ethnic groups obtain information about the state capacities and intentions? How did each case of accommodation influence the other?

Drawing on existing studies in the social movements' literature on deterrence and escalation and on the effect of repression and accommodation on dissent, this chapter will attempt to offer an understanding of variation in ethnic conflict intensity linked to state action in post-independence India.[19] Government sanctions can reduce the ability of dissident groups to mobilize by increasing the costs of protest, but they can also create micro-level incentives to protest against illegitimate repression.[20] Also, accommodation can be accompanied by

---

14 I assume a more state-centric approach which includes the state as an actor in the escalatory process and examine state repression and accommodation as a part of an ongoing interactive process between the groups and the state.

15 Cetinyan, "Ethnic bargaining"; Walter, "Information, uncertainty, and the decision to secede"; Jenne, Ethnic bargaining; Cunningham, Gleditsch, and Salehyan, "It takes two: A dyadic analysis of civil war duration and outcome."

16 Fearon, "Rationalist Explanations for War."

17 Walter, Reputation and Civil War.

18 Fearon. "Commitment Problems and the Spread of Ethnic Conflict."

19 Lichbach, "Deterrence or Escalation?"; McAdam, Tarrow, and Tilly, Dynamics of Contention; Sambanis and Zinn, "From protest to Violence."

20 Tarrow, Power in Movement. For a definition of state repression, see Davenport, "State Repression and Political Order."

repression, or used as a method to split the dissidents between co-opted moderates and radicals.[21] In the context of ethnic conflict, some scholars argue that substantial concessions like offering regional autonomy will reduce tensions.[22] Others believe that concessions and devolution of power are closely tied to an ethnic minority's willingness and capacity to revolt and secede, seeing that they can enhance the perceived legitimacy, cohesion and capacity of that group.[23] Studying different forms of state action (repression, indifference, accommodation) can help to understand why and how ethnic groups radicalize or de-radicalize their demands.

This chapter looks at secessionist conflict as the result of a process of strategic interaction between ethnic groups and the central state over a longer period of time, specifically at how it shapes the group's expectations about the costs and benefits of secession. Focusing on the dyadic relationship between the state and linguistic groups in India, it argues that the decision of ethnic groups for or against violence was shaped by the state's ways of dealing with their claims.

Evidence from India: divergent trajectories in Tamil Nadu and Punjab

Examples of potential conflict over language and ethnic differences were most visible in India in the post-colonial context. Under British rule, English was the official colonial language, and linguistic plurality did not provide the basis for the establishment of administrative units. Language-related grievances certainly existed but there was little opportunity to express those concerns.[24] Yet the language problem was already discussed prior to independence. The Indian Congress Party committed itself to a post-colonial political order of linguistically-defined states. In 1922 it decided to reorganize the branches of the Indian National Congress, not along the colonial structure of presidencies and provinces, but along language lines. In 1928 a committee headed by Motilal Nehru further outlined a vision of a future Indian independent state consisting of linguistically-defined states.[25] Following independence, several committees such as the Dar

21 Davenport, "State Repression and Political Order."

22 Gurr, "Peoples against States."

23 Group cohesion, willingness to act and capacity to act are considered to be the major factors leading to rebellion in the ethnic conflict literature, see Gurr, People Versus States. See also Horowitz, Ethnic Groups in Conflict; Hale, "The Parade of Sovereignties"; Cornell, "Autonomy as a Source of Conflict"; and Roeder, "Power-Dividing as an Alternative to Ethnic Power-Sharing."

24 Brass, "Elite Interest."

25 Schwartzberg, "Factors in the Linguistic Reorganization of Indian States."

Commission and the JVP committee were established to inquire into the basis for a reorganization of states.[26]

In this context, the question of language rationalization – the creation or establishment of a standardized language – gained political importance.[27] During the constituent assembly debates, calls were made for the linguistic reorganization of the provinces of India whose colonial boundaries did not conform to linguistic divisions. These linguistic problems were implicit in the early discussions concerning which language (and which script) would replace English as the sole official language, and which status the major regional languages and the diverse minor languages present in India should be given.[28] The constituent assembly chose a middle-way solution by deciding on a transitional 15-year period during which English would remain a national language alongside Hindi. In addition, major regional languages could continue to be used permanently in the provinces.[29] This 'constitutional compromise' promoted by Nehru was only temporary and remained open to revisions by language commissions which would meet in 1955 and 1960.[30] Although the Congress Party had supported linguistic reorganization before independence, it decided to rule out redrawing boundaries around ethnic lines following the trauma of partition of 1947.[31]

Under independent India's democratic system, the question of official languages became a problem concerning all Indians, not just the colonial elite. Minorities now criticized the unfair competition for jobs more easily accessible to those whose mother tongue was the state language. In this context, linguistic movements became vehicles for the quest for economic advancement and political power. Any policy decision regarding single or multiple languages for official and/or educational purposes had potential implications on whether or not specific linguistic communities would be able to gain better social and economic

---

26 The JVP committee was named after Jawaharlal Nehru, Vallabhai Patel and Dr. Pattabhi Sitaramayya who all sat on its board.

27 On state 'rationalization' see Weber, Economy and Society, who used the term 'rationalization' to describe the process of creating standardizing laws and practices to reinforce the uniformity of the state. More specifically on language legislation see Weber, Peasants into Frenchmen; Gellner, Nations and Nationalism; and Laitin, Language Repertoires and State Construction in Africa.

28 Austin, "Language and the Constitution"; Das Gupta, Language Conflict and National Development.

29 Austin, "Language and the Constitution."

30 Austin, "Language and the Constitution."

31 Brass, Language, Religion and Politics in North India.

opportunities.[32] During these 'dangerous decades', linguistic disputes had the potential of turning into secessionist conflicts.[33]

Hence, Prime Minister Jawaharlal Nehru and Congress followed a cautious approach in dealing with multilingualism, trying to find a balance between imposing a uniform language to hold the Union together and accommodating different regional linguistic communities.[34] At a time when the memory of the violent partition was still fresh, the Congress Party leadership hesitated to support the concept of states organized on the basis of language. They feared the rise of regional loyalties and, as a result, of secession attempts. The agitation for separatism in the Tamil homeland, the demand for an independent state for the Nagas, and the resistance of several regional groups to accept Hindi as a national language reinforced the position taken by the Congress Party.

Accordingly, the first Linguistic Provinces (or Dar) Commission constituted in 1948 warned against the reorganization of provinces on the basis of language, arguing that most reorganized states would still have large populations speaking languages other than the language of the majority.[35] It was also feared that such reorganization would negatively affect the economic development of a new Indian state. A highly centralized state system was deemed necessary to ensure sustained economic growth.[36] But the compromise over the official language of India did not appease demands for linguistic reorganization.

In 1952, violence by Telugu speakers in the southern Madras province persuaded the government to change its policy on state reorganization. New Delhi promised a Telugu-speaking state in the Andhra region (to be carved out of the Madras Province) and a national redrawing of state boundaries.[37] A States Reorganization Commission (SRC) was appointed in 1953 to evaluate different linguistic grievances and prospects for ethno-federal solutions.[38] During the SRC's consultations, language movements launched civil disobedience programs and used violence to support their autonomy demands in Tamil Nadu and in the Punjab. In order to preserve and improve their social and economic conditions, both the Tamil movement in Southern India and the Punjabi Suba movement in Northern India asked for their languages to be recognized as state languages

32 Brass, "Elite Interest."

33 Harrison, The Most Dangerous Decades; Austin, "Language and the Constitution"; Das Gupta, Language Conflict and National Development; Brass, Language, Religion and Politics in North India.

34 Brass, The Politics of India since Independence, 158-69.

35 Brass, The Politics of India since Independence, 158-69.

36 Austin, Working a Democratic Constitution.

37 Das Gupta, Language Conflict and National Development.

38 Home Department, Report of the States Reorganization Commission, 1955.

alongside the official national language. In 1956, the State Reorganization Act was passed. Cautious of taking a precedent-setting decision, the Commission shied away from any standardized formula for reorganizing states along linguistic lines.[39] Why did the newly emerging Indian state choose to deal differently with the two movements?

From separatism to integration in Tamil Nadu

Demands for more autonomy in Tamil Nadu date back to the time before independence, when the Dravidian[40] anti-Brahmin movement expanded in the early twentieth century.[41] A minority in Tamil Nadu, Brahmins were at this time considered oppressors and allies of the British colonial rulers. As the Dravidian movement became more radical after independence, its members opposed the imposition of Hindi (which, in their perspective, symbolized the dominance of the Northern Indian Brahmins) as a national language and openly demanded a separate state, "Dravida Nadu" or "Dravidistan."[42] In the post-independence period, Tamil Nadu was the first Indian state in which secessionist impulses developed.[43] How can we explain that these separatist desires had vanished by the early 1970s?

No article of the new Indian Constitution has proven more controversial than the one dealing with the issue of Hindi as the national language. After prolonged discussions, the constituent assembly accepted Hindi as the national language with a majority of only one vote (78 against 77).[44] Political mobilization on this issue was strong, as the founding of the Dravida Munnertra Kazhagam (DMK, The Dravidian Progressive Federation) party in 1949 shows, which advocated the secession of Dravida Nadu. Under these circumstances, India's Constituent Assembly postponed the implementation of Hindi until 1965 and decided that language commissions would be set up every five years to evaluate both the phasing out of the colonial language (English), and the progress of Hindi becoming the official language.[45] Furthermore, future parliaments were given the right to completely redraw state boundaries on linguistic lines (Article 3 of the Constitution).

39 Schwartzberg, "Factors in the Linguistic Reorganization of Indian States."

40 Dravidians refers to the peoples that natively speak languages belonging to the Dravidian language family. Tamil, along with other languages in South India, does not derive its roots from classical Sanskrit with Indo-Germanic roots, it is a Dravidian language.

41 Barnett, The Politics of Cultural Nationalism in South India.

42 Rudolph, ''Urban Life and Populist Radicalism."

43 Subramanian, Ethnicity and Populist Mobilization, 131.

44 Austin, "Language and the Constitution"; Das Gupta, Language Conflict and National Development.

45 Brass, Language, Religion and Politics in North India.

In spite of the turbulent political discussion that followed the Constituent Assembly's decisions on official language issues, the Tamil movement did not decide to exit the Indian Union. Political institutions and public forums in which to debate linguistic grievances seem to have functioned to such extent that loyalty to the Indian state remained high. This phenomenon was reflected in political behavior of regional parties, like the DMK. Even though it was a culturally nationalist party with potentially separatist ambitions, the DMK participated in the first post-independence elections of 1952 in the state of Madras (which changed its name to Tamil Nadu in 1968). However, the DMK was not able to compete successfully against the Congress Party, which won both a majority of parliamentary and local state assembly seats.[46] Yet by deciding to remain within the framework of established institutions and ally itself with national-level parties like the Communist Party, the DMK demonstrated its trust in the central government and its willingness to play by the constitutional rules.

A similar development could be observed a few years later, when demands to redraw state boundaries grew louder, especially from Tamil leaders.[47] After the 1955 State Reorganization Commission had presented its report, the Seventh Amendment to the Indian Constitution in 1956 reordered the political map on the basis of linguistic considerations. Although reluctant, the Indian government tried to settle the growing linguistic conflict in South India by opting for ethno-federalism and conceding regional autonomy. The creation of a Tamil-speaking state in which cultural nationalism was already strong created an incentive for the DMK to escalate demands towards advocating a territorially independent country of Tamil Nadu. But instead of encouraging secessionism, regional autonomy actually encouraged the linguistic movement to gradually de-radicalize its demands. The demand for Dravida Nadu (and an independent Tamil nation) was informally put aside and, in the early 1960s, officially dropped. This step signaled an implicit acceptance of the constitutional order in India.

Pragmatic considerations dominated the linguistic movement's decision to de-escalate its demands. First, after the reorganization of the states in 1956, the DMK feared that it could be outlawed because of its separatist program. Tamil leaders considered the central government's announcement that demands for secession would not be tolerated once the State Reorganization Act had been passed.[48] Whereas ethno-federal border rectification is usually considered a dan-

46 Stepan, "Federalism, Multi-National Societies, and 'State Nation.'"

47 For more on Nehru's position on the language issue, see King, Nehru and the Language Politics of India.

48 Widmalm, Kashmir in Comparative Perspective.

gerous precedent which can deepen ethnic demands, Indian leaders pragmatically formulated rules to govern adjustments and were able to enforce them.[49] To accommodate the demand of the linguistic movements and to avoid violence, Nehru conceded power to ethnic groups but also demanded that regional parties abandon their secessionist agenda if they wanted to participate in existing institutions. For example, the newly-passed sixteenth Amendment, Article 19, authorized sanctions against challenges to the 'integrity of India.'[50]

However, the main reason for the de-radicalization of demands was linked to changing views within the electorate. Popular support for Dravida Nadu was lacking. Since the central state had made several concessions to the Tamil movement, it became more complicated to mobilize for secession. Forums in which linguistic grievances could be voiced were available and functioning. Hence, the majority believed that it was more practical to demand a higher degree of autonomy for Tamil Nadu.[51] Waging cultural nationalist campaigns, the DMK in 1957 decided to participate again in the election for state and federal legislatures, and it firmly established itself as the second largest party in the state after Congress.[52] The more the party distanced itself from secessionist demands, the more it managed to expand its power base. Not wanting to jeopardize their now credible chances of winning the state of Madras, the DMK leaders decided in 1960 to implicitly drop their territorial nationalist aspirations. In an effort to signal their attachment to the Indian nation under duress, they explicitly discarded secession ideas when, in October 1962, India was attacked by China.[53]

Yet the fact that the demand for Dravida Nadu had been abandoned did not mean an end of language conflicts; they continued to be debated over the course of the 1960s. As stipulated in the 1950 Constitution, Hindi was supposed to become the official language by 1965. Tamil elites were particularly concerned that they would become marginalized in entrance examinations to the coveted Indian Administrative Service (IAS). Until 1962, the state of Madras had been winning 23.3 % of all places allocated in the IAS; this number was likely to be seriously reduced if Hindi became the official language. With the fear of falling behind in terms of upward mobility, lawyers, students and businessmen in January and February 1965 organized the biggest protests in Madras since the anti-British demonstrations of the 1940s. Indian Army troops intervened, arresting

49 Weiner, Party Building in a New Nation.

50 Kohli, "Can Democracies Accommodate Ethnic Nationalism?"; Stepan et al, Crafting State-Nations, 126.

51 Stepan et al, Crafting State-Nations, 126-127.

52 Barnett, The Politics of Cultural Nationalism in South India.

53 Stepan, "Federalism, Multi-National Societies, and 'State Nation," 251-252.

over 10,000 and killing more than 100 people.[54] To cope with this mounting crisis, on February 11, 1965, Prime Minister Lal Bahadur Shastri decided to postpone the introduction of Hindi as an official language "for an indefinite period of time."[55] Today, this decision remains the *de facto* policy of the central government.

In 1967, the DMK defeated the Congress Party and finally won control of Madras.[56] The DMK became the first cultural nationalist party to assume control of an Indian state. Since then, Congress has not managed to win back control of the state. It has cooperated with the DMK and another regional party, the All India Anna Dravida Munnetra Kazhagam (AIDMK). The DMK has allied itself with the Congress, and it has become increasingly integrated in the institutional structure of the Indian federation without ever giving up its cultural nationalism. Even the DMK's major cultural-nationalist competitor at the regional level, the AIADMK, routinely enters into alliances with central political parties and has forsaken its secessionist agenda.[57]

Linguistic demands in Tamil Nadu could have easily led to secessionism in the early days of Indian nation-building. However, as democratic institutions were upheld and flexible institutional solutions were found to accommodate cultural tensions, support for separatism and violence decreased. The movement's moderate elements found and used opportunities to express linguistic grievances, a practice which ensured the Tamil community's loyalty to the Indian Union. Despite the central government's hesitation to explicitly endorse the principle of linguistic states, the 1956 reorganization process brought into being political units where the dominant language and political boundaries were broadly consistent. Was this a comprehensive policy applied to all linguistic demands?

Intransigence, escalation and accommodation: A different trajectory for the Punjabi Suba movement

The accommodation of the Telugu and Tamil grievances in the 1950s led to the de facto creation of linguistic states. As a result, every language group, in theory, could have petitioned for its own state. In practice however, the 1956 Act mainly reorganized boundaries of the Southern State and ignored linguistic claims coming from other movements in Central and Northern India. All these linguistic demands emerged at the same period and were raised both in front of

54 For more on the events in Madras in 1965, see Hardgrave, "The Riots in Tamiland"; Forrester, "The Madras Anti-Hindi Agitation, 1965."

55 Quoted in Barnett, The Politics of Cultural Nationalism in South India, 134.

56 Barnett, The Politics of Cultural Nationalism in South India, 109-115.

57 Stepan et al, Crafting State-Nations, 133.

the Dar commission and the SRC. The first demand was raised by the Akali Dal (AD), who wanted to establish the state of Punjabi Suba based on the integration of Punjabi-speaking regions in the former East Punjab province. The AD argued that its demand was similar to claims for linguistic state reorganization made in other parts of India. Similar to the Tamil movement, the AD supported this linguistic reorganization as necessary to preserve the region's cultural distinctiveness and to ensure equal access to economic opportunities for their linguistic community.[58] However, the AD's request was not accepted by the SRC in 1956.[59]

Obviously, the central Indian government did not follow one distinct policy but reacted differently to various ethnic demands. In 1960, the Bombay province was separated into the two linguistically homogeneous states (Gujarat and Maharashtra), and a core Punjabi-speaking state was finally carved out of the previous heterogeneous Punjab province in 1966.[60] Why, then, did the Indian government first refuse to accommodate Punjabi demands in the 1950s? How did the central state perceive the secessionist potential of these two movements? And finally, were the Punjabi Suba movement's demands and strategies affected by the successful Tamil example?

The 1956 reorganization had neglected "ethno-national trouble-spots" such as the Punjab agitation.[61] In contrast to the Tamil movement, where linguistic and Caste cleavages conflated, religious differences and communal organizations on religious lines were more salient in the Punjabi Suba case, where the Sikh religious movement had experienced a revival since the late nineteenth century.[62] Yet due to the traumatic experience of Partition, India between the 1950s and 1970s followed a de facto rule that the government would only accommodate regionally based language claims, not those based on religious interests. Hence, ethnic movements and religious groups had to frame their demands in linguistic terms in order to be able to negotiate with the central government.[63] Some scholars have explained this inflexibility with the fact that New Delhi considered religious movements to be more likely to turn violent.[64] Minority religious autonomy was considered to be at odds with the Congress Party's

58 Nayar, Minority Politics in the Punjab, 32-34.

59 Nayar, Minority Politics in the Punjab, 32-34.

60 Brass, The Politics of India since Independence, 169.

61 Schwartzberg, "Factors in the Linguistic Reorganization of Indian States."

62 On the revival of the Sikh movement, see Brass, Language, Religion and Politics in North India, 277-402.

63 Brass, Language, Religion and Politics in North India, 277-402.

64 Kohli, "Can Democracies Accommodate Ethnic Nationalism?"; Wilkinson, Votes and Violence.

secular ideology. As a result, non-Hindu language groups such as the Punjabi Sikhs were less likely to be accommodated in the state reorganization process than the Tamil Hindus, and thus more likely to use violent strategies to obtain recognition and concessions from the central government.

The Partition precedent entered the central government's calculations when it assessed territorial demands from the Punjabi Suba movement. Pre-partition Punjab was composed of three important religious communities (Muslims, Hindus and Sikhs), with more than half the total population being Muslims. But in a diminished post-partition Punjab, most of the Muslim population was left on the Pakistani side. Punjabi Hindus identified as Hindi speakers and did not support the Punjabi Suba cause, which would have established Sikh dominance.[65] Hence, only the Sikhs actively supported a Punjabi-speaking Punjab.[66] Following the Partition and the professed secular identity of the new postcolonial Indian state, the Congress Party was therefore vigilant toward the conflation of Punjabi and Sikh ethno-nationalism. The initial perception of the government of India was that the demand from the Sikhs for a Punjabi-speaking state was merely a cover for the eventual creation of a Sikh theocratic state.[67]

In spite of these reservations, a Punjabi-speaking state was created in 1966. What led the central government to change its perception of the Punjabi Suba movement? The central government feared the dangers related to making concessions to a territory that bordered Pakistan, a situation making secessionist claims seem more likely than in geographically more isolated Tamil Nadu.[68] In addition, the postcolonial Punjab state was mostly bilingual. In contrast to other contemporary linguistic demands large sections of the population, especially the Hindi-speaking inhabitants of the Haryana region, opposed the formation of an exclusively Punjabi-speaking state in 1956.[69] Finally, the evolution of the Punjabi Suba movement's strategies and demands also had a decisive impact.

Similarly to the ethno-national movement in Tamil Nadu, the Punjabi Suba adopted varying strategies based on state action. After the failure of 1956, the AD moved away from electoral politics and negotiations with Congress to a more "agitational" approach.[70] The initial "infiltrational" strategy, which consisted of merging with Congress, helped to obtain important political concessions, such as the Parity formulas or the Sachar formula, which helped secure administrative positions and educational opportunities for Punjabi-speaking

65 Nayar, Minority Politics in the Punjab, 50.

66 Brass, Language, Religion and Politics in North India, 323-327.

67 Nayar, Minority Politics in the Punjab, 35-42, 322-323.

68 Nayar, Minority Politics in the Punjab.

69 Brass, The Politics of India since Independence, 173-174.

70 Nayar, Minority Politics in the Punjab, 202-205, 212-214, 234-236.

Sikhs.[71] In spite of these advancements, the AD still felt it needed to create a smaller, Sikh-dominated state to be able to electorally compete with Congress. As a result, the AD turned to a more agitational strategy after the SRC rejected the initial demand for the Punjabi Suba in 1956.

The agitation (*morcha*) of the late 1950s and early 1960s demonstrated a growing popular Sikh movement in support of the AD's territorial claims. Given this rising opposition, the center conceded to the Punjabi Suba the Regional Formula, which divided Punjabi-speaking and Hindi-speaking regions with separate committees in the state legislature.[72] However, this partial compromise did not last, as the Congress progressively slowed down the implementation of the formula in response to Hindu opposition to the concessions to the Akalis. In response, the Punjabi Suba movement's leader Tara Singh launched a new *morcha* in 1960-61, which led to 60,000 Akalis being arrested.[73] The AD also won very few seats in the 1962 general elections in comparison to Congress.[74] Given Tara Singh's inability to obtain Punjabi Suba through radicalized techniques, moderate leaders such as Sant Fateh Singh rebelled against his leadership and formed another faction in 1962. Contrary to Tara Singh, who publicly promoted a Sikh-dominated Punjab and Punjabi Suba, the moderate Fateh Singh systematically emphasized the linguistic principle to justify territorial reorganization.[75] After the 1956 precedent, he argued that the Punjabi Suba demand was legitimate and that further delays in accommodating their linguistic claims could be interpreted as discrimination against the Punjabis.[76] The Fateh Singh group soon became the dominant Akali faction in Punjab. The Punjabi Suba movement's strategy evolved after repeated unsuccessful attempts through agitational politics to influence Delhi. Tara Singh's AD had more and more difficulties in mobilizing support for a policy of violence.[77]

The change in the AD's strategy was a decisive factor but proved to be insufficient to achieve Punjabi Suba. Both Nehru and his successor Shastri were more sympathetic to Fateh Singh's claims of discrimination yet refused to accommodate his territorial demands. It was the Indo-Pakistani conflict of September 1965 that decisively modified the central government's perception of the movement. Just as the DMK had proven its loyalty to the Indian Union by drop-

71 Brass, Language, Religion and Politics in North India, 338-340.

72 Brass, Language, Religion and Politics in North India, 222.

73 Chima, The Sikh Separatist Insurgency in India, 29-34.

74 Chima, The Sikh Separatist Insurgency in India, 29-34.

75 Nayar, Minority Politics in the Punjab, 35-42; Brass, Language, Religion and Politics in North India, 324-326.

76 Brass, Language, Religion and Politics in North India, 325-326.

77 Nayar, Minority Politics in the Punjab, 262-269.

ping its secessionist ambitions in 1962, the AD postponed its plans to launch a new agitation movement in order to cooperate in the nation's war effort against Pakistan. Instead of exploiting the conflict to reinforce its claim for independence, the movement reaffirmed its loyalty to Delhi.[78] As a result, Congress finally conceded the division of Punjab and acceded to the AD's demands after the war. This step was facilitated by the support of the Hindu-majority Haryana region of the Punjab, which agreed to the reorganization.[79] The central government finally accepted the creation of Punjabi Suba in 1966 on the basis of the linguistic principle which had led to the first reorganization in 1956.[80]

The delayed accommodation of Punjabi linguistic demands has raised questions about center-state relations in India and the gradual process of linguistic reorganization of states. In the 1950s, the central government argued that the AD's demand for a linguistic state camouflaged an actual demand for a state in which the Sikhs would be dominant. The ambiguity had arisen because of the apparent rules of the game in India following partition and the 1956 State Reorganization Act, which did not permit Sikhs to make demands based on religion but only on language. But the central government did eventually recognize the AD's claim for a linguistic state. The change in policy between 1956 and 1966 can be described as a progressive learning process through interactions between the state and the AD. There was initially a deadlock between the Punjabi Suba movement and a central government inflexible with regard to the religious issue. Accommodation finally took root when a moderate leadership within the AD rejected the religious basis of the movement's territorial demand and the central government changed its perception of the secessionist potential of the Sikh movement.

Conclusion

The evidence from the Tamil and Punjabi cases has shown an evolving state-making process where the central Indian state modified its policies and strategies to deal with different ethnic movements over time. Some scholars have argued that variation in accommodation was a product of a screening process on part of the central Indian government. Some accounts of state reorganization in India have stressed the emergence of an overall pluralist and violence-mitigating state strategy in dealing with successive demands of language movements for

78 Chima, The Sikh Separatist Insurgency in India, 32.

79 Brass, Language, Religion and Politics in North India, 322-323.

80 Chima, The Sikh Separatist Insurgency in India, 32.

reorganization of the internal boundaries of the provinces.[81] Paul Brass has outlined four informal rules the Indian state seemed to have followed when dealing with linguistic movements in the 1950s and 1960s: First, the Indian state never accommodated groups which made explicit secessionist demands.[82] Second, the Indian state was reluctant to make concessions to linguistic minorities that were also religious minorities.[83] Third, linguistic demands needed to have popular mobilizing support instead of being elite projects.[84] Fourth, the demand needed to be supported by all the major rival language groups equally concerned with territorial reorganization.[85] Brass argues that India successfully managed linguistic tensions following these rules during the Jawarharlal Nehru years.[86] Similarly, Maya Chadda and Alfred Stepan praise the flexibility of India's federal structure, which forged an effective nation-state from a vast array of diverse and divided ethnic entities.[87]

As ingenious as these post-hoc narratives of a deliberate and uniform strategy behind the initial languages policies are, it is not evident that the Indian government has acted in such a coherent fashion. In fact, it is obvious in the SRC's report that the central government refused to set any precedent which could be emulated by other ethnic groups.[88] The study of the Tamil and Punjabi case revealed that the Indian government was more reactive than proactive during this period, making accommodations in response to popular mobilization or violence rather than trying to anticipate it.[89] At a Hyderabad meeting of the Congress party in 1953, Prime Minister Nehru referred to the issue of linguistic reorganization as a Pandora's Box and a wrong signal to give to other similar movements.[90] The government perceived of the 1956 reorganization as a concession to quell rising militancy by language groups, one which would in practice be limited to only certain cases.

The exact mechanisms accounting for the escalation of violence in ethnic groups' strategies or change in state policies are best captured in a study of the

---

81 Brass, Language, Religion and Politics in North India, 17-19; Brass, The Politics of India since Independence, 171-174.

82 Brass, The Politics of India since Independence, 172.

83 Brass, Language, Religion and Politics in North India, 17-19.

84 Brass, The Politics of India since Independence, 173.

85 Brass, The Politics of India since Independence, 173-174.

86 Brass. "Elite interest."

87 Chadda, "Integration through Internal Reorganization."; Stepan et al., Crafting State-Nations.

88 Schwartzberg, "Factors in the Linguistic Reorganization of Indian States."

89 Kohli, "Can Democracies Accommodate Ethnic Nationalism?"

90 Lok Sabha Secretariat. Lok Sabha Debates on the Report of the States Reorganisation Commission (Delhi: Lok Sabha Secretariat, 1956), 862-863.

dyadic relationship between the state and the group. The Indian government at the time wanted to make sure that certain linguistic groups' received popular support and represented actual secessionist threats before recognizing and engaging them. The government's calculations were more contingent and specific to the different movements. Over time, the evolution of the conflict was the result of a process of strategic interaction between the state and the ethnic groups in India. The evolution of state action (from indifference to concessions for example) over time and its effects on linguistic group's demands and strategies suggest a need for a more dynamic theory of secession. The relationship looks more like a trial-and-error state-making process in which groups try to identify the best solution to defend their language and culture. Depending on their repeated encounters, they chose to stay loyal to the state or to demand secession. Rather than looking at state sovereignty as a strong adherence to some strong and long-standing principles evoked in the Indian constitution, one needs to look at these interactions between the central government and ethnic groups and how their loyalty is comforted by certain concessions at given critical junctures. Only through this historical and interactive perspective is it possible to understand how the Indian government progressively built its legitimacy among many different ethnic groups present in the subcontinent.

Destiny's Children: Mediated Selves and Ambiguous Identities in the Indian Diaspora in the U.S.

Sunil Bhatia - Anjali Ram

One of the most important defining features of the twenty-first century is the complex interconnectedness between local and global practices and the creation of new forms of identity. The convoluted interplay between global and local forces has been present for centuries, but only in the last five decades have the frequency and intensity of these interchanges increased sharply.[1] These interchanges and encounters, according to Dissanayke have produced "remarkable transformations in the space of politics, economics, and culture, as newer forms of capital, originating largely in the west, began to imprint their local visibilities and inflect in unanticipated ways historically sedimented practices."[2] One facet of contemporary processes of globalization is that migration, displacement, and movement of people are shaping the ideals people pursue and identities they construct in complex ways. By drawing on our previous scholarship on diaspora and identity, we analyze how Indian immigrants living in diasporic communities in the U.S. are transformed by participating in the real, imagined, and mediated ritualized cultural practices.[3] In particular, we analyze how the history of "Indianness" that is constructed in the Indian diaspora is tied not only to the geography and the physical space of the homeland, but also shaped by the cultural importations of identity that are reconstituted by their contact with suburban America. We formulate our historical analysis of the Indian diaspora within the context of the model minority discourse that came into circulation in the 1960s and 1970s in the Unites States. Our analysis of the post 1965-Indian immigrants pays particular attention to the renovated memories, imagined communities, and cultural narratives that they use to reify and reinforce their sense of self and identity. By understanding how the language of the model minority framework was adopted by the Indian diaspora, we are able to unpack some of the roots and routes involved in the making of the history of the Indian migration in the United States.

---

1 Dissanyake, Globalization and the Experience of Culture; Inda and Rosaldo, Introduction: A World in Motion.

2 Dissanyake, Globalization and the Experience of Culture, 25.

3 Bhatia, American Karma: Race, Culture, and Identity in the Indian Diaspora; Bhatia, Rethinking Culture and Identity; Bhatia, 9/11 and Indian Diaspora; Bhatia and Ram, Rethinking "Acculturation" in Relation to Diasporic Cultures and Postcolonial Identities; Ram, Framing the Feminine; Ram, Gender, Diaspora and Bollywood.

By participating in varying degrees in community activities, religious and cultural festivals, preserving links with relations and friends back in India, developing strong social bonds with other Indian immigrants, subscribing to Indian magazines and news programs, decorating their homes with Indian handicrafts and artwork, wearing Indian clothes on special occasions and at home, regularly cooking Indian food, and so on, the Indian diaspora has routinely attempted to construct an alternative space for the expression and reification of their identity. In other words, when situated in relation to their everyday lives, their consumption of Indian cinema becomes one more activity that heightens and intensifies their cultural bifocality, as it were, as they negotiate between past and present, home and diaspora, "here" and "there."

Transnational and Diaspora Communities

Many immigrants form what we now recognize as diasporas, created with ties that span multiple nations and global spaces and considered as transforming institutional, economic, and political structures and cultures in both the host society and the homeland. *Diaspora* refers to immigrant communities that distinctly attempt to maintain real and/or imagined connections and commitments to their homeland and that recognize themselves and act as a collective community. In other words, people who simply live outside their ancestral homeland cannot automatically be considered diasporas.[4] Shuval notes that immigrant communities have a "temporal span" and typically remain immigrants for up to three generations and after that time their identification as immigrants weakens and often transforms into an ethnic identity formation. She explains, "A sense of diaspora can occur or re-occur after several generations when the group members are themselves no longer immigrants even though their predecessors were. A sense of diaspora is a feeling that is characterized by shifting periods of latency activism which occur in response to processes in the three relevant referents: the group itself, the host society and the homeland."[5] Examples of diasporic communities in the United States are those consisting of immigrants from Asia, Latin America, and Africa. However, although we do have immigrants with German ancestry, we might not necessarily have a distinct German diaspora in the United States or Canada because the largest waves of immigration have long past, and people of German ancestry have largely assimilated into the cultures of these two nation states.[6] Diasporas are usually formed when the immigrant community in question does not find its culture represented in the mainstream

4 Tölöyan, Rethinking Diaspora(s).

5 Shuval, Diaspora Migration, 33.

6 Bhatia, Interpreting the Meanings of Schooling.

host culture and when immigrants experience the absence, erasure (e.g., through intentional efforts to promote assimilation into the host's mainstream culture), and silencing of their culture by members of and practices within the host culture. Thus, for many non-European/non-White diasporic communities in particular, there is a constant and politicized negotiation of what it means to be "here" versus "there," "then" versus "now," homeland and hostland, self and other. Heated ongoing debates in the United States and other Western states over the status of immigrants and about the imperatives of immigrants to "become" Americans make clear just how politicized such debates are.

Scholars concerned with mapping an objective or classical definition of diaspora often work from a list of features or qualities that have become the criteria for defining the boundaries of the concept of diaspora. For example, Safran writes that members of the diasporic community: 1) share a history of being dispersed from a common point of origin or a homeland; 2) construct memories of the homeland and express a deep longing for the eventual return to their homeland; 3) often experience discrimination and marginality in their new location; 4) and maintain a sense of collective consciousness and solidarity with each other.[7]

The classical notion of diaspora as a typology implies a forced scattering and traumatic dispersal of people as stated in the book of Deuteronomy. The words "Babylonian exile" especially represent a "code" among Jewish history and folklore and becomes associated with the experience of alienation, exile, oppression and rootlessness. Cohen reminds us that although the word Babylon "connotes captivity and oppression, a rereading of the Babylonian period of exile" epitomizes the creation of a civilization that becomes transformed as a locus of art, learning and culture.[8] Anthias explains that the diasporic condition is not only created as a result of movement and displacement but is intricately interwoven with the cultural shifts that have occurred in both the modern and postmodern worlds. She explains that the diasporic condition:

> "is put into play through the experience of being *from* one place and of another, and it is identified with the idea of particular sentiments towards the homeland, whilst being formed by those of the place of settlement. This place is one where one is constructed in and through *difference*, and yet is one that produces differential forms of cultural accommodation or syncretism: in some version of hybridity. To treat diaspora as a condition is to pose a problem in terms of the specificities pertaining to the process of territorial and cultural shifts."[9]

7 Safran, Diaspora in Modern Societies.
8 Cohen, Rethinking Babylon, 4.
9 Anthias, Evaluating Diaspora, 555-565.

For many scholars across several disciplines, the concept of diaspora has come to represent a *condition* rather than signifying the properties of a group. The description of diaspora as a condition also serves the function of going beyond essentialist notions of race and ethnicity. Brah asserts that although the concept of the diaspora invokes images of journey, not all journeys can be described as diasporas.[10] Diasporas are not the same as travel or being a sojourner. But instead diasporic journeys are about traveling elsewhere and putting down roots. They are about arriving at a new location, settling down, and having a memory and longing for "elsewhere" or another place. This longing to be at "home" or in another "homeland" is not just based on the power of nostalgia, but rather is spurred by notions of belonging, inclusion and exclusions. Diasporic thinking allows us to reconfigure and unsettle boundaries across physical, political and cultural terrains. Diasporic movements are about border crossings, traversing across cultural spaces, but they also create "multiple identifications," "contested affiliations" and political alliances and collisions around vectors of race, ethnicity, and class.[11] Werbner argues that a diaspora community is different from an ethnic community because the members of the diaspora community have to be involved in collective displays of mobilizing cultural and material goods for their homeland by carrying out fundraising activities, engaging in political lobbying and participating in enactments of religious rituals, arts, and dances.[12]

The Indian Diaspora in the United States

The heterogeneous and diverse cultural elements of the Indian diaspora make it hard to define and articulate the concept of Indian-ness, India or Indian culture. Indian-ness or Indian culture in the diaspora is very obviously connected to the physical map of the Indian homeland. But there is no single fixed point in that vast geographical location that can be used to define the concept of Indian-ness.[13]

At the beginning of the twentieth century, one of the first groups of Indian migrants to settle in North America arrived on the Pacific coast to work on the railroad construction and the lumber mills of Bellingham, near Vancouver. These first Indian workers in North America were Punjabi Sikhs, who were mostly young farmers and experienced soldiers who had fought in the British army and were not satisfied with their service. The Sikh migration from Vancouver to California also led to an increase in the direct immigration of the Sikh

10 Brah, Cartographies of Diaspora.
11 Raghuram and Sahoo, Thinking "Indian Diaspora" for Our Time, 5.
12 Werbner, The Place which is Diaspora.
13 Bhatia, American Karma; Rudurappa, Ethnic Routes; Maira, Desis in the House.

farmers from Punjab to California. The young Sikh men who worked in the cotton farms and orchards of California were mostly in their early twenties and came from the Hoshiarpur and Jullundur districts of Punjab. The motivation of the Punjabi men to migrate to the U.S. during British India was, as Leonard observes, "primary population pressure, subdivision of land, and rural debt".[14]

The Punjabi men earned between $1.25 and $1.50 a day while working in the agriculture areas of Sacramento and San Joaquin Valley and soon distinguished themselves as laborers with a good work ethic. Their workday usually began at 4.30 a.m. and ended at 7.30 p.m.[15] Through hard work and thrift and with a tight community network, the Sikh farmers rapidly moved from being laborers to leasing land from the local banks. In a few years, the Punjabi diaspora began to grow in the agricultural areas of Sacramento, San Joaquin Valley and the Imperial Valley, and the Sikh migrants began to form small residential communities in many parts of California.

Jensen writes that by 1912 many of the farmers began to pool their assets and money to lease large acres of agricultural land. They conducted their agriculture business as a collective unit and divided their costs and profits between themselves. The Sikh migrants' business meetings with the bankers usually occurred through a spokesperson, and soon they earned reputations as excellent negotiators. Some of the Sikh farmers also earned the title of the "Rice Kings of Colusa County.[16]

Though the Punjabi migrants experienced success, incidents of prejudice and racial abuse from Americans did not cease. Leonard writes that *The Holtville Tribune* in 1910 printed an article on why the Hindus should be barred from settling in California. Both the people and the press often referred to the Sikh migrants as the "Hindu undesirable," "menace to the whole valley" and "ragheads."[17] When the Punjabi men started to gain a reputation as good farmers, the attitudes of banks and government officials, and people in general, changed. Over time, the incidents of overt racism, harassment and prejudice against the Sikhs lessened, and these so-called strange looking, foreign men with "rags" and "towels on their heads" were less "despised" and began to be perceived as "dependable" neighbors.[18]

The Alien Land Law of California, passed in 1913, disqualified all foreigners and non-citizens from owning or leasing land. Most Sikh farmers were able to beat the law by forming business partnerships with Anglo lawyers and judges

14 Leonard Making Ethnic Choices, 29.

15 Jensen, Passage from India; Leonard, Making Ethnic Choices.

16 Jensen, Passage from India, 39.

17 Leonard, Making Ethnic Choices, 45-49.

18 Leonard, Making Ethnic Choices, 29.

in California and Arizona. The Punjabi farmers found a way around this law by "working out verbal understandings with Anglo farmers, bankers, lawyers, who held land in their own names for Punjabi farmers. The director of the Holtville Bank did this, "earning for his bank the name Hindu Bank."[19]

Because of the prevalence of miscegenation laws in most states in the U.S., Sikh men were barred from marrying white women. Increasingly, the Punjabi men married Mexican women, who had been uprooted by the Mexican revolution and were working in the cotton fields of Southern California. The Punjabi-Mexican marriage alliance developed rapidly and expanded into a complex network of relationships. Ninety three percent of the wives of Punjabi men in Imperial Valley were Hispanic. Leonard writes that most of these marriages involved some courtship, and women had some choice about whom they wanted to marry. As the Punjabi-Mexican diaspora expanded, the Mexican women played a role in arranging marriages for their friends with eligible Punjabi men. The marriages between Punjabi men and Mexican women were shaped by love, convenience, loyalty, familial ties and by religious, linguistic and cultural differences. In 1917, Congress passed the Barred Zone Act that prevented all Asians (except Filipinos) from entering the United States. This Immigrant Act was intended to regulate the flow of "undesirable" immigrants, such as the mentally ill, gays, uneducated, and the poor populations. This Immigrant Act had a special provision that was called the "Asiatic Zone Act" and it was passed to mainly prevent the migration of people from China and Japan, but other countries such as India were also bound by this provision. Subsequently, the Indian migration to the United States almost came to a complete halt. Rangaswamy notes that, by the 1930s, Indians in the United States were mostly Pacific coast farmers, numbering roughly 3,000. There were about another 1,000 skilled workers, merchants and traders in the United States. Others in the Indian immigrant category included about five hundred students scattered throughout the United States, and 25 to 30 swamis or holy men."[20] With the passage of the Immigration Act of 1965, most of the new Indian migrants arriving in America were highly talented, professional/technical workers. The passage of the Immigration Act of 1965 (also known as the Hart-Celler Act) was a significant milestone within U.S history because the new legislation selected immigrants not based on the long-held policy of "national origins," but on educational qualifications and skills as well as family ties with U.S. citizens. Under this new legislation, special quotas were reserved for immigrants from countries that were described as part of the "Eastern Hemisphere." Thus, the passage of this bill facilitated the immigration of

19 Leonard, Making Ethnic Choices, 52.

20 Rangaswamy, Namaste America.

highly qualified doctors, teachers, nurses, engineers, and scientists from non-European nations. Within a relatively short period of time, the highly skilled, elite Indian professionals were being recognized for their hard work, merit and their ability to adapt to the changing work environment in the U.S. About a decade and half ago, Helwig and Helwig were one of the first small group of scholars to write a comprehensive book on the life of successful Indian professionals in the U.S. They wrote that the new Indian migrant in "America, in a short time, obtained prominent or dominant positions in many areas of the culture […]. They have made inroads into medical, engineering, scientific, and other professional fields […]. Indians are evident or dominant in particular area of business enterprise […]. In fact, they operate 28 percent (15,000) of the nation's 53,629 motels and hotels."[21] By all accounts, the immigration reform of 1965 is considered as being the most significant and profoundly influential act in the history of Indian immigration. The 1965 Immigrant Act fundamentally changed the background of the Indian migrants in the U.S. Within a very short span of time, Indian migrants in the U.S. made the transition from being "pariahs to elite".[22] Unlike the first wave of the Punjabi Sikh diaspora, the second wave of Indian migrants were mainly highly skilled professionals. They were trained as medical doctors, engineers, scientists, university professors and doctoral and postdoctoral students in mostly science related disciplines, such as chemistry, biochemistry, math, physics, biology and medicine. Prashad writes that between 1966 and 1977, 83% of Indians who migrated to the U.S. were highly skilled professionals comprised of about roughly "20,000 scientists with Ph.Ds, 40,000 engineers, and 25,000 doctors." [23] These professional Indians have made their "home" in suburban diasporas in towns and cities all across America. As "children of destiny" or "kismet," the post-1965, professional Indian diaspora acquired a slice of the "American dream" in the suburban enclaves of America, where they owned houses and had the requisite middle-class material comforts and sent their children to expensive colleges and universities.

Scholars and writers have always suggested that the Indian diaspora is very intimately connected to India as a geographical, cultural and political space. As novelist Amitav Ghosh remarks, "the spaces of India travel with the migrant," and India too "has no vocabulary for separating the migrant from India."[24] Historically, Indian immigrant communities energetically preserved their links to home through ritualized collective social gatherings, building temples in the

21 Helwig and Helwig, An Immigration Success Story, 156.

22 Rangaswamy, Namaste America, 40.

23 Prashad, Everybody was Kung Fu Fighting, 75.

24 Amitav Ghosh, The Diaspora in Indian Culture, 7.

"new world," procuring brides and bridegrooms for their children from "home," and by consuming Bollywood cinema.[25] In turn, and particularly after the post 1980s economic liberalization of the Indian economy, the government, multinational corporations, and the media peddled ways in which immigrants can recuperate a sense of homeland through discounted phone rates on festival days, investments in time-share properties in India, diasporic editions of national news magazines, and the production of "pop patriotism" as performed through popular music and film. In the next section, we explore the role Indian cinema has played in the construction of identity among the post-1965 immigrant generation. A comprehensive understanding of how Bollywood mediates immigrant identity is beyond the scope of this paper. However, no historical analysis of the Indian immigrant community can be complete without acknowledging the powerful presence of Indian cinema in the diaspora.

Bollywood and the Indian Diaspora

Symbolizing the shock and chaos of immigrant arrival the protagonist Gibreel Farishta in Rushdie's controversial novel *Satanic Verses*, tumbles from the clouds and into the waters of the English Channel. As he plummets downward he sings, "O, my shoes are Japanese, these trousers are English, if you please. On my head, red Russian hat; my heart is Indian for all that."[26] These words are the English translation of the well known Hindi film song, "Mera Joota Hai Japani." Immortalized through the film *Shri 420* (1955), this song has become a popular emblem for positing an unchanging, enduring Indian spirit, underneath a superficial garb of westernization. For instance, in the movie *Purab aur Paschim* (1970), the hero recites the words of "Mera Joota Hai Japani," to metaphorically forecast the finale where the heroine rejects her western trappings, symbolized by a blonde wig and a mini-skirt, in favor of a traditional Indian sari. As Farishta gazes down, he sees mingled with the wreckage of the plane, "broken memories", "untranslatable jokes", "severed mother tongues", and "sloughed off selves."[27] Rushdie captures the sense of how migrants are forced

25 In this paper we refer to the Hindi language cinema produced by the film industry located primarily in Mumbai (formerly known as Bombay), India. Despite the strong regional language film industries in India, the Hindi films produced in Mumbai dominate Indian cinema and has been popularly referred to as Bollywood. Recently, the term Bollywood has expanded to include a whole range of media-related products and practices that deploy the Bollywood aesthetic. However, for the purposes of this paper, we use the terms Indian cinema and Bollywood cinema interchangeably to refer to Hindi language film texts.

26 Rushdie, Satanic Verses, 5.

27 Ibid.

to negotiate their identities and re-think their location in the world. For immigrants of Indian origin, this negotiation has been often charted against the backdrop of Indian cinema. In this section, we comment on the role that Indian cinema has played in the formation of the diasporic identity and in turn how Bollywood has been shaped by its migrant audiences.

Most accounts of the globalization of Bollywood mark the enormous success of *Dilwale Dhulhaniya Le Jeyenge* (DDLJ/The Lover Wins the Bride) in 1995 as a defining moment. Prior to DDLJ, diasporic Indians were primarily spectators and consumers of Indian cinema. Scholars have pointed out the significance of DDLJ as the gateway film in the globalization of Indian cinema.[28] In the opening scene of DDLJ, we see the well-known actor, Amrish Puri as Chaudhari Baldev Singh, a middle-aged Indian storeowner in London feeding pigeons in Westminster Square. As he throws grains to the birds, he intones in his baritone, familiar to Hindi film viewers:

> "I have lived here for twenty-two years. Every day I walk on this road. And every day, this road asks me my name. It asks me: "Who is Chaudhari Baldev Singh? Where has he come from?' . . . . After spending half a lifetime here, this land is still a stranger to me and I am a stranger to it. No one knows me here, except the pigeons. They are like me. They too do not have a homeland. They go wherever they see some grain, and fill their stomachs. When will I be able to fly? I do not know. Necessity has clipped my wings. Bread has become the chains that shackle my feet. Nevertheless, one day I will definitely go . . . to my India, my homeland . . . to my Punjab."[29]

As he utters the words, he closes his eyes and the grey London skies melt into the sunny green and yellow mustard fields iconic of Punjab in North India, and a song breaks through. DDLJ chronicled the lives of Indian immigrants, their yearning for the homeland, their fear of losing their cultural values, and their desire to sustain their "Indianness." The film narrative captures the migrant moment, which articulates itself at the threshold of what Iain Chambers refers to as "an interminable discussion between a scattered historical inheritance and a heterogeneous present."[30] In other words, though cast in the melodramatic, hyperbolic vein of "Bollywood" kitsch, this film's appeal resides in its narration of the immigrant myth of the "eternal return," kept alive by continuously retelling, reliving and remembering the past. DDLJ signaled that Indian cinema was finally and officially acknowledging its diasporic audiences. From the mid-1990s onward, films featuring the diaspora have become commonplace. For the purposes

28 Bhattacharya Mehta, Bollywood, Nation, Globalization; Sharpe, Is the United States Post-Colonial.

29 Translated from Hindi.

30 Chambers, Migrancy, culture, identity, 6.

of this paper, we have chosen to primarily examine the role of Indian cinema in the diaspora before the DDLJ moment. Indeed, this film was finally a textual acknowledgment of the very powerful and pervasive role played for decades by Bollywood in the diaspora. As Athique reminds us, the globalization argument that centers on digital technologies "tends to obscure the fact that photomechanical feature films had been inherently mobile cultural artifacts for almost a century prior to this period of media acceleration."[31] In other words, even before the current tide of global media flows, Indian cinema has always provided ritualized, cultural sites for the diaspora to express and affirm identity. Prior to DDLJ, the diaspora was conspicuous by either absence or caricature in Indian cinema. However, regardless of the fact that they were not represented directly in Indian cinema, Indian diasporic audiences avidly incorporated Bollywood consumption into their everyday lives.

Before the advent of the VCR, access to Bollywood was limited to occasional communal screenings from 16mm and 35 mm reels. Punathambekar reports how these weekend screenings provided occasions and a space for Indian immigrants to enact their culture, speak in Hindi, and "participate in a ritual that was reminiscent of 'home.'" Moreover, these screenings "were marked as an exclusively Indian space, away from mainstream society, where families could meet and participate in a ritual of sharing personal and collective memories of life in India."[32] Eventually, videocassette technology expanded the access to Bollywood cinema, followed by DVDs, expansion of public exhibition venues, and finally today the availability of Bollywood movies by various digital technologies and evolved cable platforms is abundant.

By bringing distant events into everyday consciousness, as Giddens argues, popular media allows for reflexive projects of the self. Such self-reflexivity consists of sustaining coherent, yet continuously revised, narratives about one's identity, facilitated by our media experiences.[33] Contemporary memory studies likewise view remembering as a process and as ongoing acts through which people constantly transform their recollections in order to construct stable narratives of the self.[34]

Consider some of the narratives by Indian immigrant women interviewed by the second author as part of a larger study on the role of Indian cinema in the diaspora.[35] The Indian immigrant women interviewed were all part of the post-1965 generation and consistently explained their pleasure of viewing Indian cin-

31 Athique, "The Global Dispersal of Media," 189.

32 Punathambekar, "Bollywood in the Indian-American Diaspora," 154.

33 Giddens, Modernity and Self-Indetity: Self and Society in the Late Modern Age.

34 Zelizer, Reading the Past against the Grain: The Shape of Memory Studies.

35 Ram, Gender, Diaspora, and Bollywood.

ema in terms of recollecting the past. As one woman narrator explained, "you cannot really part with" Indian movies, "because that is how you grow up." She went on to comment that Indian cinema was "like your own." Another participant referred to her engagements with Bollywood by explaining how she herself is inserted into the narrative:

> "Maybe, maybe you kind of look at a Hindi movie . . . movie more subjectively as though you are a part of it . . . you know like it could happen to you or you may you know if it is set in Madras or Bombay I mean you know it maybe brings up certain . . . you know."

Although the narrator struggles to complete her statement, it is clear that for her the pleasures of viewing are bound up intimately with nostalgic identification. Some of the participants interviewed referenced specific film texts and rendered autobiographical sketches that employed cinema to structure and organize their recollections. So, for instance, one participant used the movie *Nishant*, a powerful depiction of the oppressive, feudal system that exists in villages in India, to frame her own story:

> "Like *Nishant* was one of the movies, that is a good one, that way you don't like miss Indian life you see it like . . . say this family's history is going on . . . you feel like . . . See I am from a very poor family, as I, like, sometimes I had a pair of shoes that I must have worn for the entire year, must have worn the same one, did not have a choice, so I think I am in India when I watch those things, so it gives kind of like it happens."

Similarly for another participant, the film, *Hum Aapke Hai Kaun*, captured how "things happened" in her family:

> "*Hum Aapke Hai Kaun* was more--you see--more family, what's going on, especially Hum Aap, was more like our family, it was done by Rajasthani guys so the story was almost how we have the weddings in Rajasthani, [...]."

For other narrators, Bollywood was used to maintain a continuity with the past, serving as constant reminders of their origins. Lamenting the loss of what she termed the "social aspects" among Indian immigrants, one of the participants asserted that by getting together with friends, "we make like we are in India . . . like watching movies," and she emphatically added, "we don't forget the past . . . we don't!" She went on to say that despite being in the United States for several decades, she misses India and that Bollywood cinema figures prominently in her efforts to counter feelings of loss and dislocation. In fact, she confided that she even named her eldest daughter as a reminder of her favorite Indian film heroine Rekha.

Significantly, the theme of continuity through recollection was underscored in the following comments by one of the participants when she vehemently claimed that Indian cinema is extremely important to the Indian immigrant community. According to her, it allowed:

> "our children to be educated in their own culture, to know about our own childhood, how we grew up -- children get to understand about our own culture and that in reality we are foreigners here."

Film texts for this narrator and other immigrant women that were interviewed clearly serve a very special purpose, for they permit them to reconstruct their origins, relay the past to the next generation and mark the boundaries of cultural identity. In all these accounts, Bollywood provides narrative slates that can be erased, rewritten, interpreted through recollections of the past, in order to secure stable scripts of selfhood. Such self-reflexive projects are crucial for immigrants, for whom feelings of displacement and disjuncture are paramount. Reliving and reinventing the past through film establishes a sense of continuity and certainty. Such rhetorical revivals produced in joint collaboration with Indian cinema allow these women narrators to deal with the inevitable breaks between the past and present that are caused by migration.

As Ganguly reminds us, "the stories people tell about their past have more to with the continuing shoring up of self-understanding than with historical 'truth'."[36] The immigrant narratives related to the consumption of cinema recounted here are not necessarily conveying "historical truths" about their pasts or about the India they left behind. After all, it is well known that Bollywood rarely follows conventions of realism. In fact, the unrealistic portrayals in Indian cinema have always been a cause for much denigration. In other words, the film texts themselves make no pretense of presenting "historical truths." Indian cinematic tradition has always rejected Aristotelian recommendations for mimesis in favor of grand, melodramatic, hyperbolic, metaphoric, mythologized, heroic tales that require suspensions of disbelief, which are freely given by Indian audiences. Rather, the pleasures of Bollywood for its diaspora lie in its power to facilitate and shape recollections, allow the past to be reconstructed within the present context, and provide an emotionally charged, technicolor medium through which a reified, idealized set of cultural subjectivities can be affirmed and consolidated.

Keeping alive this essentialized Indian identity that is firmly anchored to a real and imagined India is a key coping strategy that allowed the post-1965 Indian immigrant community to negotiate their place in the hierarchy of racialized discourses that positioned various non-western immigrants in relation to the mainstream white society. In what follows we unpack how the post-1965 professional Indians adopted the model minority discourse to cope with their ex-

36 Ganguly, Migrant Identities: Personal Memory and the Construction of Self-hood, 28.

periences of racism and alienation in their new world. We provide examples of how the Indian diaspora experienced racism on one level and yet were reluctant to portray themselves as "brown" people or "people of color." In particular, we examine how the discourse of racial ambiguity in the new Indian diaspora is strongly connected to the internalization of the model minority discourse.

Destiny's Children: The New Arrivals

The personal stories of the post-1965 migrants shows that these individuals, prior to their arrival in the U.S., had already amassed enough "cultural" and "linguistic capital" to succeed in the U.S. Their career paths and life trajectories in the U.S. were, in one sense, already determined in India—their stories reveal that they seemed destined to make the journey to America. Their educational stopovers at places like Yale, Stanford, the University of California, the University of Michigan, Indiana University and Rutgers ensured that these men would be able to compete for the best jobs in the most competitive organizations and multinational companies in the U.S. While it is true that their individual qualities -- such as intelligence, merit and hard work ensured their passage to the U.S., one cannot minimize the impact that their social-class positions, world-class undergraduate education in science and engineering, and familial networks had on their decisions to study in the U.S. Many Indian professionals had done their basic training in engineering at prestigious Indian universities such as the Indian Institute of Technology (IIT). Many now look back and marvel at the basic science and engineering education they received in India. Consider the interview done by the first author with Kishore, who worked at the ABC Computer Company and had graduated from one of the IIT universities. When asked the question "what was unique about the IIT education in India?" Kishore responded by saying that IIT provided very good foundations and basic training in science, engineering and mathematics. He admitted that graduate school in America was easy for him. "I had a very good, sort of fundamental basis, for the education. To me, graduate school was very easy, so I really didn't have to stretch too much in order to get the A grades, and, you know, in order to do well. I think in those things, I probably lived up to the expectations that I might have had for myself coming out of India."

Kishore's appraisal of his educational background is echoed in an episode of CBS' "60 minutes." Leslie Stahl, who did a feature on IIT for the CBS program, "60 Minutes" in June 2003 said, "Put Harvard, MIT and Princeton together, and you begin to get an idea of the status of IIT in India."[37] She pointed out that IIT has one of the most rigorous curricula in the world, and IIT graduates are known

37 Access via www.cbs.com.

to be world-class chemical, electrical and computer engineers. With an acceptance rate of less that 2%, IIT is now one of the most competitive schools in the world, said Stahl, and that most of its graduate students go on have illustrious careers in the U.S. Vinod Khosla, the founding executive officer of Sun Microsystems graduated from IIT about 30 years ago. In the "60 minutes" special, he proudly announces to the American viewers that IIT graduates have played a major role in the software development of blue-chip companies like Microsoft, Intel, IBM and Sun Microsystems.

In India, the status of IIT among middle-class families is almost mythical.[38] Students who have passed the IIT entrance tests are seen as geniuses who are guaranteed instant success. Since the rise of the city of Bangalore as a global hub of software development and a provider of low-cost technological services and call centers, IIT has begun to acquire a global brand name. The IIT undergraduate is seen as someone who is destined to work and succeed in America. Over the decades, the massive exportation of the IIT graduates -- the cream of the crop -- to the U.S. has also been the subject of much controversy. Towards the end of the "60 Minutes" feature, Stahl emphasizes how the "brain drain" from India hurts the Indian economy and research and development sector and benefits the U.S. The participants in the first author's study were aware of the "brain drain" issue, but for them, there was no other option but to migrate to America.[39]

Anil, a 51-year-old IIT graduate who was interviewed for this study, came to the U.S. in the 1980s.

"I[40]: I came to America because . . .
A: I don't know, I went to IIT, I don't know if you . . .
I: Of course!
A: And pretty much everybody came . . .
I: You went to IIT, Madras?

A: Yes, so in 1984, that was one of the things you did, and I came. So after the time, I joined IIT, I never thought I'd come to the U.S. because I never thought about what happens afterwards. After I joined IIT, it was almost, you know . . . there was no other option.

I: Yeah, in fact I've heard that."

---

38 While growing up in the town of Ambarnath in Maharashtra, India, I had friends from working-class families who were told by their parents that an IIT education would guarantee them success and social mobility in India. Many parents would select schools and colleges for their children that specifically trained their students for the IIT entrance examination.

39 Bhatia, American Karma.

40 "I" refers to the interviewer and "A" is the first initial of the participant's name.

It is interesting to note that Anil felt there were no options for him in India after he graduated from IIT. He said that out of his graduating class of 28 chemical engineers about 22 came to the U.S. in the mid-1980s. Anil emphasized that the IIT system made it very easy to apply and get admission to graduate school in the U.S. "Yeah, exactly, so it never occurred to me not to come, but I cannot say I came here because of my love for chemical engineering or something." After IIT, Anil got his Ph.D. from a well-respected engineering university in Massachusetts and then moved on to a multinational computer company in Norwich, so he could get his green card and become a permanent, legal resident in the U.S. Anil's story is not unique and is an instance of a larger pattern of migration in the Indian diaspora. Indian professionals with technology and medical backgrounds grasped the opportunities enabled by the new openness of the Immigrant Acts passed by the U.S. Congress. Inevitably, they went back to India to get married, brought back their wives and settled in various suburban pockets across the United States. The lived reality of the Indian diaspora was broad, diverse and did not uniformly subscribe to this linear portrayal of economic triumph and prosperity. However, as Khandelwal notes many Indian immigrants were consumed by their own stories of success as a model minority in the U.S. Further, the American public at large and self-serving politicians conferred this mythic status upon the Indian community.[41]

These narratives of achievement and the notion of the "model minority" became a powerful yardstick by which the post-1965 Indian immigrants measured their location in America. In this vein, Koshy observes, "The model minority position has increasingly come to define the racial identity of a significant number of South Asian Americans; it depends on the intermediary location of a group between black and white and holds a particularly powerful appeal for immigrant groups."[42] In the next section, we explore how the concept of the model minority provided the interpretive arc across which the post-1965 immigrants inscribed their sense of self, their constructions of culture, and their aspirations for future generations.

Cultural Identity, Racial Ambiguity, and the Model Minority Status

In their book, "The Myth of the Model Minority: Asian Americans Facing Racism," Rosalind Chou and Joe Feagin write about a young Chinese American woman named R.W.-- who murdered her mother by strangling her. After the murder, R.W. covered her mother's body and then made a call to the police. R.W. was a school valedictorian, a talented musician and was studying at a pres-

41 Khandelwal, Becoming American, Being Indian.

42 Koshy, Category Crisis, 287.

tigious Ivy League university. The authors note that her crime received little attention from the press, but the incident deeply unsettled the Asian American community in which R.W. and her parents lived. Chou and Feagin affirm that R.W.'s failure to complete her degree at the Ivy League school may have provoked her to attempt to commit suicide on several occasions and may have also compelled her to murder her mother. Chou and Feagin state that R.W.'s "demeanor was quiet, which likely suggested to white outsiders only a stereotyped Asian passivity. The white-created 'successful model minority' stereotype made it difficult for non-Asians around her to see her illness and encouraged silence among the Asian Americans who knew her."[43] The authors further note that many Asian American immigrants view their acculturation within the United States through a strong "white racial frame."[44] The white racial frame positions Asian Americans as high achievers, model minorities, with special aptitude for math, science, and engineering. They are considered a successful minority group because their attainments in the areas of education, income and occupation are considered on par with White Americans'. An important part of this racial framing is the view that Asian Americans don't experience racism or racial barriers in the American society. They explain that "such analyses may be correct in regard to a certain type of success measured by particular socioeconomic indicators for Asian American groups as a whole, but not in regard to the socioeconomic problems faced by large segments within these groups or in regard to the various forms of racial discrimination that most Asian Americans still face in their daily lives." [45]

The model minority myth described by Chou and Feagin is applicable to the collective mind-set of the post-1965 Indian diaspora. One point that is highlighted by many South-Asian academics is that the "myth of the model minority," which positions the Indian community as a highly qualified, professional and successful group of immigrants, also goes against them. Both professional and non-professional Indian immigrants tend to be ambivalent about the racial and ethnic discrimination they face at work and in their daily lives. The model minority myth was first created in the 1960s as a response to the introduction of the civil rights movement, and the larger demands from the African American and Mexican Americans to end discrimination and be treated as equal citizens. As a response to the demands, several white scholars, politicians, and journalists conceived the model minority myth in order to "allege that all Americans of color could achieve the American dream—and not by protesting discrimination

43 Chou and Feagin, The Myth of the Model Minority, 1.

44 Chou and Feagin, The Myth of the Model Minority, 4.

45 Chou and Feagin, The Myth of the Model Minority, 12.

in the stores and streets as African Americans and Mexican Americans were doing, but by working as "hard and quietly" as Japanese and Chinese Americans supposedly did."[46] The larger Asian-American diaspora adopted the assimilation model, conforming to the model of acculturation that did not interrogate the systemic racism on which the model is based. This internalization, in part, occurred because the second generation Asian Americans that came of age in 1960s and 1970s were strongly socialized to conform to an identity that could be described as apolitical and deracialzed. Kibria describes the racial ambivalence embedded in the model minority stereotype:

> "The model minority stereotype has a highly fluid and multidimensional set of meanings. I found my second-generation Chinese and Korean American informants to be struggling at times to resist the label of model minority, to ward off its limitations and dangers; they considered it part of their experience of racial marginality in the dominant society. But they also drew on the model minority stereotype in affirmative ways, in their efforts to make sense of and define the position of Asian Americans within the racial hierarchy of United States."[47]

The success stories of the post-1965 migrants of the Indian diaspora made them model minorities in the U.S. and the language of the model minority discourse became the criteria by which Indian immigrants began to interpret and understand their experiences in America. By and large, the men and women of the post-1965 Indian migration came from middle-class families and resided in small towns and cities. The parents of the post-1965 professional Indian migrants lived on modest salaries, but invested heavily in the education of their children. Some of the family members of these migrants were wealthy, but almost all of the participants in this study were able to come to this country because they were granted tuition waivers, full scholarships, teaching stipends and other fellowships by American universities. Once these professional migrants were in American universities, they began to rely on their advanced education, educational competence, professional networks, strong work ethic and savings to build their economic and cultural capital. The members of the post-1965 migration "came without access to or holding large amounts of capital (in dollars), thereby ensuring their place in the middle class was to be secured entirely by current income (and the moderate savings from that income),"[48]

Achieving economic success in the United States did not shield the professional class in the Indian diaspora from experiencing varying levels of racism and discrimination in their work-place and their suburban communities. For

46 Chou and Feagin, The Myth of the Model Minority, 12.

47 Kibria, Becoming Asian American, 132.

48 Prashad, The Karma of Brown Folk, 101.

many Indian immigrants their skin color, *bindis*, sari, food, "gods and goddesses," and "thick accents" become the main vehicles through which racism was directed towards the Indian diaspora by their suburban neighbors and co-workers. For example, Deepali, a biochemist, struggled to find play dates for her daughter, Karishma because her daughter was seen as different by her suburban neighbors. Venkat, a top level executive at the local computer company, talked about many painful occasions when both his children asked him why they were brown and different from white children. Neelam, a university professor, talked about how her daughter's *bindi* was ripped off by a six-year-old boy on the first day of school. Rohan, a chip designer, spoke at length about how some Indian employees felt subtle pressure from their bosses to reduce their "thick accents" so they could make the switch from working in the technical field to management level. Rohan's company subtly forced its international employees to enroll in an accent reduction course so they could be a "better fit" for mid-level management positions at their companies.

These lived experiences of the participants reveal the physical sites and cultural materials that are used to articulate their self-identity. The turban, *bindi*, saree, and accent reduction course become the materials through which the participants try to experience their difference. The educational and professional accomplishments did not protect these migrants from being the outsiders or the foreigners in this society. Despite earning high-salaries, driving luxury cars, and living in large houses in suburban Connecticut, they were still considered as brown-skinned others. The various interviews conducted with the Indian participants revealed that they were subject to moments of discrimination, overt and subtle racism, and made to feel unwanted in the society that they now called home.

In the face of experiencing difference, cultural displacement and disruption, the participants talked about temporarily taking on a universal identity or "positioning" themselves as being "race-less" in their work place, and in social and community gatherings with white co-workers and friends. They invoked notions of "individual merit," and "human nature" to explain why they are subjected to racism. In order to counter these narratives of otherness and difference, the Indian migrants produced their own scripts of self and repositioned their otherness through the language of universality and colorblind multiculturalism.

In 1900, the well-known African American scholar W. E. B. Du Bois noted that the problem of the twentieth century is the problem of the color line. Prashad takes it further and observes that, "The problem of the twenty-first century, then, is the problem of the colorblind.[49] This problem is simple: it believes

49 Prashad, Everybody was Kung Fu Fighting, 38.

that to redress racism, we need *not* to consider race in social practice, notably in the sphere of governmental action. The state, we are told, must be *above* race colorblind philosophy." He further states that there is a widespread belief in the public sphere that we have made progress on racial issues in America, but such statements ignore the larger reality that Latinos and black communities continue to experience racism in their daily lives. Colorblind multiculturalism is premised on the idea that racism involves the expression of prejudice of one party against another rather than demonstrating a pattern of systemic historical and economic injustices carried out by the dominant group against minority communities. He explains:

> "If the state acts without prejudice (that is, if it acts equally), then that is proof of the end of racism. Unequal socioeconomic conditions of today, based as they are on the racisms of the past and the present, are thereby rendered untouchable by the state. Colorblind justice privatizes inequality and racism, and it removes itself from the project of redistributive and antiracist justice. This is the genteel racism of our new millennium."[50]

The colorblind approach to understanding racism is the principal lens through which many neoconservatives, liberals, and people of color view the role of race in society. In particular, Prashad notes that many minorities who are successful in America tend to adopt a colorblind view of multiculturalism to explain their achievements. That is, these minorities typically advance the arguments that their individual effort, merit, hard work and intelligence determined their success, and that cultural factors such as race, class structures, social location, and generational privileges, played a negligible role in attaining their American dream.

Conclusion

In order to understand the success of the post 1965 Indian migration to the United States we must locate their sense of self within the larger diaspora context that has played an important role in shaping their migrant self in their new homeland. The discourse of diaspora, as Raghuram and Sahoo note, rejects the notion of culture as "dwelling" in favor of culture as "multilocale."[51] The Indian diaspora in the United States lives in "multilocale" settings and forges real and imaginary linkages between "here" and "there," and homeland and hostland. The Indian diasporic community in the U.S. carves our alternative space from the nation state. The Indian diaspora also becomes a fervent site for expressing "notions of hybridity, heterogeneity, identity fragmentation and reconstruction,

50 Prashad, Everybody was Kung Fu Fighting, 38.

51 Raghuram and Sahoo, Thinking "Indian Diaspora" for our Time, 1.

double consciousness, fractures of memory, ambivalence, roots and routes, discrepant cosmopolitanism, multilocationality and so forth."[52] Tölöyan argues that given the increase in travel, media and communication technology, more and more immigrants can be considered to be living in diasporas. [53] Similarly, Appadurai contends that "when it is juxtaposed with mass mediated images, scripts, and sensations, we have a new order of instability in the production of modern subjectivites . . . These create diasporic public spheres, phenomenon that confound theories that depend on the continued salience of the nation-state." [54]

A brief survey of the history of diasporic journeys undertaken by different groups points to both shared and unique diasporic moments and trajectories. In some instances, we notice that diasporic communities are established through the colonial experience, as can be witnessed in the formation of multicultural diasporas of people who were once a part of the European colonies and are now working in the various cosmopolitan cites of Europe – the South-Asian diaspora in Britain and the Surinamese community in The Netherlands. In other cases, such as the Indian diaspora in the United States, we see two distinct phases in their journey of migration. The first Indian migrants to the United States, over a century ago, were mainly uneducated, rural farmers from Punjab. The second migration, which began after 1965, mainly consisted of professional Indians such as engineers, doctors, and scientists. During the first phase of the migration to the U.S., many of the Punjabi Sikhs from India found their livelihood in the rural and agricultural areas of California. In the face of racial discrimination, several Punjabi men moved to the remote and alien sections of the cities and towns of California. Many of the Punjabi boarding houses were located behind Chinatown, and, in some other places, they shared accommodation with Chinese, Japanese and Mexican laborers. Jensen writes that although the Punjabi farmers gained economic acceptance in society, they were generally segregated and isolated from both the mainstream Anglo society and other ethnic communities living on the margins. The Sikh men circulated among themselves and stayed away from the Japanese and Chinese communities. The Japanese, Jensen notes, insulted the Sikhs by calling them "English slaves," and the Punjabi Sikhs found more acceptance in the Mexican-American and African-American communities.[55] A few Punjabis worked in the cities by passing off as Mexicans and blacks, because they believed that the Anglos were likely to express more preju-

---

52 Baumann, Diaspora, 71.

53 Toloyon, Rethinking Diaspora.

54 Appadurai, Modernity at Large, 40.

55 Jensen, Passage from India.

dice and bias against the Punjabi Sikhs. Most Punjabi Sikhs eventually married Hispanic women and became successful farmers in California.

In comparison to the Punjabi Sikhs, the post-1965 Indian migrants experienced a different entry point in their journey to America. Their middle-class upbringing in India, their excellent foundations in the sciences, their fluency in English, and their good work ethics propelled them into an elite segment of U.S. society. Many of these university graduates grew up being "America conscious" and were aware of what they needed to do to get into U.S. graduate schools. The formations of the Indian diaspora in the United States are born out of many arrivals and departures. Some of these arrivals and exits are imaginary, and some are based on the material and physical existence of India.

The post-1965 Indian diaspora is noteworthy for its ability to keep its transnational connections to India alive by reinventing the notion of both the "home" and the "homeland" by watching Bollywood cinema, re-enacting Indian traditional cultures and rituals in the diasporic public sphere, and making regular family trips to India. In this paper, we highlighted how watching Indian cinema, or Bollywood, has always been a major leisure activity in the Indian diaspora. In particular, we undertook an analysis of how Indian immigrant audiences have actively engaged and interpreted popular Indian cinema to mediate the constitution of their identity in the diaspora in a larger sense. Since the 1990s, with the enormous success of DDLJ where both the heroine and the hero were portrayed as British-born Indians, the Indian diaspora has finally begun to participate as a primary subject in Indian cinema. Yash Chopra, the well-known director of DDLJ, commented that earlier "we used to go abroad because of the locations. Now we are basing our characters there." The director of another box office hit set in the United States, *Pardes* (Foreign Land, 1997), Subhash Ghai commented bluntly, "My film is about American dreams and the Indian soul . . . every young person is dreamy (sic) about the place (America). But only on reaching there does he realize that there are things about himself that he cannot change." Chopra echoes such sentiments and asserted that immigrants wish to rediscover their roots after seeing such films, stating that "what they are looking for is . . . tradition." [56]Dubbed as "pop patriotism," films such as *Dilwale* and *Pardes* interpellate the migrant viewer by presenting narratives of an eternal, idyllic India, and evoking nostalgic longings for the homeland.

This continuous reworking of identity as essentialized, static, and idealized in the Indian diaspora through various real and symbolic forms plays into the ways in which Indians construct their racial identity in the United States. We have highlighted that the racial subjectivities of post-1965 Indian migrants in the

56 Quoted in Jain and Chowdhary, NRIs in Film, 20.

U.S. were embedded in the model minority discourse and were used as a strategy for assimilation in the larger American society. One important part of this model minority discourse is that it solidifies the idea that some migrant communities, through hard work, family values and educational qualifications are able to rise above their circumstances. The statement made by Phil Graham, that Indian-Americans represent the best and the brightest that the United States has to offer, reinforces the mistaken assumption that professional, well-to-do Indians have the same economic and educational opportunities as individuals from other ethnic and minority groups. Prashad writes that such statements about the cultural and material achievements of Indian migrants are used by some Americans to make unfair comparisons between Asian-American communities and black America. The model minority story that shapes the identity of so many professional Indian immigrants in the U.S. does not take into account that well-educated Indian migrants begin their lives from a different starting point than other minorities. The model minority discourse, as Prashad notes, is "based on deliberate state-selection and not based on cultural or natural selection."[57] That is, the successful "acculturation" or "assimilation" of professional Indian immigrants in the U.S. workforce is based on the special provision of the 1965 immigration act, which allowed the entry of only select, highly-qualified, transnational migrants educated in postcolonial schools and universities. For members of the Indian diaspora, their understanding of their racial identity has also impacted the way they socialized their children as second-generation Indian-Americans. By adopting a deracialzed identity and a model minority discourse, most Indian migrants preferred to dwell on socializing their children through the prism of "Indian culture" and "desi traditions" rather than through a framework that emphasized race or race-related matters at home. In sum, transnational practices and diaspora communities have become important sites for the reconstruction of culture, identity, diversity and difference. In these sites, their personhood acquires hybrid, creolized, hyphenated cultural properties and gets transformed into an "other" with multiple, shifting and conflicting identities. Our emphasis here is that diasporic identity is not just about abstract concepts, but they are rooted in lived experiences of difference and othernes.

57 Prasad, The Karma of Brown Folk, 4.

II. Ideas

Some Strategies of Indian Communists after 1947

Vijay Singh

The CPI after the Transfer of Power in 1947

At the time of the transfer of power in India in 1947 the Communist Party of India had traversed a complex history. The scattered communist groups inside the country had been united under the banner of the Workers' and Peasants' Party in November, 1925, but this party constituted a broad left formation rather than a disciplined communist organisation. The single Communist Party was unified at the end of 1933 and began to make itself felt both within the working class, and as a political force in the country as an anti-imperialist party. The mounting strength of the CPI in the trade unions and the peasantry during these years led to the party being banned in 1934. Despite this setback, by the run-up to the Second World War the party had struck deep roots in the working class particularly amongst jute, textile and railway workers. The party became legal once again in 1942 and rapidly increased its membership from four thousand members in 1942 to sixteen thousand in 1943 when the CPI was able to hold its First Congress.[58] During this period when the CPI was headed by P.C. Joshi and expanding rapidly, the party was also mired in controversy. During the Quit India movement of 1942 the CPI became isolated from the freedom movement headed by the Congress Party due to its closeness to the colonial power during the period of the People's War.[59] The CPI feared for the survival of the Soviet Union which was allied at the time with Britain and the USA. On the issue of the formation of Pakistan, as was advocated by the Muslim League, the Adhikari theses of the CPI 'On Pakistan and National Unity,' based on the premise that India was a multinational state, came to the understanding that the resolution of the Pakistan issue was a demand of the Muslim population.[60] Even though CPI support for Pakistan was dropped in April 1946 it nevertheless inflamed nationalist and communal opinion.[61]

---

58 Maslennikov, "On the leading role of working class in the national liberation movement of the colonial peoples."

59 "Record of the Discussions of Rajani Palme Dutt with M.K. Gandhi, Sardar Patel and Jawaharlal Nehru."

60 Adhikari (ed.), Pakistan and National Unity.

61 Memorandum of the Communist Party of India to the British Cabinet Mission. In: Jacob (ed.), National question in India, 235-240.

In mapping the contours of the communist movement in India after 1947 we highlight the successive changes in the political program, the political and tactical line starting from the pro-Nehru period of P.C. Joshi, the insurrectionary stance of B.T. Ranadive after the Second Congress of the CPI in 1948, and the momentary adoption of the 'Andhra line' founded on an understanding of the experiences of the Chinese Revolution in 1950 under the leadership of Rajeshwara Rao. The Ranadive and Rao lines had crushed and shattered the CPI and compelled it to seek the advice of the CPSU (B) [Bolshevik] to find a way out of the morass it found itself in. After discussions between the CPI leadership and Stalin in February and March 1951 the party under the leadership of Ajoy Ghosh adopted a number of cardinal resolutions on the party program, on policy matters, on elections and a closed statement on the tactical line. These materials were produced in the period of 'High Stalinism' and were prescribed for some years. Long after they were sidelined-following the death of Stalin they continued to haunt the communist movement for several decades. After the Twentieth Congress of the CPSU, and in its spirit, the rule of the united left government in Kerala of 1957-9 provided a new model of governance in which significant land reforms could be enacted benefiting hundreds of thousands of peasants, while retaining a formal adherence to the people's democratic revolution which was to be implemented in an unspecified distant future. It was a matter of interest that the CPI and the CPI (M) [Marxist] were able to establish themselves as a major political force in Kerala and West Bengal for decades not on the basis of the party policy of 'land to the tiller' but on the implementation of the land reform program adopted by the Congress Party but which the party itself refused to enact.

Under the general secretaryship of P.C. Joshi the CPI both during the run up to, and after, independence in 1947 unstintingly identified itself with the Congress Party headed by Jawaharlal Nehru. In the June 1947 resolution of the CPI the party recognised the limited nature of the independence accorded to India from imperialist influence, and considered that the British intended to maintain their position through the feudal princes, landlordism and big business, who had great influence over the extreme right of the Congress party. The colonial social order was retained. The Mountbatten Plan which divided the subcontinent was viewed as having made important concessions to India. The CPI gave its opinion that 'new opportunities for national advance have been won'. Accordingly, it desired the full co-operation of the popular governments and organisations for national liberation, reconstruction and unification which could be effected through the joint front of the left elements of the Congress (i.e. Nehru), the Muslim League, and the CPI itself. It argued 'The Communist Party will fully cooperate with the national leadership in the proud task of building the Indian Republic on democratic foundations.' This perspective was adopted by the entire leadership of the CPI. [62]

Other non-Soviet communist forces agreed with the CPI view, as may be seen in the writings of the British communist leader Rajani Palme Dutt and the observations of Georgi Dimitrov. In his visit to India in 1946 Dutt had advocated unity of understanding and an agreement between the Congress Party and the international communist movement which, according to Dutt, was the only way for peaceful and orderly development, going through the present phase of national freedom, advancing through unity and according to the degree of preparedness of the people, and ultimately towards a socialist India.[63] In the journal Labour Monthly that he edited Dutt continued to support this approach in the following year. In June 1947 while noting the negative aspects of the Mountbatten Plan he insisted it was a sign of progress and a retreat for imperialism. In terms similar to the CPI, whom he did not assail for failing to condemn the Congress acceptance of the British plan, he urged co-operation between the CPI and the Congress for achieving democratic advance, full independence, land reform, nationalisation and planned industrial development.[64] As is evident from the discussion with S.A. Dange on July 21st 1947, Dimitrov, too, favoured co-operation between the CPI and the Congress Party in the period shortly before the transfer of power. The Bulgarian leader asked Dange about his attitude towards Nehru and was informed that though he, Nehru, was against the CPI, the party supported him. Dimitrov suggested that an alliance be established with Nehru against British imperialism which would include communists, socialists and others supporting the Congress leader. This would enable the CPI to eschew that sectarianism which would isolate it. It was the opinion of Dange that few wanted such a broad united front because of hostility to the workers and peasants.[65] But the line of reasoning given by Dimitrov was not a universal view amongst communist leaders outside India as the transcript of the discussions between Dange and Zhdanov held in Moscow in September in the same year do not suggest any such recommendations.[66]

This trend towards the joint work of the CPI and the Congress which is evident in 1946-47 was to be soon rejected by the CPI and the CPSU (B) but would re-emerge in the post-Stalin period. Khrushchev's views on cooperating with

62 "Mountbatten Award and After. Political Resolution of the Central Committee of the Communist Part of India, 1947."

63 "Record of the discussions of Rajani, Palme, Dutt with M.K. Gandhi, Sardar Patel and Jawarharlal Nehru."

64 Dutt, "The Mountbatten Plan for India," 210-219.

65 Ganchovski, "The Days of Dimitrov as I Witnessed and Recorded Them," 316.

66 "The Discussions of S.A. Dange with the C.P.S.U."

Nehru are well-known. But this strategy was more widely accepted at the international level, for this path was also supported by the Communist Party of China. In his autobiography, the leader of the Telengana partisan warfare, P. Sundarayya pointed out: "In 1956-57, both the Soviet and the Chinese comrades advised us to forge a united alliance and go slow against the Nehru government. That way people can be mobilised without the party being seen as anti-Nehru, but if Nehru does not agree to an alliance it would be at his own peril, the Chinese suggested."[67]

However the Soviet Union in 1947 took a harder view of Indian realities. After the war the Soviet economist E. Varga had expressed the view that during the war: 'some of the colonies grew very strong economically; some colonial countries became financially independent of Britain and themselves became creditors of her'. On this basis Varga drew the conclusion that this signified a deep change in relations between the metropolis and the colonies: between Britain and India, from which the latter benefited. The war then, Varga continued, changed the political character of these colonies. As a result of the economic development of the colonies the position of the native bourgeoisie was strengthened. The views of Varga were contested by other Soviet economists at the joint conference of the Political Economy Section of the Institute of Economics and the Faculty of Political Economy of Moscow State University which was held in May, 1947.[68] They denied that the colonial character of India had fundamentally altered as metropolitan investment dominated the economy and characterised the line of Varga as upholding the 'decolonisation' thesis which had been long considered as being 'social-democratic'.[69] A special session of the

---

67 Sundarayya, An Autobiography, 361.

68 See: Varga, Izmeneniya v ekonomike kapitalizma v itoge vtoroi mirovoi voiny; Gruliow, Soviet Views on the Post-War World Economy, 20. This is a translation of the Stenographic Report of the discussion which took place in Moscow in May, 1947. It was originally published as a supplement to the November 1947 issue of World Economy and World Politics. E. Varga's views on India and the colonial question after his self-criticism are apparent in: Osnovnye voprosy ekonomiki i politiki imperializma (posle vtoroi mirovoi voiny), 293-384. After the 20th Congress of the CPSU he reverted to his 'reformist' views of 1946. I.M. Lemin placed an important role in the discussion of May 1947 by confronting the theses of Varga. He later published an influential book: Obostrenie krizisa Britanskoi imperii posle vtoroi mirovoi voiny, 1951.

69 On the question of 'decolonisation' theory see: „Dekolonizatsii Teorii" in Ekonomicheskaya Entsiklopedia Politicheskaya Ekonomia, Tom I, 374; "Revolyutsionnoe dvizhenie v kolonial'nykh i polukolonial'nykh stranakh. Tezisy," in: Kun (ed.), Komunisticheskii Internatsional v dokumentakh, 1919-1932, 832-870; Otto Kuusinen, 'The Revolutionary Movement in the Colonies', in: International Press Correspondence, Volume 8, No 68, 1225-1233; "Concluding Speech of Comrade Kuusinen on

USSR Academy of Sciences held in June 1947 further confirmed the harsh characterisation of the Indian bourgeoisie and the Congress Party leadership by leading Soviet Indologists such as Dyakov and Balabushevich. They argued that Indian capital, and the Congress, had gone over to the camp of reaction and imperialism. At the joint conference of the Institute of Economics and the Pacific Institute of the Academy of Sciences of the USSR held in 1949, V.M. Maslennikov held that the CPI was:

> "not free from the reformist influence which left its mark on the policy of the Party in the period of the Second World War. 'The Mountbatten Plan' for the partitioning of India and the granting of Dominion status to India and Pakistan which was nothing but a deal between British imperialism and the Indian bourgeois top strata, a new form of the economic and political dependence of these Dominions on British imperialism, was evaluated by the former leadership of the Communist Party of India as some kind of 'step forward' and not as a new form of attack of British imperialism on the Indian people. After the partition of India into two Dominions the leadership of the Communist Party took the decision to support the bourgeois Nehru Government and decided on the "expediency" of forming a united national front from Gandhi to the Communists."[70]

Early in 1948 the pro-Nehru understanding of the CPI under P.C. Joshi was replaced by the intransigent line under B.T. Ranadive. The 1947 December Plenum of the CPI marked this change and presaged the emergence of the new radical leadership at the Second Congress of the CPI held in February-March 1948. It was now argued that the Mountbatten Plan had not led to real, but only fake, independence with the form of subordination changing, but not the substance. The plan indicated not the retreat of imperialism, but its 'cunning counter-offensive'.[71] At the Second Congress, Ranadive in his Report on Reformist Deviation roundly condemned the stance of P. C. Joshi in its positive evaluation of the Mountbatten Plan as an advance, and its advocacy of a united front between the government and the people, for ignoring the compromising role of the Congress Party which effectively tied the working class and the CPI to a policy of co-operation with the national bourgeoisie.[72] However the Ranadive leadership went far beyond a critique of the reformism of P.C. Joshi.

---

the Colonial Question," Sixth World Congress of the Communist International, in: International Press Correspondence, Vol. 8, No. 81, 21st November 1928, 1519-1528.

70 Maslennikov, "On Leading Role of Working Class in the National Liberation Movement of the Colonial Peoples," 21.

71 Communist Party Statement of Policy, "Resolution on the Current Situation Passed by the Central Committee of the Communist Party of India at its Meeting in Bombay at its Meeting in Bombay December, 7th-16th 1947," 6.

72 Second Congress of the Communist Party of India, "Report on Reformist Deviation," 1948.

Heavily under the influence of the Yugoslav Party the CPI leaned towards effecting a socialist revolution. The Yugoslavs, in the course of their partisan warfare, had felt little need to ally with other anti-Nazi forces such as those of Draza Mihailovic who were hostile to the partisans headed by Tito.[73] After the war they gave an interpretation to the notion of people's democratic revolution such as to make it almost synonymous with the dictatorship of the proletariat and socialist revolution. There was no substantial bourgeoisie in the anti-fascist or people's front in Yugoslavia, but, anomalously, the kulaks were thoroughly mollycoddled, and included in the People's Front.[74] Nevertheless, as Stalin pointed out in a letter to Mao, there were political parties apart from the Communist Party inside the People's Front in Yugoslavia.[75] The democratic revolutions, Kardelj argued, were intertwined with socialist revolutions and this thesis was enthusiastically adopted by the leadership of the CPI, although it still maintained the strategy of people's democratic revolution at a formal level. The CPI, considered Ranadive, had to unite the working class, the peasantry, the petty-bourgeoisie and the progressive intelligentsia in its anti-capitalist strategy. No section of the bourgeoisie, large or middle, was incorporated into the strategy of the CPI. The repudiation of reformism was emphasised by support for the agrarian insurrection in Telengana which was directed against the Nizam of Hyderabad. At the time and later this whole line was dubbed as 'Trotskyite-Titoist' for its turn towards socialist revolution in what was still considered essentially a colonial country.[76]

Matters did not rest there. Ranadive formulated a perspective of fomenting revolution based on a general strike and widespread peasant jacqueries. In what became a parody of the strategy of the Bolshevik revolution it became clear the party did not have the wherewithal to organise the working class or the peasantry, let alone to launch an attempt to seize power. While the Bolshevik strategy enjoined that it must be the masses of the working class who must be the initiators of 'revolutionary violence', the Ranadive tactic was to indulge in individual terrorism by the party cadres. Attempts were made to begin an all-India railway strike through the All-India Railway Federation, but after the settlement by the socialist leadership with the government, the Ranadive group went ahead alone without any success. This tactic was tried again with a similar result. Only

73 See Clissold, Yugoslavia and the Soviet Union 1939-1973. A Documentary Survey, 132.

74 For the Soviet criticism of the pro-kulak policies of the Tito regime see Clissold, Yugoslavia and the Soviet Union 1939-1973. A Documentary Survey, 173, 189-190.

75 Telegram I.V. Stalin to Mao Tszedun, 20 April 1948. Quoted in Stalin, Sochinenia, Tom 16, chast' 1, 630.

76 Sangal, Telengana and the Rajeshwar Rao Leadership, 1.

in the CPI-dominated trade unions was some degree of success actually registered in strike actions.[77] But for the most part, as was pointed out in the party polemics at the time, individual terrorism was the order of the day. This may be considered as a recidivist throwback to the tactics of the national-revolutionary groups in Bengal and elsewhere who utilised terrorism before independence rather than as the tactics deployed by mass communist parties.

Opposition was bound to develop to this adventurism and it came from the Bombay trade unions led by S.A. Dange, CPI leaders such as Ajoy Ghosh, the disgraced 'rightist', and P.C. Joshi, who carried out a vigourous international campaign against the 'Titoism' of the Ranadive line.[78] In India polemics began against the application of (in fact in a distorted form) the Bolshevik strategy of October 1917 in Russia by the Andhra communists, which in turn was based on an imagined understanding of the strategies of the Communist Party of China before 1949. At an international level the CPGB, the Cominform and the CPSU (B) entered the fray.[79] The highly polarised polemics between Ranadive and the Andhra communists reveal major conflicts developing from highly problematical interpretations of the Russian and Chinese revolutions.

The Andhra communist critique of Ranadive had a certain political force because of its connections with the partisan struggles in Telengana where an agrarian revolt was in full operation between 1948 and 1950, directed against the despotic regime of the Nizam of Hyderabad. Some 3000 villages in an area with a total population of five million were controlled by people's power where land was distributed among the peasantry and a partisan army functioned.[80] While this model could not be significantly replicated in the capitalistically more developed Andhra region, the Andhra communists were inspired by the new democracy strategy of the CPC which had been predicated on the alliance between the Chinese communists and the Kuomintang during the anti-Japanese resistance. By April 1948 the CPC itself had switched to the strategy of establishing a people's democratic state in consonance with the prevalent international understanding that people's democratic revolution was appropriate not only in central and south-eastern Europe and Asia but also in the advanced metropolitan

---

77 Overstreet and Windmiller, Communism in India, 278-280.

78 Overstreet and Windmiller, Communism in India, 284-285.

79 "Letter of C. Rajagopalachari to J. Nehru on the advice of R.P. Dutt to Indian Communists (4th March 1951)"; "Mighty Advance of the National Liberation Movement in the Colonial and Dependent Countries."

80 Dyakov, Crisis of British Rule in India and the New Stage in the Liberation Struggles of Her Peoples, 41.

countries such as the United States and Britain.[81] In this new context the advocacy of near-socialist strategies by Kardelj or Ranadive was radically out of line.

The Andhra letter of June 1948 demanded the application of the theory of 'New Democracy' as had been adumbrated by Mao in 1940 on the grounds that Indian realities were closer to the conditions of China rather that those of Russia. It argued that the CPI should unite the working class and the entire peasantry which was to conduct partisan warfare as an immediate task.[82] This was a full-frontal assault on the prescriptions of Ranadive and socialist revolutions founded on working class insurrections and general strikes. In his broadsides against the Andhra line Ranadive argued that socialist revolution was more suitable for India as the country had achieved a high degree of capitalist development. In the rural sector this development meant that feudalism was no longer powerful and so it was impermissible to unite with the rich peasant class for a democratic revolution. The views projected by Ranadive bore a striking resemblance to those of M.N. Roy, Bukharin and Trotsky in the late 1920s. These had been categorised as the 'decolonisation' theory by the Comintern in 1928 for arguing that independent capitalist development could successfully take place under conditions of imperialism without a revolutionary rupture and the establishment of a revolutionary-democratic regime.[83] Ranadive found the advocacy of the inclusion of the rich peasants in the revolutionary alliance to be an example of rank reformism by the Andhra committee. Then Ranadive did an extraordinary thing. He extended the scope of the critique of the Andhra line to Mao himself whom he considered as the *fons et origo* of the 'deviations' which were a danger to his own understanding.[84] He continued to uphold the Telengana struggle but this struggle rapidly began to disintegrate as Indian troops entered Hyderabad state and proceeded to confront the armed peasantry. The debacle in Hyderabad state impacted on the Andhra committee, for its line was rapidly transformed into one with elements of individual terrorism not much different from the Ranadive line itself.[85]

Paradoxically, the Andhra committee prospered even as the Telengana struggle was driven into a corner by the Indian 'police action'. Indian communist opposition to the politics of Ranadive, the pressure of the Cominform and

---

81 Tse-tung, Agrarian Reform and People's Victory in China, 11; "On People's Democracy in Eastern Europe and China," 1951; Gollan, People's Democracy for Britain; Foster, "People's Front and People's Democracy."

82 Tarimela Nagireddy Memorial Trust, Vijayawada, 98-121.

83 Inprecor, "The VI World Congress of the Communist International," 1517-18.

84 "The Struggle for People's Democracy and Socialism – Some Questions of Strategy and Tactics," 71.

85 Sangal, Telengana and the Rajeshwar Rao Leadership, 53-54.

also of the CPSU (B) culminated in the January 1950 Cominform editorial which projected the Chinese path for India. In no way was this to be understood as support for a replication of the specific features of the Chinese revolution, but it stressed only the aspect of the necessity of agrarian revolution in India.[86] It was a slap in the face for Ranadive and his thesis of an immediate armed struggle for a socialist revolution in India. The Ranadive group was compelled to retreat. By May 1950 the Andhra committee was able to assume leadership of the CPI and secured the general secretaryship for Rajeshwara Rao.[87] But this group had profoundly misunderstood the implications of the Cominform editorial as it proceeded to advocate the inception of armed revolution throughout the country on the Telengana example. As had earlier occurred with the opposition to Ranadive, sections of the CPI leadership now stood up to Rajeshwara Rao. P.C. Joshi stated that conditions were not ripe for immediate armed revolution in India and posited the necessity of a return to the policies he had proposed in 1946-47. S.A. Dange, who had an important trade union base in Bombay, publicly opposed the policy of immediate armed revolt. Ajoy Ghosh and S.V. Ghate, too, came out against the policies of the Rao line which effectively formed a second, though formally different, adventurist line.[88]

A resolution to the continued crisis of the Indian communist movement was sought by a letter from the CPGB in late 1950 which argued that the CPI had misunderstood the Cominform editorial of January 1950 to mean that the immediate task of the party was to inaugurate armed struggle. The CPGB rejected the policies of Rajeshwara Rao and outlined a political perspective which was not fundamentally dissimilar to that which had been elaborated by R.P. Dutt in 1946-47.[89] While Rajeshwara Rao held on to the leadership of the CPI the crisis destroying the party continued unabated. In these circumstances the party requested the CPSU (B) to intervene to determine a path forward. Accordingly, leading members of the CPI representing different currents in the party, minus the P.C. Joshi and B.T. Ranadive groups, had meetings with the CPSU (B) leadership in Moscow in February and March 1951.

In the meetings with the Soviet party leadership, particularly Stalin, the key questions of the program and path to be adopted in the Indian revolution were thrashed out. Stalin saw the stage of revolution in India to be a part of the people's democratic revolution at its first stage. This was an anti-feudal agrarian revolution where the property of the national bourgeoisie was left untouched. It

86 "Mighty Advance of the National Liberation Movement in the Colonial and Dependent Countries."

87 Sundarayya, An Autobiography, 225.

88 Sundarayya, An Autobiography, 228-229.

89 Sundarayya, An Autobiography, 225.

was analogous to the path adopted by China. Stalin rejected the understanding that India stood before the socialist revolution. This he considered to be a 'very dangerous thesis' which had been upheld by Ranadive and which had prompted the Cominform editorial of January 1950 which indicated that India was on the Chinese road. A later phase of the people's democratic revolution was the second socialist stage which already had been embarked upon in the countries of Eastern Europe in which the national bourgeoisie was expropriated. The sharp blade of the Indian democratic revolution had to be directed at British imperialism which continued to dominate India. There was no need to take on the United States as an additional enemy. In the rural sector the entire peasantry, including the kulaks, needed to be mobilised against the feudal lords. As regards the top sections of the Indian national bourgeoisie, Stalin considered that although they had an alliance with imperialism, they had a vested interest in achieving the full independence of the country as well as building up the domestic market by the complete end of feudalism. There was no need to push the Indian bourgeoisie onto the side of the British.

Stalin launched into a devastating critique of the understanding of the CPI on partisan warfare before its proponents in Andhra and Telengana who wished to extend it to the whole of India. He rejected the understanding of the party that partisan warfare in the rural areas alone could secure the victory of the revolution in India. 'Armed struggle' was required which embraced the combination of the general strikes and uprisings of the workers alongside the partisan war of the peasants. In China matters had been different. The CPC had not practised 'armed struggle' in the peculiar circumstances of China but 'armed revolution' which signified the existence of partisan warfare together with the participation of an army of liberation. When it was compelled to break with the Kuomintang the CPC had its own armed forces. This had become the basis of partisan war but it had suffered as it had to establish itself in the forests and mountains far from the railways and the towns. It was a grievous necessity that the CPC had to be separated from the working class. Moreover the partisan regions were prone to encirclement and blockade by the forces of Chiang Kai-shek. It was only after the Chinese communists moved into Manchuria that, because they had a friendly Soviet rear, they no longer had to fear encirclement, and could consider going on to the offensive against the Kuomintang troops. Stalin noted that India had no stable rear such as that which had been available to the CPC. While India would have liberated regions and possibly also formed a liberation army in the absence of a stable rear, a partisan war could not by itself be successful and so it was necessary to have revolutionary action by the working class. Intensive work was necessary to win over the majority of the working class, prepare strikes of the workers and of the railway men, and form workers' detachments in the towns.[90]

On the specifics of the situation in Telengana, Stalin opined that it was inaccurate to assert that civil war prevailed in India. While land had been seized in Telengana it did not mean that partisan warfare was the main form of struggle in the country. Stalin held that Telengana was the beginning of the opening of the struggle, but it was not the main form of the struggle, from which India was yet far off. In his hand-written notes on a letter received from Rajeshwara Rao dated 14th February 1951 where the CPI leader asked whether partisan war needed to be withdrawn in Telengana and Tripura, Stalin commented: 'No, if the people want continue the partisan struggle'. At the same time Stalin stressed the need for the peasantry to learn to struggle for the lowering of lease rents, the lowering of the share of the harvest paid to the landlord and so on. A weak party such as the CPI should not at once speak of an armed struggle as serious difficulties would arise.[91]

Given the history of the CPI under the leadership of both Ranadive and Rao, the remarks of Stalin on the question of individual terror were very instructive. Stalin noted the inclination of Indian communists to the side of individual terror against the enemy. Yet he countered the statement of Ajoy Ghosh and S.A. Dange in their letter to him dated 14th February 1951 which suggested that communists were opposed to all types of terrorism. Stalin noted that they were in favour of the terrorist actions of the masses but against the terror actions of individual revolutionaries and persons acting outside the movement behind the back of the masses. In the discussion of 9th February 1951 on the same question Stalin stated that individual terror was such if the masses did not engage in the actions. If the masses were passive spectators then a division was created between the heroes and the masses which had been the characteristic of the Socialist Revolutionaries in Russia.[92]

Shortly after the Moscow discussions the CPI produced major materials for a party program, a statement of policy, an election statement and a closed docu-

90 "Stenographic Record of the Discussion of the Members of the Committee of the CC A-UCP(B) with the Representatives of the CC Communist Party of India on 4th and 6th February 1951"; "Record of the Discussions of J.V. Stalin with the Representatives of the C.C. of the Communist Party of India Comrades, Rao, Dange, Ghosh and Punnaiah on 9th February, 1951."

91 "Three Letters from the CPI to J.V. Stalin with the Handwritten Comments of the Soviet Leader, February 14, 1951."

92 "Three Letters from the CPI to J.V. Stalin with the Handwritten Comments of the Soviet Leader, February 14, 1951."

ment on the tactical line of the party.[93] The tactical line envisaged armed struggle taking place in the country on the basis of workers' uprisings and partisan warfare. As the second major discussion between the CPI leadership and Stalin which took place in March 1951 is still locked in the Russian archives, we cannot know what further discussions might have taken place on the question of partisan warfare and Telengana. Shortly after their return from Moscow the CPI took the decision to withdraw the armed insurrection in Telengana. In his posthumously published autobiography recorded on tape, which in part saw the light in 2009, Sundarayya records that the Telengana question was now clinched. It was agreed by all the CPI leaders that Telengana did not represent a liberation struggle in the country as a whole but only a partial bourgeois struggle which was confined to one pocket of the country, resulting in the agrarian insurrection being terminated.[94]

The new programmatic perspectives were in the framework of establishing a people's democracy in India in which under the leadership of the working class, the peasantry, the urban petty-bourgeoisie, and the middle bourgeoisie participated. The prospects of immediate armed activity were discounted. The 1951 documents united all the major sections of the CPI leadership including P.C. Joshi and B.T. Ranadive. This unity did not last very long. The advent of Khrushchev precipitated a sea-change in Soviet understanding, which engendered fresh fissures within the CPI. The CPSU ended its support for the people's democratic stage in the colonial world which had implied the leadership of the working class and replaced it with the notion of 'national democracy' which envisaged close co-operation with sections of the bourgeoisie. In India this meant an alliance of the CPI and the Nehru government. Moreover, Khrushchev's report at the Twentieth Congress of the CPSU in 1956 stressed the expanded possibilities of peaceful and parliamentary transition to socialism.[95] Such opportunities had of course been mooted earlier. In the writings of the noted political theorist A. I. Sobolev the admission of the Baltic republics into the Soviet Union in 1940 through resolutions of the parliamentary institutions of these countries, and the utilisation of parliament in Czechoslovakia in 1948 for the seizure of power and establishment of people's democracy served as major examples of this possibility.[96] The British Road to Socialism of 1951, the new party program of the CPGB, which had been examined by Stalin, also spoke in these terms. The presentation by Khrushchev did not convince major sections of the interna-

93 Sen, Documents of the History of the Communist Party of India, 1-84.
94 Sundarayya, An Autobiography, 231.
95 XX 'Sezd Kommunisticheskoi Partii Sovetskogo Soyuz,' 39-40.
96 Sobolev, People's Democracy, a New Form of Political Organization of Society.

tional communist movement that the same language was being spoken as in the Stalin period. Fears were voiced that reformist socialism was being revived.

The Twentieth Congress of the CPSU and the Peaceful, Parliamentary Road to Socialism in India

The Khrushchev period inaugurated the tripartite division in the Indian communist movement between the CPI which adopted the national democratic thesis, the CPI (M) which continued to give support to the 1951 party program and so also the understanding on people's democracy, while the CPI (ML) [Marxist-Leninist] veered towards support for a new democracy based on the earlier understanding of the Andhra committee. After the party splits the CPI was weakened, particularly after its support for Indira Gandhi in the emergency period. The CPI (ML) was formed which had a paucity of support in the working class and the peasantry. In contrast, the CPI (M), after initial repression, flourished and secured a strong government presence in the states of Kerala, West Bengal, and Tripura in the following decades until the state elections of 2011. The short-lived CPI-led government of 1957-59 in Kerala provided a model of governance which remained within the four walls of the Indian constitution and enacted major reforms, particularly agrarian reforms, which secured long-lasting electoral support for the CPI (M). The Kerala experiment initially was presented as an example of peaceful and parliamentary advance to socialism in consonance with the views projected at the Twentieth Congress of the CPSU. Later stripped of these ideological trappings it became the bedrock of successive left front governments in West Bengal, Kerala and Tripura. For some of this period the CPI (M) continued to adhere to the program and tactical line of 1951.

Kerala pioneered the notion of peaceful and parliamentary transition to socialism in India and it became the cynosure of all eyes across the world engaged with matters relating to the communist movement. As has been argued by Victor Fic, the CPI considered that after securing a parliamentary majority and organising mass movements it would be possible to break the power of the opposition parties and transform the state government machinery into an instrument of people's rule. The party would be able to inaugurate decisive political, economic and social changes in the legislature which would lead in the long term to the introduction of the dictatorship of the proletariat. In the immediate future the CPI in Kerala would have to deftly balance the preamble and the directive principles of the Indian constitution which called for the establishment of socialism and those provisions which guaranteed the existence of private property and the sanctity of civil liberties. Clearly such questions could not be resolved in Kerala alone. Nevertheless it was understood that advances could be propelled by the direct actions of the ever-expanding democratic mass organisations conjointly with legislative reform in the state assembly in the realm of agriculture, industry, education, labour relations, prices and wages. It was further proposed that the police would be expected to play a neutral role in the anticipated conflicts between the establishment and the mass organisations so that they did not take a stand between the assailants and the assailed. Similarly, pressure would be exerted on the judicial organs so that those arrested during the course of mass agitations would be released from jail. To ensure the domination of the party in the state some 1200 liaison bodies were established to co-ordinate with the ministries, police, courts and magistrates.[97] No clear vision was indicated on this logic how people's rule in the state would effect the transition to the dictatorship of the proletariat in a situation where central government power continued to exist. The traditional communist view had been that it was the responsibility of state governments to arm the people. The communist movement it should be recalled had criticised Heinrich Brandler for not doing precisely this when he was in power in Saxony and Thuringia in 1923.[98] Later left front governments in India no longer attempted to take on the burden of establishing radical people's rule. They limited their objective to coming to power to ameliorate the conditions of the masses.

The CPI ministry between 1957 and 1959 enacted landmark legislation in the realm of agrarian relations, education and affirmative action through reservation in employment for the middle, the lower castes and the tribes. All these measures struck deep into the hearts of the feudal set-up in Kerala and they evoked deep resentment amongst the landlords, vested religious educational establishments, particularly the churches, as well as amongst the upper castes.

A week after the CPI ministry was sworn in a historic ordinance was issued which prohibited the eviction of all tenants and hutment dwellers. This was done so that in the period between the announcement of agrarian reform and its enactment large-scale evictions did not take place, as had happened in many states where the Congress Party ruled.[99] The term 'tenant' was defined in a very loose manner so that it subsumed tenants, sub-tenants and even unauthorised hut dwellers. As a result no tenant was evicted from the land, and the holdings of a permanent tenant were not liable to be taken away. Moreover, the collection of

97 Fic, Kerala: Yenan of India: 1937-1969, 77-96.

98 Stalin, Sochinenia, 267; Sobolev et al., Outline History of the Communist International, 199-200.

99 This discussion on the agrarian question in Kerala is drawn from: Namboodripad, On the Agrarian Question in India; Namboodripad, The Communist Party in Kerala, 158-168; Nossiter, Communism in Kerala, 149-153; Malaviya, Kerala: A Report to the Nation, 82-97; Menon, The Kerala Agrarian Relations Bill.

rent arrears from these social sectors was forbidden. Leaseholders who possessed and occupied land could now cultivate their land without fear of eviction. In an unusual interpretation the CPI employed the term 'tiller' to include those who supervised production but who did not actually engage in manual labour. The landlords were to be paid 'fair compensation'. The land reform process could not be completed before presidential rule was imposed in Kerala in 1959. When the law was ultimately passed significant modifications were made to accommodate landed interests. Later the courts struck down some important provisions of the agrarian law which even led some analysts to argue that the final legislation had little impact. It became possible for landholders to gift away their land so that it did not become available for the rural poor. The land-ceiling for individuals and families was amended in such a way so as to decrease the amount of surplus land. An examination of the agrarian legislation in Kerala suggests that it was done basically within the framework of the recommendations of the Agrarian Reforms Committee of the Congress Party in 1949. Such was also the case with the agrarian law of 1969 by which the CPI (M) completed the task which had been started in 1957 but which it was not allowed to finish. Effectively the CPI carried out the agrarian reform policy of the Congress Party which the ruling party had not carried out, but in a way that was highly beneficial to the peasantry and the rural poor. The original ordinance which prohibited eviction and imposed a moratorium on rent payments ultimately led to agrarian reform which provided immense relief to hundreds of thousands of peasants, agricultural workers, and the rural poor. The policy of land being given to the tiller gratis and without compensation to the landlords, along with the cancellation of the agricultural debt, which was the basic CPI programme, was not to be carried out. That the bill hurt landed interests is apparent from the fact that two days after the bill completed its legislative stages a 'liberation struggle' was initiated for the dismissal of the CPI government. The constricted nature of the land reform is also clear from the fact that half a century after the promulgation of presidential rule in 1959, when it was estimated that there were 700,000 acres of surplus land available for redistribution, only some 93,000 acres were actually distributed.[100] In its election manifesto of 1946 the CPI had pledged that the 'untouchables' who formed the bulk of the landless labourers would be given first and special attention in the settling of landless labourers on fallow land.[101] This focus is not apparent in the literature generated before and after the formation of

---

100 See "Left Governments in Kerala," in http://www.cpimkerala.org/eng/brief-description--73.php?n=1, Accessed December 12, 2011.

101 Joshi, Election Manifesto of the CPI," 12.

the CPI ministry in 1957. Today the CPI (M) still speaks of confiscating surplus land and distributing it amongst the landless. All this suggests that in Kerala feudalism, far from being ended, could only be modified.

A second major field where the CPI courted controversy was on the question of continuing affirmative action for the 'backward' and 'lower' castes as well as the tribes, by the reservation of posts in government service and seats in educational institutions.[102] It is not a question frequently discussed when the CPI government of 1958-9 is examined, but the chief minister of that period, E.M.S. Namboodiripad, gives us a brief glimpse of it in his book 'The Communist Party in Kerala: Six Decades of Struggle and Advance'. This was one of the problems which were to be taken up in 1958 by the Administrative Reforms Committee, which was mandated to examine administrative efficiency in the state. It was the position of the CPI that alongside the exploitation of the property-less sections of the populace, which was based on class relations, there existed addition social oppression of the lower castes founded on the iniquities of the caste system. The Committee accepted that the oppressed castes and communities required the special protection of the legislature and the government. First it proposed the continuation of reservation of positions in education and government for the scheduled castes and scheduled tribes. Second it suggested that the 'backward' castes should have the advantages of reservation but that they should be subject to the economic criterion which would exclude the better-off sections of these communities. This was bound to be controversial as it precluded the benefits of affirmative action from the very sections which were most able to take advantage of it. The third recommendation of the Committee was that a decennial survey be conducted to determine whether sufficient progress had been made by any section of the backward communities to permit their exclusion from reservation altogether. The effect of the suggestions of the Committee was that the upper-caste and the relatively better-off sections of the 'backward' castes adopted hostile positions in relation to the CPI which was to lead to the defeat of the party in the elections of 1960. The Nair community organised a new political party called the National Democratic Party which supported reservation for the poor of all castes but was completely opposed to reservation for the 'backward' castes while backing it for the scheduled castes and tribes. A new party was also formed by the Ezhava community named the Socialist Revolutionary Party which advocated the principle that the benefits of reservation should be extended to everyone in the 'backward' communities, that is, they rejected the application of the economic criterion. Kerala society became politically polarised

---

102 Surjeet, The Communist Party in Kerala: Six Decades of Struggle and Advance, 184-191.

between the Congress Party and the CPI. Analogous to the landlords linking arms to attack land reform we find that the upper castes and upper strata of the 'backward' castes joined hands to oppose affirmative action.

The third question which split Kerala politics apart in 1958-9 was that of the Education Bill.[103] The associations of the school teachers had arisen in the Malabar region in the 1930s together with the trade union and peasant movements. The Education Bill was primarily concerned with the insecure service conditions in the Christian and other private schools as well as in the government schools. Christian schools comprised those of the Basel Mission Society in Malabar and the Syrian and other churches in Cochin and Travancore. They received no financial assistance from the government under the Raj. However the non-Christian religious communities, such as those of the Nair Service Society, set up their own schools which were aided by the government. Out of about 10,000 schools in Kerala as many as 6,000 to 7,000 were under private management and of these some 2,200 were operated by the churches. The schoolteachers' movement wanted the government to take over responsibility for education so that arbitrary functioning in the private institutions, particularly regarding hire and fire policies, was ended by the direct payment of salaries to the teachers. School teachers had formed the backbone of the nationalist and communist movements in the state and it was they who pressed for the Education Bill. At that time there were very few accepted service conditions for school teachers and no pension schemes. From the viewpoint of the government the teachers were being paid out of the government exchequer but it had no voice in appointments or service conditions. The bill did not propose the end of the system of private management in schools which had been the demand of the teachers. It had more modest propositions which were to provide for the direct payment of salaries to teachers without any deduction by private managers and to curb the power of private institutions to suspend or dismiss teachers. The second part of the bill provided for compulsory, free primary education and midday meals, textbooks and study materials for children up to the age of 14. The provision for government preparation of textbooks invited the criticism that this would lead to communist indoctrination. The education bill was passed by the Kerala legislature amidst public furore but the opposition was able to persuade the central government to withhold assent for the bill and refer it back to the state assembly.

103 Surjeet, The Communist Party in Kerala: Six Decades of Struggle and Advance, 181-184; Nossiter, Communism in Kerala, 149-153; Malaviya, Kerala: A Report to the Nation, 153-57; Malaviya, Kerala: A Report to the Nation, 26-42.

In the event, with the dissolution of the assembly the final education act was substantially modified to accommodate the private institutions.

What was called the Kerala Model was of considerable importance in the history of the communist movement in India. It showed the possibilities of radical reform within the federal structure of Indian polity. Lessons were learnt from this by both the CPI and the CPI (M). When the CPI split in 1964 the bulk of the communists in Kerala under E.M.S. Namboodripad walked over to the CPI (M) and a similar position obtained in West Bengal. The Kerala experience lay at the back of the Left Front governments in West Bengal where parallel land reforms gave valuable relief to the sharecroppers of the state. While in Kerala governance alternated between the CPI-Congress alliance and the CPI (M) governments, in West Bengal the Left Front ruled in an unbroken sequence for over three decades.

If we glance at the land reforms carried out by Left Front Government in West Bengal (questions pertaining to educational reform and affirmative action for the depressed castes, in contrast to Kerala, were never significantly prominent) a number of features strike the eye.[104] It must be conceded that much of the pressure for agrarian reform came from the poor peasant uprising in Naxalbari in North Bengal which demanded 'land to the tiller' and which led to the formation of the CPI (ML). It was under the rule of the Congress Party that the second West Bengal Land Reforms Act was passed in 1971. This enjoined a limit of 5 'standard' hectares of irrigated land (equal to 7 hectares of unirrigated land) for a family of up to five members, plus a 1/2 hectare for additional family members, with a limit of a maximum of 7 hectares for each family. About 16% of the surplus lands were appropriated by 1998, mainly under the Congress government. Of this only about 5-6 percent was actually distributed. Numerous obstacles emerged as half of the landowners declined to respond to mandatory queries about the size of their families and the surplus lands they would be required to surrender. Neither the Congress Party nor the Left Front government which came to power in 1977 had the political will to confront the big landlords to appropriate their surplus lands in a big way. Landlords were able to thwart land distribution where land had been appropriated for fear that the wages of the rural

---

104 This discussion is based on the following readings: Pranab Bardhan and Dilip Mookherjee, Determinants of Redistributive Politics: An Empirical Analysis of Land Reforms in West Bengal", http:/people.bu.edu/dilipm/publications/wbpelrefaerrevfinalsubrev.pdf accessed December 12, 2001; Bose, "Thirty Years of the Left Front Government in West Bengal," http://www.pragoti.in/node/1, accessed December 12, 2011; Mishra, "On Agrarian Transition in West Bengal"; Webster, "Panchayati Raj in West Bengal: Popular Participation for the People or the Party?" 129-163.

poor would rise, reducing their dependence on them for credits and marketing. Local government officials were able to use this appropriated land for rent-seeking purposes. Agrarian intervention by the Left Front government took the form, first, of the distribution of the limited appropriated lands by giving titles to the landless labourers; and, second, by giving hereditary tenancy rights to share-croppers and limiting the share of the crops of the landlords to 25%, or 50% if the landlord put in all material inputs. Despite the rise of neo-liberalism in India from the 1990s, land reform continued in West Bengal. By January 2011 the Left Front government in the state could boast that in 34 years of governance 11.3 lakhs acres (one lakh is equivalent to one hundred thousand) of land had been distributed among 30.4 lakh poor peasants and 15 lakh sharecroppers were granted tenurial security. Sixty-six percent of the beneficiaries of land reform belong to the depressed castes or the religious minorities. In addition homestead land (land plots for building hutments) was distributed to 3.4 lakh landless labourers. Impressive as these statistics are it is evident that big landholdings and the sharecropping system survived. The feudal remnants were modified rather than ended. It was only after the Left Front adopted a pattern of industrial development involving neo-liberalism and the linking up with Indian and foreign capital, which violently displaced the working peasantry in Nandigram and Singur and led to a number of government outrages, was the Front perceived as being detrimental to the working people. It led to the electoral debacle in West Bengal in April 2011.

The CPI government in Kerala had originally been represented as an application of a peaceful, parliamentary transition to socialism. This presentation was no longer viable after the CPI (M) was established in 1964, as it had rejected the formulations of the Twentieth Congress of the CPSU. The new logic that came to the fore was that left front governments in the states had the task of ameliorating the conditions of the working people while the transition to the people's democratic stage could only be considered once further left front governments could be brought into being in other Indian states. Such was the logic presented in West Bengal by the CPI (M). In effect the party simultaneously embraced the peaceful, parliamentary program for left front governments derived from the Twentieth Congress of the CPSU of 1956, while retaining a revolutionary program of people's democracy, envisaging the armed struggle founded on workers' general strikes and uprisings accompanied by the partisan warfare in the rural areas which was explicit in the tactical line document of 1951. Clearly one or the other had to give.

The letter of resignation which was submitted by P. Sundarayya, the general secretary of the CPI (M) to the party during the internal emergency in 1975 suggests that the Kerala practice of the peaceful, parliamentary path had prevailed in the party. This letter which was published for the first time in 1991 dealt with a wide-ranging number of issues.[105] Eleven years after the formation of the party Sundarayya argued that the CPI (M) no longer looked at matters from the point of view of a revolutionary party. The practice of the party was founded on 'deep-rooted parliamentary legalistic illusions' and on the 'possibilities of peaceful development' of the party and the movement for a long period to come. The party was deeply embroiled in revisionist habits, thinking and mode of functioning in all its mass fronts and party-building. Twenty-four years after the discussions in Moscow Sundarayya alone stood up and without mincing his words defended the programmatic and tactical perspectives of 1951. It was agreed, he continued, that the path of the Indian revolution was different from Russia and China. It would be based on the alliance of the working class and the peasantry which would synchronise the general strikes and armed insurrections of the working class in the industrial centres along with the peasant armed revolt based on guerilla bases and later liberated bases. A successful Indian revolution required the combination of the insurrection of the working class and peasantry on an all-India scale. Sundarayya then went in for the kill. He affirmed that in the name of preparing for the all-India movements of the working class and the peasantry, in fact, seeing the organisational weakness of the party and the democratic movements, the party 'unconsciously' slipped into parliamentary and constitutional forms of activity in which 'other basic tasks' of the party were neglected. Sundarayya focused on the basic flaw of the party which, put in another way, we may say that the peaceful, parliamentary model exemplified by the Kerala (and later the West Bengal experience) had dominated over the revolutionary path to people's democracy outlined in the tactical line of the CPI in 1951.

Clearly on its own terms the communist movement after the transfer of power in India was not successful in inaugurating a democratic revolution. On the question of the abolition of feudalism it chose not to emulate the agrarian revolution in Jammu and Kashmir where the landlords were expropriated without compensation by the Kashmir National Conference under the leadership of Sheikh Abdullah, or indeed the movement in Telengana where the CPI itself succeeded in wresting the lands of the landlords in important areas of Hyderabad state. In following the limited framework of the land reform policy adumbrated by the ruling Congress Party the communist movement scored important successes. While about five million acres of land were distributed in the sixty years after 1947, of these, more than one million acres were accounted for by

105 Sundarayya, My Resignation, 4-33.

West Bengal alone. The communist movement in this way buttressed the Congress Party program of simultaneously modifying and preserving the survival of feudalism but in a manner which defended the rural poor.

The communist movement exerts influence in India, despite the rise of widespread reformism, the decline in 'reformist' sectors and the expansion of the communist revolutionaries in others. As a result of diminished militancy the communist movement lost ground in the trade unions from the nineteen sixties so that today the Bharatiya Mazdoor Sangh, which is close to the communal Hindu political organisations, is the largest central trade union organisation in India. The communist parties through the multi-million membership of the trade union federations such as the All-India Trades Union Congress, the Centre of Indian Trade Unions, the All India Central Council of Trade Unions and the New Trade Union Initiative, the peasant associations such the All-India Kisan Sabha, the women's, and students' associations play a powerful role. The cultural fronts of the CPI such as the Indian People's Theatre Association and the Progressive Writers' Association exerted great influence on the cultural life of the subcontinent, extending to the Bombay film industry. The communist movement has permeated sections of the intelligentsia so that reformist Marxism commingled with nationalist influence plays an important role in the humanities and the social sciences. The communist parties have been pillars of secularism in India. At the time of the partition of the sub-continent the CPI members in India and Pakistan stood fast against the communal frenzy and in subsequent decades acted as the fulcrum of secularism. All streams of the communist movement have sustained themselves after collapse of the Soviet bloc and the rise of the market economy in China revealing the organic links of the parties with the working class and the working peoples.

The Political Power of Economic Ideas? Foreign Economic Advisors and Indian Planning in the 1950s and 1960s

David C. Engerman

> *I would not underestimate the importance of the Berlin Crisis; but I will say that in my own mind what happens to India, insofar as its economic progress is concerned in the next few years, could be... more important in the long run, than what happens in the negotiations with regard to Berlin. Richard M. Nixon, May 1959*[1]
>
> *If India fails [in her economic plan] ... I would say that the decisive struggle in the cold war in the next ten years will have been lost. John F. Kennedy, December 1959*[2]

During their campaign for the presidential election in 1960 – a process that began, in both cases, well before they earned nominations from their respective parties in the summer of 1960 – Vice President Richard Nixon and Senator John F. Kennedy (D-Mass.) had few grounds for agreement; they quarreled over everything from domestic spending to defense capabilities, from anti-corruption to anti-communism. Yet they found common ground over India, with both politicians asserting the global importance of the world's largest democracy. The Indian economy, both Kennedy and Nixon insisted, was more important than the chronic Cold War crisis over Berlin, which entered a new phase with Soviet leader Nikita Khrushchev's threats in 1958 and ended only with the erection of the wall in 1961.

The superpower tensions in India – what made it so important to both future candidates – marked the arrival of a new kind of Cold War hotspot, one defined around economic development more than geopolitical alignment, nuclear weapons, or the myriad of other issues dividing the United States and the Soviet Union in those years. Both superpowers sought to bring India into close alignment, while Indian Prime Minister Jawaharlal Nehru determinedly maintained a posture of non-alignment, engaging with nations from both Cold War blocs but beholden to neither.[3]

---

1 Quoted in Harrison, India and the United States, 144.

2 Kennedy interview with John Fischer, The Strategy of Peace, 222. Emphasis in original.

3 The best account on Indian foreign relations in the Nehruvian era focuses on military affairs: Raghavan, War and Peace in Modern India. The classic account of US policy in the region is McMahon, The Cold War on the Periphery.

This brief essay explores the geopolitics of the Indian economy in the late 1950s, especially as Cold War superpowers (and others) sought to influence Indian economic policy. While other scholars have documented the provision of western aid to India, they have focused on tangible forms – steel plants, foreign exchange resources, food, and the like.[4] But the superpowers also provided a great deal of economic advice, both solicited and uninvited, to Indian economic policy-makers and planners.[5] While the foreign advisors did not necessarily shape Indian economic policy in the ways that they had hoped, they did – perhaps inadvertently – play an important role in the domestic political disputes over Indian plans. Indeed, the presence of these advisors shows the value of considering Indian economic-policy formulation in international context.[6]

The central figures in this account are both economists and institution-builders: Prasanta Chandra Mahalanobis and Max F. Millikan. Mahalanobis, a Bengali physicist-turned-statistician-turned-economist, had a profound impact on the direction of Indian economic policy in the 1950s and 1960s, and at the same time shaped the Indian economics profession more than any other non-economist. After graduating from Calcutta's famed Presidency College and the University of Cambridge with degrees in physics, Mahalanobis grew increasingly interested in statistics. He founded and served as longtime director of the Indian Statistical Institute (ISI), a leading research and training facility that also became a key conduit between academic and policy worlds. His official connections were numerous and at times overlapping: Statistical Advisor to the Indian Cabinet, the Planning Commission's key economic advisor, and eventually a member of the Planning Commission. None of these tasks restricted Mahalanobis's movements; he traveled frequently abroad, visiting United Nations offices in New York and Geneva – as part of his service on various UN expert commis-

---

4 Discussions of American aid to India are well-summarized in Merrill, Bread and the Ballot.

5 Studies of transnational flows of economic expertise have received significant scholarly attention since the 1980s: see, for instance, the essays in Hall, (ed.), The Political Power of Economic Ideas; Valdés, Pinochet's Economists. On conversations across the East-West divide, see especially Bockman and Bernstein, "Scientific Community in a Divided World." and Bockman and Eyal, "Eastern Europe as a Laboratory for Economic Knowledge."

6 Even the best works on Indian economic planning have focused primarily on domestic rather than international politics; see for instance, Frankel, India's Political Economy, 1947-1977; Varshney and Ahmed, Battles Half Won; Rudolph and Rudolph, In Pursuit of Lakshmi.

sions – and gave lectures and seminars in the leading universities of Europe (both eastern and western), the Soviet Union, and the United States.[7]

Economist Max Millikan also had an association, albeit less direct, with physics: his father Robert won the Nobel Medal in that field for his work on the photoelectric effect. Millikan pursued a doctorate in economics, worked briefly at the Wartime Shipping Board in the 1940s, and then began teaching at the Massachusetts Institute of Technology (MIT). After a stint as an assistant director of the Central Intelligence Agency, where he established the Office of Research and Reports, Millikan returned to MIT to head its new Center for International Studies (CENIS), funded at first by his former employer. Millikan's scientific contributions did not match Mahalanobis's – there is measure of statistical sampling called the Mahalanobis Distance and no comparable honor for Millikan – yet both would seek to shape India's economy as well as its economics profession.[8] Both Mahalanobis and Millikan, furthermore, aimed to accomplish these tasks by deploying foreign economic expertise in India.

Mahalanobis and the Pursuit of Non-Aligned Expertise

Mahalanobis used foreign academic expertise to advance a domestic political agenda. He had first gotten involved in discussion about Indian economic policy in the late 1930s, after the Indian National Congress established a National Planning Committee with Nehru as chair. The Committee gathered together key figures in India's scientific elite, many of whom would lead academic and political institutions of postcolonial India.[9] In spite of the lackluster results of the Committee – in part the result of an extended hiatus during Nehru's long imprisonment during World War II – Nehru nevertheless gained from the experience a heightened enthusiasm for planning as well as confidence that Mahalanobis would be a valuable ally in implementing his economic vision.

The politician and the statistician shared a clear vision that India must undertake not just central planning but also rapid industrialization. Both men looked to the Soviet example of the early 1930s – though not, by any means, be-

7 For personal details on Mahalanobis, including many of his extensive international connections, see the highly sympathetic biography by a student: Rudra, Prasanta Chandra Mahalanobis.

8 There is no extensive biography of Millikan, but useful information appears in Blackmer, The MIT Center for International Studies. On his CIA role, see Immerman, "A Brief History of the CIA," in Theoharis, The Central Intelligence Agency, 19.

9 Zachariah, Developing India, 5. and, more generally, Prakash, Another Reason, 7. On the process and aims of the National Planning Committee, see Shah, National Planning, Principles & Administration.

cause either was a card-carrying Communist. Mahalanobis worked out a simple two-sector model of the Indian economy that shared a great deal with a key Soviet model that undergirded its early Five-Year Plans in the 1930s.[10] He concluded that only through building up steel production could India expand rapidly in a way that would establish economic independence to match its newfound political circumstances.[11] Nehru, for his part, celebrated heavy industry and large infrastructure as "temples of modern India," and expressed a strong preference for industrialization over Gandhi's vision of cottage industry in the Indian countryside.[12]

While Nehru and Mahalanobis stood at one end of the spectrum of the great economic debate of the 1930s – planning versus markets – their views were hardly out of place in India. As visions for India's economic future proliferated in the 1940s, political parties, labor unions and chambers of commerce published planning documents. These all had a great deal in common. They all expected that economic growth would be a high priority as a means to reduce poverty and develop economic independence, that a new Indian state would own significant enterprises, especially in the capital-goods sector, and that some kind of governmental direction would steer India's limited resources to maximize economic growth.[13] Two years after Indian independence in 1947, Nehru established a Planning Commission – with himself as Chairman – that functioned as what historian Benjamin Zachariah called a "parallel Cabinet." Its First Five-Year Plan began the following year. The first plan was somewhat less than the name implies; the Finance Minister of that time admitted that the Plan was a compendium of scattered individual projects taken from the various 1940s plans and collated into a single document.[14]

Within a few years, though, Nehru and Mahalanobis had established the institutional framework for a more substantial planning process and a more ambi-

10 As American economist Evsey Domar noted, this model closely resembled a key model in the USSR's first (and costly) Five Year Plan – see Domar, "A Soviet Model of Growth," in Domar, Essays in the Theory of Economic Growth.

11 Mahalanobis, "National Income, Investment, and National Development," in Mahalanobis, Talks on Planning, 9-12. Also Mahalanobis, Some Observations on the Process of Growth of National Income, 307-312.

12 Zachariah, Nehru, 140 and passim.

13 People's Plan of the Indian Federation of Labour: Banerjea and Roy, People's Plan for Economic Development of India. On the chamber of commerce plan: Thakurdas, A Brief Memorandum Outlining a Plan of Economic Development for India. Chattopadhyay, Indian Business and Economic Planning, 330-334. More generally, see Chaudhuri, "Economic Planning in India."

14 Deshmukh, Economic Developments in India, 83-85. "Parallel Cabinet" from Zachariah, Nehru, 190.

tious plan. Mahalanobis began to advise Nehru and his Planning Commission by 1954; the ISI established a beachhead in New Delhi at that time. To emphasize the intermingling of scholarly and policy work, the ISI's Delhi group was headed by Pitamber Pant, another physicist-turned economist who had previously worked as Nehru's private secretary for planning.[15] Through these institutions, Nehru and Mahalanobis began to put their marks on the Second Five-Year Plan, slated to start in 1955. It would be strikingly different from its predecessor in ambition, emphasis, and even tone. As Mahalanobis told one student, the First Plan was "an anthology" but the second must be "a drama."[16]

The Second Plan, true to Mahalanobis's word, broke dramatically from the First. It aimed to increase national income by 5% per year so that unemployment would be "liquidated" within a decade. The key to this growth would be heavy industry, which must be "expanded with all possible speed" in the public sector. Steel was a particular focus (or, for critics, fixation); the Plan called for tripling steel production in only five years. These new steel plants would permit India to industrialize rapidly without significant imports, while at the same time helping spur a more general economic expansion.[17] To promote this sector, public expenditures on heavy industry almost tripled from the first plan, to the detriment of project spending on social services and especially agriculture.[18]

Even though there was widespread agreement among the Indian political and academic elites about the need for national economic growth and for some degree of government intervention, the Second Plan's aims and assumptions came under attack. A small and fading contingent of Gandhians in the Congress Party resented the emphasis on heavy industry, preferring agriculture and village industry.[19] Others questioned the high targets for steel. Radical organizations inveighed against the plan, citing the lack of fundamental land reform, without which, they argued, there would be no way to create a more equal distribution of resources and power in the Indian countryside. The Indian Committee of the Congress for Cultural Freedom, in contrast, criticized the plan's "fantastic" tar-

---

15 Indian Statistical Institute, History and Activities, 16.

16 Rudra, Prasanta Chandra Mahalanobis, 432.

17 Unger, Rourkela. Ein 'Stahlwerk im Dschungel'. More generally, see Johnson, The Steel Industry of India.

18 Mahalanobis, "Recommendation for the Formulation of the Second Five-Year Plan" (1955), in Mahalanobis, Talks on Planning, 22. Chakravarty, Development Planning, 9. For general economic and policy debates, see Unger, Rourkela. Ein 'Stahlwerk im Dschungel', 2-5; Hanson, The Process of Planning.

19 Zachariah, Nehru, 169.

gets and worried that the only way to meet them would violate "individual liberties."[20]

Seeking to contain such debates, the Planning Commission convened a panel of twenty-one Indian economists from the country's top universities and institutes to pass judgment on the size, structure, and policies of the Nehru/Mahalanobis plan. The panel, with the exception of one dissenter, rallied behind the Plan in a hefty volume of technical papers preceded by an overall assessment. The Panel endorsed the overall aims and structure of the Second Five-Year Plan while criticizing many (even most) specific aspects of it. Indeed, the Panel's final report criticized the Plan for being insufficiently bold to achieve its aims, calling on the Planning Commission to increase the quantitative targets. The conclusion was as much a political as an economic judgment. The Panel's overall conclusions differed from the tone of the individual papers, which raised a plethora of concerns about the Planning Commission's basic assumptions and overall strategy.[21] The sole dissenter from the panel's recommendations, B.R. Shenoy, echoed the Congress for Cultural Freedom's criticism of planning in a manner befitting his membership in a group of insurgent market-oriented economists, the Montpelerin Society.[22]

Though Mahalanobis worked closely with Soviet officials, and indeed was named an Honorary Member of the Academy of Sciences of the USSR, India's economic arrangements differed markedly from those in the USSR. No major nationalization of private enterprises took place in independent India, unlike the waves of nationalization that marked post-revolutionary Russia – and, for that matter, post-World War II Britain. Indian officials like Mahalanobis expressed an abiding preference for public over private enterprise, but sought to achieve the "socialistic pattern of society" that was the Congress Party platform by expanding public enterprises, not by taking over private ones.[23]

---

20 Desai and Murthy, "The Public Sector and Targets in the Private Sector," in Indian Committee for Cultural Freedom, Studies on the Plan Frame, 27-28.

21 Panel of Economists, The Second Five Year Plan: Basic Considerations Relating to the Plan Frame; India. Planning Commission, Papers Relating to the Formulation of the Second Five Year Plan, 1, 13-14. Compare these "basic considerations" to some of the articles published in the same volume, for instance: Gupta, Notes on Objectives, etc. of the Second Five-Year Plan; Madan, The Second Five-Year Plan: Problems of Resource Mobilization.

22 Shenoy, "A Note of Dissent", in India Planning Commission, Papers Relating to the Formulation of the Second Five Year Plan, 19-20; see also Bauer, B.R. Shenoy: Stature and Impact.

23 Frankel, India's Political Economy, 3-4.

Mahalanobis's vision of a centrally planned socialist economy was apparent, to some degree, in the roster of visitors to his institute. To find suitable visitors, Mahalanobis used his excellent international connections, the result of his Cambridge training and his membership in the UN Statistical Commission. He began reaching out to economists in both Eastern and Western Europe, and spoke with American scholars during his frequent visits to New York and Geneva on UN business. His appointment to the UN's Economic Commission on the Far East helped expand his contacts among development economists all the wider.[24]

Through these and other international contacts, Mahalanobis arranged for a flurry of international visitors, often on the left side of the political spectrum. In 1955, for instance, the ISI offices in Calcutta and Delhi hosted JBS Haldane and John Strachey (UK), Charles Bettelheim (France), and Paul Baran (US) – all Marxists without party affiliation except Haldane, who was a member of the British Communist Party for most of the 1940s. There were also a number of economists closer to the mainstream of the profession, but they too tended towards the left: the Canadian-born but Harvard-based John Kenneth Galbraith, English post-Keynesians Nicholas Kaldor and Joan Robinson, and the great Polish economists Michał Kalecki and Oskar Lange. Then there were the Soviets, who came in large numbers through the mid- and late-1950s. Soviet experts included planners in government agencies as well as academic experts in development finance, applied statistics, and the Soviet version of price theory.[25]

By the end of the 1950s, Mahalanobis had also hosted most of the major western theorists of development. Nobel Laureates Ragnar Frisch (Norway), Simon Kuznets (US), and Jan Tinbergen (Netherlands), among others, took consultancies at ISI. The sheer quantity of the visitors is as impressive as their quality and academic distinction – as the following table of 1958-59 visitors by country suggests:

Table 1: Academic Visitors by Country, 1958-1959

Country	Visitors	Country	Visitors	Country	Visitors
Afghanistan	3	Germany (FRG)	2	Thailand	3

24 Rabjam K. Som, "Work with International Organizations," in Rudra, Prasanta Chandra Mahalanobis, 40-51.; Ward, Quantifying the World, 40-51.

25 Various 1950s ISI Annual Reports.

Australia	1	Germany (GDR)	5	United Kingdom	7
Belgian Congo	1	Ghana	1	United States	32
Cuba	5	Japan	9	USSR	26
Czechoslovakia	16	Netherlands	1	Yugoslavia	5
Denmark	1	Pakistan	1	Int'l Organizations	11
Finland	1	Singapore	1	TOTAL	136

These foreign experts were treated as honored guests, feted around banquet tables and seminar tables alike. Meanwhile, they were kept busy with a taxing schedule of advising, student meetings, and tours of industrial facilities all over India. They also contributed to the ISI's series called "Studies on Planning" and consulted with planning officials in New Delhi, including those affiliated with the ISI's branch there as well as members of the Delhi School of Economics.[26] Galbraith, who came to Calcutta twice in the 1950s before being appointed American ambassador to India in 1961, celebrated the Institute: "In no other place in the world at the time was there such easy and intense exchange between peoples of the socialist and the nonsocialist worlds and of the rich countries and the poor."[27]

Not all of the advising took place in India. Mahalanobis in particular had a remarkably full schedule of international travel, and frequently met with scholars and policy-makers from around the world during those trips. He cast his net widely, visiting with leading development economists in both Cambridge, Massachusetts and Cambridge, England, as well with experts on Soviet economics, planning techniques, national income estimation, and the like. It is a sign of both Mahalanobis's packed itinerary and his place within ISI that the Institute's annual reports regularly included a section on "Tours Abroad of P.C. Mahalanobis." The 1958-59 report, for instance, details foreign travels accounting for more than two months, in which he visited more than 25 cities in Austria, Belgium, Japan, the USSR, the UK, and the US.[28]

26 Table from ISI Annual Report, 1959-60, 104-110. S.R. Sen quoted in Rosen, Western Economists and Eastern Societies, 58.

27 Galbraith, A Life in Our Times, 328.

28 ISI Annual Report, 81-82. Interview with Abram Bergson, 7 December 1999.

While Mahalanobis's contacts ranged widely in both geographic and ideological terms, there was a certain leftward tilt in the orientation of the visitors. Few if any visiting economists questioned the organizational arrangements for Indian economic policy, including the key role played by the Planning Commission. The basic focus on heavy industry, similarly, was challenged by only a few visitors – and those doing so, described in more detailed below, were generally not invited by Mahalanobis himself. One reason for this acceptance of the basic parameters of the Mahalanobis-Nehru policy inhered in the nature of the advising relationship itself. Michał Kalecki, for instance, wrote a report during his 1960 visit to India that included an extensive and detailed enumeration of problems with the current arrangements. An Indian official who read this report, Kalecki recalled, "noticed with some irony that if the situation appeared so complicated, I should have perhaps recommended a change of the entire system. I replied that if a country wants to change its entire system, it makes a revolution and does not bring in foreign advisors.[29] Kalecki was unlikely the only visitor to offer advice within the broad parameters of Nehruvian economic priorities and practices.

Chicago economist Milton Friedman exhibited little such modesty – but then again he was sent by American officials, not invited by Mahalanobis. Friedman described his trip as an effort to, in his words, "counter the influence of the left-wing advice" that Mahalanobis was receiving from others. Friedman seemed determined to challenge the advice from fellow Americans – as he did that of Soviet and other East Bloc scholars. He worried especially about the India programs of the Rockefeller and Ford foundations, which were "highly sympathetic to the central planning propensities of Indian authorities."[30] But Friedman and fellow Montpellerinian Shenoy were rare market-oriented voices in a chorus dominated by planners. Though Friedman might not be the ideal neutral observer on the question of proclivities toward planning, in this particular case, he had a good point.

The Ends of Economic Advice

Mahalanobis invited such a wide range of experts not so much to learn from them – and certainly not to change his plans (or his Plans). The extraordinary number and range of experts traveling through India served to bolster his own prestige and to provide leverage for the promotion of his own views. He acknowledged these purposes in a number of public and private statements. Maha-

---

29 Kalecki, "Introduction to Annex to Financial Problems of the Third Plan," in Kalecki, Developing Economies, 217-218.

30 Friedman and Friedman, Two Lucky People, 257-262.

lanobis once compared the role of foreign experts to "airforce [*sic*] cover for the army" – visitors did not change the strategy, but helped to win the battle.[31] Elsewhere he noted that the "greatest benefit" of the visitors as reinforcing his existing plans: "through contacts with such eminent experts from many different countries we gained confidence in our way of thinking."[32] Similarly, his visits to Western Europe and the United States helped Mahalanobis, who had no formal training in economics, to overcome his "inferiority complex about economic matters." "My frequent visits to the West," Mahalanobis wrote his ISI colleague Pitamber Pant, "have not only given me greater breadth of vision but [also] have given me increasing self-confidence."[33] He gained so much self-confidence, in fact, that he boasted to a Soviet magazine about his ability to prevail in economic arguments. Asked to describe the differences of opinion between Indian planners and foreign advisors, Mahalanobis replied that "Some of them [foreign experts] express doubts about the emphasis on heavy industry.... I think that a majority of them, after a detailed discussion," come to endorse his view.[34] Mahalanobis employed foreign advisors as debating partners or as confidence-builders – but not, it seems, for advice.

Mahalanobis was no doubt overly confident in his persuasive abilities. Yet he is correct in his implication that foreign economic advisors did not shape Indian economic policy as much as they became objects in domestic disputes about the direction of the Indian economy. This was evident to at least two MIT economists, who persisted in their efforts to shape Indian policy while recognizing the relative ineffectiveness of their own efforts. Both Ian Little and Wilfred Malenbaum insisted on the value of their work while at the same time holding that the Indian plans remained a purely indigenous product.[35] They did so in the context of broader concerns among western economists that their advising in the Third World was not yielding the results they had intended or hoped. Dudley Seers, later to become a staunch critic of western development economics, published an article in one of the leading American economics journals seeking to explain "Why visiting economists fail." While Seers placed most of the blame on the hosts, he acknowledged also the inability of visitors to comprehend the policy debates into which their work was thrust. Outside expertise was not ob-

31 Quoted without citation in Clarkson, The Soviet Theory of Development, 267.

32 Mahalanobis, The Approach of Operational Research to Planning in India, 6-7.

33 Mahalanobis to Pant quoted in Khilnani, The Idea of India, 85.

34 [Mahalanobis,] "Etot plan otkryvaet Indii dorogu v budushchee: interviu d-ra Makhalanobisa," V zashchitu mira 7 (1958), no. 3, 75.

35 Little, Economic Development, 50; Malenbaum, "Who Does the Planning?," 301, 309.

jective and distant, but part of one partisan dispute or another – whether or not the visitors intended it that way.[36]

Millikan, the Center for International Studies, and Planning à l'Américaine

The role of MIT's Center for International Studies in India would neatly confirm Seers's criticisms about the role of foreign economic advisors. While fitting into the general pattern about foreign scholars' well-intentioned efforts to improve Third World economic conditions, there were some special elements of CENIS that made it especially significant in India. The Center for International Studies was established in 1952 to straddle – or perhaps to blur – the line between scholarship and policy. Created with CIA funds, the Center grew out of a classified research project on Soviet jamming of American radio broadcasts into Eastern Europe and the USSR. It soon took on a wide variety of projects, only some of which were classified research on government contract.[37]

The Center's work on economic development, in contrast to this CIA work, was funded primarily by private foundations. Millikan, together with his friend and former Yale classmate Walt Rostow, were among the early American scholars to recognize the importance of economic development to the Cold War. As early as 1953, they sought a major Ford Foundation grant to study economic development. True to the Center's mission of shaping both policy and scholarship, their proposal insisted upon "serving the basic purpose of enhancing human knowledge" while at the same time doing so "in a manner which will be of maximum use to the policy-maker as well as the scholar." Fixing quickly on India – first as the sole country study, soon joined by Indonesia and Italy – the MIT project sought to "analyze the present direction" of economic development, "define possible alternative courses of future development," and "isolate the strategic variables in these situations which can be affected by the policy and action of the governments concerned, the American government, and international agencies."[38] As their proposal made clear, MIT scholars hoped to influence not just Indian economic policy but also American policy towards India.[39]

---

36 Seers, "Why Visiting Economists Fail." See also Papanek, "Foreign Advisors and Planning Agencies," 175-176.

37 Blackmer, MIT Center for International Studies, 1; Needell, "'Truth Is Our Weapon.'"

38 Center for International Studies (CENIS) Records, "A Program of Research in Economic and Political Development", box 2, folder 1.

39 MIT efforts to shape American foreign policy are not part of the focus here, but are well-covered in Blackmer, MIT Center for International Studies, 4.; Gilman, Mandarins of the Future, chap. 5.; Rostow, Eisenhower, Kennedy, and Foreign Aid.

Millikan traveled to India in early 1954, meeting with Mahalanobis and many other economists and government officials before signing an agreement with the secretary of India's Planning Commission.[40] CENIS established an office in Delhi, located within the Planning Commission and in close touch with the ISI's Delhi branch; the office was staffed by western economists who rotated through on an annual basis. Some, such as Richard Eckhaus, Louis Lafeber, and Wilfred Malenbaum, had been working for the Center in Cambridge; others, including Ian Little and W.T. Reddaway, came from other institutions to serve in Delhi; in any case, all were in close touch with Millikan and other Cambridge officials.[41]

The MIT Center opened its Delhi office at an especially exciting time for Indian economists. By the time the Center's Delhi office was operating, the Indian Planning Commission had already established the basic parameters of the Second Five-Year Plan. Yet Indian policy-makers and economists debated the details as well as the overall priorities of the Plan, set to begin in 1955. As those debates took place, MIT economists offered a range of technical assistance, from direct advice to means to improve the economic research capabilities of Indian institutions. In that vein, Mahalanobis asked MIT and its Ford Foundation sponsors to consider donating a state-of-the-art UNIVAC computer. This equipment would provide the capability of more advanced economic modeling of the sort that was dominant in the 1960s – allowing scholars and planners to perform linear optimization, or to project results based on different assumptions. Though the request fit squarely within the grant parameters, it was rebuffed.[42] Shortly afterwards, the ISI struck a deal with the Soviets, and with great fanfare announced the delivery of a Soviet URAL computer, complete with resident technicians and training.[43] While Mahalanobis was happy to work with the Americans, he refused to become a supplicant.

---

40 CENIS Records, "Proposal for Completion of the Economic and Political Development Research Program" (1954), box 2, folder 2.

41 Blackmer, MIT Center for International Studies, 3.; Rosen, Western Economists and Eastern Societies, 5.

42 Galbraith, Ambassador's Journal, 83. Ellsworth Bunker to Fred Bartlett, 27 June 1957, in FRUS 1955-57, 8:349.

43 Indian Statistical Institute, History and Activities, 1931-1959, 20-21. What makes these computer requests all the more striking is that the institute still used the term "computer" in an older sense to refer to the people whose job was to undertake the detailed arithmetic calculations necessary for economic modeling. The shift from human to electronic computers marked a significant change indeed for the ISI. - Ibid., 3. See also Indian Statistical Institute, Report.

Even if unwilling to provide a UNIVAC computer directly to the Indian Statistical Institute, MIT economists used such computers for their own models of the Indian economy. The results of their models – which challenged the Second Plan's priorities – suggest one reason why Mahalanobis might have preferred owning an American computer to hearing American advice. From the late 1950s, and especially after a foreign exchange crisis in 1957 threatened the Second Plan, MIT economists emphasized the need for more investment in agriculture and less in steel and heavy industry. Wilfred Malenbaum, head of MIT's India project, presented one set of these results to the Ministry of Finance in late 1957; he called upon Indian planners to reduce investment allocations for public sector and heavy industry, and to increase attention to and allocations for the private sector and for agriculture in particular. He continued to hammer home this message through his residency in India in 1957-58, though with little hope of success. He concluded that Indian officials agreed with the economic analysis but were unlikely to act upon it: in spite of their acceptance of his arguments, he complained, "there seemed little disposition to take steps aimed at altering significantly the present picture."[44] Malenbaum might or might not have been right on the economics – at least he was joined by a chorus of western experts – but was certainly correct in his assessment that even the most convincing arguments would fall on deaf ears.

MIT economists' concerns about the direction of Indian planning only grew as the work on the Second Five-Year Plan gave to way to preparing the Third and Fourth Plans in the early 1960s. Economist Louis Lafeber, based in New Delhi in 1963-64, felt increasingly confident that the results of his calculations – undertaken with leading Indian economist Sukhomoy Chakravarty as well as MIT colleague Richard Eckhaus – revealed the problems of Mahalanobis's focus on heavy industry. Lafeber's discussions of the planning model brimmed with caveats about the preliminary nature of his work, the potential problems of the data, and the technical nature of his conclusions – yet at the same time he was sure that the model's "profound implications for Indian planning" meant that it would "receive attention."[45]

Both of Lafeber's predictions – about the prospects for India's planning and about the attention his model would receive – proved accurate. The Third Plan (1960-65) limped along, requiring continued foreign assistance without approaching the level of agricultural or industrial production anticipated.[46] And the

44 CENIS Records, Ministry of Finance report, attached to Douglas Ensminger to Malenbaum, box 9, folder 15; CENIS Records, Malenbaum to Trevor Swan, box 9, folder 10.

45 CENIS Records, Lafeber to Eckaus, box 10, folder 7.

46 Frankel, India's Political Economy, 1947-1977.

MIT model garnered significant attention in the policy world, especially as Cambridge-based MIT staff emphasized the model's implications in meetings with senior Indian officials. Indeed, the furor raised by this model would ultimately result in an outcry in the Indian press followed by the quiet withdrawal of CENIS from India in 1965.[47] That withdrawal marked the end of one form of economic advising – the sort of advising both funded and administered from abroad. Mahalanobis and his fellow experts believing in heavy industry had managed to defeat the best efforts of a the CENIS project – run out of one of the world's leading economics department and funded generously by one of the world's wealthiest foundations. In the end, though, advantages in wealth and wisdom mattered little; MIT's model builders – even if accurate – did not influence Indian policy. MIT economists, while challenging the Indian focus upon capital goods, at least took it seriously as a political position. This stands in sharp contrast to the dismissive attitude of other western economists; Colin Clark, for instance, insisted that the question of Indian steel plants was not a matter of economic analysis but "comparative religion."[48]

Implications

This account ends with a dog not barking – a failure of foreign economists, from MIT or elsewhere, to shape Indian economic policy. Nevertheless, it suggests important implications for understanding India's place in the Cold War world. As independent India sought advice and expertise from around the world, it sought to move beyond two patterns that defined flows of people and ideas in the twentieth century. The first pattern challenged by independent India was the one traversed, ironically, by Mahalanobis himself as well as many of his generation – between colony and metropole. For generations, the main connections for Indians – not just political and economic connections, but also intellectual ones – were with England. London was typically the first and often the last stop on the itinerary of well-traveled Indians. By the same token, Indian cultural and intellectual life revolved, to an extraordinary if understandable degree, around England. This began to change in the decade after World War I, as a handful of Indians, and especially cultural and political radicals, made their way to Germany and other destinations in continental Europe. But the German episode was relatively small in number and relatively brief in duration. By far the most im-

47 For more details, see Engerman, "West Meets East," in Staging Growth, 213-215.
48 Colin Clark, "Development Economics," 79.

portant route for Indian scholars remained through London, thence to Oxford, Cambridge, or other points.[49]

At the same time that Indian economists and policy-makers expanded their horizons and contacts beyond England, they also did so in a way that defied a second pattern of twentieth-century international relations, the Cold War division of the world into East and West. In the 1950s and 1960s, Indian students and scholars made pilgrimages to academic sites east and west. And scholars from the superpowers came to India as well. Galbraith's description of the Indian Statistical Institute as a meeting place for experts from the capitalist and communist worlds was widely shared by visitors – even if not all of them took the same pleasure that he did in that mixture. The wide range of visitors provided Mahalanobis with the confidence (not that he lacked it in any case) and the political wherewithal to promote his own vision of Indian economic growth. He, along with colleagues at the Planning Commission, managed to resist privately and later to challenge publicly American advice favoring agriculture over industry. Whether or not the outside advisors provide actual advice, they certainly provided ammunition– or, in Mahalanobis's cocky phrase, "airforce cover" – in the campaign for rapid industrialization. The range of intellectual connections routed through Calcutta and Delhi suggest the problems with assuming that Cold War divisions were replicated in global flows of knowledge and expertise. Indeed, the Cold War competition over the Indian economy was in part responsible for the number of visiting experts from the superpowers and around the world.[50]

Indian leaders' ability to maneuver suggests, furthermore, an insight no doubt clear to South Asianists but worth repeating to specialists in Cold War history. Scholars interested in the history of international development have done most of their work with the assumption that development ideas emanated from Washington (or Cambridge, Massachusetts) and traveled around the world. Historians connected the intellectual origins of development to ideas and projects of the American past, and imagined the process as one of export.[51] Yet as

---

49 Sartori, Bengal in Global Concept History, 5; Manjapra, "Communist Internationalism and Transcolonial Recognition," in Cosmopolitan Thought Zones.

50 On western integration as a parallel imperative to containment, see Berghahn, America and the Intellectual Cold Wars in Europe; Klein, Cold War Orientalism. On Communist internationalism, see the forthcoming work by Elidor Mëhilli on "The Soviet bloc as a product of globalization" and Kelly, "Defending Children's Rights."

51 For American-focused examples, see Ekbladh, The Great American Mission; Latham, Modernization as Ideology. Latham's most recent work has taken a broader perspective - Latham, The Right Kind of Revolution. Anthropologists, usually so attuned to conditions of recipient countries, have also focused on development as an imposition

this brief article suggests, American knowledge was only one of many flows in a broad and multidirectional stream of advice and information flowing through India. Indeed, a fuller accounting of the political power of economic ideas would analyze the extraordinary geographic, methodological, and political diversity of the hundreds of foreign advisors who made India a destination for economic experts. Yet as much as these visitors came to India expecting to persuade Indian policy-makers to change their Plans, the very number of visitors gave local officials room to maneuver. Paradoxically, indigenous Indian economic policies took root only because of the volume and range of international traffic.

---

from outside (usually American) institutions – for instance, Escobar, Encountering Development; Sachs, Development Dictionary.

Delhi–Metro–Polis: Public Transport, Public Opinion and National Politics

Michael Mann

Parameters of Public Transport

Looking up "Delhi Metro" in Google, the first entry is, not very surprisingly, "Delhi Metro Rail Corporation." The entry, however, is immediately followed by an article in "Wikipedia." For two reasons this article may seem surprising to the reader. First, the article is well researched based on official publications as well as plenty of newspaper articles. Altogether 124 endnotes document the meticulous scientific work which, all in all, comprises 19 printed pages. Second, the article also highlights the lack of scientific research on the Delhi Metro. Much has been written on public transport, in particular with respect to the fast growing Indian megacities, yet neither the metro in Kolkata nor the one in Delhi has been the object of much scientific consideration.[1] One may wonder why that is the case. In any case, the Wikipedia article demonstrates the attention the Delhi Metro has received from the Indian local, regional and national press. The article is written in a professional encyclopaedic style presenting a fact sheet of the Delhi Metro.

> "The Delhi Metro is a rapid transit system serving Delhi, Gurgaon and Noida in the National Capital Region of India. The network consists of six lines with a total length of 156 kilometres (97 mi) with 132 stations of which 31 are underground. It has a combination of elevated, at-grade and underground lines and uses both broad gauge and standard gauge rolling stock.
>
> The Delhi Metro is being built and operated by the Delhi Metro Rail Corporation (DMRC). As of April 2010, DMRC operates around 130 trains daily between 6:00 and 23:00 running with an interval of 3 to 4.5 minutes between trains. The trains have four coaches but there are plans to shift to six coach trains to increase capacity. The power output is supplied by 25-kilovolt, 50 Hertz alternating current through overhead catenary. The metro has an average daily ridership of 1.5 million commuters, and as of August 2010, had carried over 1.25 billion commuters since its inception."[2]

Its inception took place on December 24, 2002, and service started on the following day. Since then the Delhi Metro's history seems to have been a unique success-story. So far the Wikipedia article is the most important contribution to

---

1 Exception to the rule is: Siemiatycki, "Message in a Metro."

2 Wikipedia. " Delhi Metro," last modified March 1, 2011, http://en.wikipedia.org/wiki/Delhi_Metro.

this narrative. Lists of facts and figures demonstrate the modernity of the latest system of public transport introduced in India; modernity is represented by technological data, mileage of laid rail-tracks, number of passengers etc. Future projects underline this aspect. The official website of the DMRC is another example of how such modernity is depicted. Again it is measurable and, more importantly in the times of the Internet, able to be visualised.[3] In particular the recently established Metro Museum provides information about the history and progress of the Delhi Metro which "has revolutionized travel by providing a fast, reliable, safe and comfortable means of transport in the city characterized by rickety vehicles and unreliable operators."[4] Apart from the 'metro archive', the current self-representation is supported by selected articles from the press accessible on the homepage of the Delhi Metro.[5] Additionally, the official documentation of the DMRC provides an excellent historical and visual overview.[6]

At the same time, the modernity encapsulated in the Delhi Metro has become the national symbol of India's ability to catch up and be at par with those nations which regard themselves as bearers of modernity; the nation-states of north-western Europe and North America. In this context it is interesting to note that while metro systems in other cities around the world have had their official, sometimes even mythical, representations challenged by competing visions, "the imaginary of the Delhi Metro since the project implementation began has gone largely uncontested. … [A]t present, with such high hopes riding on the metro, those seen to be publicly critical of the project risk being dubbed anti-progress, a branding that can tarnish a political, bureaucratic or consulting career."[7] According to the Master Plan for Delhi 2021–published in 2007–, the Delhi Metro is the most ambitious prestige-project to establish Delhi as a "world-class city".[8] To become world-class and a world power seems to have been the political vision of the Indian governments at least from the beginning of the twenty-first century. And it is probably one of the reasons why the success story of the Delhi Metro is hardly ever questioned.

---

3 Delhi Metro Rail Corporation Ltd., last modified March 1, 2011, http://www.delhimetrorail.com/.

4 Delhi Metro Rail Corporation Ltd., Metro Museum, last modified March 1, 2011, http://www.delhimetrorail.com/metro-museum.aspx.

5 Delhi Metro Rail Corporation Ltd., Metro Museum, last modified March 1, 2011, http://www.delhimetrorail.com/press_releases.aspx

6 Dayal, A Dream Revisited.

7 Siemiatycki, "Message in a Metro," 290.

8 Master Plan for Delhi 2021, 1.

It will be shown in this chapter that the politics accompanying the Delhi Metro are a continuation of colonial politics, explicitly including and prolonging colonial or "western" concepts of modernity. For the Delhi Improvement Trust (DIT), established in 1937 to improve what only then became known as "Old Delhi" after the capital of British India had been moved to "New Delhi" in 1936, as well as for the Delhi Development Authority (DDA) succeeding the DIT in 1950, modernity often included, and continues to do so, the systematic exclusion of the urban poor. In contrast to recent research, there was not simply "a persistent stain of anti-poor bias"[9] but a decidedly forward policy policing, evicting, and re-settling the poor for their alleged own benefit.[10] Modernity in present-day Delhi, accomplishable through continuous improvement and development, is the slogan and the metaphor of the political elite supported by the growing middle classes to separate the better-off urbanites from the poor and the paupers. Colonial laws, colonial administrative structures and hierarchies as well as colonial town planning provided and still provide the Indian state with the authoritative means necessary to pursue such politics.

Urbanisation

To understand the role of the Delhi Metro one has to, firstly, take a theoretical look at the parameters of urbanisation and public transport. Generally seen, urbanisation going along with industrialisation (or *vice versa* as causes and consequences still cannot be sufficiently explained, which brings to mind 'the chicken and the egg') is a process which includes massive population growth of cities through in-migration of mostly rural people looking for better labour opportunities. This urbanisation process is accompanied by an increasing intensive and extensive use of natural resources, namely, water, air, soil and fuel. To be more precise, the parameters of urbanisation are, with respect to water, its supply, sewerage, groundwater pollution and, more general, sanitation. With respect to air, the issues are mostly about CO2 emissions and overall air pollution. With respect to soil, the question of land use arises, organised by municipal institutions and private enterprises and realised by housing agencies and industries.[11]

In the so called industrialised countries of the "West," urbanisation began in England in the middle of the nineteenth century and, in a rather late-coming in-

---

9 Sharan, "Claims on Cleanliness," 33.

10 For a general overview vide Priya, "Town Planning, Public Health and Delhi's Urban Poor."

11 The Master Plan for Delhi 1961 and even more so the Delhi Master Plan 2021 are lucid examples for such parameters which are the predominant categories to establish an environmentally healthy city. Cf. Master Plan for Delhi 2021.

dustrialising country like Germany, during the second half of the nineteenth century.[12] In the countries of the "southern hemisphere", urbanisation is mainly a process of the late twentieth century.[13] Yet there are some incidents of early urbanisation in Asia as for example in British India, where urbanisation (and industrialisation) of Bombay (present-day Mumbai) and Calcutta (present-day Kolkata) set in during the closing decades of the nineteenth century.[14] However, almost all other cities and towns in British India remained untouched by both processes. This was also true for Delhi, the former residence-fortress and capital city of the Mughal Empire which gradually sank into the oblivion of a provincial town after the British had occupied it in 1803.[15] In some way this overall and late onset of systematic town planning, including public transport in India, stems from the lack of, and late, town planning in Great Britain.[16]

Urbanisation made town planning a necessary tool for planning, directing and controlling urban growth with respect to the use of available resources for a steadily growing number of inhabitants. Town planning included the provision of general amenities like water supply, sewerage, electricity, land reclamation, road building, as well as the organisation of a public transport system. The latter became of particular importance, as due to town planning, quarters of residence, quarters of commerce, quarters of administration/service and zones of industry were located in different parts of the growing cities. In times of hardly existent individual transport, speedy and cheap public transport connecting all parts of a city became one of the most challenging aspects of modern town planning. However, as individual transport increased at the turn of the nineteenth century, private transport required a fast growing network of streets and roads in most industrial cities of the world. In general, traffic corridors, be they based on road or rail systems, were regarded vital for the development, basically meaning the physical expansion, of a modern city.[17]

Transport in urban environs is planned and organised along certain parameters, namely road-congestion, car-accidents and air-pollution. Looking, for ex-

---

12 Zimmermann, Die Zeit der Metropolen.

13 Feldbauer et al., Mega-Cities.

14 Among the multitude of literature I suggest the following reading: Dossal, Imperial Designs and Indian Realities; Patel and Thorner, Bombay: Metaphor for Modern India; Kidambi, The Making of an Indian Metropolis. For Calcutta see many of the articles printed in Chaudhuri (ed.), Calcutta. The Living City; and the monograph by Chattopadhyay, Representing Calcutta.

15 Gupta, Delhi between Two Empires.

16 White, Public Transport, 86-8.

17 Vide, for example, Cheape, Moving the Masses; Stadtplanung und Verkehrsentwicklung in Berlin im 19. Jahrhundert; Cherry, The Evolution of British Town Planning.

ample, at the Delhi Master Plan 2021, it becomes clear that despite massive investments in the Delhi Metro the main concern of current town planners in India, and particularly Delhi, still is the widening of arterial roads and the construction of new roads to reduce the threat of traffic jams or, turned 'positively,' to facilitate the flow of vehicles, to reduce the amount of accidents–basically for the same reason–and to reduce air-pollution including the saving of fuel/energy.[18] The reduction of these impediments to transport would indicate a statistically measurable improvement of private and public traffic. Among the many roles the Delhi Metro has to play in urban transport politics, the major one is to contribute substantially to these reductions. Seen in this context, the mass rapid transport system becomes part of a car-compatible city.[19] This issue is also mirrored by a scientific study analysing the social cost-benefits of the Delhi Metro.[20]

Transport and Modernity

Yet the Delhi Metro is more than simply a means of modern public transport in a megacity. Soon after its inception the Delhi Metro became the national icon symbolising the nation's modernity *in nuce*. The Delhi Metro has been and still is being turned into a national example of modernity which seems appropriate and desirable for other Indian megacities to follow, among them the second icon of India's modernity: Bangalore.[21] Having, however, a closer look at the categories of modernity as have been brought forward by the DMRC and in particular by its chief manager, E. Sreedharan, this article will argue that these categories are based on a western discourse of modernity. Yet more, they also reflect the British colonial state's civilising mission which in a colonial urban setting was based on segregation and sanitation, politics which the independent Indian state continued, and with respect to Delhi, particularly during the "Emergency" of 1975-77.[22]

Seen against this background it seems sensible to have a long-term view on the development of the Delhi Metro. With respect to town planning and, going along with that, concepts of modernity, neither 1947 (Independence) nor 1991

18 Master Plan for Delhi 2021, 69-71.

19 Master Plan for Delhi 2021, 69, para. 21.1 and 72, para. 12.4.1 on the synergetic effects of improved and developed rail and road systems called "Integrated Multi-Modal Transport System."

20 Murty et al., "Social Cost-Benefit Analysis of Delhi Metro".

21 Vide the profile of the Bangalore Metro Rail Corporation: http://bmrc.co.in/profile.html

22 Mann, "Town Planning and Urban Resistance in the Old City of Delhi," 251-78.

(Liberalisation) mark a caesura. This is in contradistinction to the meanwhile well established master narrative presented in the current historiography and above all the media. For example, town planning schemes for Delhi included concepts of public transport from 1961 to 2021, and the politics going along with these concepts actually demonstrate this continuity. The Delhi Metro is an especially lucid example for such continuities with respect to urban planning and politics as it reflects colonial discourses–as well as the ideology–of progress, development and modernity still in operation in 2011. This chapter will also demonstrate how far present-day planners and politicians, as well as the press, have internalised the above mentioned civilising mission and its vocabulary, reacting reflex-like to the ideology of modernity.[23]

Planning Public and Private Transport in Delhi, 1961-2006

Dramatic changes took place in the urban landscape of Delhi when British India was divided in 1947 and Delhi (New Delhi) became the capital of the independent Indian state. The new capital attracted many of the Sikh-refugees from the Panjab who had fled Pakistan to find a new home in Delhi. The municipal administration of Delhi was completely overburdened with the task of housing more than half a million refugees. The chaotic settlement policy of the post-colonial capital can still be seen in the urban map of Delhi.[24] Delhi however attracted not only refugees from Pakistan. With its growing importance as the capital of the independent state, Delhi became a new centre for business, commerce and industrial enterprises. The population of Delhi increased at such a pace that Prime Minister Jawaharlal Nehru initiated a planning committee for the National Capital Region (NCR) in 1957-8. However, town planning was still very much entrenched in colonial tradition, evident in the fact that the committee was placed with the Ministry of Health. In cooperation with the Ministry of Health and seven members of the Ford Foundation the DDA presented the Master Plan for Delhi in 1962 which was to delineate the urban development of Delhi until 1981.[25] For its farsightedness the Master Plan of Delhi became well known, even beyond India's borders.[26]

In short, the Master Plan envisaged a decentralised growth of the city which was to be facilitated by the development of so called ring-towns. These ring-towns were Loni and Ghaziabad in neighbouring federal state of Uttar Pradesh,

23 For an overview of the parameters of this modernity see Sundaram, Pirate Modernity, 1-27.

24 Kaur, "Planning Urban Chaos."

25 Delhi Gazetteer 1976, 755-9.

26 Ansari, "Strategy for the Development," 136.

Faridabad, Ballabhgarh and Gurgaon in Haryana (then still the Panjab), and Narela in the Union Territory of Delhi. Located at a distance of about 25 to 30kms from the centre of Delhi, these towns were to be developed into centres of industry, commerce and residence. Ring-roads and radial roads were to connect the capital with the ring-towns.[27] The railway as well as mass public transport did not play any particular role as the then scientific research reveals.[28] Supposedly the members of the Ford Foundation had been opting for a car-suitable city instead of an integrated transport system.[29] In 1965, however, a certain Study Team of Metropolitan Transport was set up for the first time in the Indian Union to enquire into the long-term requirements of cities like Bombay, Calcutta, Madras and Delhi. However, the initiative came to naught.[30]

Four years later, in 1969, for the first time a mass rapid rail system for Delhi emerged from a travel and transport study. Since then various government departments and municipal authorities have been engaged in exploring the issue. Different technological systems like rail, light rail, mono rail and rapid rail and even express bus systems were debated at length.[31] Over the years, and having the plans for the future development of Delhi at hand, it had become clear that the capital, metropolis and megacity would remain a low-density and fairly sprawled settlement, a vast urban agglomeration, rather than a compact city, as for example Bombay/Mumbai. Land reclamation was on top of the DDA's agenda, despite the fact that this land-consuming development seriously affected the capital's network of transport. To make traffic flow, plans simply envisaged additional circular roads, radial roads as well as flyovers and road-widening.[32] In spite of the recommendations of the Metropolitan Transport Project of Delhi for a mass rapid rail system in 1975, such a system was not placed on top of the transport-agenda of either the municipal or the governmental authorities during the 1980s.

A first rather concrete idea to plan an alternative mass and rapid transport system for Delhi came up in 1984 when the DDA and the Urban Arts Commission, established in 1974 for the aesthetic improvement of the capital city, presented a proposal to develop a multi-modal transport system which would consist of three underground mass rapid transit corridors as well as increasing the city's existing suburban railway and road transport systems.[33] Yet the proposal

27 Ansari, "Strategy for the Development," 136-9.
28 Bhatnagar et al., Transport in Modern India, 331-41.
29 Sundaram, Priate Modernity, 37-44.
30 Halder, Urban Transport in India, 238-9.
31 Siemiatycki, "Message in a Metro," 279.
32 Pucher et al., "Urban Transport Crisis in India," 187.
33 Wikipedia. " Delhi Metro," accessed March 1, 2011,

was either shelved or misplaced, in any case not given the attention it should have deserved; the Master Plan for Delhi 2001, published in 1984, only recommended a light rail transit system of 10kms, the extension of the surface rail system and a tramway.[34] This was certainly far short of the ideas and concepts that had been brought forward so far. In the meantime the problem of transport became ever more pressing since the population of Delhi had grown from 2.6 million in 1961 to 6.2 million inhabitants in 1981.[35] Population growth in other Indian cities and towns was likewise increasing, all the while causing severe problems in urban infrastructures.

It was against this background that three committees were set up in the 1980s. First, the National Transport Policy Committee (NTPC 1980) second, the National Commission on Urbanization (NCU 1988) third, the Draft National Urban Transport Policy (NTUP 1988). Taken together, all three committee reports emphasised the importance of the pattern of land use in growing cities and, at the same time, the means of adequate transportation. To optimise public transport on rail and road, the ring-railway (*vide* the attached Delhi Metro Plan) in the Delhi urban area was recommended as a viable form of efficient public transport. Still missing was a concept for a mass rapid transport system whilst the emphasis of the reports was still on the improvement and development of existing as well as new roads.[36] When planning for the Delhi Metro actually began in 1995, the multiple municipal planning organisations still had no overall concept of public transport, neither in the capital city, nor in the National Capital Region. While acknowledging the importance of Delhi as a metropolitan city and capital city, official publications do not refer to the idea of a metro system even at the end of the millennium.[37]

This suggests that at the time of the planning, the Delhi Metro was not really regarded as an urban mass rapid transport system relieving the inner and most congested parts of the city decisively from air pollution, congestion and accidents, but as an addition to the existing bus and rail services complemented by intermediate transport systems like mini-buses, taxis, three-wheelers and rickshaws.[38] This lack of planning and concept also suggests that the Delhi Metro was to offer an alternative means of transport connecting the outskirts of the megacity with the centre, and it was to offer a speedy, reliable and clean long-

---

http://en.wikipedia.org/wiki/Delhi_Metro.

34 Dayal, A Dream Revisited.

35 New Delhi Government of India Press, Census of India 1961, 36-7, Delhi, 1965; New Delhi Government of India Press, Census of India 1971- Supplement, 50, Delhi, 1971.

36 Halder, Urban Transport in India, 240-8.

37 Delhi 1999: A Fact Sheet, 30-1.

38 Delhi 1999: A Fact Sheet, 50.

distance means of transportation. Such a transport system was of particular interest for the Delhi middle classes contributing most to the vehicular 'overkill.' Living in peripheral residential quarters and ring-towns of the Delhi metropolitan area, the middle classes had a strong interest in a speedy and 'trendy,' that is modern, means of transportation, which would relieve them from using private cars, and the metro seemed to realise such imaginations.[39]

It was the massively deteriorating transport facilities in the capital-metropolis during the last quarter of the twentieth century which ultimately gave the impetus to start with the planning and construction of a mass rapid urban transport system. Numbers dramatically demonstrate the deterioration. Average traffic speed decreased from roughly 25km/h in 1972 to about 10km/h in 2001. Also, the number of vehicles in Delhi rose from 214,000 to 3,924,000 whilst the length of the urban road and street network rose from 838,000 to 2,600,000kms. This, however, means an absolute decrease in available road surface.[40] Traffic jams and accidents were not only predictable but everyday reality.[41] To make things worse, the increasing amount of buses decreased in absolute terms taking the steadily growing number of inhabitants as well as outside commuters into consideration.[42] In addition, privately operated bus lines were known for their poor service qualities and therefore the low level of commuter satisfaction.[43] The same is true, of course, for the state run bus services which are regarded as filthy, overcrowded, unreliable and involving long waiting times.[44]

Becoming aware of the increasing problems of public transport the Government of India and the Government of Delhi jointly established the Delhi Metro Rail Corporation in 1995. Planning envisaged the connection of the above mentioned ring-towns through various lines, thus linking the periphery with the centre. Additionally, interconnecting stations offered access to the ring-rail as well as other metro lines.[45] Construction started three years later and the first line, the Red Line, was opened in 2002, followed by the Yellow Line in 2004,

---

39 Cf. e.g. Saavala, Middle-Class Moralities.

40 Delhi 1999: A Fact Sheet, 49.

41 Singh, "Review of Urban Transportation in India," 85-8.

42 Singh, "Review of Urban Transportation in India," 82-3.

43 Deb and Sundar, Restructuring Urban Public Transport in India, 7; Tripta Goel, "Urban Bus Transit System in Delhi-An Assessment of the Quality of Service."

44 Singh, "Review of Urban Transportation in India," 87.; Siemiatycki, "Message in a Metro," 280.

45 Vide Delhi Metro Plan, http://en.wikipedia.org/wiki/File:Delhi_metro_rail_network.svg (4/1/2012).

the Blue Line in 2005, its branch line in 2009 and the Green and Violet Lines in 2010.[46]

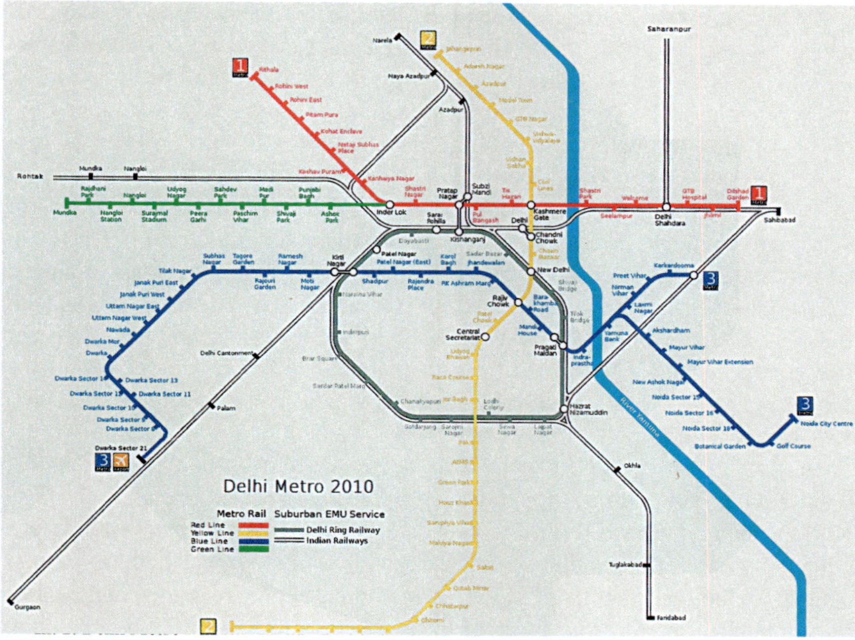

To get construction works finished on time, the DMRC was given full powers to hire people, decide on tenders and control funds. Funds were raised through a combination of the national and international finance market. The state sponsored Japanese Bank of International Cooperation provided 64 percent of the investment, the Central and Delhi State Governments provided another 28 percent while the rest was raised through DMRC property development. Technology came from various countries like Japan, Korea, France, the US and Germany. Coordination was in the hands of the DMRC whilst construction work itself was accomplished through the local workforce.[47] With such international and national backing the first line of the Delhi Metro was not only opened on time but the first phase was completed in 2006, on budget and almost three years ahead of schedule. In contrast to the beginning of the construction work which

46 Ibid., (p.1; 3-6). For an interactive route map vide http://www.delhimetrorail.com/zoom-route-map.aspx.

47 Siemiatycki, "Message in a Metro," 280. Dayal, A Dream Revisited.

was hardly commented on by the press media, completion ahead of time was hailed as "nothing short of a miracle."[48]

Be that as it may, the fact is that the Delhi Metro seems to be on sound financial footing. In 2007, the Delhi Metro claimed to be one of the only five metro systems in the world operating at a profit without government subsidies. This was achieved by keeping maintenance costs at a minimum and raising additional revenue through property development, advertisements and, last but not least, ticket sales.[49] The Delhi Metro also generates additional income by leasing out trains and stations for film shoots. Producers have to pay up to US$2,270 for every hour filming as well as security deposits and insurance fees. For the financial year ending March 2008, the DMRC reported operating revenues of almost US$70 million and a profit before tax of US$5.45 million. For the financial year 2009 numbers rose to US$164.3 and US$20.5 million respectively. And for 2010 numbers are US$160.6 and a loss of US$19.63. The loss is due to the speedy and pre-dated completion of Phase II which made high investment and timely interest repayment rather costly.[50]

In spite of the recent financial development, the chairman of the DMRC, Navin Kumar, pointed out the increasing number of passengers, as well as the "world standards [of the Delhi Metro which] should make every citizen of this country proud." Topping the facts and figures of his annual address Kumar spoke of "[t]he metro culture [which] is spreading very fast in the country. Implementation of metro projects in many big cities with 5-10 million population are already underway."[51] Taking this 'fact sheet,' the "world standards," the "world-class city" and the "metro culture" as a starting point, it is worthwhile to look at the Delhi Metro and its representation in the press media because it is here, that a certain image of the Delhi Metro was and still is created to serve national purposes.

Shaping the City and Forging the Nation

When planning for the Delhi Metro began in 1995, Anuj Dayal, former member of the Indian Railways and now the Chief Public Relations Officer of the

---

48 Wikipedia. " Delhi Metro," accessed March 1, 2011, http://en.wikipedia.org/wiki/Delhi_Metro. Quoted in Nandini Lakshman, "The Miracle-Worker of the Delhi Metro," Business Week 19.03.2007, online-version not accessible any more.

49 For property development see the website of the DMRC: "Tenders."

50 Wikipedia. "Delhi Metro," accessed March 1, 2011, http://en.wikipedia.org/wiki/Delhi_Metro.; DMRC, "Annual Report," 7, 22, 43.

51 DMRC, "Annual Report," 5.

DMRC, stated that he immediately started his "interaction with journalists with a very straight forward and simple approach. I had many friends from my earlier days in the Public Relations wing of the Indian Railways and I met many others directly and I found them extremely receptive and forthcoming." Listing more than 50 journalists from local, regional and national newspapers and magazines Dayal confessed that "[t]here are many more journalists whose names I have not mentioned here who were very helpful not only to me but to the Metro Project and without these people this project may never have become a reality." During regular meetings Dayal informed the press about technical details, planning and construction progress of the project thus publicly promoting the ambitious enterprise.[52] The Delhi Metro was not speaking for itself as a technological masterpiece but was supported and systematically promoted by the DMRC and the press.

The PR-manager and the press presented and still present the Delhi Metro as a new mass rapid system of transportation and, above that, as a symbol for the modernity of the Indian capital-megacity, a metaphor for the metropolis as well as the Indian nation. Recently, *Expressindia* reported "the fact such a high profile project was completed on time and within budget has made it a national showcase." In the same article the managing director of the DMRC, 74-year old Elattuvalapil Sreedharan, explained that "[t]he Delhi Metro is a stunning example of how a government project can be done properly." And it is also "an example for the politicians of what professionals can do if they are given a free hand."[53] The free hand was of course Sreedharan's. Three issues are at stake here: the public sector, the government and the politicians, seemingly as opposed by the professional. Yet Sreedharan's argument aims at the efficient and effective cooperation between private and public sectors which has been, so far, unique in India. The Delhi Metro therefore is a promising example for the Delhi Metropolitan Region, for the Indian nation as well as the world indicating that India is able to realise high-tech projects.

The Delhi Metro has also been described as "a shining example of what is one of the finest public sector projects in the country" as *India Today* reported in October 2009.[54] This of course shall remind the reader of the slogan "India Shining" which the BJP used during the general election campaign in 2004, thus trying to highlight and to profiteer from India's economic success. Though the slo-

---

52 Dayal, A Dream Revisited.

53 Expressindia, "Delhi Metro Showcases Public Sector Success," accessed April 13, 2007, http://expressindia.com/news/fullstory.php?newsid=84775.

54 Unnithan, "DMRC: Leading The Change," India Today, October 8, 2009, http://indiatoday.intoday.in/site/Story/65483/Cover%20Story/DMRC:+Leading+The+Change.html.

gan did not help to keep the BJP in power and though it received fierce and sarcastic critique, it obviously remained a powerful metaphor for what is regarded as the modern Indian state, the press using the slogan not for IT-businesses and party politics but for the Delhi Metro and popular politics.[55] Anything intimidating the Delhi Metro success story is taken up by the press as well. When critical voices moaned about "compromising the safety of workers and the public in a rush to complete work" this was a clear appeal to keep up and stick to the hitherto achieved standards. "Struggling" with these standards would mean to compromise on a lower level of technique, security and safety which was not to be accepted, neither by the press, nor the public, nor politicians.[56]

Now, standards however were and are not Indian but international. The Delhi Metro is praised for its profitability, environmental soundness, punctuality and efficiency.[57] Again it was Sreedharan who underlined the achievements and standards of the Delhi Metro. According to his opinion it is this sort of progress which is "competence building, motivating workers to live by his [Sreedharan's] five golden rules: integrity, professional competence, quick decisions, staying healthy and punctuality."[58] His personal standards are reflected by the Delhi Metro since it has become both the metaphor and the catalyst for achieving the basic objectives of a modern society represented through a "culture of discipline, order, routine and cleanliness."[59] Both quotes, the one from a 'man on the spot,' the other from a rather critical author, reflect and represent not only western ideals of modernity but ideals that can be traced back to colonial times, and as such of crucial importance for the British "Civilising Mission in India." Punctuality, cleanliness, order and efficiency were the categories which the British regarded as essential for the forging and the maintenance of a modern nation.[60]

Yet both men do not seem to be aware of the historical circumstance. The problem here is that the press, the manager and the author are referring to Euro-

---

55 AFP, "The Man Behind 'India Shining' Slogan," Rediff, April 2, 2004, http://www.rediff.com/money/2004/apr/02shining.htm.

56 Mathus, "City's Nightmare on Wheels," Hindustan Times, Dec. 7, 2009 http://www.hindustantimes.com/StoryPage/Print/483710.aspx.

57 IndianExpress, "Delhi Metro Among World's Top Five, Claim DMRC Officials," Indianexpress, Oct 28, 2009 http://www.indianexpress.com/news/delhi-metro-among-worlds-top-five-claim-dmrc-officials/534246/0.

58 Unnithan, "DMRC: Leading The Change," India Today, October 8, 2009, http://indiatoday.intoday.in/site/Story/65483/Cover%20Story/DMRC:+Leading+The+Change.html.

59 Siemiatycki, "Message in a Metro," 285.

60 Vide the various articles in Fischer-Tiné and Mann (eds), Colonialism as Civilizing Mission; and Watt and Mann (eds), Civilizing Missions in Colonial and Postcolonial South Asia.

pean liberal-cum-Christian virtues of the late eighteenth and nineteenth centuries that then set the standard for modernity and, at the same time, marked the difference between modern and backward civilisations and nations. In referring to these categories they today are contributing to an apparently ongoing discourse of modernity and backwardness. To demonstrate India's modernity, the press, the public and the politicians continuously point out the technological and organisational achievement, and therefore civilising effect which goes along with the construction of the Delhi Metro. The homepage of the Delhi Metro (DMRC) as well as the press coverage are only two of many indicators of this discourse. Progress is, in the first place, indicated by the use of the most modern technology, be that "Trenchless Tunnelling"[61] or the latest coaches from Bombardier.[62]

The manager, the man who stands for this progress is without doubt Elattuvalapil Sreedharan. Born in Kerala in 1932, he was educated as an engineer and joined the Southern Railway in 1954. In 1963, a huge monster-wave washed away parts of Pamban Pridge that connected Rameshwaram to mainland Tamil Nadu. The Railways set a target of six months for the bridge to be repaired while Sreedharan's employer, under whose jurisdiction the bridge came, reduced it to three months. Sreedharan was put in-charge of the execution and he restored the bridge in just 46 days. The *Railway Minister's Award* was given to him in recognition of this achievement. In 1970, as deputy chief engineer, Sreedharan was put in charge of the implementation, planning and design of the Calcutta metro, the first ever metro in India. He retired from Indian Railways in 1990. However, his services were direly needed in the same year. Under his stewardship, the Konkan Railway was constructed within just seven years. The project was unique in many respects and was highly acclaimed for its high technical standards as it covered a distance of 760 km, including 93 tunnels covering 82 km which involved tunnelling through soft soil, and had over 150 bridges.[63]

When Sreedharan was made Managing Director of the Delhi Metro in 1995 he was already well known in India for his efficient and his early completion of work. Yet, the Delhi Metro would turn him into a national hero. Even before the metro's inception he was bestowed with the "Padma Shri", the fourth highest civilian award in the Republic of India in 2001. In 2002 he was elected "Man of the Year" by the *Times of India*,[64] followed by several national and international

61 Dhillon, "Trenchless Tunnellling," The Tribune, January 29, 2004, http://www.tribuneindia.com(2004/20040129/science.htm.

62 PM News Bureau: "Bombardier to Supply Coaches to Delhi Metro", Projects Monitor, July 23, 2007, http://www.projectsmonitor.com/detailnews.asp?newsid=14184.

63 The only available and reliable biographical information on Sreedharan is, again, on Wikipedia. Cf., E. Sreedharan http://en.wikipedia.org/wiki/E._Sreedharan

64 Sreedharan is CNN-IBN IOTY - Public Service.

awards.[65] *Expressindia* stated that "Sreedharan has attained an almost hero-like status. Surveys show he is one of India's most respected persons."[66] Even when the first serious construction accident took place in July 2009, a girder collapsing and killing 12 builders, *Frontline*, the rather critical nation-wide Indian magazine still called him "something of a middle-class icon". As a consequence Sreedharan resigned from his post as Chairman of the DMRC. Yet, *Frontline* reported on the support he received from government officials as well as Congress general secretary Rahul Gandhi and the Urban Development Minister who both successfully persuaded him to continue in his post.[67]

Sreedharan's personal life-style and philosophy according to which he reads the Bhagavatgita, listens to spiritual songs and does yoga exercises every day, besides the virtues of being punctual, reliable, hard working and possessing an "iron will"[68] has been turned into a model and a shining example of how India could be improved and developed. Since Sreedharan expects his personal rules to be obeyed at least by his six project managers, and as far as possible by his subalterns and 3,500 construction workers, the Delhi Metro has become a model-enterprise, a model for the city and its inhabitants, and a model for the nation and its population. Sreedharan explains that "I have created an organization which has got a unique work culture and organizational values. The team consists of hard-working, dedicated and professionally competent people." And thinking about the role of the Delhi Metro he stated that "[w]e are keen that the philosophy to have a metro system in all cities with a population of over 3 million, is adopted as a national policy."[69] Without doubt, the man, the management and the metro have become a symbol of national integrity.

Yet one has to be aware of the fact that the "free hand" which Sreedharan possesses to accomplish his "gigantic task"[70] is based on colonial administrative

---

65 Wikipedia, E. Sreedharan., "Awards and Accolades".

66 ExpressIndia, "Delhi Metro Showcases Public Sector Success," Apr 13, 2007, http://expressindia.com/news/fullstory.php?newsid=84775.

67 Mahaprashastra, "Metro Crash," Frontline 26,16 Aug 01-14, 2009, http://expressindia.com/news/fullstory.php?newsid=84775.

68 Unnithan, "DMRC: Leading The Change," India Today, October 8, 2009, http://indiatoday.intoday.in/site/Story/65483/Cover%20Story/DMRC:+Leading+The+Change.html.; Amy Yee, "Delhi's Subway Builder," Forbes Magazine, Oct 5, 2009, http://www.hvk.org/articles/0509/272.html.

69 International Railway Journal, "Delhi Metro Expands to Tackle City's Growing Pains," FindArticles, February 2006, http://findarticles.com/p/articles/mi_m0BQQ/is_2_46/ai_n16071120/.

70 Ibid. One is also reminded of the gigantic technological enterprises like the construction of the railway and the canal systems including bridges, tunnels, barrages, dams etcetera in British India as well as the USA's and the Soviet Union's or, later Egypt's

structures supporting current needs of organisation and speedy construction. Organisation, however, started late in comparison to the mass rapid transport systems in other megacities of the world. In India, however, an extended struggle between the central state, the federal state and the city governments over which level has ultimate control over the urban mass transportation system, combined with a general paucity of funds for large-scale projects, has resulted in under investment in such projects.[71] The Calcutta/Kolkata metro is the saddest example for such underfunding, although the Delhi Metro, due to its exceptional funding-scheme, is hitherto the exception to the rule. Yet, underfunding of Indian municipalities and the struggle over competencies and control on various state levels is part of the colonial heritage. For example, the Lieutenant-Governor for Delhi was ex-officio chairman of the DDA. He was appointed by the central government and vested with a veto over any democratic urban/municipal institution and organisation.[72]

Similarly, underfunding was a chronic problem for all cities and towns in British India. Even in those cities with an "Improvement Trust," by far the smallest number, and in Delhi, the latest to join 'the club' of Improvement Trusts, finances were regulated by the provincial government. Municipal authorities had to apply for credit, funds and public works and it was the personal discretion of the governor or lieutenant-governor to grant finances and approve projects. The history of the "Improvement Trusts" is a lucid and, at the same time, sad example of a colonial regime which re-distributed public money and public resources from bottom to top of the society to finance the military, home-pensions and prestigious projects like the planning, layout and construction of pompous civil lines including public buildings.[73] Lahore, Agra, Lakhnau, Kanpur and New Delhi are perhaps the most telling examples of how the British re-invested public money to improve their urban living quarters and environs. Separating the civil and military lines (cantonments) from Indian towns and cities, the British literally cemented social, cultural and racial segregation through settlement politics.[74]

The latter aspect is of particular interest when looking at the re-construction of the environs of Delhi's metro stations. Land reclamation for erecting the

---

Asswan-Dam and China's many dam-constructions. Gigantic projects seem to manifest a nation's possibilities and power.

71 Siemiatycki, "Message in a Metro", 279.

72 Mann, "Town Planning and Urban Resistance in the Old City of Delhi," 261.

73 Cf. Kidambi, Making of an Indian Metropolis, 71-113; Gupta, Delhi Between Two Empires, 125-56; Mann, "Delhi's Belly," 1-31.; Mann and Sehrawat, "A City With a View," 543-70.; Metcalf, An Imperial Vision.

74 Grewal, "Urban Morphology under Colonial Rule."

mostly over-ground track-system, but more importantly, to erect the spacious metro stations, became vital for the construction of the Delhi Metro. The prospect of having the Commonwealth Games in 2010 in the metropolis gave a strong impetus to push through many local projects, in particular land-reclamation, slum-clearance and re-building the areas surrounding metro stations. Like the Asia Exhibition in 1972 and the Asian Games of 1982, the Commonwealth Games worked as a catalyst to promote and to push the gigantic project.[75] The beautification of individual stations with mosaics and galleries indicating, for example, nearby sightseeing spots for tourists or promoting commercial issues are only one aspect of the DMRC improvement scheme.[76] The other, more visible and of more consequence, is the slum-clearance programme in the immediate vicinity of stations thus expanding the effect of the metro far beyond the actual track. In fact, it became a major target of both the DMRC and the DDA to develop the urban landscape.

Especially the vicinity of the metro stations of Seelampur and Shadara became the object of urban re-structuring. In the impoverished neighbourhoods of both stations, vast areas of *jhuggi-jhompries* and *bastis* [77] including commercial shacks have been cleared and replaced by more sanitary, and more formalised buildings. In "more affluent parts, information technology parks, shopping malls, cafes, restaurants, cinemas and housing projects have been proposed to capitalise on the increased accessibility provided by the metro. Thus, following on their mandate, planners have sought to extend the metro benefits beyond the station walls, and bring increased cleanliness and order to the community."[78] The DMRC has become a major land-development agency with plans to improve the land it was able to acquire with the help of the DDA along the metro lines. "In recent years, the proposed route alignment has thus been shifted as DMRC officials seek to find locations that can be most profitably developed for high-end business parks, amusement parks and residential developments that

---

75 Moorthy, "On the Transformation of Delhi in View of the 2010 Commonwealth Games", Frontline 23, April 07, 2006, http://www.flonnet.com/fl2306/stories/20060407003109900.htm.

76 Ramachandran, "Delhi Metro Gets a Handicrafts Gallery," The Hindu, February 09, 2010, http://www.thehindu.com/2010/09/02/stories/2010090252320200htm.

77 A basti can be described as a little village or a large cluster of houses within a city indicating a segregated area of small shacks with its own lane system and generally lacking any sort of amenities like public latrines, sewerage, lightning, electricity etc. The term jhuggi jhompri is derived from Hindustani meaning clustered ramshackle hutments of a temporary character. Often jhuggi jhompris turn into stable and permanent settlements: bastis.

78 Siemiatycki, "Message in a Metro," 285-6.

will provide the necessary return on investment to make the overall project viable."[79]

Historical precedents

The politics of slum-clearance, re-settlement, town improvement and beautification have a long tradition originating in colonial times, further developed in the 1950s and in the case of Delhi dramatically pushed during the Emergency. Slum-clearing schemes were elaborated by the Delhi Improvement Trust (DIT) set up in 1937 just a couple of years after the capital of British India had actually moved to newly completed New Delhi. To relieve "Old" Delhi[80] from what the British regarded as overcrowding, filth, lack of sanitation and unhealthy living conditions, the DIT, in accordance with the Town Improvement Act of the United Provinces of Agra and Oudh, worked out massive and comprehensive slum-clearance and re-housing programmes. These clearance schemes provided for the improvement or demolition of houses generally regarded as unfit for habitation. The DIT and the Delhi Metropolitan Council (DMC) were empowered to clear settlements, rebuild dwellings and resettle people without having any clear guidelines for such far reaching measures.[81]

A legal framework was set up by the DIT in 1956 in the form of the Slum Areas Improvement and Clearance Act that provided a comprehensive law for politicians and municipal authorities. In 1957 the DIT was replaced by the DDA under the provisions of the Delhi Development Act of the same year. Together with the officials of the Ministry of Health and the Ford Foundation this committee elaborated, as mentioned above, the Master Plan for Delhi until 1961. Despite its acclaims there were also certain deficits. First, as has already been referred to, the composition of the planning group suggests the emphasis was on individual rather than on public transport. Second, the plan did not indicate a shift of paradigms and perceptions regarding slums, slum dwellers and the poor.[82] A first wave of slum-clearances destroyed many parts of Old Delhi in the 1960s. A second wave followed during the Emergency of 1975-77 when Sanjay Gandhi, son and designated successor of Indira Gandhi, bulldozed what he and

79 Siemiatycki, "Message in a Metro," 288.

80 Old Delhi as a municipal/administrative entity comprises, besides the Walled City also Sabzimandi, Saddar Bazaar, Karolbagh and Paharganj, basically urban extensions of the nineteenth century.

81 Mann, "Town Planning and Urban Resistance in the Old City of Delhi," 257.

82 A critical assessment of the 1962 Delhi Master Plan after forty years after its publication is provided by K.T. Ravindran, "A Stage of Siege." The poor and the Delhi Metro are of special interest.

the DDA regarded as slums, evicted and forcefully resettled many poor people from Old Delhi.[83]

After the Emergency, Jagmohan, the then acting vice-chairman of the DDA, in his book *Island of Truth,* which reads as some sort of reminiscence of glorious yet bygone days, explains his personal view of the slum clearance and resettlement programme executed during the Emergency.

> "What were my motivations, my objectives, my outlook? I have always believed in the destiny of the city, in its historic role, in its being a spiritual workshop of the nation, in its capacity to impart urbanity and civility to the rural migrant, and in its ability to weave the dismembered threads of our national existence into a strong and well-knit fabric. I have made earnest efforts to make Delhi an ideal city, a model for other cities to follow, a city which should be an organ of love and justice [...]."[84]

In nuce Jagmohan acquaints the reader with the multifarious roles of Delhi. First of all there is a historical role. Delhi is an ancient urban region having served many rulers as place of residence, the British being the last ones. Also, various important battles have been fought near Panipat, locus of Delhi's Indira Gandhi International Airport, and the wider region is also the home of the famous *Mahabharata* which is regarded as a national epos. Second, taking up the ongoing in-migration since Independence and the massive increase of the urban population, Jagmohan reminds the reader of the civilising aspect of a city providing 'in-flowing' peasants the chance of a social uplift. Consequently, the rural migrant must be freed from his backward rural habits. However, according to Jagmohan's (and the former British) perception, living in *bastis* and *jhuggi-jhompris* is a continuation of such rural habits. Hence, demolishing these settlements and resettling its people becomes an act of civilising, ultimately aiming at the improvement and betterment of the affected people. Idealistically the evicted and resettled poor should welcome such measures since they are meant for their own benefit.[85] Resistance thus becomes an act of ungratefulness and, last but not least, uncivilised behaviour.

In sum, the capital city is the "spiritual workshop of the nation" meaning the nation is forged in Delhi which is why Jagmohan turned the city into a model for the nation during the Emergency. Of course the city has to play that role for some time to come. Delhi is the national showcase where the "dismembered threads" of the nation are knit into a strong fabric which is essential for a strong

83 Mann, "Town Planning and Urban Resistance in the Old City of Delhi," 260-1; Tarlo, Unsettling Memories.

84 Jagmohan, Island of Truth, 170.

85 Rather cynically, a re-settlement colony established during the Emergency on the eastern bank of the Yamuna was called "Welcome," Tarlo, "Welcome to History," 51-74. Today "Welcome" has got a metro station.

nation. To a large extent the nation's enemy is not necessarily external but even worse internal, epitomised by the city's "slum" population. Delhi however is the nation and the nation is Delhi, embraced through love and justice. In short, Jagmohan rather opts for simple and therefore strong unity than for the nation's actual slogan of "unity in diversity" which seems to be a marker of 'creeping' weakness. Pursuing his policy as DDA vice-chairman, he was backed by Indira Gandhi who told her people after declaring Emergency Rule "to get on with the job of nation building" thereby also justifying slum-clearances in Delhi as a necessary programme for "improving the living conditions of the poor."[86]

More revealing is the history behind this story. As indicated above, these kinds of improvement and development strategies were an essential means to legitimise colonial rule in India. According to this concept of colonial legitimacy British-European civilisation stood against Indian-Asian savagery. The gap between the civilised and the uncivilised was turned into a mandate of colonial uplifting. Yet, uplifting, improving and developing was not only part of the British self-claimed 'external' determination but, at the same time, part of an 'internal' civilising mission. It has been pointed out in a seminal study on the reciprocal influences of the British civilising mission, attitudes in India and its repercussions on British politics at home, that the idea of progress was developed in England as well as in India, categorising the Other, in particular both the poor and the savage, as symbols of backwardness. This backwardness legitimised constant policing, surveillance and control whether in Britain or in British India. Whilst London became the laboratory for programmes of internal social uplift, British India was turned into the seedbed of a comprehensive civilising mission when, in particular, tribals, savage by definition, and Indians at large, backward by definition, were turned into objects of canting philanthropic-humanitarian treatment.[87]

What becomes even more interesting is the fact that the post-colonial Indian state did not only prolong, perpetuate and intensify the colonial regime's construct of legitimacy, but used it as the British and many other European nation states of the nineteenth and twentieth centuries did to homogenise the imagined national population. Paupers and poor do not fit in such an imagined community which is precisely the reason why they become the object of continuous policing, surveillance and control. Basically the post-colonial Indian state continues to pursue a politics of national identity building that stems from the nineteenth century European context. The question is not only whether the post-colonial

86 Drieberg and Jag Mohan, Emergency in India, 76-9.

87 Marriott, The Other Empire: Metropolis, India and Progress in the Colonial Imagination.

Indian state has internalised the European civilising mission concept[88] but also, extending the timeline further with the Delhi Metro railway-line right into the twenty-first century, whether the Indian state which has since the Emergency overcome its status as an 'innocent' and continuously 'victimised' post-colonial state, is pursuing national politics with the tools of the nineteenth and twentieth centuries.

Conculsion

The Delhi Metro is presently one of the most important tools with which the government pursues the idea of forging the nation. Instrumentalising the Delhi Metro in the context of the Commonwealth Games of 2010, the central, state and city governments justified the forceful eviction of beggars from the streets of Delhi. Beggars were and still are seen as a nuisance which has to be stopped. If Delhi wants to keep its status as a "world-class city" which it has attained through the Delhi Metro, beggars will have to disappear since they represent a "third-world city." Official authorities claim to have removed about 100,000 beggars just in time before thousands of national and international guests visited Delhi for the Commonwealth Games.[89] However, few critical voices ask whether the "gap between the Metro and the rest" will not split the urban society.[90] Given the role Delhi has to play as a national showcase one may ask whether the Delhi Metro has not, in the meantime, become the symbol of national abilities and inequalities. Yet, in spite of the critical voices about the social impact of the Delhi Metro it seems that the vast majority of the press reports and the public opinion at large still clings to the role of the Delhi Metro as a symbol of national importance.

That national importance is also indicated by the developments in Delhi after Independence. The capital city became 'flooded' with refugees from mostly urban centres in the Panjab like Rawalpindi, Lahore and Multan. Yet, from the 1970s onwards regional and transregional in-migration started to bring urban and rural people into Delhi. Settling the refugees as well as the later in-migrants created multiple identities preventing a single overarching or, rather, specific urban culture. The extravagant multiple urban universes manifested in the many

---

88 Vide some of the articles in Watt and Mann, (eds), Civilizing Missions in Colonial and Postcolonial South Asia, which emphasise that particular role, however, in specific contexts.

89 Mahaprashastra, "War on Beggars," Frontline 27, July 02, 2010, http://www.flonnet.com/fl2713/stories/20100702271309800.htm.

90 Chaudhary, "Mind the Gap between the Metro and the Rest," India Today, January 29, 2011, http://indiatoday.indiatoday.in/site/articlePrint.jsp?aid=128059.

living quarters of Delhi's urban agglomeration in the South, the Southeast and the Southwest, make up today's city; a city which is rapidly changing, unmatched by any other contemporary Indian city. It is also for this reason that Delhi has become a metaphor for India and its history, as it stands for diversity and unity. Delhi never "is" but is a metaphor for many things. For many of its inhabitants Delhi "is who we think we are" or, more wishfully, "is what we would like to be," and in some way idealistically, "looks like what we would like to be."[91] Against this background it becomes clear that the Delhi Metro is indeed a metaphor for the city, the region and the nation as it not only symbolises ideals of a "world-class city" but the realities of a living city.

Now it seems also understandable that even critical comments on 'mishaps' like overcrowded coaches pushing off Delhi University students, and unreliable feeder-bus services from nearby residential areas, do not really criticise the Delhi Metro but, on the contrary, emphasise the need to further keep up the "world-class" standard for the metropolis's privileged classes.[92] The overall benefits of the Delhi Metro remain highly acclaimed and unchallenged. It seems to be public common sense, at least for the middle classes of Delhi and other major cities of India that the Delhi Metro is indeed a symbol of modernity, a metaphor for India's claimed status as a major power, an image which if spoilt would most likely cause national public outcry. The growing middle classes do represent the Indian nation. Ironically, the middle classes have always supported governmental politics of marginalisation especially in an urban environment. They were keen to see towns and cities modernised and expanded into new clean zones for their own use, with the squalor-ridden slums eradicated and the poor kept at bay and under control.[93] Interestingly, the British authorities regarded the middle class as an 'embryo' of the future Indian civilised society which once more justified harsh and violent action against the poor.[94]

The same is true for the slum-clearance programmes in Delhi after 1937. Again, the middle class mostly represented by Indian government officials and

91 Sengupta, Delhi Metropolitan, 1-2, 15, 19.

92 Matur, "Feeder Service or the Lack of It," Hindustan Times, December 07, 2009, http://www.hindustantimes.com/StoryPage/Print/484059.aspx.; Matur, "Crowded Stations, Slow Trains," Hindustan Times, November 19, 2009, http://www.hindustantimes.com/StoryPage/Print/477845.aspx.; Vatsala, "Metro Traffic Pushes DU Students Off Track," Mid-Day, July 12, http://www.mid-day.com/news/2010/dec/071210-News-Delhi-Metro-traffic-miss-classes-crucial-exams.htm.

93 Meller, "Urbanization and the Introduction of Modern Town Planning Ideas in India," 330-50. Meller, Patrick Geddes, 220-1.

94 Gooptu, The Politics of the Urban Poor, 66-70, 73-4, 77-82.

urban traders, agreed with the radical renovation of "Old Delhi". Until today *bastis* and *jhuggi-jhompris* are simply seen as ugly stains in an otherwise clean urban environment. To discriminate the irregular (and illegal) settlements and their inhabitants, the city authorities used a metaphorical language describing the *bastis* and *jhuggi-jhompris* as cancer which has to be removed from the urban body to prevent metastases spreading into the still unaffected body. Even Jawaharlal Nehru used this rather abusive language.[95] It was again used during the 1975-77 clearances and is still part of the political and press language to defame the poor. The language, the concept and the planning of urban development are part and parcel of a colonial administrative and legal legacy regarding the city as the living space of civilised urbanites. The poor, actually 'peasants living in an urban environment,' either defer to that politics or disappear from the public.

Substantial critique springs from academia. One article points towards the increasing prevalence of infrastructure mega projects around the world and, at the same time, the evidence which suggests such projects often fail to achieve their stated benefits.[96] The Delhi Metro, however, seems to be the exception to the rule. High expectations were, so far, actually met by reality.[97] The Delhi Metro was rewarded with national and international awards in particular for its environmental-cum-energy saving aspects again indicating the "world-class" status.[98] Yet such mega projects are, in any case, capital intensive enterprises. In spite of the sound financial funding and punctual repayment it has also been criticised for exactly those reasons; the Delhi Metro mainly serves capitalist interests like, for example, mono-rail industries, the light-rail industries and, last but not least, the DMRC as a land-development agency.[99] Apart from such 'ideological issues', the capital used to construct an urban mass rapid transport system at the cost of US$51 to US$76 million per km could have been used to develop a 30 to 50km bus network served by modern buses. This would have benefited 30 to 50 times more people that the current metro system.[100]

Yet buses do not seem to represent modernity. Though they certainly stand for mobility they also stand for old fashioned means of transportation in a megacity and a "world-class city." One either travels by car or by metro. Using three-wheelers, taxis, and buses which are regarded as intermediate transport systems

95 Mann, "Town Planning and Urban Resistance in the Old City of Delhi," 271.
96 Siemiatycki, "Message in a Metro," 211.
97 The State of the Indian Cities 2001, 61-3.
98 Wikipedia. " Delhi Metro," accessed March 1, 2011, http://en.wikipedia.org/wiki/Delhi_Metro.
99 Tiwari, "Urban Transport in Indian Cities," 3.
100 Tiwari, "Urban Transport in Indian Cities," 2.

means to refer to conventional and therefore not modern transport systems. If the Delhi Metro is a metaphor for modernity, mobility as such, represented by the Delhi Metro, is likewise a metaphor for modernity. Rapid urban transport systems, as has been indicated above, can be used best to put a modern nation on a media stage, be that in the press, be that on TV or in Bollywood films. In contrast, endless clusters of buses, taxis, cars and in particular two- and three-wheelers are simply the worst to be imagined by a modern nation. However, looking beyond such imaginations the Delhi Metro was, of course, a necessary means of improving public transport in a fast growing megacity. To critically approach the problem, several points have to be taken into consideration.

First: Without doubt, the Delhi Metro rather serves the Delhi well-off urbanites living in the periphery than the mostly poor people of the densely populated quarters of the megacity. Metro-polis therefore exists for 1.5 million daily riders,[101] that is a little more than 10 per cent of Delhi's present population. Uncomfortable bus rides in overcrowded buses stuck in regular traffic congestion will be the norm for the vast majority of public transport users. It is not the Delhi Metro as such, and the middle classes it serves in general, which has to be criticised but the way the whole system has been implemented. The metro network connecting the outskirts of the city is only one indicator of its exclusionary nature, serving a certain clientele and systematically barring and evicting the poor - the other side of that then shining medal. Missing feeder bus systems even at the outskirts of the city where the middle classes reside further demonstrate this rather fragmentary concept of public transport. Generally speaking, a holistic approach taking into consideration the needs of public transport of as many inhabitants as possible would have been much more appropriate.

Secondly: With respect to town planning, all Master Plans of Delhi (1961, 1981, 2021) do lay emphasis on motor vehicles on roads. The Delhi ring-rail as well as the Delhi Metro are just parts of an additional - yet not substantial transport system. Despite daily time-consuming congestion, individual transport still seems to be the most modern way of mobility. Taking the metro is "hip" and, at the same time, necessary for urban long distance commuters, but when, for example, feeder systems are inefficient or, even worse, non-existent, individual transport is or seems much more reliable than the Delhi Metro. Therefore it is not the Delhi Metro as a means of a rapid urban mass transport system which must be criticised but the planning and the politics of the Delhi Metro represented by the DDA, the DMRC, the Delhi Municipal Corporation and the central government. Part of that planning is to instrumentalise the ideas of the mid-

101 Wikipedia. " Delhi Metro," accessed March 1, 2011, http://en.wikipedia.org/wiki/Delhi_Metro.

dle classes with respect to modernity and mobility. Strict separation and segregation as essentials of colonial town planning, yet to some extent also reflecting brahmanic ideals of purity, became part of the post-independent Indian state, thus prolonging ideas of colonial and caste society instead of overcoming them.

Thirdly: So far the Delhi Metro only serves a small minority of Delhi's inhabitants. The majority of its population is still not being taken into consideration. Modernisation, it seems, is reserved for particular segments of the population making modernisation rather fragmentary. This kind of fragmented modernity in an urban context has been termed "Indischer Inselurbanismus"[102] (Indian insular urbanism) indicating islands of modernity in an urban environment. However, coming back to the question in how far the media propagated the modernity of the Delhi Metro, it seems that those who aren't the 'profiteers' of the Delhi Metro, and therefore of rapid mobility and modernity, nevertheless do appreciate its existence for rather imaginative local and national aspects. Seen against this background the Delhi Metro indeed works as a unique tool for shaping the city and forging the nation, giving a majority of its inhabitants the feeling of living in a modern city and being members of a modern society with world-class aspirations.

102 Vide various articles in Archplus 185, 2007.

India's *Ville Radieuse*: Modernist Town Planning in Chandigarh

Boris Niclas-Tölle

Chandigarh

To Western minds it might appear surprising that one of the "fathers" of twentieth-century modernism erected his master work in India. The city of Chandigarh, situated at the foothills of the Himalayas, was planned by the Frenchman Charles Jeanneret, better known as Le Corbusier, and his team of architects during the 1940s and 1950s. Chandigarh is commonly considered a vestige of the modernist kind of town planning closest to the concepts developed by the International Congresses of Modern Architecture during the 1930s. Those concepts not only influenced the reconstruction and transformation of cities in Europe after World War Two but also had an impact on efforts to modernize African, Latin American and Asian countries. Modernism's rejection of traditionalist Western architecture made it especially attractive to those governments eager to underline their countries' independence from former European colonial powers. In this context, modernism became more than an architectural style or a philosophy of design: It became part of a broad modernization project that included industrial and economic development as well as the transformation of the respective societies. As recent research on the global history of modernization today suggests, this endeavor manifested itself in heterogeneous ways, many of which have not been investigated so far.[1]

One of the countries which actively participated in the modernization project was India in the Nehru era. Jawaharlal Nehru, independent India's first prime minister, pursued a modernization policy to develop India's economy and society. Already during the 1930s, he had aligned himself with a fraction of the National Congress that advocated public commitment to accelerate India's industrialization process. In planning their country's future, many Indians looked abroad for examples: Apart from the European Industrial Revolution, Japan served as a case in point: Japan had developed from a feudal, rural society into a Pacific national power in less than fifty years. Hence, the strong Meiji government was seen as a paragon for India's development.[2] Similarly, the Russian experience with rapid industrialization inspired many Indian nationalists dreaming

1 Engerman and Unger, "Towards a Global History of Modernization."
2 Lajpat Rai, The Evolution of Japan and other Papers.

of a strong and rich Indian nation.[3] Hence, when India became independent in 1947, the government opted for a strategy of import substitution industrialization to make the national economy independent from costly imports. To execute such a strategy in a short time, a powerful government and a central planning agency were considered necessary.[4] The construction of new towns, which was integrated into India's Five Year Plans, helped to legitimize the centralism promoted by Nehru and his allies. Modern towns, as prestige projects, rendered the country's modernization achievements visible by dramatically changing the appearance of the nation's cityscapes. Displaying efficiency and technical abilities strengthened India's national self-consciousness and demonstrated the country's independence on an international level.

Chandigarh's construction had an even deeper national meaning. The city was to secure governance over India's western borderlands, where the political situation was very unstable. 1947's partition had caused the division of the federal state of Punjab and the loss of its capital Lahore.[5] During the succeeding civil war, refugee groups of Muslims and Sikhs migrated in opposite directions. When the groups met, they often clashed violently, leading to brutal massacres which caused several tens of thousands of casualties.[6] Against the background of this regional conflict and an increasing tension over the state of Kashmir, establishing an Indian national Identity in the area was deemed a project of national importance.[7] The symbolic relevance was reflected in the name of Chandigarh, which can be translated as "Chandi's Fortress". Chandi is believed to be a manifestation of the Hindu goddess Shakti, who represents the constant transformation of the world.[8] By conjuring a Hinduist spirit as eponym of the new capital of Punjab, India clearly demarcated its parts of the divided state as Indian sovereign territory. The founding of Chandigarh also indicated the Nehru government's strong self-consciousness and the influence of Hindu nationalism.

In Nehru's view, Chandigarh was primarily a project to demonstrate India's emancipation from the former colonial powers. His office repeatedly stated that it was of central concern to the Indian nation to construct a modern Indian town without relying on British or American aid.[9] Applying Western modernist prin-

---

3 Saha, "Technological Revolution in Industry - How the Russians did it."

4 Nayar, "Nationalist Planning for Autarchy and State Hegemony. Development Strategy under Nehru."

5 Sarin, Urban Planning in the Third World, 13.

6 Kulke and Rothermund, Geschichte Indiens, 326-339; Ludden, Geschichte Indiens, 214-244.

7 Ludden, Geschichte Indiens, 237-241.

8 Prakash, Chandigarh's Le Corbusier, 8.

9 Prakash, Chandigarh's Le Corbusier, 39-43.

ciples of town planning did not seem to question this autonomy. Nehru believed that industrialization and technological development had to be accompanied by urbanization. To prevent the wild, unhealthy growth of cities and to avoid chaos, town planning techniques had to be applied. Since Europe had the longest experience with industrialization-related urbanization, it made sense to import and adapt European techniques.

The Functional City

Most contemporary urban centers in Europe developed during the transformation from agrarian to industrial societies during the nineteenth century. Famines and unemployment caused migration into towns, a tendency reinforced by the high demand for labor around the centers of industrialization. Enormous growth and the subsequent scarcity of living space led to a rapidly decreasing quality of life in the cities, which conservative and anti-modernist critics soon denounced as Western civilization's nemesis.[10]

With the beginning of the twentieth century, confidence grew that most of the problems of urban life could be solved by modern instruments. Technological progress and new scientific findings such as the evolution theory fundamentally changed the self-understanding of societies. Science was to improve human life. Hence, in 1915, biologist Patrick Geddes demanded a new science of town planning.[11] He recommended a broad education as well as scientific centers for local scientific town planning in every city. Other approaches like Ebenezer Howard's concept of the garden city aimed to combine the relative advantages of city life and country dwelling by promoting mass transit systems that would enable commuting between the city centre and the outlying districts.

Driven by pragmatic and theoretical approaches like Howard's and Geddes's a new concept of town planning emerged which did not seek to solve modern society's problems by rejecting modernity but by applying its very principles. Arguing that science had made industrialization possible, science was to provide the means of revoking industrialization's negative impacts. As enthusiasm for planning grew, traditional understandings of urban and social space changed dramatically. The "Victorian slum" became a synonym of horror, and nineteenth-century warnings of the collapse of society served to legitimize calls for large-scale urban planning.

In the late 1920s, the concept of the Functional City came into being when members of the modern architecture movement sought to apply the principles of functional architecture to an urban situation. They believed that improving liv-

10 Bahrdt, Die moderne Großstadt, 35-39; Oswald, Die überschätzte Stadt, 65-72.

11 Geddes, Cities in Evolution, 97-108.

ing conditions could be achieved by an efficient arrangement of modern building blocks instead of lowering population density and decentralizing urban spaces.[12] In 1928, the first International Congress of Modern Architecture (CIAM; in French: Congrès Internationaux d'Architecture Moderne) convened at La Sarraz, Switzerland. CIAM had been initiated by the Parisian architects Le Corbusier and Gabriel Guévrékian and the Swiss art historian Siegfried Giedion. Their goal was to establish an international architectural avant-garde to contain the influence of academic neoclassicism which was predominant at that time.[13] At La Sarraz, a group of European architects approved a declaration demanding a fundamental restructuring of cities by allotment of land, traffic regulation and legislation. Urban spaces were to be aligned rationally with the functions of living, working and recreation, and they were to rely exclusively on modern architecture.[14]

Zoning was not a novel concept at the time. In 1919, the Frenchman Tony Garnier had published a plan for an industrial town that included the functional zoning of living sectors, public facilities and industrial areas.[15] In the Netherlands and the United States, a practice of functional, zone-based planning had been established in the 1920s.[16] What was new about CIAM's zoning was the radical rejection of traditionally grown urbanity and academic architecture, which, in the eyes of the avant-garde, represented obsolete structures unable to renew themselves. Also, CIAM's members demanded that planning and rebuilding projects should be organized by the government, not by private investors. In his drafts of the "Radiant City," Le Corbusier presented the vision of a completely transformed and functionally zoned town. Industry complexes, apartment buildings, administrative high-rise buildings, elevated highways, parking lots and public parks were aligned onto a strictly geometric chess-board grid. Aggressive and charismatic, Le Corbusier and his fraction within CIAM were able to gain public recognition as CIAM's opinion leaders throughout the 1930s. In 1941, Le Corbusier published the statements of CIAM's Athens conference as the "Athens Charter."[17] Although the architect Josép Lluis Sert used the same material in his volume "Can Our Cities Survive?"[18], Le Corbusier's Charter prevailed to be regarded as the main reference work for modern town planning.

---

12 Le Corbusier, The Radiant City, 104-111.

13 Mumford, The CIAM Discourse on Urbanism 1928-1960, 9.

14 Declaration of La Sarraz in Hilpert, Le Corbusiers 'Charta von Athen,' 102-111.

15 Garnier, Die ideale Industriestadt.

16 Mumford, The CIAM Discourse on Urbanism 1928-1960, 25.

17 Hilpert, Le Corbusiers 'Charta von Athen,' 113-215.

18 Sert, Can Our Cities Survive?.

Modernist town planning in the West

The orthodox concept of the functional city along the lines of the "Ville Radieuse" met with stark skepticism in Europe, and Le Corbusier was not able to realize his radical plans. However, the basic principles of functional town planning fundamentally influenced town planning practices during the second half of the twentieth century. In 1942, the reconstruction of war-shattered London was planned by Patrick Abercrombie and J.H. Forshaw.[19] The plan applied several of the functional principles laid down in the Athens Charter and awarded a central government authority control over the reconstruction efforts. According to MARS, the British CIAM group, London's reconstruction was one of the first publicly funded projects to apply modern planning principles onto an existing social organism.[20] In post-war Germany, town planning principles comparable to those used by the Nazis were continued. There seemed little reason to be critical of that continuity since similar kinds of planning were practiced abroad, too.[21] The ideas of Athens had spread and been accepted as a modern development technique throughout Europe and beyond, neglecting the contradictions between the different political systems. While national and regional differences existed, of course, European nations' post-war town planning practices shared an emphasis on functionalism and decentralization. The reconstruction of devastated cities like Warsaw, London, Rotterdam,[22] Hamburg, Bremen and Frankfurt; the founding of new satellite towns like Sennestadt[23]; the construction of British "New Towns"; and the rapid growth of suburbs in many countries of the industrialized world mirrored this trend.[24]

Functionalism's Economic Origins

Two major characteristics of modern functional town planning are seriality and the rejection of architectural ornaments. In the eyes of the critics, these characteristics translated into dangerous monotony. Modern planners, however, embraced and propagated monotony as an expression of rationality and order. Yet functionalism should not be reduced to stylistic preferences. One also needs to take into consideration the material logic of economic development and industrialization. Siegfried Giedion, art historian and founding member of CIAM, de-

19 Abercrombie, Greater London Plan 1944.

20 Mumford, The CIAM Discourse on Urbanism 1928-1960, 123.

21 Durth and Gutschow, Träume in Trümmern I, 193-196.

22 Durth and Gutschow, Träume in Trümmern I, 285-325; Durth and Gutschow, Träume in Trümmern II.

23 Reichow, Die autogerechte Stadt.

24 Hall, Cities of Tomorrow, 274-318.

scribed the buildings of the Chicago School of Architecture as the first manifestation of functional architecture.[25] He emphasized that the Chicago School was shaped less by academic theories than by a pragmatic attitude stemming from new technological possibilities and economic demands. In Chicago, architects were confronted with the rapid speed of city growth and exploding real estate prices. In reaction, they applied new construction techniques to build high-rise buildings of constantly increasing size.[26] Concrete casting under freezing conditions allowed for construction to continue during winter-times, while floodlights and the installation of protective construction systems made construction during night-times and rainfall possible. According to Giedion, it was under these conditions that functionalism evolved. Consequently, functionalism was called "Commercial Style" by contemporaries.[27] Similarly, Giedion argued that the German Bauhaus architects developed their modernist ideas in the context of industrial construction projects.[28] Here, economic factors played a similar role as in the case of Chicago's skyscrapers. Therefore, functionalism and rationalism in architecture came initially to be seen as the result of economic efficiency; only later did an aesthetic school develop that declared them to be the rationale of modern design.

This was also true for functional town planning. Long before Le Corbusier's idealized plans came into existence, Tony Garnier's "Citè Industrielle" had been completely tailored to the needs of the local industry and its employees. Functional town planning later applied the logic of industrialization to urban development.[29] CIAM's 1928 foundation paper stated that "real economic efficiency will be the fruit of rationalization and standardization that will be as applicable onto architectural planning as onto industrial methods of construction."[30] The appeal to industrial concepts was driven by the egalitarian promise of industrialization to provide low-priced high quality by means of serial mass production. The declaration of La Sarraz defined "economic efficiency" as a "production that suffices to satisfy the needs of mankind."[31]

Functional town planning was successful because it allowed for the reconstruction of industrialized nations with industrial methods. The claim of modern planning to be unpolitical, non-academic and free of historical ballast promoted

25 Giedion, Raum, Zeit, Architektur, 244-258.
26 Condit, The Chicago School of Architecture, 14-25.
27 Condit, The Chicago School of Architecture, 26-27.
28 Giedion, Raum, Zeit, Architektur, 306.
29 Guillien, The Taylorized Beauty of the Mechanical.
30 Hilpert, Le Corbusiers 'Charta von Athen,' 96.
31 Hilpert, Le Corbusiers 'Charta von Athen,' 96.

the international establishment of functionalism as a means of development in non-Western countries, as the example of Chandigarh suggests.

Modern town planning in India

Colonialism left lasting marks on Indian architecture in the first half of the twentieth century. Until 1947, the majority of architectural and town planning projects were executed by the British administration. Imperial style reflected British rule, hence Indian elements were not given much room for a long time. In the late nineteenth century, the evolution of an Indian middle class and the enthusiasm of some Westerners for India's ancient architecture led to the emergence of the Indian-Saracen style. This style, a mix of European Gothic covered with an abundance of allegedly Indian ornamentation, reflected the spatial logics of traditional Indian architecture only superficially.[32] Similarly, town planning before 1947 mainly served colonial interests and usually correlated with contemporary European and British trends. Most importantly, town planning served to represent British colonial power (especially in the construction of New Delhi), to construct cheap dwellings for the workers of the growing textile industry, and to prevent epidemics through measures of urban hygiene. While measures like the widening of streets or the construction of living space were useful in principle, British planning authorities like the Improvement Trust in Calcutta often displayed overt racist attitudes in their considerations and in actions like the destruction of Indian and Chinese living quarters.[33]

Discussion about modern architecture in India began in the 1930s, when independence seemed to be within reach. Interestingly, many Indians found modernism attractive not because of its rationalism, its international character, or its rejection of conservative values. Instead, modern architecture was generally perceived as a Western style, which made it even more interesting. Young architects who had studied in Europe admired its modernity and wanted India to embrace precisely the Western characteristics it seemed to embody.[34] Hence, the debate about modern architecture reflected the conflict in which many Indians found themselves in the mid-twentieth century. Gandhi's propagation of the spinning wheel emphasized India's cultural independence, but at the same time it was a symbol of pre-modern manufacturing practices. To embrace modernity, which the Nehru government did, meant accepting Western paradigms as well as a degree of continuity in dependence on the former colonial power. This was

32 Evenson, The Indian Metropolis, 82-112.

33 Evenson, The Indian Metropolis, 130-132.

34 Evenson, The Indian Metropolis, 180-181.

especially true with regard to town planning, a field in which India relied on British expertise for a long time after independence.[35]

In the case of Chandigarh, this continuity was apparent, too. The special representative of the government of Punjab, A.L. Fletcher, based his plans for the new city on Patrick Abercrombie's Greater London Plan of 1943. Fletcher was a follower of the British town planning avant-garde. His plan for Chandigarh envisioned a network of three connected "New Towns", of which one was planned as a classical garden city while the other two should be a university and an administrative town.[36] Indian chief engineer P.L. Verma criticized Fletcher's plans for being too close to the British tradition of town planning and not integrating Indian realities. The connection of the three satellite towns would have required a degree of motorization among the Indian population that was far from given in India in 1948. Furthermore, Verma estimated that the planned population limit of 200,000 was set far too low; he expected a faster industrial development and a large migration of refugees from Pakistan into the city. The latter had not been accounted for by Fletcher at all. At Verma's urging, Fletcher was relieved from the project in November 1948, and Chandigarh was conceptualized as a town for 500,000 inhabitants.[37] When Verma and Fletcher's successor, P. N. Thapar, wanted to travel to Europe to find a new town planner for Chandigarh, Nehru intervened. Fearing that a European town planner would develop a similarly 'alien' concept like Fletcher, Nehru insisted they engage a planner who was familiar with India. The American Albert Mayer seemed to be the perfect candidate. Mayer had established himself as a town planner during Roosevelt's New Deal, and he had worked as an engineer in India in the early 1940s. Since 1946, he had been advising the Indian government and was close to Nehru. Therefore, Mayer was Nehru's first choice for planning Chandigarh, and Mayer developed the first master plan for the town. However, before construction had begun Mayer's most important architect, Matthew Nowicky, died in an airplane crash. Thapar and Verma used this tragedy to travel to Europe to look for a European architect. Mayer had coordinated his works mainly from his office in New York, which had caused some discontent on the Indian side. Hence, Thapar and Verma argued that the new team should be obliged to work in India.[38] Obviously, Thapar and Verma acted in opposition against Nehru, who tried to cancel the trip to Europe but failed.[39]

35 Evenson, The Indian Metropolis, 182-184.
36 Prakash, Chandigarh's Le Corbusier, 36.
37 Prakash, Chandigarh's Le Corbusier, 37-39.
38 Sarin, Urban Planning in the Third World, 39.
39 Prakash, Chandigarh's Le Corbusier, 43.

In France, Verma and Thapar met Le Corbusier. Although he was already famous for his influence on modern town planning, he had not been able to realize any of his plans except for a few single buildings. His latest project, the reconstruction of the two French coastal towns La Rochelle and St. Dié, had failed due to the resistance of the local population.[40] Verma and Thapar were not impressed with his Maison d'Unité, and Le Corbusiér's enthusiasm for the Chandigarh project remained limited. He declared that if he would plan Chandigarh at all, he would do it in France, which caused Verma and Thapar to continue their journey to Great Britain, where they met the architect couple Edwin Maxwell Fry and Jane Beverley Drew.[41] Fry and Drew were the first architects who reacted positively to the plan from the very beginning. Both had already worked on projects in the British colonies in Africa and the Middle East and were familiar with the special conditions of projects in tropical areas.[42] It was Drew's enthusiasm that encouraged them to instantly sign a contract that obliged them to three years of work in India. Drew and Fry also lobbied Le Corbusier to join the project on the condition that he could mostly work in France. Also, his brother Pierre Jeannerett was engaged as an additional architect.[43] The contracts were signed in 1950. Although Le Corbusier presented Chandigarh publicly as a "good deed with bad payment" in 1958,[44] his letters to Fry and Drew show that he perceived the project as a possibility to finally realize the Athens Charter. He wrote: "After 22 years of CIAM action the moment to be heard has arrived to realize a magnificent work. [...]. It is a grand victory for CIAM, it is also an occasion for proving that the CIAM congresses are capable of real action."[45]

In 1951, the team travelled to India and began its work. Le Corbusier was given full control over the project to prevent internal conflicts during the creation of the master plan. Maxwell Fry, who was qualified to work as a town planner, too, abstained from being involved in the design of the master plan out of respect for Le Corbusier's personality. Instead, he focused on planning the dwelling sectors in cooperation with Jane Drew.[46] Albert Mayer desperately tried to regain control over the project, but being situated in New York and facing a dedicated group on site he could not but fail. Deeply frustrated, he left the project the same year. Meanwhile, Le Corbusier finally had achieved his goal to create a complete city exclusively under his personal directive.

40 Mumford, The CIAM Discourse on Urbanism 1928-1960, 156.
41 Evenson, Chandigarh, 25-27.
42 Prakash, Chandigarh's Le Corbusier, 43.
43 Sarin, Urban Planning in the Third World, 39-41.
44 Evenson, Chandigarh, 26.
45 Quote taken from Sarin, Urban Planning in the Third World, 42-43.
46 Fry, "Le Corbusier at Chandigarh."

The Realization of the Athens Charter

Le Corbusier made Chandigarh into a strictly rectangular-shaped city with a Cartesian chess-board structure. By choosing this form, Le Corbusier emphasized his personal preference of straight lines and rectangles, very much in contrast to Albert Mayer's earlier master plan.[47] In planning to shape the city like a leaf, Mayer had followed the latest trend of organic design prevalent in Europe at the time.[48] Le Corbusier distinctly opposed this trend and revived his own (by then rather outdated) design of the "Ville Radieuse".

Different from comparable construction projects in Europe and the United States, Chandigarh was a pioneer settlement. American Greenbelt towns, British New Towns and satellite towns throughout Europe were constructed to reduce population density in existing urban centers. They were usually planned in the context of a larger scaled regional planning. Contrastingly, the motive to build Chandigarh was to create an urban centre. It was not embedded in a larger regional plan. By abandoning Fletcher's original idea to divide the town in three separate satellite cities, the planners of Chandigarh focused on creating a single, densely populated urban centre. This decision made apparent the inherent limitations of the Athens Charter, which was supposed to offer solutions to existing urban problems in Europe. The charter was not meant to provide a construction plan for a completely new town. Rather, it was a collection of basic principles of planning and construction. As radically different as they were from established principles, they did not include recommendations for the actual shape of a city. Therefore, the Athens Charter could be applied to large scale decentralized regional projects as well as to centralized ones such as Chandigarh.

As described above, the primary idea of the Athens Charter and modern town planning was the functional differentiation of urban space. Consequently, Chandigarh was divided into several sectors and zones meant to serve the functions of working, dwelling, leisure and traffic. A more detailed comparison of the master plan and the Athens Charter can illuminate how the charter was implemented in Chandigarh. Since Le Corbusier considered Chandigarh the prime example of the Athens Charter in practice, it makes sense to base such a comparison on his versions of the master plan.[49]

---

47 Kalia, Chandigarh, 91-92.

48 Reichow, Organische Stadtbaukunst.

49 Sarin, "Chandigarh as a Place to Live in."

Dwelling

The charter's most essential demand was the improvement of urban dwelling conditions. A minimal living standard should be provided for every inhabitant of the town to grant the possibility of living in dignity. To achieve this, the dwelling sectors in each town were to be constructed in the best topographic and climatic areas. They should be arranged and constructed under hygienic aspects, which primarily meant to provide a sufficient flow of fresh air and insulation in every building. To prevent adverse effects through noise and pollution, buildings should not be positioned parallel to traffic lanes. Population density should not exceed a specific degree, and every individual should be provided a minimum amount of living space. The amount of this minimum individual space had been calculated by CIAM experts, who argued that it should be implemented as a universal human right. The construction of multi-story buildings should enable a high population density while maintaining a low housing density. Large green spaces between the blocs were supposed to prevent buildings obstructing each other.[50]

Since the 1920s, it was an established practice among modern town planners to segment large settlements into smaller neighborhood units. Those were seen as "germ-cells" of society and were grouped around establishments to provide for immediate demands such as minor commercial areas, schools or sports clubs. Chandigarh was organized following a similar neighborhood principle. It was originally divided into 25 sectors. According to the master plan, possible future additions were to be built in a southward direction.[51] Each sector of the city was planned to contain four villages of 150 buildings each, which was the average size of Punjab villages at the time. The spaces between the villages should be used for small shopping areas and public facilities.

Population density was not regulated but depended on the inhabitants' income. The northern sectors were planned for the upper classes and featured larger buildings and estates, while the lower classes were to live in the southern, more densely settled parts of the city. At the northern sectors, population density was as low as 5,000 inhabitants per sector, while most of the southern sectors contained up to 20,000 inhabitants. Originally, Le Corbusier had planned to increase population density in the north before expanding the town southwards. Due to the fact that this would have meant redistribution at the cost of Chandigarh's upper classes, this part of the plan was ignored by the respective authorities in charge.[52] Although Le Corbusier distanced himself from egalitarian de-

50 Hilpert, Le Corbusiers 'Charta von Athen,' 131-135.

51 Joshi, Documenting Chandigarh, 30.

52 Sarin, Urban Planning in the Third World, 73.

mands to provide the same living space for everyone, his master plan answered to the essential demands of the Athens charter. It did not include any attempts to remove social inequality. However, a minimum living space, hygienic urban conditions as well as water and an energy supply were provided to even the poorest sectors of Chandigarh.[53]

Leisure

The Athens charter defined leisure quite narrowly as sports and recreation in nature. Youth centers and clubs should be provided for children and adolescents, but even those facilities were simply relegated to "green spaces."[54] Le Corbusier commented on a city's leisure function with the following words: "A leisure program has to be set up that allows activities of all kinds: To walk – alone or with company – in the beauty of nature, sports of all kinds, [...]; entertainment such as concerts, open-air performances, games in a stadium, various competitions."[55] Following these demands, extensive green spaces were planned at Chandigarh. All sectors were enclosed by more or less broad greenbelts; housing spaces were limited in favor of abundant plantings. Public green spaces were accessible in close vicinity to every house. In most of these spaces, public facilities were placed. Additionally, the establishment of local recreation areas was an integral part of the plan. To the north, an artificial lake was built. To assure its function as a recreation area, construction at its shores was prohibited. Le Corbusier also declared the banks of a river crossing the town a park and called it the "Valley of Leisure."[56] As impressive as these measures were, they cannot hide the fact that "leisure" was limited to very few activities. Apart from some sports clubs, there were no amusement areas, no "downtown," no sector that would encourage cultural development. The reason for this was the strictly rational philosophy of the Athens Charter, which defined "leisure" as an act of compensation for modern life by experiencing nature and conducting physical regeneration. It can be assumed that everything that exceeded such a rational understanding of leisure was not forgotten but consciously rejected.

Work

The Athens charter distinguished between three kinds of work functions and assigned each of them different locations. Industrial facilities should be placed

53 Sarin, "Chandigarh as a Place to Live in."
54 Hilpert, Le Corbusiers 'Charta von Athen,' 138-140.
55 Hilpert, Le Corbusiers 'Charta von Athen,' 139.
56 Evenson, Chandigarh, 34.

outside the town and as close as possible to long-distance traffic lanes. They should be segregated from living areas by large greenbelts. Due to the "urban character" of their activities, trade and repair businesses should be set up at the "most intense points" of the city. Administration and service enterprises should be concentrated in a "business city."[57] Since Chandigarh's purpose was to be a political centre, no industry sector was planned. There were some minor supply businesses intended to be in the city's vicinity, but this did not include any heavy industry. Much more important were the government and administration buildings. At sector one, an elevated plain at the north-east of the city, the famous capitol complex was placed. The area housing the federal state government was designed by Le Corbusier himself. Spaciously arranging sculptures and buildings, he created an extensive and monumental plaza that resembles imperial monumentality. Le Corbusier was immediately criticized for segregating the government complex from the city and for applying such an oppressive design. Clearly, the goal to create a public compound of convention and communication as a germ cell of democracy was not achieved.[58]

Via the "Valley of Leisure," the capitol complex was connected to sector 17, where the pedestrian area of the "Bridge Market" was supposed to function as the business sector of the city. Here, the urban administration, several banks and shopping centers were located. That sector 17 did not grow into a bustling city centre was due to the fact that soon after Chandigarh's construction began, the idea of a central business district was abandoned in favor of a decentralized commercial concept.[59] Astonishingly, semi-industrial trade and repair businesses as envisioned in the Athens Charter seem to have been completely neglected in the master plan. It has to be assumed that Le Corbusier did not differentiate between general service enterprises and more technical oriented workshops that require a more specialized infrastructure.

Traffic

Traffic in the functional city was required to provide a fast and direct connection to all sectors of town. The contradiction between zoning and the demand of short distances between homes and workplaces could only be resolved by a traffic plan that allowed an uninterrupted flow of high-speed traffic within the city. To provide this, traffic in the modern city was to be spatially separated by velocities. Pedestrians and vehicles should move on separate lanes that should not overlap at any point. Vehicles should be differentiated by speed classes and

57 Hilpert, Le Corbusiers 'Charta von Athen,' 143-145.

58 Prakash, Chandigarh's Le Corbusier, 71-122.

59 Sarin, Urban Planning in the Third World, 90-95.

drive on respective lanes that should be separated through different height levels, which meant the construction of bridges, tunnels and highways. High-speed lanes should be shielded by large greenbelts.[60] Regarding traffic, the Athens Charter relied completely on individual car traffic; trams, buses, trains or other concepts of public mass transit were not included. Chandigarh was aligned to car traffic as well. By cross-linking high-speed lanes, highways, feeder roads and generous parking lots, every citizen should be connected to the city's high-speed road network. Le Corbusier developed a system of seven standardized road types, calling them simply "Vs", an abbreviation for the French "voie" (road). V1s were regional highways that transported cars to and from the town. V2s and V3s were inner city highways that formed the characteristic grid of the city. Inside the sectors, the roads further ramified into smaller ways up to the V7s, which were reserved for pedestrians and bike traffic.[61] Traffic signals were avoided and substituted by roundabouts and clover-leaf solutions at crossroads and intersections.

Real Estate Speculation

To be able to realize the Athens Charter, direct control over the whole construction area was deemed necessary. The fragmentation of urban areas caused by private real estate speculation was seen as a contemporary illness. To solve this problem, the planning process and all construction sites were to be nationalized. Le Corbusier's version of the Athens Charter demanded uncompromised state control over private property and a society-oriented, holistic urban development that ruled out private interest.[62] By preventing speculation, the planners hoped to be able to control real estate and accommodation prices. Only that way would it be possible to provide minimum living standards to all income classes. To make all this possible, a powerful government organization was founded. The "Chandigarh Planning Organization" (CPO) had control over the entire territory that had been nationalized for this purpose. In the process of nationalization, several village dwellers were expropriated and could only be relocated under threat of lethal force. In post-colonial Punjab, this incident presented a moral burden on which the new capital was built.[63]

When Chandigarh was constructed, housing for 90 percent of the government employees could be completed during the first construction phase. The rental prices for the apartments and houses, which that had been designed by ar-

60 Hilpert, Le Corbusiers 'Charta von Athen,' 149-151.

61 Evenson, Chandigarh, 32-33.

62 Hilpert, Le Corbusiers „Charta von Athen,' 165-166.

63 Evenson, Chandigarh, 7.

chitects Maxwell, Drew and Jeanneret, were fixed at ten percent of the respective employee's salary.[64] Although the prices were very low, even the lowest income class apartments were equipped with modern kitchens, sanitary facilities and a tap water supply.[65] Infrastructure was constructed completely by the CPO. By selling selected developed estates with increased land value to private investors, the public construction program was supposed to be able to fund itself over the years. When private investors wanted to construct buildings themselves, they had to comply with very strict regulations defined by the master plan. To fund urban construction by selling developed land was generally a common funding strategy at this time. Therefore, the rising land value that would pose a severe problem some years later was not perceived as such in the early years. Instead, it was acclaimed as an indicator of the success of modern planning.[66]

Chandigarh's Development: A Failure of Utopian Modernism?

Originally, Chandigarh had been planned as an administrative town. As such, it was to be exclusively inhabited by government employees and service suppliers. The thousands of construction workers who built the city had not been forgotten. Once construction of the city was completed, they were to move on to other construction sites. Given the national development plan, according to which construction projects were to be executed throughout all of India, this expectation appeared reasonable at the time. If an economic miracle had happened in India, a nation-wide demand of work would have made it possible to employ all the workers at other sites. Yet such an economic miracle did not happen. Although the government tried hard to implement the national economic development plans, it could not easily solve the problem of massive poverty which India was characterized by. Most construction workers stayed in Chandigarh, and large numbers of unemployed people, who had heard about the good job opportunities at the construction site, migrated to the developing city. In the first years, the CPO had organized advertising campaigns to attract workers, but after a short time more workers were available than were required. Most of them were uprooted refugees from Pakistan, or economic refugees from the poor neighboring states. Many had left their villages because agricultural yields were low and they suffered from the social injustices of India's caste system.[67] Migration into Chandigarh was further reinforced by the families many workers brought. Hence, the population density grew much higher than expected, requir-

64 Sarin, Urban Planning in the Third World, 64.
65 Joshi, Documenting Chandigarh, 43-45.
66 Sarin, Urban Planning in the Third World, 60.
67 Sarin, Urban Planning in the Third World, 145-148.

ing a better supply infrastructure, which in turn opened up new job opportunities, which attracted more migrants.

In principle, the massive influx of migrants into the city was not a problem because the master plan included the possibility to expand the city southwards. However, many of the incoming migrants were unemployed and lacking specialized training. Also, they did not bring any capital to Chandigarh. Therefore, the massive rush of people overstrained the funding plans of public housing projects which aimed to draw money by selling developed estates to private investors. Madhu Sarin argues that this strategy never could have worked in a Third World country since the majority of the population simply did not have the financial resources to be able to afford the acquisition of building plots, not to mention developed real estate.[68] From a 1982 perspective, this critique may be justified. However, it implies that the Indian planners should have acted on the assumption of a permanently desolate economic situation in India. This would have meant to assume a failure of their plans for accelerated industrialization and modernization. Hence, they tried to realize the master plan despite considerable underfunding.

The integration of the newcomers into the southern parts of the city proved problematic because the intended densification of the privileged northern sectors was skipped. Consequently, an immense additional demand for expensive infrastructure arose in the city's south. Furthermore, when the jurisdiction of Chandigarh as a capital was extended not only to Punjab but also to Haryana, an increased number of government employees were required. Their rising demand for subsidized housing could not be funded through the sale of developed estates. When the CPO started to sell undeveloped building plots, prices for land rapidly increased. Many residents could afford the emerging high real estate prices only by subleasing parts of their living space, which resulted in the high population density modern planning was meant to prevent.[69]

Poverty also affected the traffic and business situation. Chandigarh provided an outstanding infrastructure for individual car traffic. Yet the majority of people were too poor to afford a car. In 1982, the predominant means of transport was still bikes and rickshaws. The administration was not able to fund the operation of a comprehensive public transit system.[70] Therefore, the functional segregation failed due to insufficient individual mobility. Throughout the city, small markets and stores emerged. Since most vendors could not afford to rent stores,

68 Sarin, Urban Planning in the Third World, 77-80.
69 Sarin, Urban Planning in the Third World, 74-90.
70 Sarin, Urban Planning in the Third World, 98-99.

most commodity trade happened on the streets, specifically on the back of *rehris*, hand-drawn transport carts.[71]

All these problems suggest that Chandigarh as a project failed. But what exactly was it that failed? The unforeseen growth of the number of poor inhabitants made it financially impossible to provide everyone with a minimum living standard. Well-developed urban areas became a scarce good which only the privileged classes could afford. The living situation in Chandigarh became just what the Athens Charter had attempted to fight. Contemporary reports therefore rarely shared the enthusiasm that had accompanied the project of Chandigarh during the initial years of construction. Beginning in the 1960s, several authors criticized modern town planning and functional zoning in particular. Publications such as Jane Jacobs' *Death and Life of Great American Cities* and Paul Bahrdt's sociological critique *The Modern Metropolis*, and titles such as *The Murdered City* or *The Inhospitality of Our Cities* attacked the secluding effects of functional zoning.[72] What initially had been advertised as an objective and rational regulatory measure against urban chaos was increasingly deemed monotonous, boring and suffocating. Alternative concepts of mixed-use, functional overlapping and urban heterogeneity gained support.[73] Post-modern concepts of town planning such as "Collage City" by Colin Rowe and Fred Koetter appeared and were advertised since the 1970s.[74] As the discussion about modern town planning continued, it became clear that functional zoning was not the only issue that caused opposition against modern town planning. Angelus Eisinger argues that the actual problem was the self-image of modern planning.[75] Modern architects had understood themselves as social engineers or surgeons, as experts who were the only ones qualified to save urban societies through spatial rearrangement and optimizing their efficiency. It was their arrogance to impose agendas on entire societies without any interest in feedback or participation of the respective populations. Their plans were based on abstract drafts, mostly designed to look impressive on a sketch board. In his critique, Eisinger sides with Lewis Mumford, who in the 1940s argued against the modernist avant-garde when he rejected to honor Josép Lluis Sért's *Can Our Cities Survive?* by writing an introduction. He justified his decision by criticizing the limitation of town planning to the four basic functions "Living, Dwelling, Work, and Recreation",

71 Sarin, Urban Planning in the Third World, 182-205.

72 Jacobs, Death and Life of Great American Cities; Bahrdt, Die moderne Großstadt; Siedler, Niggemeyer and Angreß, Die gemordete Stadt; Mitscherlich, Die Unwirtlichkeit unserer Städte.

73 Wolfrum, "Funktionale Stadt I Patchwork City."

74 Rowe and Koetter, "Collage City."

75 Eisinger, Die Stadt der Architekten, 62-72.

which he deemed insufficient for a democratic society.[76] In principle, the anti-modernist criticism of the 1960s followed a similar stance. Zoning was seen as constraint of an urban pluralism of functions that was considered essential for the heterogeneity of a democratic society.

In the 1970s and 1980s, authors like Robert Fishman and Peter Hall declared the attempt to plan a complex society insane and impossible to realize.[77] Fishman rejected the idea that a society could be planned in an industrial manner. To him, Le Corbusier's visions implied a rejection of democracy and favored a society governed by an aristocratic elite of experts. In 1998, James C. Scott described "high-modernism s" abstract idea of a society in which the individual's needs were reduced to simplified materialistic minimum requirements.[78] He interpreted the attempt to provide minimum dwelling standards for everyone as a variant of authoritarian egalitarianism that he associated with socialist dictatorships. From this perspective, towns like Chandigarh have frequently been rejected as realizations of Fordist dwelling machines, born from a technocratic vision of the 1920s. The monumental proliferation of public space and the exaggerated segregation of functional zones constrained individual communication with society. Instead of creating a modern democratic society, modernist towns achieved the exact opposite, namely the elimination of social communication.

Chandigarh in the Twenty-First Century

Chandigarh today is populated by twice as many people as was foreseen by the master plan. A 2002 study by the Massachusetts Institute of Technology projected further intense population growth.[79] Therefore, the study recommends the use of idle spaces to increase housing density. Examples for such spaces are the greenbelts that segregate the V2 and V3 roads from the dwelling sectors. Subsequent to such a densification, it would be profitable to install a public transit system such as a tram line to increase the population's mobility. While the MIT study focuses on parks and green spaces for conversion, a study by the High School for Architecture, Urban Design and Planning of Ahmedabad emphasizes the development potential of undeveloped, so-called "left-over" areas.[80] The authors of both studies recognize that the biggest obstruction for such a strategy is the non-compliant attitude of the city's elites, who live in the less densely popu-

76 Mumford, The CIAM Discourse on Urbanism 1928-1960, 132-134.

77 Fishman, Urban Utopias in the Twentieth Century, 265-277; Hall, Cities of Tomorrow, 203-240.

78 Scott, Seeing Like a State, 115.

79 Agrawal, "Privatizing the Public."

80 Doshi, et al, "In Search of India's Future Cities."

lated northern areas. By using idle spaces, densification could be achieved without having to access their estates. Doing so, however, would neutralize the function of the greenbelts that segregate the dwelling zones from the streets.

The discussion shows how much the Athens Charter prevails to address basic questions of town planning. A carefully defined and controlled population density influences not only the living quality in a city but also the ability to use urban spaces effectively. The necessity to provide public transit systems demonstrates that the charter's emphasis on effective traffic systems has not lost actuality over the last 50 years. The fact that the contemporary focus has changed from individual car traffic to rail-based mass transit systems results from a global paradigm shift due to economic and ecological reasons. However, individual car traffic is on the rise in India, and whatever the future traffic systems in Chandigarh will bring it will constitute a challenge for town planners to connect society to the urban traffic-flow. Here, Chandigarh profits more from its modernist heritage than it has had to suffer from it. Today, the city is proudly said to be the "cleanest and greenest city" of India.[81] Plans for an inner city railway system began in 2008.[82] Uncontrolled growth, social segregation and the funding of public housing projects will remain the biggest challenges to the city, but town planning can only marginally intervene here. These factors depend on India's national economic development, which at this moment seems to be arriving where it aimed to be for the last 50 years.

Conclusion

Chandigarh today is usually considered a failure. In his detailed account of Chandigarh's history, Ravi Kalia points out several planning mistakes such as the absence of a larger regional planning and their effects. Kalia's conclusion bears a remarkable diagnosis: "The underlying assumption of the planners was that the city has a civilizing influence and that urbanization leads to modernization. [...]. Available evidence, however, indicates that cities in South Asian countries do not necessarily have a modernizing influence. [...]. The assumptions of the Chandigarh master plan were based on the consumption patterns of the middle classes of the industrialized countries of the West."[83] Similar inter-

81 Rediff, "Chandigar cleanest of all," accessed on July 29, 2011. http://news.rediff.com/slide-show/2010/may/11/slide-show-1-chandigarh-cleanest-of-all.htm.

82 The Times of India, "Chandigarh Metro Map," Accessed on July 29, 2011. http://articles.timesofindia.indiatimes.com/2008-01-17/chandigarh/27743116_1_chandigarh-metro-map-mohaliand panchkula/

83 Kalia, Chandigarh, 146-147.

pretations of Chandigarh's failure have been formulated by other scholars, too. Charles Correa describes Chandigarh as "just too modern to be a real Indian town,"[84] while Sunil Khilnani claims that "Chandigarh failed to produce a society of secular individuals or a modernist politics."[85] Just like the post-modern critics, Kalia and Correa interpret urban modernism as a utopian concept that should transform societies into something they were not. By emphasizing the distinctly Western origins of modernism and the impossibility of imposing this kind of modernism onto a South Asian society, their allegation of utopianism is reinforced. Interestingly, emphasizing the allegation that the utopian project was imposed on Indian society leads exactly to the opposite of emancipation from Western discourses. Rather, the putative finding of a "natural Indianness" that cannot be combined with "Western modernism", dictated by an authoritarian socialist-like government, aligns itself with an anti-modernist discourse that condemns modern planning as anti-liberal centralism.

In Europe, the modernist avant-garde continuously defended modernism against allegations of embodying an authoritarian utopianism. Its members claimed that society had already changed and that it was the city alone that remained in a state of pre-modern backwardness. To them, reconstructing the city was not a transformation of society but the adaption of living conditions to a new status quo. The emphasis on central authority was rooted in the perception of social crises and demand for concerted action. In Europe, this concerted action successfully transformed urbanity, providing unprecedented achievements in traffic, urban hygiene and living conditions in general. However, Europe in the mid-century was far more industrialized and technologically developed than India. Applying European modernist concepts, which were presented as a functional adaptation to a changed social reality, to early post-colonial India indeed seems to have been based on a one-sided perception of Indian reality.

Nevertheless, Vikramaditya Prakash argues that it would be wrong to understand "Indian" and "modern" as a contradiction. He emphasizes the role of Chandigarh as a true expression of a distinct Indian modernism.[86] As such, its construction was not an isolated utopian act but part of a nation-wide attempt to accelerate the process of industrialization and modernization. Significantly, the national development policy of the Nehru government was discussed in a similar way on the political and economic levels. Yet the city of Chandigarh was never meant to transform society. It was designed to reflect independent India's modernity, and when the accelerated industrialization of India slowed down, so did

84 Correa, "Chandigarh: The View from Benares."

85 Khilnani, The Idea of India, 135.

86 Prakash, Chandigarh's Le Corbusier, 25-28.

the social development of society. This also affected the situation in the city of Chandigarh. Since the town had been built for a modern industrialized society, the setbacks of Indian modernization became eminently visible.

It seems rather cynical to argue that modern town planning failed in Chandigarh because it was a Western idea, incompatible with the realities of Indian society. This would mean to declare poverty an inherent aspect of Indian culture and any attempt to fight it impossible to achieve. The post-modern critique of certain aspects may be justified from an architectural and town planning perspective. However, it does not address the main problem of Chandigarh, which today is a vast area of unofficial settlements, which mostly consist of slums, and an official settlement area characterized by social inequality and segregation. One solution for this problem would be a comprehensive public housing program to lower the demand for living quarters and to ease pressure on the real estate market. Such a program would have to attend to certain minimum standards as they were demanded by CIAM's Athens Charter of 1933. Certainly, urban development discourses of the last 50 years would have to be critically reflected and urban sociological findings would have to be taken into account. Resigning from a comprehensive town planning due to an exaggerated dichotomy between planning and a putative freedom of culture cannot be the solution.

The case of Chandigarh demonstrates the limits of post-modern theoretical approaches, which emerged from the perspective of an economically satisfied post-war society of standardized "suburbias," where the existence-threatening conditions of the industrial age had been replaced by an intellectual discomfort of an overly ordered society. To post-modern historiography, modernism ends with the paradigmatic changes of the 1960s and 1970s. In countries such as India, though, modernism has not lost all of its potential, as a 1980s project in Indore, Ahmadabad, demonstrates.[87] In the township of Aranya, the development agency constructed the infrastructure for a large settlement consisting of several public facilities, traffic lanes, water supply, a sewage drain and jointly used sanitation facilities. Construction of housing at the particular plots was left to the inhabitants. Although monotonous serial housing was abandoned, which gave everyone the chance to realize their own design visions, the concept applies approaches of modern town planning very similar to those formulated in the 1930s. In this case, modern and post-modern approaches supplement each other.

87 Bhatt and Scriver, After the Masters, 98.

III. Resources

The First Stages of India's Nuclear Policy[1]

Hans-Joachim Bieber

Nuclear planning before independence

On the eve of independence, India was still a largely agrarian society. Although there was some industry, mainly textile processing and steel production, and even a relatively extensive rail network, more than 70% of the country's population worked in agriculture; only about 10% were employed in manufacturing and industry, and 14% in the service sector.[2] In 1939, the generating capacity of British India's power plants amounted to just about one million kilowatts; electrification had occurred in only 17% of all communities with more than 5,000 inhabitants. The majority of the population relied on the use of wood and cow dung as the most important source of energy.[3] Future energy needs depended on the speed and extent of India's industrialization. The members of the independence movement had various ideas on what industrialization was to accomplish. According to Mahatma Gandhi, the movement's charismatic leader well into the 1930s, industrialization was to satisfy the Indian population's basic material needs. Gandhi wanted to preserve (or restore) agrarian social structures and maintain traditional trades and crafts. Moreover, he wished to retain cultural values such as simplicity, sense of community, and spirituality. By the time independence came within reach, however, the Indian National Congress, the political organization of the independence movement, was led by Jawaharlal Nehru. And Nehru's vision of India's future was influenced by European models, particularly by the Soviet combination of industrialization, socialism, and a centrally planned economy.[4] Accordingly, he emphasized the need to produce sufficient amounts of energy, above all electric energy.

---

1 A first version of this article appeared as Bieber, "Zur Frühgeschichte der indischen Nuklearpolitik."

2 Dharma, The Cambridge Economic History of India, vol. 2, 535.

3 As early as the early 1950s, India's annual per-capita consumption of electric energy amounted to only 14 kwh, as opposed to 1100 kwh in Great Britain, 2207 in the USA, and 3905 in Canada. See Government of India, Planning Commission: The 1st Five Year Plan, New Delhi 1952, 342.

4 For Gandhi's relationship to Nehru and the differences in their respective ideas see Rothermund, Gandhi und Nehru.

The occurrence of fossil fuels in India was limited and consisted mostly of poor-quality coal in areas far from industrial centers. One way of meeting growing energy demands was the use of hydropower, which became prominent in India in later years. Already prior to independence, however, Nehru was also interested in harnessing a technology that was totally new at the time and had not yet anywhere been tested on a large industrial scale, namely nuclear technology. A young Indian physicist, Homi Bhabha, had drawn Nehru's attention to this possibility. Bhabha belonged to the international elite of young nuclear physicists and had lived in Europe until 1939. Born into a wealthy Parsee family in Bombay in 1909 and a relative of the Tata family, India's most prominent entrepreneurs, Bhabha studied mechanical engineering and physics in Great Britain in the 1920s. While working on his doctorate, he visited nuclear physicists throughout Europe who were considered authorities in their field. After 1936, he rapidly attained fame by presenting his work on cosmic rays and quantum electrodynamics.[5] The outbreak of the war took him by surprise; he was vacationing in India and could not return to Europe. Although he accepted a position funded by the Tata Corporation at the Indian Institute of Science (IIS) in Bangalore, he appeared to be planning to return to Great Britain or to move to the United States. However, when, around 1942 it became clear that India was moving closer towards independence he began to consider the possibility of staying in his native country for good. In this context, he started investigating the question of how India could satisfy its electrical energy needs following the end of colonial rule.

As early as January 1943, Bhabha stated in a lecture he gave in Bombay that the use of nuclear energy for civilian purposes was "definitely in sight [...] within a decade or so." He continued to argue that nuclear energy presented a great opportunity and a vital necessity for independent India.[6] In 1944, he developed a plan for an institute for fundamental research in nuclear physics and cosmic radiation. Like many of his European contemporaries in the natural sciences, Bhabha was convinced that basic research was a prerequisite to achieve

---

5 Treatments of Bhabha's scientific research in the 1930s can be found in Penney, "Homi Jehangir Bhaba", 39; Kragh, Dirac, 195; Singh, Some Eminent Indian Scientists, 7; Brown et al, 20th Century Physics, 392; Cassidy, Werner Heisenberg, 495. Bhabha's contributions were so outstanding that, in 1941, he became a Fellow of the Royal Society (FRS) and was later nominated for the Nobel Prize: Anderson, Building Scientific Institutions in India, 92.

6 Quoted in Illustrated Weekly of India, August 19, 1945. Regarding Bhabha's predictions, see the interview in Times of India, August 11, 1945; also Government of India, Department of Atomic Energy: Ten Years of Atomic Energy in India 1954-64, 4.

scientific excellence in applied research.[7] In June 1945, the management of the Tata Company decided to fund the establishment of an institute for fundamental research in physics and mathematics and to name Bhabha as director. Given an annual budget of Rs 80,000 (at the time roughly equivalent to $17,000), the Tata Institute for Fundamental Research (TIFR) had to begin its work on a rather modest level. Initially, it was affiliated with the Indian Institute of Science (IIS) in Bangalore.[8]

A few weeks later, the United States dropped atomic bombs on Hiroshima and Nagasaki. India's political and intellectual elite was shocked. Bhabha, however, showed professional respect and spoke of the "beginning of a new epoch." By this he did not mean a new age of human self-destruction but one of "nuclear energy."[9] It was most probably due to his influence that a weekend supplement of the *Times of India*, India's most respected daily newspaper, ten days after the bombings hailed the availability of a limitless and nearly cost-free source of energy. Mankind would henceforth be able to live "in a Utopia like the dreams of Edward Bellamy," a society in which labor would be limited to a few hours per day and a few years of adulthood. The newspaper also pointed to new possibilities in the battle against cancer and bone marrow disease, easing house work, the construction of an "electronic express train" that would reduce travel time between Bombay and Calcutta to one hour, and the construction of space stations and spacecraft able to reach Mars and Venus.[10]

A short time later, the Indian independence movement appeared to have made a policy decision in favor of promoting nuclear research. During his time in prison (1942 to 1945), Nehru had Bhabha provide him with literature on new scientific developments such as the theory of relativity and quantum theory. In early 1947, Nehru stated that the ability to harness nuclear power provided mankind with vast amounts of energy, which would lead to far-reaching social changes. Probably mirroring Bhabha's interests and perhaps inspired by him, Nehru concluded that India could not afford to neglect this new opportunity "because it might be used for war." He emphasized: "In India we want to de-

---

7 Bhabhas remarks on his intentions regarding the founding of the TIFR, made on the occasion of the opening of new buildings of the institute in 1962 and quoted by Bhabha's successor as director of the institute, in: Menon, Scientific Research in the Developing Nations, 103.

8 On the establishment of the TIFR see Menon, Homi J. Bhabha, 428; Ramanna, Perspectives of India's Nuclear Policy.

9 Bhabha in an interview with the Times of India, Aug. 11, 1945. For the reaction of the Indian elite on the dropping of the atomic bombs see the editorial in Times of India, August 9, 1945.

10 "Autolycus: As I See It." Illustrated Weekly of India, August 19, 1945, 27.

velop it [nuclear technology] and we will develop it to the fullest, [...] in cooperation with the rest of the world and for peaceful purposes."[11]

Indian scientists and politicians used the period between the end of the war and independence to prepare for India's nuclear future. In December 1945, the TIFR moved to Bombay, Bhabha's home town, and began to expand, with the support of the Tata trust and the local government. Its staff increased by roughly 30% annually.[12] In January 1946, the National Institute of Sciences appointed a committee on nuclear research to investigate possibilities for the civilian use of nuclear power and to help establish India's representation in the United Nations Atomic Energy Commission. Meeting at the TIFR in Bombay, the committee considered creating a government monopoly on thorium and other fissionable minerals.[13] Research conducted by the Manhattan Project and made public by the United States after the war had demonstrated that a uranium isotope (U-223) could be produced by splitting thorium with high-velocity neutrons.[14] In India, this discovery was considered to be "the most important revelation since the atomic bomb itself."[15] Owing to extensive deposits of monazite sand in southern India, the country ranked second only to Brazil in possessing the world's largest occurrence of thorium oxide, thus giving thorium the reputation of being one of India's most important commodities. In January 1947, the Indian Science Congress passed a resolution according to which all fissionable minerals were to be placed under government ownership and to be mined solely under government supervision, off limits to foreigners. Soon thereafter, Nehru paved the way for the necessary legislation.[16] At the same time, Indian physicists used contacts es-

---

11 "Nehru's speech on the occasion of the opening of the Indian Science Congress in Delhi." Times of India, January 4, 1947. On Nehru's access to scientific literature with the aid of Bhabha during the former's imprisonment, Singh, Jawaharlal Nehru on Science and Society, XVIII.

12 "Bhabha's speech on the occasion of the opening of new TIFR facilities in February of 1962." Times of India, January 16, 1962.

13 See Times of India, April 29, 1947; Anderson, Building Scientific Institutions in India, 39. In addition to Bhabha, the committee consisted of the physicist Meghnad Saha, professor at the University of Calcutta and FRS since 1927; of the chemist Shanti Swarup Bhatnagar, FRS, Secretary General of the Council of Scientific and Industrial Research (CSIR), and India's most influential manager of scientific research; and of K.S. Krishnan, head of the physics department at Allahabad University and designated director of the National Physical Laboratory in Delhi.

14 Smyth, "Atomic Energy for Military Purposes," 7, 27, 38.

15 Times of India, March 29, 1945.

16 Cf. his speech to the National Mineral Policy Conference in New Delhi on January 13, 1947, printed in: Nehru, Selected Works, Second Series, I, 430, and his statement of February 27, 1947, ibid., II, 604 ff.

tablished prior to the war and the country's ties to the British Empire to revive international scientific cooperation.[17] In this context, famous scientists from abroad were invited to India, initially to the Indian Science Congress in January 1947.[18]

India's nuclear program 1947-64

After gaining independence, the new Indian nation invested remarkable efforts and costs to achieve its nuclear goals. As early as December 1947, a Board of Atomic Research was appointed under Bhabha's direction. Nehru, who not only was prime minister and foreign secretary in India's first government but was responsible for science and research as well, assured Bhabha that he would do his best to provide him with "all the necessary facilities."[19] The Indian government urged the Durbar of Travancore, which was not yet part of the Indian federation, to terminate its 1946 agreement with Great Britain on the export of monazite sand. New Delhi then signed an agreement with the Durbar to ensure government control over this seemingly promising mineral.[20] In the summer of 1948, the Indian parliament passed the Atomic Energy Act, granting the government general authority over all activities aimed at utilizing nuclear energy for peaceful means.[21] To execute this act, an Atomic Energy Commission (AEC) was appointed. It replaced the Board of Atomic Research. Its members, however, were largely the same; again, Bhabha became director. The AEC enjoyed extensive autonomy, enabling Bhabha to steer the development of nuclear research according to his own ideas.[22] In 1949, the TIFR moved to a new facility six times

---

17 See Times of India, June 12 and September 10, 1946; Richards, Sir Shanti Swarup Bhatnagar, 186; Hill, "The Ethical Dilemma of Science," 313.

18 10 Scientists from Great Britain participated, including the physicists Patrick Blackett and Charles Darwin, director of the British National Physical Laboratory. Moreover, there were five participants from the United States, four from Canada, three from the Soviet Union, and one each from France and China; see Times of India, January 7, 1947; Richards, Sir Shanti Swarup Bhatnagar, 229 f.; Nehru, Selected Works, Second Series, I, 377, note 4.

19 Nehru to Bhabha, December 2, 1947, in Nehru, Selected Works, Second Series, IV, 554; cf. also Times of India, December 1, 1947 and June 8, 1948.

20 See Nehru to Bhatnagar, January 14, 1948, in Nehru, Selected Works, Second Series, V, 353; On the 1946 agreement between Travancore and Great Britain, Times of India, March 29, 1946.

21 For a discussion of the accompanying debates, see Abraham, The Making of the Indian Atomic Bomb, 48.

22 On the founding of the AEC, see Abraham, The Making of the Indian Atomic Bomb, 60. Initially, the AEC consisted of only Bhabha, Bhatnagar, and Krishnan.

larger than the old one. An additional institute for research in nuclear physics was opened in Calcutta. Departments of nuclear physics were established at the universities of Delhi, Ahmedabad, Aligarh, and at the IIS in Bangalore. After Travancore joined the Indian Union, the federal government and the provincial government of Travancore-Cochin founded a joint venture leading to the establishment, in 1951, of a plant in southern India for processing of monazite sand; production began in August 1952.[23] The AEC built facilities for using monazite residue and copper waste to obtain thorium and uranium.[24] In 1954, Nehru laid the corner stone for the new, highly modern facilities at the TIFR. The creation of new research teams in chemistry, metallurgy, and electrical engineering helped make the institute the center of nuclear research in India.[25] In the summer of 1954, a government department dedicated solely to nuclear technology, the Department of Atomic Energy (DAE), was established and given responsibility for the AEC. Though formally under the directorship of the prime minister, the department was *de facto* led by an undersecretary; again, the post was given to Bhabha, who remained head of the AEC and director of the TIFR. As undersecretary, he had direct access to the prime minister and hence excellent chances of implementing his plans.[26] In November 1954, Nehru hosted a two-day conference in Delhi to approve a three-stage plan for the further development of harnessing nuclear energy. The first stage called for the construction of reactors fueled by natural uranium to produce energy and plutonium. The second stage was supposed to see the building of reactors to obtain uranium-233 from thorium with the help of plutonium. In the third stage, breeders fueled by thorium and uranium-233 were to be constructed. The long-term objective was the creation of a complete nuclear complex to apply nuclear technology to as many civilian uses as possible. The plan was tailored to India's specific needs: Initially it focused on the use of natural uranium, which was available in many countries and even in small amounts in India itself. Eventually, though, the aim was to transform natural uranium into plutonium and to change thorium into uranium-233, which would render the construction of uranium-enrichment plants or the impor-

---

23 See Nehru's remarks made in his speech on the occasion of the opening of the plant in December of 1952 Nehru, Selected Works, Second Series, XX, 107.

24 See The Journal of Commerce, Ten Years of Atomic Energy, 8.

25 See Times of India, January 2, 1954; Anderson, Building Scientific Institutions in India, 36-96; Nehru's speech on this occasion in Nehru, Selected Works, Second Series, XXIV, 198.

26 On the establishment of the DEA and its relationship to the AEC, see Chowdhry, Change-in-Organizations, 120; Singh, Management of Scientific Research, 143; Anderson, Building Scientific Institutions in India, 39-66; Ramanna, Perspectives of India's Nuclear Policy, 8; Sharma, India's Nuclear Estate, 24.

tation of enriched uranium unnecessary and thereby keep India independent from foreign countries. What was necessary was the construction of reprocessing plants, and that meant a closed fuel cycle. The plan mirrored remarkable self-confidence. At the time the transformation of thorium into uranium-233 was still very new. There was little to no expertise available regarding the use of thorium as a nuclear fuel, breeder technology and reprocessing. Whether it would be possible to realize the ambitious plan and how much effort would be required was totally unknown.[27]

Shortly after the 1954 conference, construction of the Atomic Energy Establishment (AEE) began. Located on Trombay Island, in close proximity to Bombay and the TIFR, this center was devoted to research in all areas of nuclear technology, ranging from the building and operation of reactors to the production of fuel rods, nuclear fuel, and heavy water. The directorship was given to Bhabha, who continued to serve in his other capacities as well. In August 1956, India's first research reactor – the first reactor in Asia to be built outside of the Soviet Union – became critical.[28] The reactor was allegedly designed and, for the most part, built in India; but in fact most of the construction plans as well as vital components originated in Great Britain.[29] In the same year, India acquired a second research reactor from Canada, equipped with natural uranium and moderated by heavy water.[30] By early 1957, construction of the AEE had progressed so far that Nehru could officially open the center.[31] The building of a plant for fuel rods began in the same year, and in 1958 a third research reactor was erected.[32] In February 1959, India announced that it had produced the first pure uranium metal; in June 1960, the production of the first fuel element (again the first Asian one not manufactured in the Soviet Union) was made public.[33] In July

---

27 The speeches of Bhabha and Nehru are printed in Times of India, November 27, 1954. Those of Nehru, Selected Works, Second Series, XXVII, 416. On this conference, also see "Ten Years of Atomic Energy", 9. Sharma, India's Nuclear Estate, 19; Agarwal, India's Nuclear Development Plans and Policies, 22; Abraham, The Making of the Indian Atomic Bomb, 75.

28 See Times of India, July 5, 1957 and October 30, 1960.

29 See Abraham, The Making of the Indian Atomic Bomb, 82.

30 Ramanna, Development of Nuclear Energy in India 1947-1973, in Nanda, Science and Technology, 103.

31 See Times of India, January 20, 1957; Nehru's opening speech in Singh, Management of Scientific Research, 141. On the development and organization of the AEE see Chowdhry, Change-in-Organizations, 122; Sharma, India's Nuclear Estate, 122.

32 See Bulletin of the Indian Embassy in Bonn, June 1957; The Journal of Commerce, "Ten Years of Atomic Energy," 16, 23, 26.

33 See Times of India, February 10, 1959; The Journal of Commerce, Ten Years of Atomic Energy, 18.

1960, the second research reactor became critical, the third in 1961. In the same year construction of a reprocessing plant began. Soon thereafter, a mine to extract uranium ore was opened in Bihar and a plant to produce heavy water was put into operation in Punjab.[34] In 1965, India exported heavy water to Belgium, thereby becoming the first country other than the United States to supply this technologically sophisticated product to Western Europe.[35] In the same year, the reprocessing plant was opened – at a time when such plants were in operation in only four other countries (France, Great Britain, the Soviet Union, and the United States).[36]

By the late 1950s, the use of nuclear power plants to generate electric energy seemed to have become a definite possibility for the near future. Bhabha in early 1957 announced that, in the course of India's Second Five-Year Plan, the country would erect its first reactors for generating electricity and producing plutonium to supply the subsequent generation of reactors. Furthermore, he stated that the commercial use of thorium-powered breeders would be possible by the mid-1960s.[37] In the fall of 1958, the AEC estimated that first-generation nuclear reactors would reach a capacity of 1,000 MW in 1965; that second-generation reactors, powered by thorium and plutonium, would achieve an additional level of 250 to 330 MW in 1967; and that, starting in 1969, another 230 MW would be attained annually by breeders. Breeder capacity was projected to amount to 1,600 MW by 1974 and 12,000 MW by 1984.[38]

At the end of 1958, the Indian government decided to build the first nuclear reactor and to consider the construction of two or three additional plants by

---

34 See Times of India, January 1, 1954, March 23, 1957 and June 7, 1957; The Journal of Commerce, Ten Years of Atomic Energy, 20.

35 See Government of India, Department of Atomic Energy: Annual Report 1965/66, 3, 59.

36 See Bhabha's remarks in a radio interview of August 1964, in Jain, Nuclear India, 147; and his remarks on the occasion of the opening of the plant, in Times of India, January 23, 1965.

37 See his comments made at the opening of the AEE in January of 1957 Times of India, January 21, 1957; also Bhabha, On the Economics of Atomic Power Development in India and the Indian Atomic Energy Program, in Science and Culture 23/4, 222; the report of his lecture at the University of Mysore in February of 1958, in The Mining Journal, Feb. 28, 1958.

38 See Bhabha and Prasad, A Study of the Contribution of Atomic Energy to a Power Programme in India, in Proceedings of the 2nd United Nations International Conference on the Peaceful Uses of Atomic Energy, 95; Sharma, India's Nuclear Estate, 48.

1964.[39] In 1960, Tarapur, located on India's western coast and roughly 60 miles north of Bombay, was selected as the site of the first reactor. In 1962, a site in Rajasthan was selected for the second reactor, and in 1964, Kalpakkam near Madras in southern India was designated to become the site for the third reactor. India's first nuclear power plant, a light-water reactor powered by enriched uranium, was purchased in the United States. The second plant, which contained two reactors with a capacity of 200 MW each, fueled by natural uranium and using heavy water, was purchased in Canada.[40] The third plant was constructed in India itself. In 1964, Bhabha predicted that by the end of the twentieth century most of India's demand for electricity would be met by nuclear-generated power and that any additional subsequent demand would be satisfied exclusively by nuclear energy. He believed that his country's atomic energy program could be said "to have reached maturity" and that the goal of self-sufficiency had been achieved. India, Bhabha maintained, could "look forward to the period ahead as a developed and mature atomic power, but one whose efforts are solely directed toward using atomic energy for peaceful purposes."[41] In fact, India remained largely dependent on foreign support, especially in the area of reprocessing and the production of heavy water. Nevertheless, the country's achievements were not only unique for a so-called Third World nation but also surpassed the state of nuclear technology in many industrialized countries.[42]

---

39 See Times of India, November 28, 1958; the announcement of India's president to both houses of the Indian Parliament on Feb. 9, 1959, Lok Sabha Debates (LSD), 2nd series, vol. 25, column 24.

40 On the selection of locations, see Times of India, August 17, 1962; DAE, Annual Report 1965/66, 3; David Hart: Nuclear Power in India, London 1983, 38. – India's decision to choose as its first nuclear power plant one that did not conform to the government's envisaged action plan and the country's ensuing dependence on enriched uranium from abroad can probably be explained by the fact that the USA offered favorable terms of sale and that the US-built reactor seemed capable of providing electrical power swiftly. This was in Bhabha's interests as there was a growing discrepancy between his forecasts and the accompanying funding for nuclear development on the one hand and the related practical benefits on the other. Concerns thus began to be voiced about the potential success of India's nuclear program. See Pathak "Nuclear Policy of India," 51; Bothwell, "Nucleus: The History of Atomic Energy of Canada Limited," 350; Abraham, The Making of the Indian Atomic Bomb, 91; Perkovich, India's Nuclear Bomb, 56, 78, 519.

41 Bhabha in a radio interview in August of 1964, cited in Jain, Nuclear India, vol. 2, 150.

42 See Perkovich, India's Nuclear Bomb, 64.; Mullenbach, Civilian Nuclear Power, 250; Hart, Nuclear Power in India, 32.

Motives for India's early nuclear program

One motive for India's early and energetic embracing of nuclear technology was the conviction, expressed repeatedly by Bhabha and Nehru, that nuclear fission had started a revolution "equally big or bigger" than the industrial revolution of the nineteenth century, which was going to rapidly change the world.[43] Nehru saw India's failure to be part of the industrial revolution as one of the main reasons why India had become a "slave country."[44] If India were to miss out on the revolution in nuclear technology as well, he added, the country would lose its last chance to enjoy a modern future. He believed that nuclear technology would enable India to circumvent the reliance on coal, and that this would permit the country to leap from the "age of cow dung" directly into the modern age, perhaps even to the forefront of technological advancement.[45] India's expectations focused above all on the possibility of using nuclear energy to produce energy, which according to Nehru symbolized "almost any kind of progress."[46] Added to this was the belief that nuclear energy would be relatively cheap. Bhabha never ceased to claim that the costs for building and operating nuclear power plants in regions far removed from coal deposits were no longer (or would soon no longer be) higher than those needed for conventional power plants.[47] The Indian government also expected to use nuclear energy to power trains and ships and to effect far-reaching changes in pharmaceutics, medicine, food production, and food preservation. At a later stage, so-called peaceful nuclear explosions were to be conducted to construct ports and transportation routes as well as to exploit ore, oil, and natural gas deposits.[48] All of these expectations conformed to those existing in industrialized nations; they were underscored at the 1955 United Nations Conference in Geneva on the peaceful uses of nuclear energy.

The faster nuclear technology developed in industrialized countries the stronger the conviction became in India that such progress was inevitable; under these conditions, the question whether nuclear energy was desirable or not be-

---

43 Nehru in a speech on the occasion of laying the cornerstone for the new TIFR buildings on Jan. 1, 1954, Nehru, Selected Works, Second Series, XXIV, 199.

44 See Nehru's speech on the introduction of the Atomic Energy Act at the constitutional convention in July of 1948, in Singh, 64.

45 Nehru in a speech to researchers, students, and high-ranking civil servants in Calcutta, quoted in Auszüge aus der Weltpresse, November 4, 1955.

46 Nehru's speech at the inauguration of the Canadian research reactor on January 16, 1961. Quoted in Times of India, January 17, 1961.

47 See his speech on the occasion of the 50th anniversary of the Indian Institute of Science in Bangalore on February 5, 1959, Times of India, February 6, 1959.

48 The official government documents from the 1950s, printed passim in Jain 1974, Nuclear India, vol. 2.

came obsolete. As Nehru claimed in 1957, India had the choice to either move forward with nuclear technology or to fail and allow other nations to progress.[49] India's commitment to nuclear technology was supported by the assumption of many industrialized countries that the modernization of so-called underdeveloped nations could be accelerated with the help of nuclear energy; for example, portable reactors would allow obtaining water from extreme depths, thereby making arid or desert regions arable.[50] For this reason, Indian politicians considered the importance of nuclear energy for underdeveloped countries greater than for industrialized nations, which had alternative energy sources at their disposal.[51] Accordingly, India supported newly independent African and Southeast Asian countries interested in obtaining nuclear technology.[52]

The hopes, however, which India placed in the use and potential benefit of nuclear technology appeared to be higher than those of many of the industrialized nations. India was attempting to conduct cutting-edge research at a time when it had neither the basic facilities nor the scientists and technicians to do so. By the mid-1950s, India was the lead advocate of breeder/plutonium technology and the use of thorium as a nuclear fuel. In the field of nuclear fusion it had much stronger expectations than the industrialized nations[53] and hardly any other country placed as much importance on attaining self-reliance or self-sufficiency

---

49 See his speech on the occasion of the opening of the AEE, Times of India, January 21, 1957.

50 See for example the paper of the UN-Department of Economic and Social Affairs for the 1955 Geneva Conference on the Peaceful Uses of Atomic Energy in Jain, Nuclear India, vol. 2, 23; United Nations Economic Applications of Atomic Energy, Power Generation and Industrial and Agricultural Uses, 13.

51 See Nehru's letter to Bhatnagar of Mar. 20, 1952, in Nehru, Selected Works, Second Series, XVII, 299; his speech to the Indian parliament of May 10, 1954, ibid. Even at the Bandung conference of April 1955, one of the most important meetings of Asian and African heads of state in the 1950s, emphasis was placed on the "particular significance of the development of nuclear energy for peaceful purposes for the Asian-African countries," see the final communiqué in Appadorai, Select Documents on India's Foreign Policy and Relations: 1947-1972, 545.

52 See Times of India, July 25, 1956 and April 27, 1956.

53 In his speech at the opening of the 1955 Geneva United Nations Conference on the Peaceful Uses of Atomic Energy Bhabha predicted that controlled nuclear fusion and its use for power production would be possible within two decades; see Proceedings of the International Conference on the Peaceful Uses of Atomic Energy, 35. In 1960, anticipation was expressed in the Indian parliament that India's scientists would be the first to succeed in harnessing nuclear fusion for peaceful uses and that this would occur soon, see LSD, 2nd ser., vol. 44, column 2003.

as India.[54] All of this indicates that India's early engagement in nuclear technology was motivated by factors other than economic ones. Indeed, these factors become obvious when we examine India's contemporary discourse.

In the post-1947 years, Indians repeatedly expressed the need to demonstrate that their country was no less capable of scientific and technological achievement than industrialized countries. This need was rooted in the country's defining experience of having been the recurring object of cultural disdain during colonial rule. India's educated classes probably felt more victimized by such disrespect than did members of other social levels, with whom the British had had little or no contact. Many years after independence, one of the most prominent authors of Indian origin still referred to India as a "wounded nation."[55] Independent achievements in what was believed to be the most promising future technology were supposed to rehabilitate Indian civilization and prove to the former colonial power or to the West in general that the disdain directed towards India had been unjustified. For example, in the 1940s and 1950s Indians referred to Asia as the "mother of culture" and to India's intellectual tradition as having been an early form of modern scientific thought.[56] In physics, the atomistic theories of ancient Indian thought were repeatedly pointed out. India's long-time chief delegate to the United Nations, and later Secretary for Defense, Krishna Menon, explained: "The notion that there was no difference between mass and energy [...] was perhaps revolutionary to the Western world, [...] not so to the Oriental mind. A child in India would speak of matter and energy as the same."[57] At the same time, India's involvement in nuclear technology was to demonstrate at home and abroad the ability of the newly independent state to modernize and to remove the intellectual shackles of "communalism, provincial-

---

54 See Nehru's speech given at the opening of the Plant for Rare Earths in December of 1952, in Nehru, Selected Works, Second Series, XX, 110. His speech to the Indian parliament on March 25, 1954, ibid. and his remarks, at the same forum, of May 30, 1956 and of April 10, 1958. Also Bhabha's speech given at the inauguration of the AEE in January 1957: A printed version was distributed by the press office of the Indian government and can be found in the Political Archives of the German Foreign Office.

55 Naipaul, "India: A Wounded Nation." Also see Majumdar, History of the Freedom Movement in India, 293; Rothermund, Indische Geschichte in Grundzügen, 92; Eliade, Indisches Tagebuch, 351.

56 The quotation is from Nehru's speech given at the All Indian Students' Congress in Delhi on December 31, 1946, Nehru, Selected Works, Second Series, I, 390.

57 Quoted in Jain, Nuclear India, vol. 2, 5. Nehru himself often spoke of a link between nuclear physics and ancient Asian – in this case, Buddhist – concepts of the characteristics of matter and of the relation between matter and mind, see Bonn, Die indische Herausforderung, 202; Abraham, The Making of the Indian Atomic Bomb, 27.

ism, castism and linguism."[58] To use the terminology of the Western Enlightenment, India wanted to emerge from its self-incurred immaturity.

The country's participation in nuclear technology was also an expression of its desire to develop its own models for the future – models drawing on Indian traditions but aiming at rapid social and technological modernization. This was to be done by avoiding the destructive aspects such innovation had brought about in industrialized nations, and by evading ideological interference. Nehru once summarized his ideal as a "kind of marriage of ancient Indian philosophy and modern scientific knowledge," of ancient Indian and modern Western thought.[59] In his speech at the inauguration ceremony at the AEE in 1957, he referred to the island of Elephanta, located next to Trombay, the site of the AEE. Elephanta is home to caves with 1,300-year-old Hindu sanctuaries that continue to be the destination of pilgrimages. For Nehru, Elephanta represented "something of lasting value and significance," while Trombay stood for modern technology. Mankind, he thus concluded, was as incapable of living in isolation on an island such as Elephanta as it was of relying solely on nuclear reactors. What was needed, he said, was a "combination of Elephanta and the Swimming Pool Reactor, a proper balance in life."[60]

Motives such as these gave India's early involvement in nuclear technology high symbolic value. They demonstrated the orientation of the newly independent country towards the future and expressed India's cultural, spiritual, and political renaissance. They revealed India's new self-awareness, its transcendence of established ways of thinking as well as its desire and ability to modernize. They demonstrated the country's pride in its cultural traditions and its determination to end the humiliation and domination on the part of foreign powers once and for all. They also helped India to secure its newly won political independence economically and technologically and to restore its pre-colonial cultural and political parity with the West. The farther the newly independent nation advanced in constructing and expanding its nuclear research facilities, the more these facilities came to be symbols and catalysts of national pride.[61]

The cultural aspects behind India's early involvement in nuclear technology can serve to explain some political and technological particularities of the coun-

58 Nehru, "Opening speech to the Indian Parliamentary and Scientific Committee 1961," Times of India, August 28, 1961.

59 Nehru, "Speech on the 100th birthday of the Bengali physicist and botanist J. C. Bose," Times of India, December 1, 1958.

60 Quoted in Times of India, January 21, 1957.

61 See the remarks of representatives Sharma, Mukerjee, and Rao during the parliamentary debate on the DAE on August 18, 1960 and of representatives Sharma, Dwivedy, Kalva, and Mathur during the debate on August 19, 1961.

try's nuclear program, among them the desire to attain self-reliance. On the technological level, this desire was revealed in the key decision first to build reactors fueled by natural uranium and then to proceed as quickly as possible to the construction of breeders using thorium. Politically, the goal to become self-reliant was expressed in the country's refusal to allow foreign powers to influence or obstruct its development of nuclear technology. Owing to India's experience during colonial rule, Indian politicians and researchers feared that the industrialized powers might attempt to monopolize the use of nuclear energy and impede or even prevent the use of such energy in underdeveloped nations in order to keep them economically and politically dependent.[62] Consequently, India refused to grant supplying countries supervision and regulation rights on reactors, nuclear fuel, and other related materials delivered to India as long as those rights were not mutual.[63] In addition, India distrusted suggestions to have the international exchange of fissionable materials and nuclear technology controlled by an international organization with the right to supervise the acquisition of nuclear fuel and technology but would waive that right when it came to overseeing the respective activities of exporting countries. For India, an unequal division into "atomic haves" and "atomic have nots" was nothing more than "atomic colonialism." No nation, India's leaders maintained, was willing to accept "a colonial position" any longer.[64] In this respect, India considered itself an advocate of the other former colonies and of those countries which, while not yet independent and/or involved in nuclear technology, might want to use nuclear technology in the future.[65]

---

62 Nehru, Speech of July 24, 1957, Times of India, July 25, 1957; Nehru's letter of October 26, 1955 to the Chief Ministers of the Indian Federal States, in Nehru, Letters to Chief Ministers 1947-64, vol. 4, 293.

63 During the negotiations with Canada on the delivery of a research reactor, Bhabha agreed to a commitment on the part of India to utilize the reactor for peaceful uses only but limited Canadian inspection rights to the first supply of nuclear fuel delivered from Canada. See Bothwell 1988, 350; Abraham, The Making of the Indian Atomic Bomb, 120. In the 1963 agreement with the USA on the delivery of the first Indian nuclear power plant, India initially allowed inspections to be conducted by joint US-Indian teams only in order to ensure the principle of equality. Not until 1967 did India recognize the IAEA as the supervisory body for both plants; in 1971, the IAEA assumed responsibility for the safeguards. One of the main reasons why India constructed its third nuclear power plant itself (a replica of the plant delivered by Canada) was that the country was able to avoid having to bind itself to external supervision; see Fischer, History of the International Atomic Energy Agency, 176.

64 Nehru, Speech to the Indian parliament on July 24, 1957, Bulletin of the Indian Embassy in Bonn.

65 See Bhabha's statement at a conference on the IAEA charter in Sept. of 1956.

Political characteristics of the early Indian nuclear program

In addition to cultural factors, India's early nuclear energy program had a special political characteristic, one which may seem surprising from today's perspective: the exclusive focus on peaceful uses of nuclear energy. Nehru repeatedly assured "that whatever might happen, whatever the circumstances, we shall never use this atomic energy for evil purposes."[66] However, India never denied its technological potential for developing nuclear weapons. At the end of 1959, Bhabha informed the Indian parliament of the country's ability to produce nuclear weapons without foreign assistance. At the beginning of 1961, he estimated that it would take about two years for this to occur.[67] The government was then all the more emphatic in expressing its objective to develop its nuclear program for peaceful uses only.[68] Until the early 1960s, this objective was shared by all parties of the Indian parliament.[69]

On an international level, India supported a general renunciation of and a ban on nuclear weapons. It spoke out in favor of non-violent solutions to conflicts between nations, or, as Nehru once remarked, of taking "the Gandhian path, of unity, love and cooperation" rather than "the path of violence, as symbolized by the atom bomb."[70] A renunciation of the use of nuclear weapons by the major powers, however, failed to come about. The superpowers increased the potential effect of nuclear weapons by developing the H-bomb, which – as was demonstrated repeatedly in test explosions – had a destructive capacity exponentially surpassing that of the atomic bombs dropped on Japan. India responded by insisting that the use of these weapons, too, be renounced and banned. As a first step toward that goal, New Delhi advocated an end to nuclear arms testing and to the nuclear arms race; it also called for a prohibition on the transfer of nuclear arms to countries not yet in possession of such weapons.[71] In 1956, Indian physicists published an accusatory report on the effects of radioac-

66 Nehru at the inauguration of the AEE in early 1957, cited in Singh, 100; Beaton and Maddox: The Spread of Nuclear Weapons, 143; Agarwal, India's Nuclear Development Plans and Policies, 20.

67 See Times of India, December 16, 1959; Bhabha, Press conference in New Delhi in early February of 1961, Times of India, February 3, 1961.

68 Menon, Speech January 31, 1958, Times of India, February 1, 1958; India's representative to UN, Statement of April 5, 1962, Times of India, April 6, 1962.

69 See, for example, the parliamentary debates of August 10, 1960 on the DAE and of August 19, 1961.

70 Nehru, Selected Works, Second Series, XIII, 22.

71 For pertinent statements by Nehru see Gopal, Jawaharlal Nehru: An Anthology, 394. On India's position on nuclear armament and disarmament in the 1950s and early 60s, see Wittner, One World or None, 307.

tive fallout on the atmosphere, on food and water, and on the life of future generations. Nehru wrote the foreword, and the Indian government distributed the report worldwide.[72] The views expressed were again shared by all political parties in India and by those sectors of the press involved in forming the opinions of the country's elite.[73]

As united as Indians were in opposing the use of nuclear weapons, security considerations did play a role (at least behind the scenes) in shaping India's early nuclear policies. Bhabha repeatedly stated in personal conversations that he wished to keep a "military option" open.[74] At times, Nehru, too, did not categorically reject the option of producing nuclear weapons in India. He sometimes referred to India's determination not to lag behind other nations in the possible use of nuclear energy for military purposes.[75] Nevertheless, in the 1950s and early 1960s, such remarks received little attention. Neither published documents of the US Department of State nor reports from the German Federal Republic's diplomatic representatives assigned to India expressed the belief that India's nuclear program included a policy of using nuclear power for military aims. India, after all, did not have the necessary technology needed to build nuclear weapons, let alone the required deployment systems. Its army was not known to be involved in nuclear planning, and since neither China nor Pakistan possessed nuclear arms, there was no need to feel threatened. In addition, any indication by India to develop its own nuclear weapons would have been inconsistent with Nehru's policy of peace and his desire to pursue alternatives to the military policies of the superpowers. As the German Federal Republic's ambassador to India stated in 1964, such an indication would have dealt a "death blow" to the credibility of Indian foreign policy, particularly toward the Third World countries.[76]

That is why India's nuclear program was seen and supported internationally as being part of a policy of civilian modernization. After the United States abandoned its initial reservations vis-à-vis the export of civilian nuclear technology in 1953 by establishing its Atoms for Peace program, British, Australian, and French physicists began to advise India in the planning of the Atomic Energy

72 Nuclear Explosions and Their Effects, Delhi 1956.

73 See the resolution of May 22, 1957 by the lower house of India's parliament on the testing of nuclear weapons, in Appadorai 1985, 558; September 1957 resolution by representatives of all parties of the lower house for the UN General Assembly, Times of India, September 17, 1957.

74 See Blackett's interview in Bhatia, India's Nuclear Bomb, 114; Perkovich, India's Nuclear Bomb, 33, 58.

75 See Zinkin, Challenges in India, 19; Smith, India's Ad Hoc Arsenal, 179.

76 Report of November 13, 1964 by the German Federal Republic's ambassador in New Delhi.

Establishment.[77] Canada supplied uranium and in 1956 delivered a research reactor with the unusually high capacity of 40 MW. The procurement agreement enabled several hundred Indian scientists and engineers to go to Canada to receive training, which Canada paid for.[78] Great Britain supplied fuel elements. The United States delivered heavy water, supplied the AEE with literature, and participated in the training of Indian nuclear experts.[79] Norway, Sweden, Yugoslavia, and Israel cooperated with India as well. Later, the Federal Republic of Germany participated and, to a very limited extent, the Soviet Union. Physicists from abroad came to India in increasing numbers to attend the annual Indian Science Congress, the inauguration of research institutes, and scientific conferences.[80] They also came to conduct research, specifically at TIFR, which already by the 1950s was among the world's leading institutes in research on cosmic radiation, as international scientists emphasized repeatedly.[81] Indian universities and research institutions established ties to famous international scientists by conferring academic honors. Niels Bohr, for example, was given an honorary doctorate at the University of Bombay in 1960; John Cockcroft was made an honorary member of TIFR in 1964.[82]

The cultural factors motivating India's nuclear program produced certain peculiarities of its implementation, too. These, however, must be seen in connection with the country's general conditions, such as huge economic and social problems, the limited scope of formal education among the great majority of its

---

77 On the Atoms for Peace program see Hewlett and Holl, Atoms for Peace and War, 9; Pilat, Atoms for Peace: A Future after 50 years?; On the help of foreign scientists in the planning of the AEE see J. Singh 1973, 148; Sharma, India's Nuclear Estate, 22.

78 On Canadian-Indian cooperation in nuclear programs, see Bhabha, The Canada-India Reactor: An Exercise in International Cooperation; Bothwell 1988, 350; Abraham, The Making of the Indian Atomic Bomb, 89; Perkovich, India's Nuclear Bomb, 27.

79 See Times of India, March 20, 1955, February 16, 1956 and August 15, 1959; Sharma, India's Nuclear Estate, 22; Perkovich, India's Nuclear Bomb, 30.

80 The inauguration of the AEE in January 1957 was attended by Cockcroft and Sir Edward Plowden, Head of the British atomic energy agency; the Nobel Prize recipient Hideki Yukawa, at the time the most famous Japanese nuclear physicist; Nesmeyanov, President of the Soviet Academy of Sciences. Even China and Pakistan sent high-ranking representatives as those two countries did not yet seem to feel threatened by India's developments in nuclear technology. See Times of India, January 9, 20, and 21, 1957.

81 As early as 1955, the Australian nuclear physicist Oliphant referred to the TIFR as an emerging "Mecca" for research in elementary particles; see Times of India, February 25, 1955.

82 On Bohr see Times of India, January 5, 1960; on Cockcroft, Times of India, March 16, 1965.

inhabitants, and – by Western standards – weaknesses in its democratic system. Thus India's political and financial investments in nuclear technology appeared to be relatively greater than those of many industrialized nations.[83] In addition, the country's high-ranking representatives never missed an opportunity to publicly celebrate advancements in India's nuclear program.[84] Moreover, the political consensus on involvement in nuclear technology may have been greater in India than in other countries. What was definitely greater was the lack of public criticism and parliamentary supervision. Only rarely in the 1950s and 1960s did the Indian parliament hold debates on the country's nuclear program. When such debate did occur, most speakers, regardless of their party, praised the work of the AEC and the DAE. At most, details of the program were questioned. Often, however, the speakers advocated a more rapid development and even greater funding for nuclear research.[85] Until the end of the 1950s, India's print media contained few critical references to this topic.

Furthermore, the bonds between scientific interest and political decision-making were stronger in India than in many other democratic countries. This also applied to the autonomy and exclusive status of India's nuclear complex, understood here as an ensemble of respective facilities for research and development and of bodies exerting political decision and control. Bhabha was not only the director of the TIFR and the AEE; he also headed the AEC and served as undersecretary of the responsible ministry, thus combining scientific leadership and political decision-making. Formally, the DAE, the political arm of In-

---

83 At home and abroad, Nehru showed himself to be one of the most ardent supporters of nuclear technology; see, for example, his speech on the introduction of the Atomic Energy Act at the Constituent Assembly of 1948, in: Nehru, Selected Works, Second Series, V, 421 ff. Information on the amount of funding provided by the Indian federal government for nuclear research is scant and inconsistent. Most probably, however, such funding made up the largest part of research and development expenditures. According to statements made by Nehru to the Indian parliament, funding amounted to roughly 10 million Rs annually during the first half of the 1950s (see House of the People, Parliamentary Debates, part 2, 6th session 1954, vol. 5, column 7032). Allocations for the DAE rose from 10 million to 120 million between 1954 and 1957 (see the printed text of Nehru's speech of July 24, 1957 to the lower house of the Indian parliament in Times of India, July 25, 1957). According to US-government estimates, India spent approximately 220 million dollars on nuclear research from 1954 to 1964, see Perkovich, India's Nuclear Bomb, 69.

84 Nehru personally opened many of the nuclear research institutes, reactors, and plants. See Times of India, December 26, 1952, January 9, 1957, January 17, 1961 and January 16, 1962.

85 See the parliamentary debates of May 10, 1954, April 10, 1958 and August 19, 1961; Perkovich, India's Nuclear Bomb, 39.

dia's nuclear program, was directed by Nehru. But Nehru was known to rely solely on Bhabha for advice on matters concerning nuclear policy – matters with which the Cabinet was never involved.[86] Consequently, under Bhabha's directorship the AEC became the planning and control center of India's nuclear program, with the DAE serving as its assisting body. Apart from Bhabha, only two other scientists were members of the AEC in the 1950s. Both of them were so convinced of the importance of utilizing nuclear energy for the purpose of modernizing India and making the country economically prosperous that they refused to allow critical voices in their midst who might question forecasts, planning, and demands for funding. The commission's deliberations were rarely publicized, and its decisions were treated as government secrets.[87] The exclusiveness and lack of transparency surrounding this decision-making process as well as Bhabha's political influence were reinforced by the close ties of trust and understanding between Bhabha and Nehru. Both men belonged to India's upper class and had a wide range of connections in society. Both had studied in England and were admirers of European music, literature, and visual arts. They both believed that Western science and technology were indispensable to India's modernization. This common background allowed them to relate to each other. Their friendship was so close that they met every two weeks, and Bhabha became one of only two individuals not related to Nehru who addressed the later as *bhai* (brother).[88]

These factors, which reinforced each other, served to strengthen and solidify the distinct features of the early stages of India's nuclear energy program. The exclusiveness and lack of transparency characteristic of the country's nuclear complex increased in 1958. At that time, the AEC, at Bhabha's urging, was given responsibility for formulating DAE policy and implementing it and freed

86 Kapur, India's Nuclear Politics, in Poulose 1978, 173. Kapur mentions as advisors, in addition to Bhabha, the diplomat Sardar Panikkar as well as Krishna Menon, who was the long-time Indian representative to the United Nations and who later served as Minister for Defense. Gupta, India and Disarmament, in: Nanda, Indian Foreign Policy: The Nehru Years, 251. He refers moreover to M.J. Desai, who served as Undersecretary in the Ministry of External Affairs, and to V.C. Trivedi, the long-time Indian delegate at the Geneva Convention on Disarmament. On the overall functioning of the Indian cabinet under Nehru see Brecher, Succession in India, 94.

87 Using the secrecy clause contained in the Atomic Energy Act, the government withheld specific information on the budget of the DAE and the country's nuclear program. Accordingly, it even refused to provide the names of the participating scientists, see the remarks made by the Minister of Science, Mishra, to the lower house of the Indian parliament on March 13, 1953; Sharma, India's Nuclear Estate, 22; Abraham, The Making of the Indian Atomic Bomb, 61.

88 See Menon 1967, 435; Gopal, Nehru, 67.

from "all non-essential restrictions or needlessly inelastic rules." This fortified the position of Bhabha, who continued to serve as undersecretary of the DAE.[89] He became known as "a moghul of the nuclear establishment," as the "uncrowned king of the scientific world in India."[90] He benefited from the fact that his fame and influence were increasing internationally, too, owing to no small extent to Nehru's active support. For example, Nehru arranged to have Bhabha appointed president of the 1955 United Nations Conference on the Peaceful Uses of Atomic Energy.[91] This appointment made Bhabha a truly international figure. He had offices in Vienna, London, Paris, Washington, and Montreal, friends all over the world, and was a member of numerous research organizations abroad.[92] His international visibility strengthened his political influence in India and helped render the country's nuclear program more resistant to criticism. When his feasibility calculations began to be questioned, both the DAE and Nehru countered the critique by pointing out that India's involvement in nuclear technology was indispensable to the country's future and therefore had to be evaluated independent of financial considerations.[93] Pertinent criticism was not to be heard in parliament either.[94] Attempts by some government officials to stall India's nuclear program – not so much on factual grounds but due to annoyance with the program's preferred status and treatment – also failed because of the "Nehru-Bhabha-effect."[95]

The personality cult evolving around Bhabha and the unconditional support for his policies in the centers for nuclear research strengthened the exclusive po-

89 Nehru's, Announcement of April 23, 1958 to parliament, 117; Abraham, The Making of the Indian Atomic Bomb, 97.

90 Sharma, India's Nuclear Estate, 32. On Bhabha's public reputation also see the parliamentary debates of Aug. 10, 1960, LSD, 2nd ser., vol. 44, column 2000.

91 Anderson, Building Scientific Institutions in India, 66; Rigden, Rabi: Scientist and Citizen, 243.

92 Sharma, India's Nuclear Estate, 24; Penney, Biographical Memoirs of Fellows of the Royal Society, 35.

93 On the criticism and counterproposals see Times of India, August 11, 1959; a letter to the editor in ibid., August 18, 1960 and the relevant editorial of September 2, 1960. On the rejection of that criticism see the AEC Communique, Times of India, August 14, 1959. The letter of the AEC Public Relations Officer in ibid., September 1, 1959. Bhabha's statement of December 15, 1959 to the parliamentary committee on nuclear policy, ibid., December 16, 1959; Nehru to the India Parliament, Speeches of December 18, 1959, LSD, August 4, 1960, August. 10, 1960, August 19, 1961; also Perkovich, India's Nuclear Bomb, 38.

94 Speech Mukerjee, LSD, August 10, 1960; those of representatives Sharma and Bharucha of August 16, 1961, ibid.

95 Raghavan, Opposition to Atomic Colonialism, 26.

sition of nuclear research in India even further.[96] Due to their largely autonomous status, their high standards in recruiting staff, and their interdisciplinary approach, the research centers set new quality standards. They benefitted from excellent international contacts and were involved in world-class research. They became "islands of self-confidence," the likes of which were found nowhere else in Indian science and research.[97] Nevertheless, the centers formed a type of "closed-door society"[98] and sealed themselves off from the public. The result was a stifling of any public discourse on political and technological alternatives to India's energy policy and thus of any discussion on relevant alternatives that might have proved more useful or sensible.

The enormous hopes and expectations with which India started its nuclear program proved to be highly exaggerated, if not unfounded. Nuclear energy began to contribute noticeably to India's electricity supply much later than projected by Bhabha.[99] The first nuclear plants were unexpectedly susceptible to faults, and construction of further plants occurred much more slowly than initially planned. Thorium-fueled reactors have remained in the experimental stage until today. The dream of the breeders is over, and the prognosis for when nuclear fusion will solve the energy problems of mankind remains at 50 years – just as it was 50 years ago.

Finally, the cultural motives behind India's early nuclear policies provided for amendments to policy plans in the event of a change in general conditions. Such changes occurred when China attacked India in October of 1962, when Pakistan attacked Kashmir in 1965, and when the 1968 non-proliferation treaty was signed. After China tested its first nuclear weapon, parts of the Indian public demanded that India produce its own atomic weapons. These demands increased during the 1960s.[100] Although the Indian government continued to adhere to its previous policies, it now did so with decreasing emphasis. At the same time, India (not least for domestic reasons) increasingly stood by its re-

---

96 Khanna, Transfer of Technology: BARC Faces an Uphill Task, in Times of India, June 5, 1974; Anderson, Building Scientific Institutions in India, 86; Sharma, India's Nuclear Estate, 17.

97 Morehouse 1968, 10, 50; Ramanna, Perspectives of India's Nuclear Policy, 26; Anderson, Building Scientific Institutions in India, 2, 78. At Bhabha's funeral in January 1967, Vikram Sarabhai, his successor as head of India's AEC, spoke of the "Islands of self-confidence" as being Bhabha's legacy, see Times of India, January 13, 1967.

98 According to Spenta Wadia, a TIFR physicist, in an interview given in the mid 1980s, in Malchow and Tayebi, Menschen in Bombay, 162.

99 World Nuclear Association, Nuclear Power in India (www.world-nuclear.og/info/inf.53.html).

100 See, for example, the parliamentary debates of November 27 and December 11, 1964 on the respective draft of the resolution, LSD.

fusal to subject its nuclear technology to internationally imposed supervision and limitations, from which the recognized nuclear powers had been exempted. Upon the signing of the 1968 Non-Proliferation Treaty, India's feared two-class world of atomic haves and atomic have nots was becoming a reality. Consequently, nuclear arms were seen as a status symbol of the world powers, and India rejected the treaty although it supported its goals in principle. The country's interest in developing its own nuclear arms increased, not so much on military grounds but for reasons of self-respect and to demonstrate its insistence on being treated internationally as a coequal. India's first testing of a nuclear device in 1974, referred to as a "peaceful nuclear explosion," was by no means a surprise.

Conclusion

This change in policy in the late 1960s and early 1970s cannot be treated here in further detail, nor can we cover the disappointment which set in when it became clear that the economic expectations tied to the civilian use of nuclear energy were unrealistic. What this article has shown is that India's early involvement in nuclear research and technology did not rest on economic and energy considerations alone. Cultural factors, particularly India's colonial experience of having been ruled, exploited and disdained, played a decisive role in shaping India's nuclear policy (and in other fields of India's modernization policies, too). Together with domestic political factors, those cultural factors determined India's later decision to build nuclear weapons; one might even argue that they were more influential than military considerations. It seems likely that the symbolic value nuclear arms possessed for India was and is higher than the West, with its emphasis on security policies, is inclined to recognize.[101]

101 Cf. Bieber, "Die Atombombe als Statussymbol"; Bieber, "Kernwaffen."

Indian Globalisms: From Population Control to Reproductive Tourism

Mohan Rao

Could men but come awake – enchantments keep
Their noblest faculties held fast in sleep
And frightful dreams and real fears, alas!
Before their soggy haunted vision pass
Not least the reverend Thomas Malthus with his trick
Of killing conscience with arithmetic. James MacAullay[1]

I.

From its conception, population control has been a global project. While Malthusians were concerned about poverty in their own countries, neo-Malthusians looked across at poor countries around the world. While Malthus could only suggest moral restraint to control births, neo-Malthusians came equipped with contraceptive technology. As the ideas of race congealed in the late nineteenth century, the social science disciplines that were framed in a racial discourse, justifying colonialism, were primarily anthropology and the short-lived science of phrenology. It nevertheless spilled into other disciplines such as psychology, although it lies at the heart of socio-biology even today.

Colonialism was a function of the formation of modern nation states, commencing in the eighteenth century, and preceded ideas of race by more than a century. Thus while colonialism was not impelled by ideas of race, colonial consolidation was made possible by this ideological discourse. In India itself it was a combination of Victorian utilitarianism, eugenics and fears generated by the events of 1857 that led to the hardening, indeed some have argued, the discovery of race. Thus we had categorisations of martial and non-martial races, of Muslims as a race and so on. At the same time, both the formation of ideas of nascent Hindu nationhood, and the discovery of an ancient Aryan heritage, along with the work of Indologists like Max Müller and others came together with ideas of a Hindu race harking back to a golden age. Its reverberations shake the world we live in today, threatening to tear apart the India we know, as the Hindu Right seeks to turn the nation into a "pure" Hindu state.

---

1 MacAullay, A Vision of Ceremony. Quoted in Clark, Population Growth and Land Use, 157.

Charles Darwin's *The Descent of Man*, published in 1871, provided a significant measure of inspiration to the birth of the eugenics movement.[2] The ideas of competitive struggle, natural selection and the survival of the fittest, when applied to the social arrangements of human societies, had frightening consequences, not to mention deep ethical and moral implications. Racial purity and improvement of the racial stock were the prime concerns of the eugenics movement. The eugenics movement was named by one of its illustrious founders, a cousin of Darwin's, Francis Galton, who pioneered the use of statistics on human populations.

Eugenics had two sets of action on its agenda: the positive eugenics of Galton and the negative eugenics of Clapperton. Those who received the attention of the latter at one time or the other were criminals, the mentally retarded, the insane, the tuberculous, lepers, alcoholics, epileptics, the "feeble minded," the "degenerate," immigrants and of course the poor, who apparently bred all these characteristics. For example, it is noted with alarm:

> "In Degeneracy healthy aspirations no longer exist, the struggle for survival the higher in the organism against the lower having ceased and the cells having conformed in a mass to a lower grade of being... There is no greater menace to a race than is furnished by such sturdy degenerates."[3]

Darwin, the most influential of scientists, himself canonised his cousin's ideas.[4] Given the overwhelming influence of Darwin, it is not surprising that many commentators at this time introduced Darwinian metaphors to social arrangements. Social Darwinists, believing that biology was destiny, at least for the poor, thus began to identify an extraordinary series of social and behavioural facts as heritable. It was not far from this to asserting that only the "fit" should be encouraged to procreate and the "unfit" discouraged.

There were profound inconsistencies, not to mention logical absurdities, in the arguments of the Social Darwinists. One was, of course that the unfit were by definition not given to wider social concerns; indeed they were often feeble-minded – that catch-all category including the mentally subnormal and a whole range of social "misfits." They could thus hardly be called upon to sacrifice their reproduction for the larger good of society, for the future of the race. If voluntary eugenic measures were not of much use with this category of people, what

2 Greer, Sex and Destiny: The Politics of Human Fertility, 266.

3 Greer, Sex and Destiny: The Politics of Human Fertility, 266.

4 Darwin wrote: "We now know, through the admirable labours of Mr. Galton, that genius tends to be inherited". Quoted in Kevles, In the Name of Eugenics: Genetics and the Uses of Human Heredity, 20.

about some element of coercion?[5] But coercion invited state interference, and in one of the private areas of individual liberty at that. But was coercion really necessary if, in the struggle for survival, nature red in tooth and claw, by definition the unfit would be weeded out?

Eugenics held great appeal for influential people on both sides of the Atlantic. In *Mein Kampf*, Adolf Hitler wrote:

> "Because the inferior are always numerically superior to the better, the former would multiply so much faster – if they have the same possibility to survive and reproduce – that the better necessarily would be placed in the background. Therefore a correction has to be made to the advantage of the better. The nature (sic) offers such a correction by exposing the inferior to difficult living conditions which reduce their number. Concerning the rest the nature (sic) does not allow them to reproduce indiscriminately, but makes a relentless selection according to their strength and health conditions."[6]

Hitler included among others, Jews, communists, homosexuals and gypsies in his grand design. The most extreme "correction" he offered to nature's lethal ways was the so-called Final Solution.

In the United States the eugenics movement gained momentum early in the twentieth century mainly at the instance of natural scientists convinced by Galton that "genius" was a heritable characteristic. The rediscovery of Mendel's work in 1900 led to the formation of the American Breeders Association in 1903. In 1906, a Eugenics Section of the Association was established to "emphasise the value of superior blood and the menace to society of inferior blood."[7] The American eugenic movement was involved with legislation to restrict immigration for "unrestricted immigration," especially of those not Anglo-Saxon or Nordic, was described as the "annihilator of our native stock."[8] The eugenicists were also instrumental in initiating legislation and carrying out eugenic sterilisations on the institutionalised mentally "sub-normal," the epilep-

---

5 This continues to have enormous appeal today in India, as the spate of "disincentives" in the Indian family planning programme would attest.

6 Hitler, Mein Kampf. Quoted in Bondestam and Bergstrom, Poverty and Population Control, 16.

7 Hodgson, "The Ideological Origins of the Population Association of America," 1.

8 Had these immigration laws not been tightened for eugenic reasons, a large number of Jews might perhaps have escaped the death camps. The Nazi sterilisation laws were influenced by contemporary American laws, upheld by the liberal justice Oliver Wendell Holmes, who argued that they were "better for all the world". See Brunius, Better for All the World: The Secret History of Forced Sterilisations and America's Quest for Racial Purity.

tic and the psychotic.[9] Indeed, the eugenicist Leon F. Whitney wrote, "We cannot but admire the foresight of the [German] plan [of sterilising people] and realise by this action Germany is going to make herself a stronger nation." He also observed that, "the Negroes furnished six times as many sub-normals as did the native – born whites."[10] Echoing Whitney, M. S. Golwalkar, the founder of the Rashtriya Swayamevak Sangh (RSS),[11] wrote in 1947:

> "To keep up the purity of the Race and its culture, Germany shocked the world by her purging the country of the Semitic Races, the Jews. Race pride at its highest has been manifested here. Germany has also shown how well-nigh impossible it is for races and cultures, having differences going to the root, to be assimilated into one united whole, a good lesson for us in Hindustan to learn and profit by."[12]

Meanwhile, in London, the Eugenic Society, in 1930, encouraged by the Report of the Joint Committee of the Board of Education – which had found that "mentally deficient parents create centres of degeneracy and disease which welfare

---

9 Such laws for eugenic sterilisations were enacted in the USSR, Canada, and in the Scandinavian countries.

10 Greer, Sex and Destiny: The Politics of Human Fertility, 274.

11 The RSS (or Rashtriya Swayam Sevak Sangh) is the shadowy head of a group of right-wing Hindu organisations collectively called the Sangh Parivar, or the Sangh family. The RSS is a male, largely upper-caste, cadre-based organisation involved in ideological work and in behind-the-scenes-politics. Its parliamentary wing is the Bharatiya Janata Party (BJP), which headed a coalition government from 1998 to 2004. The prime minister at that time, Mr. Vajpayee, is an RSS member, as is the then second-in-command, Mr. Advani. Indeed most leaders in the BJP come from RSS ranks. The Sangh family also comprises the more militant Vishwa Hindu Parishad, which has played a large role in violence against Muslims and Christians, along with another organisation, the Bajrang Dal. The women's wing of the RSS is named the Rashtriya Swayam Sevika Sangh; the Bajrang Dal wing is named the Durga Vahini. The Sangh Parivar also has organisations working among students and tribals, a worker's wing and – extremely important for fund-raising – an organisation known as the Hindu Sevak Sangh in the United States and the United Kingdom. Upper caste professional Hindus in these countries, searching for identity, for myths and symbols, are massive donors. There are enormous problems with the characterisation of the Sangh Parivar as Hindu fundamentalist or Hindu nationalist. They do not represent Hindus, and indeed seem to be deeply ashamed of Hinduism, wishing to transform it into a more "masculine" religion, like Christianity or Islam. There are of course no fundamentals in Hinduism. Their claim to be nationalistic is equally moot since they played an extremely marginal role, if at all, in India's freedom struggle. Indeed the assassin of Mahatma Gandhi, a good and proper Hindu, was a member of the Sangh Parivar as it then existed. However, this is how they are referred to, especially in the Western literature and media, and following this, in India.

12 Golwalkar, "We, Or Our Nationhood Redefined, Bharat Publications," 10.

work can never reach"[13] – began concerted lobbying and propaganda for a Eugenic Sterilisation Bill. Associated with this effort were a press baron, the noted author H.G. Wells, Darwin's son Major Darwin, and Julian Huxley. The last, who later became a lion of the population control movement, wrote:

> "The principle of supplementing the segregation of defectives by sterilisation in certain cases is to my mind very important, and indeed very essential, if we are to prevent the gradual deterioration of our racial stock."[14]

Eugenics was also tied to the destiny of the imperial nation. Such a nation, it was felt, required much more than merely economic and military power. It also demanded an efficient way of ensuring that its population was kept fresh, energetic, efficient and productive by ensuring that its fresh flow of population was mainly recruited from the "better stock." Imperial anxiety about national fitness was also occasioned by British fears of the German naval strength and that the Boer War (1899-1902) revealed what appeared to be a shockingly low standard of health among male recruits, linking together questions of public health and national welfare. It was these anxieties, these fears that led to the 1904 *Report on the Physical Deterioration of the Population*. It was these concerns, too, that led Sidney and Beatrice Webb to make their plea for a welfare state in their 1910 treatise on the need for state sponsored public health, *The State and the Doctor*.[15]

Eugenics was scientifically discredited by that famous biologist (and friend of India) J.B.S. Haldane. But it was Hermann Muller's discovery of mutation in the early 1940s that denuded it of the very last vestiges of scientific respectability. The eugenic lobby now turned to what they called crypto-eugenics or population control. In 1956, the British Eugenics Society decided in a resolution:

> "That the Society should pursue eugenic ends by less obvious means, that is by a policy of crypto-eugenics. The Society's activities in crypto-eugenics should by pursued vigourously, and specifically that the Society should increase its monetary support of the Family Planning Association and the International Planned Parenthood Federation."[16]

II.

India was integrated into the global world of capitalism with the battle of Plassey in 1757. The colonial loot of the "jewel" in Britain's crown was both instantaneous and staggering. It has been estimated that the treasure taken from

13 Kevles, In the Name of Eugenics: Genetics and the Uses of Human Heredity, 88
14 Greer, Sex and Destiny: The Politics of Human Fertility, 270.
15 Oakley, The Captured Womb: A History of Medical Care of Pregnant Women.
16 Greer, Sex and Destiny: The Politics of Human Fertility, 278.

India alone between Plassey and Waterloo was an astounding 500 million pounds to 1 billion pounds.[17] Its impact on the industrial revolution in England was equally instantaneous and has been noted in the following words: "The Bengal plunder began to arrive in London, and the effect appears to have been instantaneous [...]. At once in 1759, the Bank (of England) issued 10 and 15 pound notes [...] and the industrial revolution began with the year 1760."[18]

Thus while India provided a large chunk of the capital for England's industrialisation, she also began the process of her own impoverishment and deindustrialisation. India was systematically deindustrialised and became in turn a market for Lancashire cottons: In 1820 India took 11 million yards; by 1840 it took 145 million yards. Unable to bear the unfair competition, spinners and weavers in India, suffered destitution. Spinning and weaving in urban India were wiped out; the rural artisans, immiserated, were ready victims for the famines that loomed over India in the nineteenth century.

The ideas of Malthus were now resurrected as an explanation of Indian poverty, especially to colonial administrators taught at Haileybury College before they set sail to India. As far back as early in the nineteenth century European travellers, setting the tone for later colonial administrators supervising the plundering of India, invoked Malthus as an explanation for poverty in India. For example, Abbe Dubois,[19] after surveying the destruction of the Indian weaving industry and the consequent pauperisation of her artisans, and indeed after linking this to the mills of England, remarks:

> "Of these causes (of misery) the chief one is the rapid increase of population. Judging by my own personal knowledge [...] of Mysore and the districts of Baramahl and Coimbatore, I should say that they increased by 25 per cent in the last 25 years [...]. Some modern political economists have held that a progressive increase in the population is one of the most unequivocal signs of a country's prosperity and wealth. In Europe this argument may be logical enough, but I do not think that it can be applied to India; in fact, I am persuaded that as the population increases, so in proportion do want and misery. For this theory of the economists to hold good in all respects the resources and industries of the inhabitants ought to develop rapidly; but in a country where the inhabitants are notoriously apathetic and indolent, where customs and institutions are so many insurmountable barriers against a better order of things, and where it is more or less a sacred duty to let things as they are, I have every reason to

17 Patnaik, "On the Political Economy of Underdevelopment."

18 Adams, cited in Patnaik, "On the Political Economy of Underdevelopment," 198.

19 Abbe Dubois, a Catholic priest, escaping the anti-clerical blood purges in the aftermath of the French Revolution traveled extensively through South India. His journals were purchased by the East India Company, whose members were trying to better understand the creatures they were ruling.

> believe that a considerable increase in the population should be looked upon as a calamity rather than as a blessing."[20]

Thus was assiduously constructed the image of the Other, of Orientalism, of seething poor overpopulated tropics, in a swoon of customs and habits, ineradicable and unchanging.[21] Colonial policy exonerated the responsibility of creating a relative surplus population in India. In addition to the destruction of her cottage industry, British agricultural policy – of commercialisation and revenue extraction through the Permanent Settlement Act – impoverished vast sections of the Indian peasantry.[22] This dispossessed peasantry did not have the option that their English counterparts did, of turning into proletarians, working in the industries, for British free trade policies actively hindered industrialisation. India was thus integrated into the world economy as an exporter of primary commodities with a virtually stagnant, vast and immiserated agricultural sector and no industrial sector to speak of. The spectre of Malthus loomed large over India even in the nineteenth century when there was little population growth and the Indian population was stalked by periodic and terrible famines taking the toll of an estimated 30 million deaths.

Focusing on population growth as an explanation for Indian poverty is therefore seriously misleading. It nonetheless held great appeal to not only colonialists, but leading sections of the Indian population. For example, Wattal's influential work entitled *The Population Problem in India: A Census Study*, published in 1916, commences with Malthus' law of population, concluding that the "alarming" growth of the Indian population was responsible for widespread poverty and ill-health.[23] Mass, for instance, has noted that by the 1930s "significant layers of the native elites adopted neo-Malthusian views."[24] Margaret Sanger therefore had a ready and receptive audience.

The first family planning clinic in India was opened in 1925 by Karve, who later went on to assist in the formulation of official policy as a member of the National Sub-Committee on Population. The Indian chapter of the Neo-Malthusian League was inaugurated in Madras in 1928.[25] In 1930, the world's first government-sponsored birth control clinic was inaugurated at the behest of the Maharaja of Mysore. Madras followed with the establishment of birth control clinics in state hospitals in 1933. In 1935 in Bombay the Family Hygiene Society was established; the Society brought out a journal quaintly entitled *The*

20 Dubois, Hindu Manners, Customs and Ceremonies, Translated by Beauchamp, 93-94.
21 Said, Orientalism.
22 Patnaik, "On the Political Economy of Underdevelopment."
23 Wattal, The Population Problem in India: A Census Study, 11.
24 Mass, "An Historical Sketch of the American Population Control Movement," 651.
25 Bose and Desai, Studies in the Social Dynamics of Primary Health Care.

Journal of Marriage Hygiene. In the same year Margaret Sanger undertook a triumphant nation-wide tour, winning friends and influencing people, although she left Mahatma Gandhi singularly unimpressed. One such apostle, Lady Dhanvantri Rama Rao, invited her to address the All India Women's Conference.[26]

In 1938 Lady Rama Rao and Margaret Sanger organised the First Family Hygiene Conference in Bombay. They were assisted by an Indian millionaire whose American wife shared Sanger's conviction that India was poised at the precipice of a population explosion, and who had therefore established the Watamull Foundation to control it.[27] Also in 1938, the Indian National Congress established a National Planning Committee under the chairmanship of Jawaharlal Nehru. The deliberations of one of the Sub-Committees, chaired by Radhakamal Mukherjee, were devoted to the question of population. Its concerns were largely eugenic in nature. It deplored the fact that "attention to eugenics or race culture are matters hardly yet in the public consciousness of this country" and went on to say:

> "Man, who has come to the stage of development where he is anxious to breed carefully such species of the lower animals as dogs or horses to obtain very specific qualities in particular specimens of the species, has not yet realised apparently the possibilities inherent in careful scientific breeding of the human race."[28]

It was early in the twentieth century too that we see the birth of what is today called Saffron Demography.[29] As early as 1909 U.N. Mukherji, in the wake of the partition of Bengal and colonial initiatives towards communal representation under the Minto Morley reforms, had written a book entitled *Hindus: A Dying Race*, which went on to influence many tracts and publications by the Hindu Maha Sabha, the parent organisation of the RSS. This book seemed to meet a widespread demand, going in to many reprints, feeding into Hindu communalism, and helping create it. It had a special appeal to Hindu communalists, who, in the face of demands for separate representation emanating from both Muslims and the lower-castes, were anxious to create a monolithic Hindu community. Whipping up anxiety about Muslims would be one way to weld together hugely

---

26 Lakshmanna, Population Control and Family Planning in India.

27 Greer, Sex and Destiny: The Politics of Human Fertility.

28 National Planning Committee, Report of the Sub-Committee on Population, 17.

29 "Saffron Demography" is how Patricia and Roger Jeffery describe the myths and lies around the use of demography by the Sangh Parivar; saffron is the colour that the Sangh claim represents Hindus. See Jeffery, Confronting Saffron Demography: Religion, Fertility and Women's Status in India.

diverse, and often antagonistic, castes into one community, erasing the structural divisions in caste society.

As the work of Sanjam Ahluwalia[30] has shown, the construction of the discourse of over-population in colonial India was wedded to the project of nationalism, to modernity, and to some varieties of feminism. The authors of the project were a motley lot: A substantial section of the Indian political elite (with the notable exception of M.K. Gandhi), predominantly male medical practitioners, Western feminists, the early Indian feminist movement, colonial authorities, a section of indigenous medical practitioners and, of course, the Hindu fundamentalists. Their concerns were equally varied: To harness procreation towards a racially superior country, to hasten economic development, to reduce maternal and child deaths, to decrease the birth rate of the poor, the unfit and the Other, including here the lower castes and Muslims and, finally, to create a modern Indian family, and indeed the modern Indian woman. This Indian woman would be modern, wedded to her husband and the nation, thus exercising reproductive restraint. Prudent, a good mother, and god-fearing she would, above all, be unlike the materialist Western woman.

Something striking that Ahluwalia notes is that while Sanger and Stopes tried to influence the medical profession and the political elite, they made no efforts at all to reach out to either Periyar or Ambedkar, fierce proponents of both modernism and of birth control, although not for eugenic or neo-Malthusian reasons. Both Periyar and Ambedkar, lower caste leaders, and the latter a framer of the egalitarian Indian Constitution, called for birth control to liberate women from the tyranny of caste, the family and patriarchy, which obviously was too radical for Sanger. As Ahluwalia notes: "Even while these Western advocates (of population control) espoused somewhat radical ideas about gender politics, their class affiliations and political programme were clearly middle class. Ambedkar's social base and his radical programme of social transformation made him an unsuitable ally."[31]

Sanger tried very hard indeed to win over Gandhi, but was rebuffed. Gandhi argued instead that "If it is contended that birth control is necessary for the nation because of over-population, I dispute the proposition. It has never been proved. In my opinion, by a proper land system, better agriculture and a supplementary industry, this country is capable of supporting twice as many people as there are today."[32] Gandhi was also opposed to birth control for other reasons. He believed that sex represented sinful indulgence, a lowly animal instinct

30 Ahluwalia, Reproductive Restraints: Birth Control in India 1877-1947.

31 Ahluwalia, Reproductive Restraints: Birth Control in India 1877-1947, 63.

32 Ahluwalia, Reproductive Restraints: Birth Control in India 1877-1947, 79.

meant merely for procreation. Ahluwalia observes that "Gandhi stripped women of sexual desires and reaffirmed motherhood as the natural vocation for women."[33]

Middle class women entering nationalist politics, in a space created for them by Gandhi, were deeply troubled and divided. While they fiercely supported Gandhi's nationalist agenda, they felt strongly about birth control too – for reasons of health of women and children, among others. Thus Begum Hamid Ali called for finding "a safe and really cheap type of contraceptive which may be popularised or given free at clinics established for the purpose."[34] Kamala Devi Chattopadhyay called for birth control because "All imperialistic minded rulers encourage large families ...The other reason is because women freed from the penalty of undesired motherhood will deal a death blow to man's vested interest in her. He can no more chain and enslave her."[35] Lakshmi Bai Rajwade, who was to become a forceful advocate of state-provided family planning in the National Sub-Committee on Health, argued that child and maternal mortality were directly related to frequent child birth.

Nevertheless, all these upper-caste women were careful to state that they did not intend contraceptives to rock the familial boat. As men did, they too reified the sacred duties of motherhood, even as they sought that this should be performed in a more rational, prudent, manner. Although, to its credit, the Indian women's movement was utterly untouched by communal concerns, they were nevertheless united by dysgenic fears that the poor were breeding too much in relation to the middle classes.

The Second World War diverted the attention of planners from such concerns. But in 1949 the Family Planning Committee was formed in Bombay with Lady Rama Rao as president. In 1951, it was renamed the Family Planning Association of India. The FPAI has been a major force shaping population policy in the country. Indeed it takes credit for "playing an active role in inducting the first Planning Commission to incorporate family planning in health."[36]

It was in this period, the 1950s, that the population control lobby was consolidated. Hugh M. Moore, an American millionaire, established the Hugh Moore Fund, which published a pamphlet called *The Population Bomb* in 1954. The Ford Foundation joined Moore and the Rockefeller Foundation in their activities. In 1952, Margaret Sanger and Lady Rama Rao launched the Interna-

---

33 Ahluwalia, Reproductive Restraints: Birth Control in India 1877-1947, 78.

34 Ahluwalia, Reproductive Restraints: Birth Control in India 1877-1947, 96.

35 Ahluwalia, Reproductive Restraints: Birth Control in India 1877-1947, 105.

36 Family Planning Association of India, FPAI All India Council 1973-75, 1.

tional Planned Parenthood Federation (IPPF) in Bombay. One of the most influential people invited to this conference was C.P. Blacker, who noted:

> "Nor need we question that a husband and wife living in squalor and ignorance who already have a large number of children not being reared properly might well be considered unfit to have additional children. Yet many parents of these various unfit types keep producing unduly large numbers of children, chiefly because through ignorance or indifference – and often against their will – they let Nature take its course. To combat this situation, eugenists favour the spread of birth control."[37]

The IPPF became a major force in the population control movement across the globe. The funding for the IPPF initially came from the Hugh Moore Fund and Rockefeller Foundation.

The latter, together with The Milbank Memorial Fund, founded an Office of Population Research at Princeton University. The office included leading demographers such as Kingsley Davis and Frank Notestein. When Rockefeller founded The Population Council both these demographers took up employment there.[38] Hugh Moore founded the World Population Emergency Campaign in 1960 with funds from his foundation and from Du Pont. The president of the World Bank ran the campaign. The primary aim of the World Population Emergency Campaign was to create and reinforce First World fears of a population "explosion" in Third World countries with dire consequences for the entire globe.[39] It has been suggested that the revolution in Cuba provided additional impetus to these fears.[40] The Emergency Campaign and the Population Council began a systematic and powerful campaign to influence American policymakers to include population control as a component of US aid to Third World countries. Neo-Malthusianism had thus arrived on the world agenda. Inevitably, India – always at the forefront of the family planning movement's field of vision – saw neo-Malthusianism thrust forcefully on its official policy and programmes. They not only funded research but were also involved in training demographers, doctors and statisticians. It is not surprising then that large and influential sections of Indians fervently uphold these neo-Malthusian ideas.

III.

India was at the heart of global population concerns, especially in relation to China, for at least until 1979 Chinese population policy was profoundly indifferent to the West. It was felt that population control had to be made to work in

37 Greer, Sex and Destiny: The Politics of Human Fertility, 341.
38 Gordon, Women's Body, Women's Right.
39 George, How the Other Half Dies.
40 Mass, "An Historical Sketch of the American Population Control Movement."

India to stave off communism.[41] The elite in India are as convinced as the colonialists were that poverty in India is primarily due to overpopulation. Thus neo-Malthusian ideas shaped Indian population policy as it lurched from one approach to another, reaching its apogee during the period of internal emergency in the country between 1975 and 1977, when, officially it was admitted that 1776 people had died as a result of "excesses" committed in the family planning programme. Coercion of various sorts, strings of incentives and disincentives continued to characterise the programme, until the entire public health system became suborned for family planning.[42] Funding for the family planning programme continued to increase in relation to health, although officially, following the ICPD at Cairo, targets were removed. There were few critical voices, and these few were ignored in the population control planning juggernaut.[43]

Over the last twenty years since India embarked upon Structural Adjustment Programmes at the behest of the World Bank and the International Monetary Fund, we have witnessed a sharp decline in the state's commitment to public health, never very marked. Thus today our country has the fifth lowest public health expenditure in the world. As the National Health Policy (NHP) report of 2002 admitted, this is, at 0.9 per cent of the GDP, lower than the average in even Sub Saharan Africa.[44] Along with decreasing state spending on health, policy measures have encouraged the growth of the private sector in health care so that today we have the largest, and least regulated, private health care industry in the world. Evidence from across the country indicates that access to health care has declined sharply over this period. The policy of levying user fees has impacted negatively upon access to public health facilities, especially for poor and marginalised communities, and to women.[45] With the sharp rise in health care costs, as the NHP report of 2002 acknowledges, medical expenditure has emerged as one of the leading causes of indebtedness.

Equally significant have been other changes. Inter-regional, rural-urban, gender and economic class differentials in access to health care in India are well documented. Since the onset of liberalisation policies, these have considerably

41 Ross, The Malthus Factor: Poverty, Politics and Population in Capitalist Development.

42 Rao, From Population Control to Reproductive Health: Malthusian Arithmetic.

43 Since the 1980s, the health and Indian women's movements have critically examined the health and population control programs in India and have managed to stall the introduction of potentially coercive injectables and implants, besides campaigning against incentives and disincentives in the program, in particular the Two Child Norm.

44 Government of India, Ministry of Health and Family Welfare, National Health Policy, New Delhi.

45 Government of India, Ministry of Health and Family Welfare, Report of the Commission on Macroeconomics and Health, New Delhi.

widened. The decline in public investments was matched with growing subsidies to the private sector in health care in a variety of ways.[46] State support for private health care grew with the initiation of private-public partnerships (PPP) that took a variety of forms.[47] Private funds made their entry through these partnerships. For instance, under the aegis of Global Alliance for Vaccines and Immunisation (GAVI) and the WHO, plans are underway in the Ministry of Health and Family Welfare to introduce a range of utterly unnecessary vaccines in a replay of "let them eat cake."[48] It is truly remarkable that GAVI conditions for support include a guarantee for "reasonable prices," support for credible and sustainable markets, and prohibitions on compulsory licensing. India has taken the support of GAVI for the introduction of the hepatitis B vaccine in selected pilot projects. The result is the creation of new markets along with the neglect of the determinants of diseases in populations.[49] What these strategies effectively do is undermine comprehensive public health care: Routine immunisation rates have dropped in several states in the country. Thus the poetry of PPPs is another case of the sucking up of resources, what the French call *actione capillaire*.

Such arrangements have also led to the burgeoning of high-technology diagnostic centres in urban areas, with excess capacities. But interestingly, government employees can now obtain reimbursement for medical expenditure at these institutions, creating effective demand for high cost medical care. Between 1984 and 1986 over 60 diagnostic centres entered the market with an investment of Rs. 20,000 million.[50] Thus Mumbai has thirteen body scanners, Delhi eleven, Chennai eight, Kolkata three, Pune three and Hyderabad two.[51] In such a situation, not warranted by public health considerations, there has occurred the irrational and overuse of such technologies, with Say's Law coming into play: Supply in the health sector, if it is over-determined, creates demand. The oversupply of doctors in the private sector has also led to unnecessary or over-medication of healthy people.[52] Given differential emoluments, it also sucks out personnel from the public health system, with significant internal migration. Policy-led

---

46 Baru, Private Health in India: Social Characteristics and Trends.

47 Two states, Andhra Pradesh and Gujarat, have entered into PPPs in the health sector with Satyam computers, at considerable cost to the state exchequer. Satyam has recently been revealed to be India's biggest corporate fraud. The PPPs continue, however.

48 Chakravarthy, "Role of the World Health Organisation."

49 Puliyel and Madhavi, "Vaccines: Policy for Public Good or Private Profit?"

50 Nandraj, Muraleedharan et al, Private Health Sector in India: Review and Annotated Bibliography.

51 Jesani and Anantharam, Private Sector and Privatisation in Health Care Services.

52 Nandraj, "Beyond the Law and the Lord: Quality of Private Health Care."

development of health tourism has contributed to this.[53] Thus while India produces more than enough doctors – but not enough nurses – for her public health system, she is in fact facing an acute crisis in human health resources for the public health system.[54] Over the same period there has been a burgeoning of medical colleges in the private sector, charging astonishing capitation fees. This has not surprisingly led to appalling standards of medical care, but also to high dowry rates.[55]

Suffering a huge crisis of human resources in the public health sector, despite the overproduction of doctors, India has also emerged as a major exporter of health human resources.[56] The loss of skilled workers does indeed bring some benefits to the migrants and their families; it also leads to foreign exchange flows for the country of origin. Nevertheless, it also places a strain on public provisioning and public financing of education. It is estimated for instance that 4,000 to 5,000 doctors, trained at public expense, emigrate every year, at an estimated cost of USD 160 million to the Indian exchequer.[57] A study carried out at India's premier public medical institution, the AIIMS in New Delhi, estimated that 50 per cent of doctors trained here have migrated overseas as well as internally to the private sector between 1989 and 2000. This study had certain extremely interesting findings: It showed that privileged upper-castes tended to migrate abroad in much more significant numbers.[58] This could be expected from the fact that migration to the West over the last few decades has primarily comprised upper caste professionals, but it also means that affirmative action,

53 There if a flourishing trade, a black market of body parts, in the private sector in India, including reproductive ones. Newspapers frequently report kidney removal scandals. There is also a burgeoning industry in assisted reproduction, including commercial surrogacy.

54 Rao et al., India's Health Resource Crises: Too Many and Yet Too Few.

55 Srinivas, "Changing Values in India Today," 933-38.

56 There is indeed a great deal of anecdotal evidence about unemployment among doctors in India, concentrated in urban areas, and fiercely competing for practice with little attention to medical norms or rational prescription practices. Reflecting this, it appears that doctors are the second largest category of applicants to the Indian Administrative Services exams. But, of course, we have no firm data. If data from the government sector in India is unreliable, there is in fact little data on the private sector which is even averse to academic enquiries. Thus we have no recent data on the private sector health care in India, let alone systematic epidemiological data.

57 Voluntary Health Association of India, Report of the Independent Commission on Health in India, New Delhi.

58 Kaushik et al., High-end physician migration from India, Bulletin of the World Health Organization.

with reservation of seats for the backward castes, has important public health implications. [59]

Initiatives like the Global Commission on Macroeconomics and Health have been pungently, and indeed accurately, described as "neither public health nor macroeconomics."[60] Thus, while state institutions have been criticised for their failure to deliver, there is simply no explanation as to why this has occurred, or indeed why the private sector is supposed to work better. There is an assumption that India is characterised by widespread state presence in all sectors of the economy and polity. In the case of the health sector, this is simply not the case. Along with a weak state sector, an unregulated and powerful private health care sector raises several issues of universal care, of comprehensive care and above all, of equality. Failing this, efforts at tinkering through projects carry the risk of consolidating the dual health care system that the country now possesses: One weak and under-funded for the vast majority of the population with no access to primary health care, and the other largely urban-based curative high technology health care for a minority of the population whose public health needs are taken care of. Larger macro-economic changes that have increased regional, rural-urban and class inequalities have compounded the problem. It is thus not surprising to note that despite the fact that economic growth over the nineties has been described as shining, India's position on the Human Development Index (HDI) globally, never shining to begin with, has fallen further into areas of darkness, from 127 to 132.[61]

Yet another scheme has been the provision of a range of incentives to the private sector in health through provision of land at throw-away prices, grants of customs duty exemptions for import of sophisticated medical technology, and loans from financial institutions at low interest rates. These incentives have been provided for both private for-profit and not-for-profit institutions. The period thus witnessed the emergence of a corporate health sector, increasingly influen-

---

59 The question of reservations, or affirmative action, for the backward castes in India is a hugely divisive political issue playing out on familiar tropes from racist debates in the West, with of course peculiarly Indian complexities. Doctors, largely upper caste, and the dominant section in the media, also largely upper caste, have opposed reservations on the grounds of merit, on the grounds of maintaining standards and so on. Indeed, they implicitly argue that characteristics such as intelligence, merit and efficiency have a genetic basis. In their protest, medical students have swept streets and polished shoes, considered quintessentially lower caste occupations. See Abhay, "Anti-Quota protests: complaints against students."

60 Narayana, "A Review of Health and Economics," 960-964.

61 Rao, "Health in the Age of Globalised Governance," in Kameshwar, Globalisation, Governance and Reforms in India.

tial in policy setting. A study indicated that these schemes had been utilised primarily by urban-based institutions that had not always provided free services to the poor as they were expected to as per the terms of the contractual agreement.[62] Further, there were no mechanisms to monitor these projects, with the government's limited institutional ability to do so. The Qureshi Committee was set up by the Government to examine the violations, by private hospitals, of the terms of their agreements. This Committee found gross violations on every commitment made. In short, the public had been diddled, with the government watching benignly on.[63] The Qureshi Committee report of course gathers dust.

What it has spawned is India's integration into the global reproductive tourism industry, estimated to be worth three billion USD in the United States alone.[64] Within six years of the birth of the world's first test tube baby in 1978, the Government of India sponsored work on in vitro fertilisation (IVF) at the Institute for Research in Reproduction in Mumbai in 1982. This initiative was soon taken over by the booming private sector in health, especially the corporate sector now emerging with state assistance. According to the Indian Council of Medical Research, there were an estimated 250 IVF clinics in 2005. The Indian Society for Assisted Reproduction has a membership of more than 600. What is interesting is that these clinics have now moved to smaller cities and towns to exploit the market in these areas, and indeed to create them.[65] India has emerged as a destination for people wishing both to have assisted reproduction and for surrogacy. Indeed the surrogacy business alone is said to be worth USD 445 million.[66] The cost of hiring a surrogate in India ranges from USD 6,000 to 8,000, as against about USD 80,000 in the United States. Although there are wide variations, the cost of IVF in India is about USD 500 for each cycle, compared to USD 5,000 in the United States. What is also important to bear in mind is that the assisted reproduction technology industry also offers a regular supply of spare ova to another industry, namely the stem cell therapy industry, also unregulated in India. India has announced a public private partnership with three

62 Bhat, "Private Health Care Sector in India: Issues Arising out of its Growth and the Role of the State in Strengthening Public-Private Interaction."

63 Government of Delhi, "High Level Committee for Hospitals in Delhi: Enquiry Report", Justice A.S. Qureshi Committee, New Delhi.

64 Spar, The Baby Business: How Money, Science and Politics Drive the Commerce of Conception. This should be treated with abundant caution, because the figure is constantly inflated by those wishing for the industry to grow, indeed to flourish.

65 Sama, Constructing Conceptions: The Mapping of Assisted Reproductive Technologies in India.

66 Warner, "Outsourced Wombs."

European pharmaceutical companies and the British government for stem cell research.[67]

The growth of reproductive tourism is justified as a win-win situation: Women from abroad, desperate to bear biological babies, can now do so while Indian surrogates earn money. The government has now reluctantly come up with a bill to regulate this booming market. But the bill, drafted at the behest of the very industry it seeks to regulate, is meant not so much to offer protection to the women surrogates as to the industry.[68] The irony of course is that by the same logic, the government need not ban the sale of body organs, as it does. Although the framework to justify reproductive tourism is also "reproductive choice," there is no attention paid to the idea of reproductive justice.[69] Studies indicate that women hiring themselves out as surrogates almost invariably do so out of economic necessity,[70] and indeed are exploited by a range of middle men and women.

As India integrates with the global economy, striving to assert herself on the global stage, boasting of an impressive economic growth rate and the ability to withstand the global meltdown, one way to do so appears to be the foreign exchange it earns through reproductive tourism. As the French have it, *plus ça change, plus c'est la même chose*. India rushes into globalisation, by turning sexual and reproductive slavery into globalised commodities.

---

67 The Hindu, Editorial, October 23, 2007.

68 Qadeer and John, "The Business and Ethics of Surrogacy," 10-12.

69 Fried, "The Politics of Abortion: A Note," in Rao and Sexton, Markets and Malthus: Population, Gender and Health in Neo-liberal Times.

70 Pande, "Not an 'Angel', Not a 'Whore': Surrogates as 'Dirty' Workers in India," 141-173.

Employment and Unemployment in a Global Economy: The Indian Case

Dietmar Rothermund

Globalization and Employment

Independent India had resisted the pressure of the world market for a long time. Under colonial rule, India had been an "open economy" with a vengeance. It was only under the impact of the Great Depression that the British introduced some protective tariffs aimed at defending the Indian market against foreign competitors, especially the Japanese. These tariffs were combined with "imperial preference" which enabled the British to retain their market share.[1] Indian entrepreneurs then supported the national movement and hoped to get genuine protection from the government of independent India. In this they were not disappointed, but they had to accept a highly regulated "mixed economy" under the tutelage of the state. Nehru wanted to industrialize India as fast as possible and he saw in import substitution the best way of doing this. India has a huge home market and therefore this policy was initially highly successful. But Nehru also restricted internal competition as he felt that it would be wasteful for a poor country. This, however, encouraged the production of goods of poor quality which could not have been exported abroad. Since "export pessimism" prevailed in India, there was no interest in the export market. India managed to delink itself from the world market for several decades. Indira Gandhi stressed "self-reliance" and strengthened India's restrictive economic policy even further although at that time the limits of import substitution had been reached. Unemployment had increased in India and there was also the pressing problem of a negative balance of trade.

There were two items which India had to import for the survival of its industry: investment goods and oil. The two oil price shocks of the 1970s affected India's balance of trade very badly. In her second term of office (1980-84) Indira Gandhi cautiously liberalized the Indian economy to some extent and Rajiv Gandhi then followed the same line. Unfortunately, liberalization was attempted by reducing protectionism rather than also doing away with the internal controls inhibiting competition. Lower tariffs ushered in a rise of imports. Since customs duties accrued exclusively to the central government, Rajiv Gandhi's government was flooded with funds which it invested in the public sector so as to increase employment. This only added useless manpower to an unprofitable sector

---

1 Rothermund, India in the Great Depression, 142.

of the economy, thus making its later liberalization even more difficult.[2] Finally, the balance of payments crisis of 1991 forced the government to cut the Gordian Knot which tied down the Indian economy. It then responded very positively to the subsequent structural adjustment. The private sector now forged ahead and unleashed a new economic dynamism. Investment increased but employment did not rise to the same extent. Economists even spoke of "jobless growth." Only in some fields as in the rapid expansion of IT- related services did employment increase by leaps and bounds. This was possible due to India's great pool of highly skilled manpower. Here globalization proved to be a great boon for India.

Employment in the Organized and the Unorganized Sector of the Economy

The most peculiar feature of the Indian economy is its division into a fairly small organized sector and a huge unorganized sector. The conditions of employment in these two sectors are very different. The worker in the organized sector is protected by labour laws, enjoys relative high wages and cannot be easily dismissed. The labour laws were not initially a product of socialist policies. They were introduced in the nineteenth century by the British colonial rulers at the behest of British industrialists at home who wanted to curtail the competition of cheap labour in India. In independent India, politicians with socialist sympathies did not wish to reduce the protection of labour which by now had become a privilege guarded by trade unions. The role of those unions will be discussed later on. Here it may suffice to state that the rigidity of the Indian labour market, which has often been criticized by economists, has a venerable tradition and cannot be overcome very easily. Indian industrialists reacted to this rigidity by hiring only very few "regular" workers and supplementing their workforce with temporary workers or outsourcing a large part of their production. This contributed to the growth of the unorganized or "informal" sector which grew much faster than the organized one.[3]

The unorganized sector in which about 90 per cent of India's workforce is employed by small entrepreneurs is not bound by rigid laws. "Hire and fire" in the most primitive capitalist fashion is the rule in this sector. Some workers in this sector can avoid being fired by working diligently at low wages for many years. They are by no means all unskilled but are often experts in their respective trades. A typical workshop in the unorganized sector has a boss who may even be a graduate engineer and no more than 10 workers. Such small shops are

2 Rothermund, Liberalising India, 13.
3 Ghose, "Informal Labour", 289

hardly taxed and their workers do not belong to unions. These shops usually form clusters, sharing essential machines and producing parts for "regular" industries. They do not aim at increasing their economies of scale as they would then lose their tax exemption. Instead of "vertical" integration, the entrepreneurs active in this sector may practice a kind of "horizontal" integration. If such an entrepreneur has capital to spare he invests it in a neighbor's firm who runs a similar small shop. In a study of the textile industry in Tiruppur, this type of investment has been described as "fraternal capital."[4]

India's has provided striking examples of the "disorganizing" of industries. The transformation of the cotton textile industry is a case in point.[5] In earlier times this industry consisted of large mills, mostly concentrated in Ahmedabad and Mumbai. The mill owners were constrained by a textile policy of the Indian government which did not permit them to modernize their machines and favored the hand looms which generated more employment. The government did not notice or did not wish to take note of the fact that the old hand looms had been replaced by power looms Initially these were often power looms discarded by the mills, but subsequently the small entrepreneurs running sheds with about four looms each also modernized their equipment. The great strike in the Mumbai mills in the 1980s helped to hasten this transformation. The mill owners could not make both ends meet any longer. They closed down their mills, which were taken over by the state as "sick industries." The workers who had continued their strike lost their jobs and then manned the power looms where they had to work for lower wages. The fantastic result of all this was that within a few years the decentralized power looms produced as much as all the mills had produced earlier – at a much lower cost. Nowadays there exist about 426,000 power loom units in India, employing altogether about 5 million workers and producing 1.4 billion sq. m of cloth per year.[6] Their drawback is outmoded technology. The modern shuttle-less loom is conspicuous by its absence not only in the power loom workshops but even in those mills which have survived. This is a handicap also for the workforce which is not trained in the modern methods of textile production. But the story of the "disorganized" cotton textile industry shows the enormous resilience of the unorganized sector which is the backbone of India's industrial growth. Unfortunately this resilience is based on a brutal exploitation of labour. Many workers in this sector experience increasing "casualization,"[7] i.

4 Chari, Fraternal Capital.
5 Rothermund, "Industrialization of India," 484.
6 Chandra, "Textile and Apparel Industry," 526.
7 Papola, "Employment Trends," 134.

e. they are at the beck and call of the employer who hires them whenever he needs them.

One of India's thriving export industries, the cutting of diamonds, has also profited from cheap labour in the informal sector. Indian jewelers have discovered that the so-called industrial diamonds can also be used for bracelets. These diamonds are small and had so far been used only for industrial instruments. Indian artisans can cut and polish these small precious stones so perfectly that they fit into elegant ornaments.[8] In Gujarat there are many workshops in which these small diamonds are prepared for the jewelers. When export demand recedes, these workers are laid off and hired again when the business improves. The informal sector swarms with such activities.

Dharavi in Mumbai, the largest slum in Asia, with about one million inhabitants, is a surprising monument to the productivity of labour in India's unorganized sector.[9] Social scientists doing field research in this slum have found out that the people here are not really poor, they just cannot afford to pay the high rents for ordinary housing in the metropolis. Only about 5 per cent of the people in Mumbai have an income which would enable them to buy a house. Around 40 per cent of the inhabitants of the metropolis live in houses in which they were born. They would not be able to buy them at current prices. A strict Rent Control Act protects tenants, but it also discourages builders from providing flats for rent.[10] Thus life in the slums is for many citizens of Mumbai the only option. Many of the slum dwellers are self-employed and run small shops and tiny factories. The total annual output of the Dharavi slum economy is estimated at US$1.5 billion.[11] Presumably there are what may be called "economies of connectivity" in this slum economy. Large firms in the organized sector profit from economies of scale, small self-employed slum entrepreneurs benefit from lending each other a helping hand.

The persistence of the unorganized sector in India has puzzled many observers. Ever since W. Arthur Lewis proposed his theory of a dual economy in which the organized sector can draw on the unlimited supply of labour of the unorganized or informal sector, many economists have hoped for a transition of the labour force of developing countries to modern employment and an increase in the productivity of labour. However, this does not happen in India where there is not a dual economy but where two parallel economies coexist and develop along different lines.[12] Instead of the organized sector absorbing the unor-

8 Rothermund, India, 96.

9 Menon, "Slums," 481.

10 Gandhi, "Affordability of Housing in Mumbai."

11 Nilekani, Imagining India, 311.

12 Ghose, "Informal Labour," 291.

ganized one, it profits from "outsourcing" the manufacture of parts and of other ancillary activities which the unorganized sector supplies at a low cost. It is not only in the secondary but also in the tertiary sector of the economy that the two parallel economies exist. Domestic service is a case in point. The Indian middle-class employs millions of domestic servants. Whereas this middle class mostly works in the organized sector, its servants are an integral part of the unorganized sector. It is estimated that this class consists of about 40 to 50 million households. Each household would employ at least one servant. The vast army of domestic servants dwarfs total employment in the organized industrial sector. Another large informal service group is that of the street vendors or hawkers in the cities.[13] They are usually self-employed, their trade is considered to be illegal and this makes them easy prey for the police and other authorities which extract bribes from them for not interfering with their business. Small-scale manufacturing units in the informal sector often depend on these hawkers for the sale of their products. There are estimates that about 10 million street vendors operate in the cities of India. Many of them had earlier worked in the textile mills which were closed down when the power looms rose to prominence.

The Role of Trade Unions

Trade unions usually pay attention only to laborers in the formal sector of the economy whose jobs are protected by legislation.[14] According to the statistics of the Ministry of Labour about 24 million Indian workers are organized in unions. The two oldest unions are the All-India Trade Union Congress (AITUC) affiliated with the CPI, it has 2.7 million members, and the Indian National Trade Union Congress (INTUC) affiliated to the Congress party with a membership of about 2.4 million. The AITUC was founded in 1920 by the Indian nationalist Lala Lajpatrai. It participated in the freedom movement and prominent Congress leaders like Nehru served as its presidents. In the 1940s it was taken over by the Communists, and this is why INTUC was founded in 1947 as a Congress union. Most of the other parties also have unions affiliated with them. The Bharatiya Janata Party has the Bharatiya Mazdoor Sangh (Indian Workers Association) which claims to be the largest Indian trade union with about 6.2 million members. It was founded in 1955 by the leaders of the erstwhile Bharatiya Jana Sangh. The Socialists founded their own union in 1948 after leaving the Congress party - the Hind Mazdoor Sabha (Workers Assembly of India) and it has 3.3 million members. Although the socialist parties have practically disappeared from the Indian political scene, the socialists are still active in the labour move-

13 Bhowmik, "Street Vendors," 504.

14 Nagaraj, "Trade Unions," 534.

ment. The CPI(Marxist) founded its own trade union in 1970, the Centre for Indian Trade Unions (CITU) with 3.2 million members. The fact that all unions are affiliated with political parties implies that they may get involved in political campaigns which may not be in the immediate interest of the workers.

All Indian trade unions have difficulties in collecting fees from their members. This also means that their functionaries can rarely hope for regular pay. Some of them extort money from the industrialists by threatening to stir up trouble. There are also more subtle means of extracting bribes from industrialists. The entrepreneurs have to break all kinds of labour laws in order to get their work done. The labour union leader could act as a whistleblower, but if he keeps quiet he will receive a bribe. The other partner in such a deal who expects a bribe is the factory inspector sent by the government.[15] These inspectors were introduced by the British in the nineteenth century when the first Factories Act was passed in 1881. This act was amended in independent India in 1948 and 1987. The powers of the inspectors were confirmed by these amendments.

The union leaders are rarely workers, they are mostly "outsiders,"[16] many of them lawyers who know how to defend workers before tribunals. Since wages are normally determined by awards in India and there is hardly any collective bargaining, the defense of individual workers who have been retrenched is the most important work of union functionaries. Due to the links between unions and political parties, the union leaders are usually party cadres who will obey the commands of their political leaders. In the 1960s and 1970s when the Indian economy stagnated and unemployment increased, there were many strikes organized by union leaders. Indira Gandhi was irritated by these strikes and suppressed them during the Emergency (1975-1976), but to placate the workers she introduced new legislation in 1976 which stipulated that a company employing more than 300 workers must get the permission of the government for the retrenchment of each individual worker. When she was back in power she even lowered the limit to 100 in 1982.[17] This tied the hands of entrepreneurs and prevented them from hiring workers. This legislation also increased the "discretionary" powers of factory inspectors.

In recent years there has been a decline in the interest of workers in trade unions. The "outsiders" as union leaders have failed to protect the interests of the workers. Trade unionism in India is characterized by an almost total absence

15 Nilekani, Imagining India, 310.

16 Morris, "Growth of Large-Scale Industry," 666.

17 Nilekani, Imagining India, 305.

of shop floor democracy.[18] If the workers lose interest in "outside" leaders they are not going to generate leadership from among themselves.

The Migration of Labour

Indian labour has often been induced to migrate to distant places in order to earn a living. After African slaves were no longer available, because slavery had been abolished, Indian coolies were transported as "indentured laborers" to Fiji and Malaya, South Africa and Trinidad and many other places overseas. In India they were made to work in the coal mines of Bihar and the tea plantations of Assam. In our times there has been a substantial migration to the countries around the Persian Gulf where millions of Indian workers earned so much that their remittances helped to fill the gap in India's balance of payments in the 1970s and 1980s when India's balance of trade was negative. When I asked Indira Gandhi in 1981 whether she was afraid of a crisis which might arise if these millions of workers would be suddenly sent home by the Arab authorities, she replied: "The Arabs need us" – and confidently denied that there was any problem at all.[19] Actually, the Gulf War of 1990 did cause a return of Indian workers from Kuwait, but soon thereafter migration to the Persian Gulf resumed.

There is another Indian migration of a more permanent type: the "brain drain" of highly educated Indian experts who settle in the USA. By now about two million Indians live there and many of them have become American citizens. For some time this "brain drain" has been deplored in India, but in recent times some Indians who have lived and worked for several years in America have returned to India in order to set up their own business, making good use of the networks which they have established abroad.

In addition to this overseas migration there is also a substantial internal migration in India. Studies based on the National Sample Surveys have shown that migrants who have settled elsewhere in India have usually improved their economic position. Labour migration is thus a very positive phenomenon.[20] But in general, Indians stick to their places of origin. Census statistics show that only 3.5 per cent of the people of India live in a district other than that in which they were born, as against 7 per cent in China.[21] Linguistic barriers may be a real obstacle to migration. India's many languages are not just dialects but veritable languages which are quite "foreign" to each other. Moreover, the degree of urbanization is relatively low in India. The forces which pull peasants into the ur-

18 Nagaraj, "Trade Unions," 536.

19 Rothermund, India, 234.

20 Özden and Sewadeh, 'How Important is Migration?,' 294.

21 Özden and Sewadeh, 'How Important is Migration?,' 295.

ban crucible of the city are not as strong in India as elsewhere. Nevertheless, there are notable "corridors of migration," the most important of which connects Uttar Pradesh with Maharashtra (Mumbai). A somewhat smaller corridor connects South India with Mumbai.[22]

The migrants are not necessarily welcome in the places to which they flock. Local labour fears their competition for jobs. A militant political party of Maharashtra, the "Shiv Sena," has as its main aim the restriction of the migration of workers from other states into Mumbai. In the 1990s it even formed a state government of Maharashtra in coalition with the Bharatiya Janata Party and tried to extend its activities to other regions of Maharashtra outside the metropolis. But the main plank in its platform continues to be the xenophobic reaction to "outsiders." However, the fear that the Indian cities will be overwhelmed by landless laborers in search of better opportunities for earning a living is unfounded. There is evidence that the rate of rural-urban migration has slowed down in India in recent times.[23] This is not due to economic progress in the countryside but rather to the "push-back" factor of the cities which cannot accommodate more migrants.

Regional Disparities and the Phases of the Demographic Transition

The usual expectation concerning regional economic development is based on convergence rather than divergence. Regional disparities are considered to be temporary aberrations rather than permanent features. But in India economic growth has accentuated these disparities rather than propelling them towards convergence. For instance, in 1980 the Panjab, the richest Indian state, had a per capita income which was three times that of Bihar, the poorest state, in 1998 the Punjab had five times that of Bihar.[24] The disparities of Indian states with regard to the prevalence of poverty are also very pronounced. Studies based on surveys (1999) have identified two distinct groups of states, of which the first one is much better off than the national average of 29 per cent of people living below the poverty line and the second one is very poor. The first group consists of Haryana and Panjab (11.8), Kerala (14.5), Gujarat (15.4), and Himachal Pradesh (17.5); the second group includes Bihar (46.9), Orissa (46.3), Madhya Pradesh (36.8) and Uttar Pradesh (33). It is interesting to compare these figures with those of 1973. At that time the national average was 54.9 and the deviation from that average by some of the states just mentioned was less pronounced, e.g. Bihar (61.9), Kerala (59.8), Uttar Pradesh (57.1), Gujarat (48.2). Only the Panjab

22 Özden and Sewadeh, 'How Important is Migration?,' 298.

23 Kundu, "Changing Agrarian System and Rural-Urban Linkages," 194.

24 Dhillon, "Fiscal Policy Reforms," 189.

(28.2) and Himachal Pradesh (26.4) were comparatively well placed even at that time. Kerala registered rapid progress in the intervening period and Gujarat also did very well. This shows that there are not only persistent disparities but also striking differences in the trajectories of development. These trajectories, however, are again influenced by rather different circumstances. Gujarat, for instance, registered substantial industrial growth whereas Kerala benefited from the remittances of the many Keralites working in the Gulf states.[25]

Regional disparities have also marked the pattern of demographic change in India which has emerged after the "population explosion" of the 1960s and 1970s. The demographic transition usually begins with a decline of the death rate which is then followed by a decline of the birth rate until a low level equilibrium at the replacement rate is reached. This is in contrast with the earlier equilibrium at high death rates and high birth rates which prevailed for many centuries. The fall of death rates in India was caused by advances in public health and modern medicine which eliminated epidemics. In the late nineteenth and early twentieth centuries there were deviations from this path due to famines and the toll taken by the so called "Spanish Influenza" (1918). From the 1920s to 2001 the death rate then fell from about 38 to 8 per thousand births, in the same period the average life expectancy at birth rose from about 26.8 to 64 years. Infant mortality also showed a pattern of progressive decline. In 1951 and 1961 the infant mortality rate was 146 per 1000 births. It slowly declined to 110 in 1981. In the subsequent two decades it came down to 63. This obviously reflects an improvement in medical care. The number of medical doctors increased from 62,000 in 1951 to 625,000 in 2004. The doctors used to congregate in urban areas in earlier years, but now many of them work in small towns in the countryside where they are accessible to the rural population.[26] While death rates fell at a rapid rate, birth rates responded to this trend only very slowly. Initially they fell from about 47 in 1921 to 40 per 1000 in 1941, but then they started to rise once more to 42 in 1961. The difference between birth rate and death rate amounted to nearly 20 in 1961 and this caused the increase which was seen as a "population explosion." After 1961 the birth rate fell again, but it kept its distance from the death rate at about 20 until 1991.

The Government of India was for a long time preoccupied with "family planning" so as to counteract the "population explosion." In the 1970s highly controversial methods of forced sterilization were adopted. These methods had to be abandoned due to large scale protests. Even the term "family planning" had to be changed to the more benign "family welfare." It then emerged that the

25 Rothermund, India, 210.
26 Rothermund, India, 176.

voluntary adoption of birth control has made great progress in India in recent years. The Census of 2001 showed the birth rate had come down to about 25 while the death rate stood at 8 per 1000. Population density has increased in India in keeping with its population growth. In 1951 on the average 117 people inhabited one sq. km; in 2001 there were 324. Projections for 2026 show that by that time the average will be 448; four states will have more than 900 people per sq. km: Bihar, Kerala, Uttar Pradesh and West Bengal.[27]

The fall in the birth rate is caused by the reduction of the total fertility rate (TFR) which refers to the average number of children which a woman would bear in her lifetime. This reduction of TFR has been quite noticeable in recent years. It has ushered in a phase of demographic transition during which a "demographic dividend" will accrue in India. The young people who reach the age of employment will have to take care of fewer dependents and can thus save more of their income. Projections for the year 2011 show that India has a population of about 1.2 billion of which 65 per cent are in the age group from 15 to 64 and 29 per cent are less than 15 years old, for 2001 the respective percentages were 60 and 35. The "demographic dividend" will be even more obvious by 2026 when the respective percentages are estimated to be 69 and 23. Of course, there will also be an increase in the number of old age dependents above the age of 64 years. But this is comparatively small, from about 5 per cent in 2001 to about 6 per cent in 2011; by 2026 it is supposed to be 8 per cent. When the aging population grows, the "dividend" turns negative, but this is a problem which India is going to face only after several decades. However, there are important regional differences in this respect. For Kerala and Tamil Nadu the "dividend" had already reached its highest point before 2001 and it will turn negative in 2011. By contrast Uttar Pradesh and Bihar may benefit from it only around 2026 when it has turned negative in most other states.[28]

There are estimates that the "dividend" may enable India to add 3 per cent to its rate of economic growth per year. But this naturally depends on the gainful employment of the age group between 15 and 64 years. If the present trend of economic growth continues, it may actually be possible to find employment for all of them, provided that India escapes from the trap of "jobless" growth. This would require deliberate efforts to create more opportunities for employment because there has been a consistent trend of the declining employment elasticity in recent years. A high elasticity means that an increase of economic growth would be immediately reflected in an increase of employment. A low elasticity may be due to the higher productivity of labour; i.e. those already employed

---

27 Rothermund, India, 177.
28 Rothermund, India, 179.

would be able to cope with additional work. Agriculture which had so far been able to absorb the additions to the labour force due to the increase of population has recently shown zero elasticity. This is an ominous sign indicating a future rise in unemployment. Only a shift towards horticulture and animal husbandry may create more employment in the countryside. The total number of those who have to be employed in India in 2026 is going to amount to 925 million. This corresponds to 65 per cent of the population. From 1971 to 1991 this percentage had increased from 52 to 59 per cent of a much smaller population. The progress towards 65 per cent is a direct reflection of the "demographic dividend." The Planning Commission is aware of the problems faced by India in this respect. In the paper on the approach to the Eleventh Five Year Plan it states: "All avenues for increasing employment [...] must be explored. If we fail to do so, the demographic dividend can turn into a demographic nightmare." Perhaps the export of labour-intensive products would offer the best prospects for the employment of India's huge labour force.

The regional disparities in the demographic transition are related to differences in social traditions. The patriarchal custom of looking upon women mainly as agents for bearing children and giving them no scope for practicing birth control according to their own wishes is an impediment to family planning. A high TFR and a slow rate of its decline are characteristic for several North Indian states. In Uttar Pradesh the TFR stood at 4.83 in 1997 and 4.33 in 2001. This was well above the national average of 3.49 and 2.89 respectively. The figures for Bihar were very similar to those of Uttar Pradesh: 4.89 and 4.40. Rajasthan with 4.41 and 3.54 also showed the same pattern, but here the rate of decline was much more pronounced than in the two other Northern states. Projections for 2011 when the replacement rate (2.1) should be reached throughout India according to the National Population Policy show the following TFR for the Northern states: Uttar Pradesh 3.42, Bihar 3.49, Rajasthan 2.24. The fact that the national average of 2.1 may be achieved by 2011 would only be due to a compensation effect. The states of Southern India are expected to have a TFR below the replacement rate at about 1.7.[29]

The discrepancy between the North and South could actually lead to an intensified North-South migration which could have political repercussions due to the competition for jobs. In addition to giving rise to migration the North-South discrepancy has another dimension which could precipitate political tensions. Parliamentary constituencies should have a similar number of voters throughout India. It is stipulated in the Indian constitution that each decade the census could lead to a revision of constituencies. The North would then get more parliamen-

29 Rothermund, India, 183.

tary seats and the South would lose some. Those states which fail to reach the targets of the National Population Policy would thus be rewarded, while those who have met their target would be punished. In order to avoid a clash of interests, the number of constituencies was "frozen" in the 1970s. After the 2001 census a revision would have been due, but then a new compromise was found: The delimitation of constituencies may be changed within states, but there will be no change in the number of parliamentary seats which would be to the disadvantage of the states of Southern India. A constitutional amendment has postponed the date of adjustment to 2026. By that time the contrast between the North and the South will be even more pronounced and the Northern vote would be significantly "devalued." It would depend on the political power equation prevailing at that time whether there will be an adjustment or not. Demography may become a political minefield.[30]

The Problem of Rural Underemployment

The fact that India is home to the largest number of poor people in the world is directly related to the retention of two-thirds of its labour force in the rural areas where the productivity of labour is extremely low. A look at the contributions of the primary, secondary and tertiary sector to the Indian economy could give the impression that India is a very modern country. The tertiary sector takes the lead, it is followed by the secondary sector and the primary sector contributes less than one fifth of the Gross Domestic Product. This picture changes dramatically when one takes into consideration how the labour force is distributed among the three sectors. The tertiary sector has been spearheaded by information technology (IT) in recent years. It is estimated, that including all its support staff, IT employs about five million workers.[31] It was beneficial for those working in IT that it was classified as "service" rather than industry, because in this way it was unencumbered by the many rules and regulations which restrict the growth of industry in India. Of course, the tertiary sector consists of only a very small percentage of IT-related activities. The domestic servants and street vendors mentioned above also belong to the tertiary sector. But if we look at the lower strata of the primary sector of the economy we find about 75 million agricultural laborers (1991), most of them landless and dependent on working for others. In the period from 1951 to 1991 India's population grew from 361 to 844 million, the number of cultivators increased from 70 to 110 million, and that of agricultural laborers from 27 to 75 million.[32] The net cultivated area remained

---

30 Rothermund, India, 183.

31 Rothermund, India, 109.

32 Padhi, "Agricultural Labour in India," 27.

about the same at 140 million hectares. Before the Green Revolution there had been some expansion of the cultivated area, but this consisted of marginal soils which did not yield any harvest in the great drought of 1965-66. The Green Revolution then depended on an increase of the irrigated area from about 20 million hectares in 1961 to 47 million in 1991. Much of this irrigation was due to the spread of tube wells. In 1961 just about 135,000 hectares were irrigated by means of tube wells, by 1991 this area had grown to 11 million hectares.[33] This amounted to nearly a quarter of all irrigated land. But tube well irrigation leads to a dangerous exploitation of groundwater. In many parts of India the water table has been lowered at a frightening speed. This then forces the cultivators to get deeper tube wells – a veritable "race to the bottom." The exploitation of groundwater is not the only ecological problem caused by the Green Revolution. The massive application of nitrogenous fertilizers has ruined the soil in many places. In addition to such ecological problems there are also socioeconomic ones associated with the Green Revolution. Economists previously assumed that the impact of the Green Revolution was "neutral to scale," i. e. big and small peasants could equally benefit from it. But it turned out that rich peasants were in a much better position to reap the harvest of the Green Revolution, whereas the poor remained poor.

In the new era of expanding irrigation, marginal soils were no longer cultivated. The increase in the number of cultivators must therefore have led to a shrinking of the size of their holdings from an average of about 2 to 1.2 hectares. But the number of agricultural laborers had also increased. By 1991 there were on average 0.5 workers per hectare as against 0.19 in 1951. Irrigated land may have required more labour for its cultivation, but nevertheless there must have been an oversupply of labour without a commensurate increase in productivity. In fact, in the period in which the share of agriculture in GDP decreased from 50 to 20 per cent, the numbers of agricultural laborers remained rather high. Nevertheless, an increase in real wages of about 60 per cent for an agricultural labour could be noticed in the period from 1983 to 1999.[34] This may be due to an increase in non-farm work in the rural areas, but little is known about these changes in rural employment.

In general, the mismatch between land and labour has increased the incidence of rural underemployment. In earlier times, cultivators who owned more land than they could cultivate with their family members employed laborers whom they maintained throughout the year. They had to do this in order to be sure that in the peak seasons of ploughing and harvesting they had enough help.

33 Bronger, Indien, 363.
34 Kotwal, "Employment and Poverty," 128.

With the rise of a huge "reserve army of labour" in the Indian countryside, the cultivators dispensed with permanent helpers and hired laborers whenever they needed them. This meant that in the off-season the laborers were unemployed for about one hundred days. In order to alleviate rural poverty the government has introduced several "food for work" programs and employment guarantee schemes.[35] The early programs started in the 1970s, but it was found that targeting was a major problem. How to ensure that the programs reached the people in need of them? Moreover, it appeared that administrative costs and corruption severely curtailed the amounts which reached the poor. The latest and largest of these schemes is the Mahatama Gandhi National Rural Employment Guarantee Act (MGNREGA) introduced in 2005. Its financial dimension would approximate 1 per cent of GDP. It stipulates that one member of each rural household could claim employment under this act for 100 days in a year. Since the wages are low (Rs.60 per day), it was presumed that nobody who is not poor would show up for this work. The guarantee also included a payment of wages even if the government was unable to provide work for the applicant. The Right to Information Act passed in the same year would ensure that applicants deprived of their entitlements by officials could ask for an inspection of the relevant files. This is by far the most comprehensive measure aimed at solving the problem of rural poverty and underemployment.[36] It is still too early to evaluate its success.

Indian Labour enters the World Market

It has been rightly argued that globalization has greatly increased the mobility of capital but not of labour. However, the increase in world trade has also contributed to the mobility of goods. Labour does not need to move if its products can be freely transferred to all parts of the globe. This is how India's enormous labour force can find employment in an expanding world market. India is still far behind China in this respect, but it is catching up fast. Moreover, while China has already spent its "demographic dividend," India is still enjoying it.

India's entry into the world labour market will, of course, also cause some problems. The growing employment of Indians producing goods and services for the world market will depress wages in advanced countries. Global "wage compression" is a new phenomenon affecting labour everywhere. But there is also another aspect of these changes in the global labour market. Many lines of production in advanced countries will no longer be profitable and may have to be given up completely. But "moving up market" has always been associated with innovation and further economic growth.

---

35 Gaiha, "Employment Guarantee Schemes," 129.

36 Rothermund, India, 215.

The medialisation of post-colonial Indian society: National and transnational dynamics

Nadja-Christina Schneider

Introduction

'Old' and 'new' media alike have been booming to such an extent during the last three decades that media development in India can be viewed as a driving force of India's new 'economic miracle.' It is very interesting to observe that not only the internet, television, and mobile phone industry is growing at a tremendous speed, but also 'traditional' media such as the press and the radio. In times of a recurrent debate about the crisis of print media or the oft-heard assessment that print has no future, the Indian newspaper market keeps growing and has attracted the interest of transnational corporations and multinational companies.

While this unprecedented media boom is one of the factors which have made India an interesting target for foreign direct investments, Indian media corporations do not seem to find it too difficult to adapt to the rules of an increased media globalization. They are actively pursuing business beyond the borders of the Indian state. It is quite evident that this development is intrinsically linked with the economic liberalization and subsequent enforcement of a consumption-oriented market economy in the 1980s and 1990s. Not only have the country's largest media companies benefited from this development, they have shaped it decisively. And yet the analysis of media or medialisation processes after 1947 cannot and should not be reduced to these dynamics. A closer look at each medium of communication reveals a unique interplay of factors and dynamics – on the national as well as on the transnational level – that are responsible for the burgeoning (or shrinking) of media and related markets.

If one compares the press and television, a fairly inconsistent picture of contemporary media developments in India emerges, with notable differences in the respective narratives. With regard to the Indian press, for example, one could follow Robin Jeffrey who argues that the suspension of the Emergency in March 1977, which had been declared in June 1975, marked the decisive point of departure for the totally unexpected boom of the Indian newspaper market.[1] Concerning the recent history of Indian television, however, the two key events would be the Asian Games in 1982 (introduction of color TV) and the beginning of the satellite age in India in 1991, when Rupert Murdoch's STAR TV began broadcasting to India from Hong Kong.

---

1 See Jeffrey, India's Newspaper Revolution, 38.

This article will offer an overview of some of the most significant trends and aspects of media development in postcolonial India. It will do so by focusing on the perception, debates, and critiques that were unleashed by the progression of medialised communication in India. Using the example of the recent newspaper boom, the first section will illuminate some of the key factors that shaped and established print media as a true 'mass medium' in India. This finding challenges the long-held belief that the press is an 'elitist' and 'predominantly urban' medium, as the following statement suggests: "In a country like India with its high percentage of illiterates, there is little chance of the press ever becoming an actual mass medium."[2] I would like to avoid such a one-sided depiction of the commercialization of the print media (without questioning the commercialization process as such, which accompanied the print media's rapid expansion and paved the ground for it, especially in less urbanized regions of the country). As Jeffrey argues, new public spheres or domains are always the harbinger of new 'consumer spheres.' Accordingly, we need to acknowledge that the commercialization of the media seems to be a viable, though ambiguous way of including non-urban or less urbanized areas in public discourse, and that this discourse proceeds not only on the national level but also on the local and regional levels of Indian society.

In the second section, the focus will be on the state-owned TV channel *Doordarshan* and the family-oriented format of the 'soap opera,' which was introduced to Indian audiences in the early 1980s and experienced a unique career in the following years. With regard to crucial moments in the medialisation of postcolonial Indian society, the impact of TV serials cannot be underestimated. Initially, they were conceptualized to foster 'social change,' 'development' and, above all, 'national integration.' Yet soon they turned out to be a catalyst for the breakthrough of a consumption-oriented market economy in India and, perhaps even more significantly, for the shaping of a new religious consumer sphere, which emerged side-by-side with the political ascent of Hindu nationalism in the 1980s and 1990s.

The third and final section will look into the debates that followed the rapid medialisation processes during the 1980s and 1990s. It will focus on the discourse of media and/or cultural imperialism and on India's new role as an aspiring media power in the South Asian region (and beyond).

2 See Singhal and Rogers, India's Communication Revolution, 54; Sharma, "India and Its Media," 264.

I. Transformation of the press after Independence: Farewell to the "golden age" of the press, commercialization, and the triumphal procession of print media in the 1980s and 1990s

In view of the consolidation of the press during the first half of the twentieth century, many authors subscribe to the idea of an incorruptible political press striving for objective truth and justice – very much like the ideal type of the fourth power in a state. To consider critical journalism a political task, not a business, was only possible as long as newspaper owners, editors and journalists shared a vision of providing a service to the nation. Being a journalist was seen as a vocation (not just a job), the 'inner strength' of the press as stemming from the individual courage of actors who again and again pointed at social injustices that the rich and mighty would have preferred to gloss over:

> "When India was in bondage, the press made a mission to preach Swaraj and Nationalism at the cost of risks – risk is the touchstone that tests the sincerity of the pioneer. The pioneer journalists held the view that the newspaper was an adviser, guide and helper to the public. Its first duty was to put forward a certain policy which was good for the country."[3]

As a consequence, the 'loss' of the anti-colonial project was retrospectively regarded as the main reason for a grave disorientation of the Indian press after independence. Sonwalkar argues that newspapers missed the opportunity to reposition themselves politically and thus propagated a more or less unconditional pro-government attitude, at least until Nehru's death in 1964.[4] Raghavan, however, attaches more importance to the fact that many of the formerly British-owned as well as several of the 'nationalist' English-language newspapers were purchased by entrepreneurs following their business interests, which, according

3 Agrawal, Press, Public Opinion and Government in India, 16-17.

4 Sonwalkar, "'Murdochization' of the Indian press," 824. Until independence, newspaper publishing in India could be subsumed under three broad categories: First of all, the so-called "establishment press" (or Anglo-Indian newspapers), e.g. The Statesman, The Pioneer or The Times of India. Secondly, the category of the so-called "national" or "nationalist" press (English newspapers owned by Indians), e.g. The National Herald, The Hindustan Times, The Hindu or The Indian Express. And thirdly, the category of the anti-colonial, Indian-language press, e.g. Ananda Bazar Patrika (Bengali), Kesari (Marathi), Sandesh (Gujarati), Bombay Samachar (Gujarati), Mathrubhumi (Malayalam) or Aaj (Hindi). (See also Nair, "Growth and Structural Transformation of Newspaper Industry in India,"; Raghavan, The Press in India.; Ståhlberg, Lucknow Daily and Schneider, 'Kultur' und 'kultureller Differenz' im indischen Mediensystem. Sonwalkar estimates the total number of newspapers within the second and third category amounted up to 4.000 newspapers and magazines – in English as well as in many Indian languages (Sonwalkar, "'Murdochization' of the Indian press," 823).

to Raghavan, explains why they followed a pro-government course after 1947.[5] Whatever the decisive factor may have been, the consequence was that the old ideal of 'enlightening journalism' was challenged by the new image of 'professional,' primarily market-oriented journalism, and that they entered into a tense coexistence. The profound changes in the sphere of journalism have led many critics to idealize the past and express a very pessimistic view of journalism's present condition in India which, in their view, has "lost its soul."[6]

Jeffrey considers this kind of nostalgia for a "golden press age" to be one of the universal myths that contribute to the legend of every "national" press:

> "Laments were common for lost, golden days when independent editors, left alone by enlightened proprietors, wrote fine prose and uplifted fellow citizens. Yet evidence from elsewhere suggested that the myth of the independent editor and the golden age was part of the saga of newspapers everywhere, not something specific to Indian-language dailies."[7]

Moreover, the fact that the Second World War marked the end of an era in which the press had been carried by an idea or political intention was something that was felt with great regret in other parts of the world, too. Rosenberg speaks of a global wave of nostalgia that went along with a profound critique of contemporary developments in journalism all over the world. This critique gained strength in view of the worldwide process of deregulation and privatization since the 1980s. Today, few newspapers emerge as "public institutions" working at the service of society, whereas most of them make an appearance as commercial enterprises that constantly have to fight for market shares, especially vis-à-vis the digital media.[8]

Most markedly, media criticism in India expresses a deep-seated skepticism about the consumption-oriented market economy. Hardly any other economic sector symbolizes the latest developments of capitalism as visibly as the globally expanding media industry. This is especially true for the print media sector in India. The fact that even those newspapers that had gained a reputation for their commitment in the struggle for Independence could no longer be distinguished from other, profit-oriented newspapers, and that they were among the pioneers of an increased commercialization of the print media sector in India was considered especially problematic in this context.[9]

---

5 Raghavan, The Press in India, 110.

6 See Joglekar, "The Print Media," 7-12; Chakraborty and Bhattacharya, News behind Newspapers, chapter 1; Bhatt, "New Trends in the Press," 3-4.

7 Jeffrey, India's Newspaper Revolution, 151.

8 Rosenberg, "Das Journalisten-Ich," 110-112.

9 See Vardhe, "Clash of Titans," 108-109.

What was the structural framework within which this development took place, and which role did the government play in this framework? After Independence, the Press Commission (founded in 1952) suggested the establishment of two institutions, the Registrar of Newspapers for India (RNI) and the Press Council. The newly founded Registrar of Newspapers for India, based on the functions and obligations detailed in the Press and Registration of Books Act of 1867, was to monitor the development of the print media sector and to collect statistical material. As an autonomous body, the Press Council was to monitor all developments that could potentially harm the freedom of the press. Furthermore, the Press Council was expected to promote the incorporation of self-regulating mechanisms into the structures of the press sector.

Hence, the independent state in principle supported the private character of newspaper companies and, consequently, the market-based operation of the Indian newspaper sector:

> "The trends in ownership and organization of newspapers, which were beginning to be apparent in the late colonial period, became fully visible by the beginning of the 1950s. The report of the First Press Commission (FPS), took note of these trends. Importantly, the profit motive replaced the idealistic and missionary spirit of the former days. The individually owned or family concerns got converted into joint stock companies and the number of papers under the control of each individual concern increased, leading to concentration of ownership. [...] The process of transformation of press from a craft to a commercial venture was thus complete."[10]

However, it would be wrong to conclude that the state was going to refrain from influencing and exerting control over newspapers. Outwardly, the image of an independent Indian press free from any form of censorship was upheld, true to Nehru's repeatedly quoted motto "I would rather have a completely free press with all the dangers in the wrong use of the freedom than a suppressed or regulated press."[11] But in practice the state used inconspicuous means of interference, such as issuing printing licenses and, more importantly, placing government advertisements. As long as nearly no private advertising existed, governing parties enjoyed a monopoly and made ample use of their privilege – a practice which had been put in place in the 1920s under British rule and which the post-colonial government adopted ceaselessly.

Until the gradual replacement of 'government advertising' by 'corporate advertising' in the course of the liberalization of the Indian economy in the late 1980s and early 1990s, successive Indian governments used their advertising monopoly to influence the press for their interests. "The use of advertising to

---

10 Nair, "Growth and Structural Transformation of Newspaper Industry in India," 4183.

11 Quoted in Joglekar, "The Print Media," 8.

punish, reward and thereby seek to influence newspapers became part of the repertoire of political parties in government."[12] Hence, during the first decades following Independence the press and the state became interdependent. The danger resulting from too much interference by the state or from pre-emptive self-censorship by the press was often pointed out. Many observers were also critical of the fact that the English-language press received by far the largest amount of government advertising budgets, while non-English (Indian- or regional-language) newspapers were clearly disadvantaged.[13] The unequal treatment was partly based on the central government's assumption that the non-English-language press was "less national" and "less modern" and exhibited more "communalist tendencies" than the English-language press – an attitude remarkably similar to the stance the British colonial administration had taken vis-à-vis the so-called "vernacular" press.[14]

This was further aggravated by the fact that the huge potential of Indian- and regional-language advertising had been underrated for decades. Only when market research became more prominent in the 1970s and 1980s was this misperception corrected. Especially the results of the second National Readership Survey (NRS) in 1978 can be regarded as a breakthrough in this context. Eight years after completion of the first NRS, newspaper readership in India had grown by 65 per cent in cities. When the second survey was conducted in 1978, approximately 48 million people were regularly reading a newspaper or magazine. The biggest growth rates were registered in so-called Class III cities with populations between 20,000 and 50,000 people. This increase in readership alone demonstrates that the print media sector had achieved a considerable success in the history of the Indian market economy. At the same time, this development also led to speculations about the potential readership in less urbanized or rural regions.[15]

Only five per cent of the total number of newspapers distributed throughout India at the beginning of the 1970s reached the rural regions of the country, in-

12 Jeffrey, India´s Newspaper Revolution, 60.

13 Jeffrey, India´s Newspaper Revolution, 63. As Jeffrey points out, the Press Commission addressed this imbalance already in the 1950s.

14 See Naregal, Language, Politics, Elites, and the Public Sphere, 1-13; Jeffrey, "Breaking News," 7. On the problem of the linguistic hierarchization of the Indian press and the dichotomy between 'English-language' and 'Indian-language' press, see Schneider, Zur Darstellung von 'Kultur' und 'kultureller Differenz' im indischen Mediensystem, 131-156.

15 Jeffrey, India´s Newspaper Revolution, 65-66. According to Kumar, a total of 15,814 newspapers and magazines in more than 75 languages were published or distributed in India in 1978 (Kumar, Mass Communication in India, 12).

dicating how large the urban-rural divide used to be.[16] By the mid-1980s, the English- and Indian-language press reached 37.2 percent of the urban and 7.1 percent of the rural population.[17] From the 1990s onwards, however, the urban-rural divide began to diminish. According to the 1998 Indian Readership Survey (IRS), 58 percent of the grown-up population (persons older than 15 years) in urban settings and 25 percent of the rural grown-up population were regular readers of daily newspapers.[18]

Table 1: Varying growth dynamics of the press in the linguistic regions of India: Shares of selected states of the total circulation of daily newspapers between 1964-1997[19]

Federal	1964	1978	1991	1997
Maharashtra	20,08	17,17	14,70	12,62
Tamil Nadu	17,04	9,31	6,49	3,88
West Bengal	11,28	11,73	5,72	5,20
Kerala	10,82	10,95	6,52	5,53
Uttar Pradesh	5,22	6,66	16,32	16,17
Gujarat	5,10	6,52	7,34	6,16

16 See Chandrasekhar, "Analysing Indian Language Newspaper Readership"; Agrawal, Press, Public Opinion and Government in India, 16. When interpreting these numbers, one certainly needs to take into account that newspapers were and are often read out by a literate person, which means that in addition to the circulation, one also needs to take the actual readership into account. In India, readership numbers differ significantly depending on the region and social context (see Schneider, Zur Darstellung von 'Kultur' und 'kultureller Differenz' im indischen Mediensystem, 99). In 2003, the total readership number (newspapers & magazines) was 242 million, according to Joshi and Bhatia, 156 million of these were newspaper readers and 86 million of other publications. (Joshi and Bhatia, "Medien in Indien," 878).

17 Kumar, Mass Communication in India, 53.

18 Jeffrey, India´s Newspaper Revolution, 3. Despite the fact that there was still a considerable urban-rural divide in the 1990s, the diminution of this gap continued in the 2000s (Schneider, 2005:98). Currently, it is very interesting to note that the readership of online editions of Indian newspapers is of special interest to marketing companies. Besides the relatively high number of readers abroad, these online offerings are also frequently used by readers in smaller towns in India.

19 The Indian Year Book, quoted in Nair, Growth and Structural Transformation of Newspaper Industry in India, 4184.

Karnataka	4,47	6,23	4,84	3,66
Andhra Pradesh	3,34	5,24	4,40	4,20
Madhya Pradesh	2,59	3,58	6,73	9,33
Punjab	2,44	3,21	4,50	3,59
Bihar	2,39	3,27	8,81	4,64
Rajasthan	0,37	2,57	3,64	6,19
Orissa	0,37	1,30	3,20	3,86
Assam	0,37	0,88	0,28	1,48

The rise of market research in India (and its surprising findings) not only led to an expansion of regional markets and the inclusion of completely new segments but also caused an unprecedented boom in the advertising sector.

Between 1981 and 1996, the budget of the biggest advertising agencies increased from 320 to 4,200 Caror Rupees, i.e., 13 times, according to Jeffrey (1 caror = 10 million). The English-language press was not the only one to benefit from this increase; the Indian-language press did too. From the mid-1980s onwards, approximately half of the total amount invested into advertising went into the Indian-language sector:

> "The increases in advertising expenditure in the 1980s and 1990s were so large that their volume alone would have provided rising revenue to Indian-language publications able to attract the attention of advertisers. But "print" was now accepted to mean print in Indian languages as well as English. During the 1980s, the Indian-language press captured a larger proportion of print advertising expenditure than ever before."[20]

During the same period, the entertainment media emerged as another major competitor for these rising advertising expenditures. At the beginning of the 1980s, the state-owned TV channel *Doordarshan* had already begun to show commercials. Another major rival appeared in 1991 in the guise of satellite and cable television.[21] As a consequence, the share of advertising expenditure for print media sank from approximately 75 percent in 1985 to approximately 60 percent in 1997.[22] Initially, this had no palpable ramifications for the print media sector, seeing that, "driven by the 'liberalization' of the Indian economy and the

20 Jeffrey, India´s Newspaper Revolution, 60.

21 See Naregal, "Cable Communications in Mumbai," 289.

22 Jeffrey, India´s Newspaper Revolution, 62.

arrival of multi-national corporations, advertising expanded at 'frenetic pace'".[23] For individual newspapers or magazines within this sector, however, the rise of entertainment media intensified competition. The same was true of the 'shooting stars' among the Hindi and regional-language press as well as the English-language press. Against the background of a steadily growing middle class, the latter could no longer claim exclusive access to the audience with the highest purchasing power.[24] The result was increased commercialization – if not commodification – of news and news-making and the use of fairly aggressive marketing strategies in order to woo more advertisers. Although advertisers, not readers, bring in the money, large advertising budgets are tied to consumption-oriented audiences. Hence, many newspapers made ample use of numbers and statistics based on the latest market research surveys in their marketing campaigns. "To remain financially viable, most media must sell markets (readers) to buyers (advertisers). This dependency can directly influence media performance."[25]

In view of these profound changes within the print media sector, Indian newspapers since the late 1990s were accused of 'selling' their readers to big companies instead of pursuing their genuine task, namely enlightening citizens and acting as a watchdog over the state. My own analysis of all advertisements for Indian newspapers published in the printed edition of the weekly magazine *Outlook* between January and July 2003 supports the conclusion that potential advertisers were considered more important than readers, as they were in most cases only referred to in terms of their education, social status and purchasing power. It is also interesting to note how strongly the advertising strategies of successful newspapers such as *Mathrubhumi* (Malayalam), *Hitavada* (English), *Sanmarg Hindi Daily* and *Dainik Jagran* (Hindi) resembled each other: In most cases, 'convincing' numbers from the latest Readership Surveys (either NRS or IRS) were quoted, along with explicit reference to the purchasing power of the respective reading audience. I would like to illustrate this specific advertising tactic by quoting from three campaigns run by newspaper companies which ran between January and July 2003. By analyzing these campaigns, I would also like to stress the need to acknowledge the increasing importance of advertising and public relations, both as a distinct field of research as well as an important factor in recent media developments in India.

---

23 Jeffrey, India's Newspaper Revolution, 62.

24 See also Chandrasekhar, "Analysing Indian Language Newspaper Readership."

25 Klaehn, "A Critical Review and Assessment of Herman and Chomsky's Propaganda Model," 11.

Advertisement from the *Mathrubhumi* campaign (*Outlook* 2003):

> "Kalyan silks, what I started as a small showroom in Thrissur has now transformed itself into a well-known brand in Kerala. Mathrubhumi, with its staggering readership of 75.48 lakhs (source NRS 2002) has ensured me good reach among all categories of people. And its credibility as a newspaper has added punch to my advertising. This is what I call a double impact."

Advertisement from the *Hitavada* campaign (*Outlook* 2003):

> "The Hitavada- English Readers. Educated Readers. Affluent Readers. 303,000 Readers. Can your media plan afford not to reach them? IRS 2002 certifies what you already knew – the highest read English daily of Central India."

Advertisement from the *Dainik Jagran* campaign for the regional editions in Bihar and Punjab (*Outlook* 2003):

> "The rising popularity graph of Dainik Jagran in Bihar ensures a rising sales graph for your client [...]. For the simple reason that over 70% of its readership are in the SEC AB segment. Surprised? Good, for there's even more. Its readers possess the best purchasing power. [...] So go ahead, make your client happy. Now that you know how.
>
> Now there's a solid media option to reach out to readers in Punjab. [...] What's more interesting is the fact that this readership has come from readers who matter. Which means now you have a winner for clients wanting to advertise in Punjab."

Considering the fact that *Dainik Jagran*, at present the most successful and widely read newspaper in India, especially in the 1990s cultivated the image of a down-to-earth, non-elitist newspaper, it is remarkable that the paper would nevertheless make use of the same advertising tactics by referring to "readers who matter." [26] The close interplay of market research and newspapers as well as the strong direction of advertising tactics towards potential advertisers can partly be explained by the increased occurrence of so-called price wars. At the beginning of the 1990s, this extremely aggressive marketing technique was first introduced by the *Times of India* but soon found many imitators among the Indian-language or regional press. The basic idea of a price war is to undermine the dominant position of a newspaper in a specific locality by systematically reducing the price for a single copy of one's own paper and thereby forcing the rival to do the same.[27] Subsequently, prices for newspapers fell to such a low level that sales

---

26 For a detailed analysis of the Hindi press and its rapid growth since the 1980s and 1990s, see Ninan, Headlines from the Heartland; Ståhlberg, Lucknow Daily; Neyazi "Cultural imperialism or vernacular modernity?".

27 See, for instance, Vardhe, "Clash of Titans," 108.

alone could not cover the costs of production and distribution; consequently, wooing of advertisers increased significantly.[28]

The emergence of a multilingual "consumer sphere"

The continuously rising growth rates in newspaper readership since the end of the 1970s can be explained by the interplay of several factors. A major factor was the end of the Emergency in 1977. The darkest period of Indian democracy, as it is often referred to, was characterized by sharp censorship measures, the manipulation of media content, and a massive curtailment of the freedom of the press.[29] When the Emergency ended, an enormous demand for information about the events during this phase had accumulated in Indian society, as Jeffrey argues:

> "[...] inside the bottle into which Mrs Gandhi had jammed a cork in 1975, immense curiosity built up. Once she was defeated in the 1977 elections, tens of millions of people searched eagerly for news of what had happened around them in the previous nineteen months [...]. In three years – between the depths of the "emergency" in 1976 and 1979, the years before Mrs Gandhi returned to power – newspaper circulations rose 40 per cent for daily newspapers and 34 per cent for periodicals. [...] People wanted to read about themselves."[30]

Moreover, by the end of the 1970s, migration contributed to an increase in information by Indian society. Millions of people either had relatives or friends in the United States, Europe or in some other industrialized country. Informal communication channels carried new images and ideas of a more 'comfortable', better life to India.[31] These images very much resembled those projected by advertising agencies in consumption-oriented market economies. Consequently, the demand for information that characterized the immediate post-Emergency period was accompanied by a sharp increase in the demand for consumer goods. This prompted the Indian government to initiate the first careful step towards the opening and the deregulation of the Indian economy.[32]

Similarly, the Indian government began to show its willingness to improve press technologies and the media infrastructure. New printing machines were

---

28 See also Schneider, Zur Darstellung von 'Kultur' und 'kultureller Differenz' im indischen Mediensystem, 124-128.

29 See Ramadorai and Bhattacharya, "India," 1173-1176.

30 Jeffrey, India's Newspaper Revolution, 38; see also Rajagopal, Politics after Television, 177.

31 See the contribution by Sunil Bhatia and Anjali Ram in this volume.

32 See Appadurai, Modernity at Large, 4; Jeffrey, India's Newspaper Revolution, 39; Schneider, Zur Darstellung von 'Kultur' und 'kultureller Differenz' im indischen Mediensystem, Chapter 1, 4.

imported. The development of new photo composition programs facilitated the use of the various scripts used in India for printing. These technological innovations allowed the Indian-language press in all parts of the country to catch up and expand at a tremendous pace.[33] Another very important factor in this process was the regional differentiation and localization of newspaper contents and editorial offices. The regional-language press in particular benefited from market research, which enabled decision-makers to assess the real potential for their newspapers in less urbanized and in rural areas. They realized their potential at a tremendous pace. The oft-cited pioneer of this profound transformation of the Indian newspaper was the Telugu press, especially the daily newspaper *Eenadu*, which was founded in 1974 by Ramoji Rao, one of India's most successful and renowned media entrepreneurs.[34] Until today, *Eenadu* is by far the most widely read newspaper in Andhra Pradesh and one of the most successful Indian-language newspapers.

Jeffrey brilliantly describes the fundamental paradox in the relationship between consumption-oriented market economies and print media: Newspapers are essential for spreading the "liberal idea." Without the existence of media the circulation of diverse opinions, not to mention the idea of a freedom of thought is simply impossible. At the same time, the "limousines" carrying liberalism are maintained, polished and set in motion by explicit economic interests.[35] Jeffrey argues that even if newspapers expand mainly because companies consider more and more parts of the population potential "consumers" not only of news but also of the products advertised in the newspapers, this development should not be judged as a negative development. Prior to the 1990s, there was hardly any reporting on local news in India, due to the lack of logistics and personnel plus the high costs of local news reporting compared to national and international news. Local news coverage could only set in once market research surveys had confirmed that it was possible to earn money in this field.[36]

Thus, while new public spheres are always pioneers of new 'consumer spheres,' they also open up new opportunities for the participation of inhabitants of less urbanized and rural areas in public discourses. Those discourses do not take place exclusively on a national level but on regional and local levels, too, and they are inextricably linked to various kinds of enter-, info- or politainment as well as to advertising and public relations. Under these circumstances, one may wonder how and if this reality is compatible with the concept of a liberal

---

33 Jeffrey, India´s Newspaper Revolution, 42.

34 Jeffrey, India´s Newspaper Revolution, 107.

35 Jeffrey, India´s Newspaper Revolution, 75.

36 Jeffrey, India´s Newspaper Revolution, 88.

public sphere. This challenge notwithstanding, in trying to understand the dynamics of medialisation processes it does not seem useful to establish new classifications and hierarchies implied in labels such as the 'informed elites' versus the 'entertained masses.' In fact, the media and media companies actively blur the differences and boundaries between these categories, genres and journalistic formats, as the development of the Indian press since the 1980s suggests.[37] In order to properly assess the mechanisms of how, under the condition of largely medialised communications, meaning is constructed in India, one needs to consider the interplay and amalgamation of journalism, entertainment, public relations and advertising.[38]

II. Expansion and transformation of state owned television channel *Doordarshan*: "Soap operas for social change" versus "cultural homogenisation" and growing consumerism

Television was introduced in India as a state monopoly in 1959. The national broadcasting services as well as the state owned TV channel *Doordarshan* were controlled by the Ministry of Information and Broadcasting until the 1990s.

Until the beginning of the 1980s, *Doordarshan* was primarily conceptualized as a tool to popularize development and education programs. However, television remained a comparatively slow-growing medium prior to 1982. It was Prime Minister Rajiv Gandhi who set the course for an integrated television campaign aimed at the propagation of the market economy and a new vision of 'national culture' via *Doordarshan*. As many authors have observed, Rajiv Gandhi possessed a clear vision of the "synergy effects" this configuration could generate for his government.[39] In the News and Entertainment Program of 1982, the Congress government proposed that the ideological construction of a 'national family' should be propagated through new, family-oriented entertainment productions. In 1984, TV serials modeled on South American telenovelas were introduced in India. Telenovela-style serials took on a variety of forms in different so-called developing countries. What they had in common was that they were heavily influenced by the transnational discourse on development, as Man-

---

37 Similarly, the division or binary categorization of the Indian print media into a supposedly "national" (i.e. English-language) vs. "regional" (i.e. Indian-language press) is equally misleading and deeply problematic. For a detailed discussion, see Rajagopal, Politics After Television.; Rawat, Press & Prejudice, 1-21; Schneider, Zur Darstellung von 'Kultur' und 'kultureller Differenz' im indischen Mediensystem, 131-160.

38 See also Dörner, Politainment, 42; Mazzarella, Shoveling Smoke; Brosius, India's Middle Class.

39 Rajagopal, "Consumer Identity and Image-Based Politics"; Mankekar, Screening Culture, Viewing Politics, 50; Chakravarty and Gooptu, "Imagination," 87-107.

kekar points out. At the time, television was regarded as a "panacea" against underdevelopment.[40] Following the social learning theory, viewers were expected to adopt the 'progressive' attitudes of the protagonists in the interest of development. Yet in India the main 'development boost' could be observed in the numbers of viewers and the enormous demand for TV sets. As the characters in the TV serials increasingly displayed consumption-oriented attitudes, the didactic component was pushed to the background. The shift in emphasis was closely tied to the increased presence of sponsoring and advertisements before, after and during the serials.

The first Indian telenovela was the very successful "Hum Log" ("People like us"), which was screened between 1984 and 1985 and reached an average of fifty million viewers.[41] "Hum Log" was about an Indian family with two children struggling for a better life, and trying to realize this vision by acquiring education as well as consumer goods. So it was already apparent in the very first serial that the "dream of a better life" was constructed along very similar lines as in Western market economies.[42] The huge success of "Hum Log" seemed to prove that development-oriented information could be 'packaged' in a careful combination of entertainment and education.

For the private business sector, the sweeping success of serials meant above all a large and permanent consumer audience, which led to an increasing interest in *Doordarshan* and to the production or sponsoring of 40 serials that were to follow "Hum Log" between 1984 and 1987.[43] A so-called Commercial Sponsorship Scheme had already been introduced in 1983. It allowed for the transmission of commercial spots on TV as well as the sponsoring of serials and thus paved the way for private investment in the state-owned TV sector. For instance, "Hum Log" was sponsored by Nestlé and consequently emerged as the decisive vehicle for products distributed by Nestlé in India, among them Maggi noodles. As Mankekar brilliantly illustrates, the consumption of Maggi noodles, which had been introduced to the Indian market in 1982, rose three times between 1983 and 1984, from 1,600 to 5,000 tons.[44] Not only foreign multinationals but Indian companies, too, benefited from their continuous presence on *Doordarshan*, either in the form of commercial spots or through the sponsoring of serials. However, sales figures increased most clearly when the Ramayan epic was broadcast at the beginning of the 1990s and broke all previous records (see below). Accordingly, it can be argued that the huge success of TV serials on

40 Mankekar, Screening Culture, Viewing Politics, 71.
41 Singhal and Rogers, India's Communication Revolution, 88-91.
42 See Ninan, Through the Magic Window, 127.
43 See Thomas and Kumar, "Copied from without and cloned from within," 136.
44 Mankekar, Screening Culture, Viewing Politics, 82.

Doordarshan was an important reason for the triumph of the market economy in India.

The radical modification of the modernization project and of the ideology of progress as they had been promulgated by the Congress party under Jawaharlal Nehru was anticipated by state-controlled television in the 1980s. From then onwards, 'development' and 'progress' rarely referred to a material, legal and social improvement of the 'underprivileged' but to the purchasing power of a growing Indian middle class and the general economic growth it was supposed to spur. Similar to the discourse of the *Wirtschaftswunder* ('economic miracle') in the Federal Republic of Germany during the 1950s, it was suggested that Indian citizens could significantly contribute to their country's progress through consumption.

Entertainment serials in India were and still are explicitly family-oriented. As Mankekar argues, their "social messages" indicate that the viewing families are supposed to perceive of themselves as an embodiment of the "national family."[45] This aspect is best exemplified by the popular serial "Buniyaad" ("The foundation"): "[T]he trials of a post-Partition (Punjabi, refugee, Hindu) family trying to stay intact symbolizes the struggles of the post-Partition Indian nation to 'keep united'".[46] A crucial element of this identity construction was the deliberate promotion of different forms of expression of "modernity", because the differences of role and status within the "Hindu middle class family" imply a variety of specific patterns of consumption. However, it is important to note that the "lifestyle" of middle class families in serials and commercial spots was represented by the entire family and not so much by individuals. So while the "serial family" represented the plurality and cohesion of the Indian "national family," it also manifested itself as a "unit of consumption."[47] The consumption-oriented lifestyle of urban middle classes blended "traditional attributes", ascribed to wives, mothers and daughters-in-law, with "modern attributes," which were primarily ascribed to husbands, sons and occasionally young (unmarried) daughters and together produced a "genuine Indian" way of life. In its totality, it was supposed to be modern and traditional at the same time, progressive and conservative, globally oriented with respect to the requirements of consumer goods, locally oriented with a strong emphasis on a unique, non-Western culture. As Mazzarella puts it: "Indian Soul, International Feel."[48] It is very interesting to observe that this concept of the Indian family as a "unit of consumption"

45 See also Munshi, Prime Time Soap Operas on Indian Television, 1-33.
46 Mankekar, Screening Culture, Viewing Politics, 74.
47 Mankekar, Screening Culture, Viewing Politics, 85.
48 Mazzarella, "'Very Bombay'," 33.

still prevails today. For instance, a recently published market research study by Juxt Consult & Indicus Analytics is titled "Great Indian Families. Understanding the Indian 'Families' as Unit of Consumption (2009)."[49]

Obviously, TV serials primarily aimed at the urban Indian middle and upper classes. They played a crucial role in the propagation of a renewed construct of "Indianness": They emphasized the importance of tradition and the preservation of the joint family by constantly reevaluating an "authentic Indian culture" as opposed to "Western culture." Both versions of modernity were embodied by women: "Western" modernity, which was supposedly threatening Indian social structures, and a "successful Indian" modernity, which was deeply rooted in "Indian traditions":

> "They portray a rejection of Western influences usually symbolized by the modern woman who disrupts the joint family and she is alienated from Indian traditions and values. The good woman is always the one who lives within the confines of the family and protects it from these external forces of modernity and disruption. At the same time within this outward façade of traditions, modernity is ever present in the form of educated career women and women as career makers. It is this mix which makes the series palatable to the middle and upper class audience, as rituals are sold with fun and frolic."[50]

The gradual disappearance of development-oriented messages from TV serials on *Doordarshan* in the 1980s and 1990s was paralleled by the emergence of consumerism as a new indicator of India's modernity. Meanwhile, advertisements increasingly used the motif of the "strong nation". It is striking to see how interchangeable commercial and political advertising were in those decades.[51] Rajagopal explains these particular "synergy effects" as the result of an unprecedented centralization of cultural production. While centralization led to an accelerated circulation of similar narratives, slogans and symbols in areas as distinct as media, economy and politics, it also meant that public discourse generally passed through an increasingly smaller number of interdependent channels.[52] According to Chakravarty and Gooptu, it was the advertising industry which managed to provide the aesthetic images and truly "animate" nationalist messages, especially in the 1990s.[53] Similarly, Mazzarella conceptualizes the

---

49 "Great Indian Families. Understanding the Indian 'Families' as Unit of Consumption," Slideshare, accessed March 30, 2011, http://www.slideshare.net/indicusanalytics/great-indian-families-2009?type=powerpoint.

50 Kidwai, "Images of Muslim Women in Indian Television Serials," 154.

51 See also Schneider, Zur Darstellung von 'Kultur' und 'kultureller Differenz' im indischen Mediensystem, 38ff.

52 Rajagopal, "Consumer Identity and Image-Based Politics," 5.

53 Chakravarty and Gooptu, "Imagi-nation," 90.

advertising business as a "particularly compelling point of mediation between the local and the global, between culture and capital" in contemporary India.[54]

"Mobility" is the core image of countless advertising campaigns. Chakravarty and Gooptu argue that it can be regarded as the central metaphor of contemporary Indian media culture as such.[55] It refers to the aspirations of "upwardly mobile" classes and to their desire for personal "freedom of movement," another metaphor appropriated and converted by consumerism that finds its expression in an increasing number of Indian car-drivers or tourists. On a more abstract level, "mobility" is linked to the general progress of the Indian nation.[56]

As Rajagopal describes, the great euphoria about the global wave of deregulation in the last two decades of the twentieth century was intrinsically tied to a renewed rise of nationalism and the so-called neo-nationalist movements. In contrast to societies whose national identity was based on the topoi of uniqueness, civilizational or cultural supremacy, racial or ethnic unity (or homogeneity), and a sort of "global mission," cultural nationalism in India at that time had not yet been disseminated beyond the high-caste upper classes. From the beginning to the mid-1980s, however, the growing Indian middle class began to set course toward consolidation, both socio-economically and with regard to political influence.[57]

Parallel to this process, observers stated that the Congress government was increasingly using Hindu symbols and rituals in public functions. Against this background, Muslims in India felt openly discriminated against and became disillusioned with the Congress government.[58] Contrary to rosy campaign promises, their socio-economic situation had not improved significantly; their disaffection grew stronger as the Hindu middle class continued to prosper. Accordingly, Indian Muslims felt increasingly isolated from the national mainstream, a feeling that was fueled by demands for a strong centralized state and the "cultural homogeneity" of a "Hindu nation." Hindu symbols also gradually began to dominate the visualization and medialisation of Indian "national culture" and "progress" on *Doordarshan*.[59]

---

54 Mazzarella, Shoveling Smoke, 3.

55 Chakravarty and Gooptu, "Imagi-nation," 99.

56 Even Gandhi and his spinning wheel were appropriated by advertising campaigns and converted into yet another "national" symbol of mobility. For instance, Bajaj coined the following famous slogan in an advertising campaign which was widely publicized in 2001: "Often, all it takes to move a nation, are just two wheels. Bajaj Auto Ltd.".

57 Rajagopal, "Consumer Identity and Image-Based Politics," 1659.

58 See William Gould's contribution in this volume.

59 Hasan, Legacy of a Divided Nation, 262; Mankekar, Screening Culture, Viewing Politics, 10.

The aesthetic and discursive rapprochement to the political project of Hindu nationalism reached its climax with the broadcasting of the "Ramayana" epic on *Doordarshan* in the early 1990s. Commercially speaking, the huge success of this serial mirrors another significant increase in the sales of consumer goods advertised during the commercial breaks.[60] On the other hand, the screening of the "Ramayan" serial coincided with the most critical phase of the so-called Ramjanmabhumi campaign for the erection of a Hindu temple at the site of the Babri mosque in Ayodhya. This does not mean that the Ramayan serial directly contributed to the escalation of violence between Hindus and Muslims after the demolition of the Babri Masjid in Ayodhya in December 1992, as has been stated so often by media critics. Nor can television be blamed for the growing polarization of Indian society in the 1980s and 1990s. One could rather describe it as a longer process during which the concepts of "nation," "culture" and "community" were reconfigured in a way that they increasingly overlapped with the projection of a "Hindu national culture and religion." In that perspective, television would seem to have reflected this process initially and, by doing so, to have influenced its visual form and content.[61]

It is therefore important to consider the logical analogies that both product advertising and political propaganda follow in consumption-oriented market economies: For one, they emphasize the "freedom of choice" and "empowerment" of consumers/voters. Second, they suggest that individuals are able to "get in shape" and face the challenges of the future only by acquiring the "right" image, the "right" identity and the "right" products. As Rajagopal observes, this elementary logic of consumerism found wide acceptance among the upwardly mobile (Hindu) middle class in the second half of the 1980s. What followed, accordingly, was the shift from a "consumerist celebration of a 'Hindu' identity" to a collective identity."[62] The consolidation of a coalition of high-caste Hindu groups with hegemonic tendencies in those years took place parallel to the construction of a consumption-oriented Indian nation as transmitted by state-owned TV (and other media) and the advertising industry. But that was not all. It also marks the success of the Sangh Parivar's (family of [Hindu nationalist] organisations) media strategists, who, within the framework of the Ramjanmabhumi campaign, employed the new projection of a "Hindu" consumer culture to further their political interests.

60 Rajagopal, "Consumer Identity and Image-Based Politics," 1664; Mankekar, Screening Culture, Viewing Politics, 81.

61 See also Ghosh "Media and the Aftermath."

62 Rajagopal, "Consumer Identity and Image-Based Politics," 1664.

Under the government of the National Democratic Alliance (NDA) in the 1990s, the BJP strove for an inclusion of the so-called Indian Diaspora within this (trans-) national, political and economic project. As a result, the identity politics of the Indian state were gradually expanded to Non-Resident Indians (NRIs) and Persons of Indian Origin (PIOs), especially to those who lived in the United States and Great Britain.[63] The mobilization of a perceived "cultural difference" of the Indian "Diaspora" in those countries followed both political and economic interests, especially the increase of investments in India or the transfer of money to relatives in India.

Earlier, the allegedly "westernized" and "culturally uprooted" NRIs had been the target of much ridicule and caricature in India. But in the 1990s, the attitude towards Indians abroad changed significantly, if not totally, seeing that the newly constructed "national family" reserved a place for them at their table.[64] Hence, they were "re-integrated" as highly esteemed members of the family. Owing to this image of "success," the NRI has sometimes been re-named as "Global Indian." He (very rarely "she") is no longer characterized by the fact of his non-residence in the "motherland" but rather by his mobility, which is now seen as something that contributes to the myth of the Indian nation.[65]

III. Outlook: The discourse of cultural imperialism and India's new role as an expanding media power in the 1990s and 2000s

The rapid expansion of transnationally active media corporations in the 1990s led to the recurrence of the debate on "cultural imperialism" in India as well as in other nation states in South and Southeast Asia. While the forced rhetorical dissociation from the "West" influenced the renewed imagination and actual integration of an "Asian culture and community," Indian media companies were quick to adapt to the new rules of media globalization and began to expand beyond India's borders.

In the mid-1990s, when the controversy over the question whether foreign direct investments (FDI) into the Indian print media sector should be allowed or not had reached a first peak, statements like the following one were common:

---

63 See for instance, Walton-Roberts, "Globalization, national autonomy and non-resident Indians," 53-69.

64 See also Desai "Die Ausbürgerung Einheimischer und die Einbürgerung von Ausländern."

65 See Schneider, "Media culture, advertising and consumerism in India," 829-832.

> "The print media seeking to ride into India with hi-tech might and propagandist power to consolidate the West's cultural conquest will make Indians un-Indian and our politicians welcoming economic recolonisation."[66]

V.R. Krishna Iyer, a former Supreme Court judge, worked hard to mobilise public opinion against the intended opening of the Indian print market. He was convinced that every Indian was bound to support the "Operation Rescue of Indian print media." Among the opponents of FDI into the Indian press sector were some of the most powerful press companies in the country, especially the Times of India Group, the Hindu Group and the Eenadu Group. Although the potential weakening of their market position was most probably the main reason for this attitude, editorials and lead articles published in their newspapers depicted the question of FDI as a major threat to India's culture. Besides "cultural imperialism," terms such as "India's threatened sovereignty" or a "new form of colonialism" were frequently used in this debate.[67] Similar statements were made on the political level. The oppositional alliance comprised, among others, the Congress party, the Indian Newspaper Society, the Indian Press Council and all-Indian trade union federations. Congress Party spokesman Anand Sharma announced that his party maintained its position as had been declared in the 1950s. As early as 1954, the first Press Commission of India had emphatically warned against allowing foreign players to enter the Indian press sector. The recommendation led to the legal prohibition of foreign direct investments in 1955. Forty-seven years later, it seemed that the opponents of FDI would be successful again: The pro-FDI draft bill pushed by the BJP-led government was voted down in a parliamentary committee in February 2002.

At first sight, the stance of the Congress Party may be surprising, for the Congress of the 1990s and the early 2000s surely was no longer a strict supporter of the idea of economic self-reliance and autonomy vis-à-vis the former colonial powers. Ever since the reforms at the beginning of the 1990s, Congress had come to symbolize the economic liberalization of the country. It had been the driving force behind the opening up of Indian television as an advertising market for sponsors and advertisers from abroad. In view of this, how can the fierce opposition against the opening of the Indian press to FDI be explained? The answer lies partly in the historical meaning of the press and in its anchoring in collective memory as the "national" medium per se – not only in terms of its geographical scope but also with regard to the emergence of an Indian public

66 Iyer, "Foreign Print Media Incarnating as Indian Fourth Estate?"

67 See also Sonwalkar, "Opposition to the Entry of the Foreign Press in India, 1991-1995"; Schneider, Zur Darstellung von 'Kultur' und 'kultureller Differenz' im indischen Mediensystem, 66-70.

sphere based on anti-colonialism. In its initial phase, the Indian press was a product of the reform movements of the nineteenth century and the struggle for national self-determination in the first half of the twentieth century. What many of the leading figures of those movements had in common was the fact that they were also the pioneers of Indian journalism. Well-known names such as Ram Mohan Roy, Jawaharlal Nehru and especially Mohandas Karamchand Gandhi were inextricably linked with the political history of the country and with the history of journalism in India. It is against this historical background that the ideal of non-corruptible journalism with a strong political focus is still the measuring stick which is applied to the postcolonial and increasingly market-oriented journalism of today.

Apart from the nostalgic idealization of the Indian press, one also needs to take into account the alleged "invasion from the sky," i.e., the introduction of satellite television. In this "invasion" scenario, which could be observed in a number of postcolonial states in Asia during the 1990s, Western print media or satellite channels came to symbolize the deeply felt threat to the integrity of cultural and geographical regions as well as of nationally defined borders. What formed the basis of this scenario was the persistent idea of an unchallenged and dominant "centre of power" in the West, which was supposedly trying to maintain its colonial domination over the "periphery" according to the logic of a borderless corporate capitalism.

This "discourse of complaint and protest," as media researcher Ien Ang calls it, was inspired by the widely received theory of Herbert Schiller, who equates cultural imperialism with media imperialism.[68] As Ang rightly criticizes, it is rather reductionist to consider media as powerful agents who permeate all social and cultural textures and, more importantly, as the sole cause of abrupt socio-cultural changes.[69] Tomlinson and other cultural and media theorists have repeatedly argued against the idea of a homogenized global culture as a result of media globalization. They also question the idea of an unchallenged "centre of power" in the West vis-à-vis its countless "peripheries."[70] Interestingly, however, some of the states in South and Southeast Asia argued for the promotion of a new "Asian perspective" as the foundation for their own global ambitions. According to Ang, it was this discursive shift which marked the transition of the

---

68 Ang, "Globalisierung der Medien, kultureller Imperialismus und der Aufstieg Asiens," 565.

69 Ang, "Globalisierung der Medien, kultureller Imperialismus und der Aufstieg Asiens," 565.

70 Tomlinson, "Internationalismus, Globalisierung und kultureller Imperialismus."

anti-colonial or post-colonial climate to what could be termed a "neocivilizational climate."[71]

In lieu of a specific national identity, the renewed Asianism stressed the importance of Asia as a transnational cultural community, one which was to present itself as united on the "cultural terrain" in order to promote transregional economic integration.[72] Of course those efforts have not rendered the nation state irrelevant. On the contrary: In India, following a phase of deregulation during which the state had seemingly retreated from the media sector, attempts to re-regulate it became visible in the beginning of the 2000s, with the effect of limiting the scope of action for foreign as well as for Indian media companies.[73]

When the new FDI policy for the Indian press sector was enforced in June 2002, the former opponents quickly began to look around for partners in Great Britain, Australia or in the United States. Again, it was the big newspaper groups in India which benefited from it. They are also the biggest players in other media sectors in India, while a number of smaller publishing houses have been driven out of the market.

The expansion of Indian media corporations in the region of South Asia and beyond proves most evidently that the dynamics of media capitalism or media globalization are no longer exclusively generated in the "West" and directed towards an (equally imaginary) "rest". They have become very real in all kinds of directions.

> "Instances of cultural/media imperialism within the South figure less in western media studies, but there seems to be enough evidence now to suggest that they increasingly complicate regional politics. The notion of mediascapes as cultural 'battlegrounds' is often evoked in economic terms, but this can well extend to politics as well, as the situation in South Asia suggests. For example, elites of Pakistan, Nepal, Bangladesh and Sri Lanka not infrequently speak of Indian cultural imperialism. [...].
>
> The source of domination is clearly not necessarily in the North or West; it can emanate from and within the South as well. In some locales, the threat posed by the local and the regional may be perceived to be more serious."[74]

---

71 Ang, "Globalisierung der Medien, kultureller Imperialismus und der Aufstieg Asiens," 580.

72 Ang, "Globalisierung der Medien, kultureller Imperialismus und der Aufstieg Asiens," 580.

73 See Schneider, Zur Darstellung von 'Kultur' und 'kultureller Differenz' im indischen Mediensystem, 7-14.

74 Sonwalkar, "India," 506.

Thus, as Sonwalkar very pointedly argues, the fear of a "Murdochization" of the Indian media sector is not a danger that comes from the outside, for India has generated its own "media barons."

IV. Power

Foreign Policy and the Success of India's Democracy

Jennifer Bussell

What is the role of foreign policy in domestic politics? This chapter poses this question to the case of India, and to the specific ways in which the links between foreign and domestic policy may shed new light on the nature of India's democracy. The 'surprise' of successful democratic politics in India has garnered significant public and academic attention, but the explanations provided have focused almost exclusively on the nature of domestic characteristics and institutions. Here, I posit that an analysis of India's foreign relations in the period between Independence and the economic reforms of the 1990s can further extend our understanding of the ways in which India's democracy was consolidated. In particular, an evaluation of the contribution foreign policy made to the availability of resources for offsetting the social costs of industrial development, as well as to the nature of domestic political competition, helps to highlight the need for more explicit attention to the relationship between international and domestic politics.

India's post-Independence foreign policy has, on its own, received significant academic attention, and for good reasons. India played a formative and leading role in the Non-Aligned Movement, while also maintaining relations, to varying degrees, with both the Soviet Union and the United States during the Cold War. At the same time, analysts of Indian democracy throughout the twentieth century have questioned both the viability and the quality of democratic practice in a large, poor, and ethnically diverse setting. Those who applaud Indian 'exceptionalism' highlight historic structural choices, including those of both Independence movement leaders in their commitment to a secular, liberal democracy and British colonists who moved toward democracy during the transition to independence, as well as ongoing efforts to maintain fair elections, mediate ethnic conflict, and promote economic growth.

Fewer analyses have explored the links between these two areas and the relevance of transnational relations to the stability of Indian democracy, particularly during the Cold War era considered in this volume. I address the relationship between foreign policy actions and domestic politics by asking a set of related questions: As a founder and leader of the Non-Aligned Movement, did India's stance on Cold War relations play a role in stabilizing domestic politics? How did domestic notions of democracy interact with India's foreign policy agenda and relationships with other countries? Did relations with foreign powers, including with regard to aid and arms purchases, interact with domestic politics in important ways?

Drawing on theories of international relations, I explore these questions through an examination of India's foreign policy in this period, its strategic choices about the acceptance of foreign aid, and its specific relationship with major world and regional powers. I show that foreign policy, while not the major driver of domestic politics in this period, played an important role in shoring up democratic processes, particularly in comparison to many other decolonized nations during this period.

What this chapter does not do is question the relevance of existing arguments explaining the success of India's democracy; this analysis is intended to complement these accounts, rather than contradict them. This is in line with the literature as it stands, which does not point to one single cause of success and rather emphasizes a set of interrelated factors that have together supported democratic practice, even through a dangerous interlude of authoritarianism. I posit that these rich explanations can be further strengthened by additional attention to the ways in which previously identified relevant factors, such as the important role of Nehru's leadership, were also shaped by international affairs. Thus, my goal in this discussion is to highlight how foreign policy in the pre-1991 period served as an additional buttress for India's democracy.

Perspectives on India's Democracy

Varshney presents the basic puzzle of Indian democracy: "Democratic theory holds that poverty, widespread illiteracy, and a deeply hierarchical social structure are inhospitable conditions for the functioning of democracy. Yet except for 18 months in 1975-77, India has maintained its democratic institutions ever since it became independent of Britain in 1947."[1] High levels of poverty have persisted in India since Independence, literacy rates have improved but remain low in many places, and both religious and caste-based divides continue to define large parts of social life. Despite these conditions, as Varshney describes, the press remains free, the judiciary is largely free from executive interference, and peaceful transfers of power occur on a regular basis at both the national and sub-national levels. Simply put, "for more than five decades India's democracy has succeeded against considerable odds."[2]

These outcomes are contrary both to the expectations of democratic theorists and to the empirical experience of most other countries. Democratic theorists

1 Varshney, "Why Democracy Survives," 36.

2 Kohli, The Success of India's Democracy, 1.

note that democracy was instituted in India at a time "when the population was overwhelmingly agricultural, illiterate, occupationally much less specialized than in a [developed] country, and highly traditional and rule-bound in behavior and beliefs,"[3] all characteristics that should make it more difficult to sustain viable democratic practice. According to Ganguly, India's experience also challenges the "expert consensus that some 'floor' level of economic growth is needed before democracy can consolidate."[4]

In his review of India's paradoxical democracy, Varshney highlights four sets of arguments that he posits contribute together to a successful democratic outcome, focusing on historical, economic, leadership, and ethnic characteristics. Prior to Independence, the combination of British "experiments with partial self-rule" and the evolution of the Congress Party from an upper-middle-class group to a mass party, entailed both that there was an institutional foundation for competitive politics and that "when the Congress finally came to power at all levels of government beginning in 1947, it had years of invaluable seasoning under its belt, giving India an advantage unknown to many other decolonized nations."[5]

The particular democratic institutions then put in place by the framers of the Indian Constitution helped to facilitate a transition from semi-democracy under colonialism to a full-fledged, independent democracy. This is supported by the findings of a recent multi-country empirical analysis, in which Adserà and Boix show that the constitutional framework of a country can, in two areas, have an effect on the stability of democratic regimes.[6] First, they find that in low income, developing countries, presidential regimes, rather than parliamentarian, are associated with an increased likelihood of democratic collapse. Because presidents have fewer constraints, and more opportunities, to extract rents from the state, it is more likely that they will destabilize the regime. Second, the authors show that federalism is correlated with greater democratic stability, which they associate with greater decentralization of policy-making, more homogenous political units, and a decreased ability of state actors to extract massive amounts of rents. These findings are important for the Indian case, because they highlight the stabilizing qualities of two primary institutions put into place in the wake of Independence: a parliamentary system and federalist state. From the perspective of institutional alternatives, and given India's wealth of characteristics that democratic theory associates with democratic instability, the best possible institutional

3 Dahl, Democracy and Its Critics, 253.
4 Ganguly, "Six Decades of Democracy," 32.
5 Varshney, "Why Democracy Survives," 37-38.
6 Adserà and Boix, "Constitutions and Democratic Breakdowns."

configuration for stabilizing democracy is exactly what it has, a parliamentary federalist state.

The economics of democracy are also important, and Varshney highlights the strategic choices made by Prime Minister Nehru with regard to tradeoffs between industrialization and protection of the mass population dependent on agriculture. India was able to industrialize while maintaining a substantial peasantry and democratic institutions, in contrast to the theoretical expectations of Moore,[7] because Nehru "realized that one could not give suffrage to rural India and at the same time extract huge quantities of food from it at below-market prices."[8] Instead, and this is an important point to which I will return below, "resources for industrialization came not from agriculture, but from urban savings and foreign aid (including wheat from the United States)."[9]

Finally, Varshney identifies the relevance of leadership, particularly that of Nehru, for democratic consolidation.[10] Nehru's appreciation for democratic constraints meant that he willingly worked within the institutions set up during the transition from colonial rule and accepted situations, such as judicial rulings, in which his opinion was not aligned with outcomes. More generally, Varshney posits that most of India's political leaders followed this model in the early post-Independence years, when the country's democracy was at the greatest risk of failure.[11] "The democratic temper of India's first-generation leaders contributed handsomely to building up the system's democratic base. Once such a solid base was in place, it became hard completely to undermine the democratic edifice."[12]

These combined arguments highlight the relationship between the democratic institutions, both formal and informal, established by India's rising leaders before and just after Independence, the restraint that these same leaders displayed in allowing themselves to be constrained by the institutions of their making, and the recognition leaders showed of rapid industrialization's threats to their overall goals of democratic development. More generally, Kohli argues that understanding India's democracy requires a focus on the negotiation of power distributions within society, which "draws attention to such factors such

7 Moore, Social Origins of Dictatorship and Democracy.

8 Varshney, "Why Democracy Survives," 42.

9 Varshney, "Why Democracy Survives," 42.

10 Because it is less relevant to the later discussion of foreign policy in this essay, I do not focus here on Varshney's arguments about the relevance of ethnic relations to India's democracy.

11 Varshney, "Why Democracy Survives," 48.

12 Varshney, "Why Democracy Survives," 48.

as leadership strategies, in design of political institutions, and the political role of diverse social groups, or, in short, to the interaction of the state and society."[13]

What I offer in the following sections is a new perspective on India's democratic consolidation. I posit that it was India's foreign policy that in many cases helped leaders to navigate these domestic societal alignments. This was particularly the case with regard to choices over tradeoffs between economic development and democracy, in which foreign relations played an important role in supporting democratic practice by alleviating pressures that could, under other circumstances, push elites toward authoritarianism.

India's Foreign Policy after Independence

Analyses to date of India's democracy offer powerful explanations for India's democratic stability in general, but these accounts rarely take into account the temporal context of India's emergence as a democracy. India achieved independence at a moment of significant conflict between two global powers. In many post-colonial states, similar origins resulted in a polarization of sorts that rarely led to consolidated democracy, as I discuss in more detail below. Thus, India was not just successful in its democracy, but it was successful at a moment in time when very few of its peer nations achieved the same goal. The question, then, is not just why did India succeed, but why was India different?

To answer this question, I posit that we must first look to the ways in which India dealt with external actors, before then considering how these choices interacted with internal conditions. India's foreign policy strategies in the post-Independence era have been well documented, so I will focus on the philosophies underlying India's approach to international relations and the significance of this approach relative to that of other developing countries at the time. In particular, I offer a brief account of the specific elements of India's foreign policy that, I will argue, display a direct or indirect relationship with the practice of domestic politics in the post-Independence period.

A primary element of India's international stance was the development of an *independent* foreign policy agenda. Analysts note that India's political leadership, and particularly that of Prime Minister Nehru, believed that "recent, hard-won freedom from the colonial yoke would … be meaningless unless it found expression in the international arena. Being subcontinental in size, too, ruled out an assumption of client status for India. An independent voice was not merely a choice, it was an imperative."[14] Thus, India was not only a 'new' country; it was

13 Kohli, The Success of India's Democracy, 1.
14 Chandra, India after Independence, 149.

a country whose leaders perceived a role for it internationally that would require autonomous actions.

What was less clear at the time of Independence, however, was what this type of self-sufficient foreign policy might look like in the context of an international arena in which the United States and the Soviet Union were quickly establishing themselves as the poles of an international system. Because the United Kingdom, India's former colonial power, was not playing a predominant role in this emerging international power play, the choice of an alignment strategy for India was not immediately obvious. What was clear was that an alignment strategy of some sort would necessarily be one of the first and most important foreign policy decisions the country's leaders would need to make.

Prime Minister Nehru took this policy opening, born both of India's first democratically elected government and the fluidity of the post-World War II period, as an opportunity to shape a new stance on foreign relations that reflected an aversion to aligning with either of the emerging world powers. Instead, Nehru and other domestic leaders saw India as a power in its own right and one that would potentially see greater costs than benefits from siding with either the United States or the Soviet Union. Nehru's strategy of non-alignment emerged from this perspective.

Non-alignment, in short, emphasized a refusal to join any international bloc or alliance, so as to ensure the country's freedom to act in its own interests internationally. The five principles underlying non-alignment, as outlined by Nehru in 1954 and codified in an agreement on trade between the Tibet region of China and India, included mutual respect for territorial integrity between countries, mutual non-aggression, mutual non-interference in domestic affairs, equality and mutual benefit, and peaceful co-existence.[15] In taking this stand with regard to all external affairs, India could not justifiably commit to support the actions of other states, through alignment with an international bloc, which might go against these principles.

The non-alignment strategy was not intended to be the singular approach of one, albeit large, nation. Instead, Nehru felt that non-alignment was an important tactic for all former colonies. As Chandra et al. describe, "Nehru's understanding was that newly independent, poor countries of Asia and Africa had nothing to gain and everything to lose by falling for the temptation of joining the military blocs of the big powers. They would end up being used as pawns in contests for power of no relevance to them."[16]

15 United Nations, Treaty Series, 70.

16 Chandra et al., India after Independence, 149.

The risks of alignment to newly independent states were not, to Nehru's mind, purely, or even largely, international. Instead, Nehru saw the inherently *domestic* implications of foreign relations. For those countries emerging from colonial controls and attempting to build new countries, the most prominent needs of policy-makers "were to fight poverty, and illiteracy and disease, and these could not be met by joining military blocs. On the contrary, India and other similarly placed countries needed peace and quiet to get on with the business of development."[17] So, while India's size demanded that it play an international role, this role itself did not entail that India ignore its domestic policy agenda, or that of what it considered its peer states. Foreign policy itself was directly linked to internal goals.

On the basis of both non-alignment and the desire for a strong, independent international role, India engaged, or chose not to engage, in a diverse set of foreign policy activities. In terms of international alliances, India did not side with the United States or the Soviet Union in the Cold War, as I address below, but it also did not choose to engage in broader partnerships that, by default, also linked it to one or another side of this power struggle. In particular, it "neither joined nor approved of the Baghdad Pact, the Manila Treaty, SEATO, and CENTO which joined countries of West and East Asia to the western bloc."[18] In doing so, Indian officials operationalized non-alignment as a proactive strategy to retain control over foreign relations. As Nayar and Paul posit, "What underlay the refusal to join either power bloc was the fierce determination to be independent and master of one's own foreign policy rather than handing over its management to the superpower leading one bloc or the other."[19] This focus on "foreign policy autonomy" is arguably seen as "the most fundamental aspect of Nehru's foreign policy."[20]

More specifically with regard to bilateral relations with the United States and the Soviet Union, while the balance of India's activities vacillated over the decades under consideration, at no time was either country explicitly ignored for the sake of relations with the other. Hardgrave and Kochanek argue that India's non-alignment was "a tightrope act of attempting to balance its close relationship with the Soviet Union and its desire to maintain friendly relations with the United States and the West."[21] However, the strategy can also be seen as an attempt, at least in the early post-Independence years, to balance against the power of the United States post-World War II while the Soviet Union was gain-

17 Chandra et al., India after Independence, 149.
18 Chandra et al., India after Independence, 149.
19 Nayar and Paul, India in the World Order, 124.
20 Nayar and Paul, India in the World Order, 124.
21 Hardgrave and Kochanek, India, 475.

ing strength. As a result, others argue that it was in "this circumstance of the U.S. as a hegemonic power and the assertion by India of foreign-policy independence that were sown the seeds of the largely conflictual relationship between the two states, casting them as adversaries for a long time to come."[22] Thus, relations between the three states experienced an ebb and flow over the following decades, often influenced by interactions with other large neighbors such as Pakistan and China, but overall India was able to maintain its non-alignment strategy to a reasonable extent through the initial decades of her independence.

Arms purchases represented a primary element of negotiation within India's foreign policy strategy, and are an area often emphasized by analysts of non-alignment. To some extent, India is perceived to have relied heavily on Soviet suppliers for arms, such that it was relatively dependent on the U.S.S.R. for these purchases by the late 1970s.[23] However, under Nehru's leadership, India purchased military equipment from France, the United States, the United Kingdom, Sweden, Japan, and Germany, as well as from the Soviets.[24] Thus, "dependence on any one country was avoided and better bargains could be driven since potential partners knew that rivals existed."[25]

A similar diversification strategy was pursued for domestic economic development. The United States government did not support Nehru's strategy for a planned economy and thus was relatively unwilling to provide direct assistance for industrial development, despite efforts by some academics to promote support for India's economic growth.[26] The Soviet Union, on the other hand, saw a stronger reflection of its own domestic strategies in India's economic plans and actively supported heavy industry development by the public sector.[27] The U.S. and other Western countries were instead willing to provide financial and in-kind assistance to back broader developmental goals. India's leaders saw the potential benefits of both types of support and thus "sought to secure its independence by balancing its dependence on the West for aid and loans with Soviet credits and technical assistance."[28]

In all of these ways, and particularly through the efforts of Prime Minister Nehru, India attempted to create an environment in which state leaders could make choices on international policy issues on the basis of *India's* interests, not

---

22 Nayar and Paul, India in the World Order, 125.
23 Hardgrave and Kochanek, India, 475.
24 Chandra et al., India after Independence, 151.
25 Chandra et al., India after Independence, 151.
26 Engerman, "West meets East' and Rosen, Western Economists.
27 Chandra et al., India after Independence 159.
28 Hardgrave and Kochanek, India, 475.

the interests of any partner or bloc leader. This ability was, to Nehru, the defining feature of an independent India. As he put it, "What does independence consist of? It consists fundamentally and basically of foreign relations. That is the test of independence .... Once foreign relations go out of your hands into the charge of somebody else, to that extent and in that measure you are not independent."[29] Thus, while foreign policy was seen as the key to national independence, it can also be understood as an expression of India's own democratic idealism. The pressure to join a particular military bloc was perceived to be a threat to the country's ability to take each situation and determine an appropriate course of action based on the specific nature of the problem at hand, not any previous promise to support a particular actor. "Non-alignment meant having the freedom to decide each issue on its merits, to weigh what was right or wrong and then take a stand in favor of right."[30]

India's independent stance also served as an example to other states. "Non-alignment came to symbolize the struggle of India and other newly independent nations to retain their independence from colonialism and imperialism. India being the first to become independent rightly gave the lead to other ex-colonies in this respect."[31] Other states were enabled to engage internationally in a similar way and over the following decades the Non-Aligned Movement came to play a role in international politics. "In the UN, for example, whose membership had swollen with their [post-colonial states'] entry, the one country, one vote system enabled the non-aligned bloc, often helped by the Soviets, to check dominations by the western bloc. Non-alignment thus advanced the process of democratization of international relations."[32]

Other post-colonial states, however, were somewhat constrained in their ability to fully act on this example. Nehru noted that, "I can understand some of the smaller countries of Asia being forced by circumstances to bow down before some of the greater Powers and becoming practically satellites of those Powers, because they cannot help it [...]. But I do not think that consideration applies to India."[33] Thus, the differences between India and other post-colonial states should not be completely ignored. It is perhaps explicitly these differences that enabled India to take advantage of non-alignment and, in doing so, increase the probability that its democracy would succeed. It is to this argument that I now turn.

---

29 As quoted in Nayar and Paul, India in the World Order, 127.

30 Chandra et al., India after Independence, 149.

31 Chandra et al., India after Independence, 150.

32 Chandra et al., India after Independence, 150.

33 As quoted in Nayar and Paul, India in the World Order, 130.

International Politics and India's Democracy

As noted above, analysts have made great strides toward understanding how Indian democracy survived and consolidated in the face of substantial obstacles. But these analyses have focused almost entirely on the nature of domestic institutions and constraints. In light of the last section's discussion, this focus seems somewhat limited. Prime Minister Nehru himself clearly believed that international politics were directly relevant to the Indian state's ability to pursue its domestic goals. International relations theorists would likely agree, arguing that the nature of global power relations and the placement of a country within the international sphere can have important effects on domestic politics. Given India's emergence from colonialism, like many other developing countries, during a period of major international upheaval, it seems only appropriate to consider how the play of international politics may also have contributed in important ways to the development of Indian democracy.

In this section, I argue that by promoting non-alignment, Nehru removed the possibility of relying on a single external actor for support, but in doing so, created the potential opportunity to acquire even greater external resources for domestic needs than might otherwise have been the case. A commitment to democratic practice tied Nehru's hands with regard to non-democratic domestic behavior – he had to rely on a functioning state within the confines set up by the Constitution – but his emphasis on non-alignment as a key element of foreign policy increased his ability to draw on multiple sources of support, without strong conditions, and to promote stable economic growth within a democratic regime. At the same time, non-alignment also restricted support for any domestic interests that could potentially have threatened the Congress Party's dominance during the early years of democracy, such as the Communist Party(ies). Thus, Nehru's government was able to establish basic democratic practice within a largely one-party state, which, while not authoritarian,[34] possessed many elements of state control that have been associated with planned economic development in other contexts.

This argument is informed by analyses of the relationship between domestic and international politics. Gourevitch offered one of the first accounts of how international relations can affect domestic outcomes by stating, in its simplistic form, that, "political development is shaped by war and trade."[35] In other words, "the distribution of power among states" and the nature of international economic relations can have an important effect on domestic politics.[36] More spe-

34 Huntington, Political Order.

35 Gourevitch, "Second Image Reversed," 883.

36 Gourevitch, "Second Image Reversed," 882.

cifically, according to Gourevitch, state leaders are expected to make domestic policy choices that enhance or protect their position in the international state system. Because "the anarchy of the international environment poses a threat to states within it: the threat of being conquered, occupied, annihilated or made subservient," states are given an incentive "to organize themselves internally so as to meet these external challenges."[37] Put otherwise, "War is like the market: it punishes some forms of organization and rewards others."[38] Following this logic, and because states differ in their placement within the international system, we should expect to see differing choices over domestic political structures. "The vulnerability of states to such pressures is not uniform since some occupy a more exposed position than others. Hence, the pressure for certain organizational forms differs."[39]

In the case of India, as noted above, Prime Minister Nehru believed that India was too large, and thus too important in the international system, to play a subservient role internationally. This belief was fundamental for shaping India's stance on non-alignment. Yet, this did not imply that Nehru must impose an authoritarian government domestically. Instead, India could potentially use this international role to help ensure the success of the electoral system preferred by political elites, representative democracy. But what were the mechanisms by which this could occur?

Later work helps to provide insights into the mechanisms linking international and domestic policy outcomes. Analyses such as those by authors in the Keohane and Milner[40] edited volume and Goldstein[41] addressed the more specific relationship between international actors and domestic economic outcomes, while another stream of research has focused on the link between international factors and the *emergence* of democracy,[42] as well as the *deepening* of democracy.[43] Rudra's analysis is perhaps the most germane here, as it focuses on the role of greater participation in globalized markets on the nature of democratic consolidation. A key element of her argument emphasizes the role for "safety nets" in "providing social stability and maintaining political support for the existing authorities."[44] This social support is a necessary element of increased par-

37 Gourevitch, "Second Image Reversed," 896.

38 Gourevitch, "Second Image Reversed," 896.

39 Gourevitch, "Second Image Reversed," 896.

40 Keohane and Milner, Internationalization and Domestic Politics.

41 Goldstein, "International Law and Domestic Institutions" and "International Institutions and Domestic Politics."

42 Pevehouse, "Democracy from the Outside-In?"

43 Rudra, "Globalization and the Strengthening of Democracy."

44 Rudra, "Globalization and the Strengthening of Democracy," 705.

ticipation in global markets because it helps to offset the threat of economic and political instability for elites who could be threatened by the effects of increased market competition on the poor majority.

Rudra's argument is relevant for the Indian case because it highlights the implications of an important theory of economic development often attributed to Huntington[45] in which development requires a strong, if not authoritarian, state hand to manage the significant social and economic dislocation that occurs during the process of industrialization. The poor, often dependent on subsistence agriculture, face economic dislocation from industrialization and the resulting instability can threaten the government. In a democratic regime, this can take the form of an electoral threat, which viably puts the ruling, democratically elected government at risk. In an authoritarian regime, the state has more substantial resources available to put down this threat, through the use of force, and so may have a greater chance of retaining power.

However, in democratically run states, government overthrow is not a predetermined outcome. In those cases where the government can offset economic threats to large segments of the population, perhaps most generally through social welfare spending,[46] elites may be able to balance the benefits of economic growth with stable democratic practice. This evokes the more general argument made by Polanyi regarding the importance of social protection in shifting from feudal to capitalist economic practice, and highlights the even greater importance of this protection in those regimes that rely on majoritarian rule for their stability.[47]

This dynamic was particularly relevant for maintaining domestic democracy in India, because it helps to explain the moderate development strategy taken by the Indian state. "Nehru was aware of the formidable, novel and unprecedented character of his effort to develop the country economically on the basis of a democratic and civil libertarian political structure. No other country had attempted this so far."[48] In practice, this meant that state leaders, rather than pursuing rapid growth at the cost of social welfare or forsaking growth altogether, looked to find a balance between these strategies. Unlike "most other nations and societies [that] had used authoritarian and administrative measures and institutions during the period of their economic take-off," India did not push economic growth beyond the bounds that could be managed by the state in terms of retaining social and political stability. "Nehru was aware that his path of development might

45 Huntington, Political Order.
46 Rudra, "Globalization and the Strengthening of Democracy."
47 Polanyi, The Great Transformation.
48 Chandra et al., India After Independence, 176-177.

slow down the rate of economic development. But the Indian people, he felt, were willing to pay this price for the sake of a democratic political order."[49]

This perspective, in general, is not new to analysts of Indian democracy.[50] What I propose to contribute here is the theoretical and empirical observation that planned industrial development alongside strong state support for social welfare was *enabled* by Nehru's strategy of non-alignment. Even with a moderate economic development strategy, political stability implied a need for resources to support the demands of social development if the state embarked on a substantial process of industrial development. These resources were available to the Indian state in large part as a result of a foreign policy strategy that maximized leverage in relations with foreign powers.

As noted earlier, India relied predominantly on the Soviet Union for industrial development support. The U.S.S.R. "readily came forward with assistance in the building of the Bhilai steel plant in 1956,"[51] as well as other plants in the future. One analyst noted that, in "1973-74, it was estimated that '30 per cent of India's steel, 35 per cent of [her] oil, 20 per cent of [her] electrical power, 65 per cent of heavy electrical equipment and 85 per cent of our heavy machine-making machines are produced in projects set up with Soviet aid.'"[52] While Western powers also supported steel plants, such as the British in Durgapur and the Germans in Rourkela, the United States was much less interested in providing support to the growth of India's planned economy.[53]

With regard to support for general economic development, however, the US, as well as other Western powers, was substantially more generous. During the period 1961 to 1969, the United States gave India, on average, $667 million per year in aid.[54] This represented more than 50 percent of the total direct aid received by India from foreign sources during this period,[55] which is estimated at just over a billion U.S. dollars.[56] This aid was important in absolute terms, but also because the ability to draw on multiple international sources for support meant not only that India would not be disproportionately reliant on any particular partner, but also because it potentially enabled a larger amount of economic support overall. Thus, India was in a better position than most of its peer states

---

49 Chandra et al., India after Independence, 176-177.

50 Varshney, "Why Democracy Survives."

51 Chandra et al., India After Independence, 159.

52 Chandra et al., India after Independence, 176-177.

53 Chandra et al., India after Independence, 176-177. See also Hilger, "Revolutionsideologie, Systemkonkurrenz oder Entwicklungspolitik?"

54 Government of the United States, Statistical Abstracts.

55 Government of India, External Assistance Brochure.

56 This is based on an average exchange rate in 1969 of U.S. $1 = Rs. 7.5.

in terms of its ability to access international resources. This seems doubly important when we consider the post-independence experiences of many of these peers with regard to democratic consolidation.

I have already emphasized the Cold War context of India's decision both to engage in a strategy of non-alignment and, in doing so, to create the potential to receive aid from both sides of the great power divide. However, the importance of this strategy to India's democracy is made starker through reflection on the experiences of India's peer newly independent states during the same period. While this era in many regions marked the end of the colonialism, the indirect influence of the Cold War powers on other states, particularly developing countries, entailed an important shift in the nature of international influence.

Recent empirical analysis highlights the relationship between international interests and domestic politics during the Cold War era. Building on evidence from African country case studies, Dunning argues that "During the Cold War, foreign donors prioritized strategic considerations and the spread of their political influence in sub-Saharan Africa ... [which] may have diminished the credibility of donors' threats to make the disbursement of further aid conditional on the adoption of domestic democratic reforms."[57] In other words, the competition between the Soviet Union and the United States for influence in post-colonial Africa states (and elsewhere) affected these powers' ability to influence domestic outcomes. Under these conditions, "to the extent that donors actually prefer to promote democracy among recipient countries, threats to make aid conditional on the fulfillment of democratic reforms may not be credible, because withholding aid from autocratic countries could mean losing clients to the other Cold War power."[58] As a result, aid-interested countries may potentially resist the adoption of democratic practices while still benefiting from aid, even from those countries with an interest in promoting democracy.

Dunning examines this hypothesis in the African context, using data on aid receipt and democratic outcomes both during and after the Cold War. In the pre-1987 period, he finds no relationship between overseas development assistance (ODA) from OECD countries and state scores on Freedom House's democracy ratings. This finding is consistent with the idea that Western powers were willing to provide aid regardless of domestic political conditions. In the post-1987 period, however, ODA is positively associated with democracy scores.[59] These

57 Dunning, "Conditioning the Effects of Aid," 410.
58 Dunning, "Conditioning the Effects of Aid," 411.
59 Dunning, "Conditioning the Effects of Aid," 417-418.

findings "lend support to the hypothesis that the impact of aid on regime type varies between the Cold War and the post-Cold War periods."[60]

The underlying logic of this relationship dynamic is that client states used the threat of defection to the other patron to minimize pressure on domestic leaders to enact and follow strong democratic institutions. These states tended not to have strong state institutions endowed to them by previous colonial administrations,[61] let alone the same experience with, and ideology of, democracy that existed among the first leaders of India. Because they could threaten to switch between international blocs, they did not have pressure to gain this experience or shift their ideological inclinations. As a result, many state leaders, relying on authoritarian or semi-authoritarian strategies, utilized the threat of defection to extract rents from the aid provided by their patrons. The extraction of state resources for personal use has been common across Africa,[62] and sources of international aid only increased these resources.

Yet, this logic also implies that most client states were also strategically aligned with only one major bloc in the Cold War. If states used the *threat* of defection to their advantage, then they could not logically use that threat against both sides, assuming at least minimal transparency in international alignments, which seems reasonable during the Cold War period. Indeed, at least in the 1960s, analysis of African countries' foreign policy actions showed strong tendencies toward one or the other sides of the international divide.[63] Thus, these states, in general, did not have the same leverage that India did to extract resources from both the Communist bloc and the West. Alignment implied access to rents without pressure to promote particular domestic institutions, but it also entailed fewer sources of aid in the international community. Thus, while both the aligned African states and non-aligned India were able to evolve domestic political institutions according to the interests of domestic political elites, India had access to a wider range of external resources to support this process. In India, this meant the consolidation of democratic institutions, whereas in many African states, a pattern of semi-authoritarian extractive rule was substantially more likely to evolve during the Cold War period.

This argument, that access to diverse sources of aid helped India to negotiate the dynamics of industrialization and democracy, is only one side of the non-alignment coin. Prime Minister Nehru's foreign policy strategy also had a second important implication for India's domestic political affairs. By maintaining

60 Dunning, "Conditioning the Effects of Aid," 419.

61 Leonard and Straus, Africa's Stalled Development, 10.

62 Bratton and van de Walle, Democratic Experiments in Africa, 66-68.

63 McGowan, "Africa and Non-Alignment," 289.

a relationship with both the United States and the Soviet Union during the Cold War, India's government elites did not alienate either side to an extent that could be detrimental to the ruling Congress Party's hold on power. In particular, the relatively warm relationship between Nehru and Soviet elites meant that leaders of parties in competition with the Congress Party could not take advantage of Soviet largess in order to quickly build a viable opposition. Specifically, "Indo-Soviet relations served to undercut the Communist Party of India and to 'domesticate' the communist movement in India."[64]

The weakening of domestic opposition in this manner, at least temporarily, helped to strengthen the hold of the Congress Party on national power while not invalidating democratic practice. Alternate parties continued to compete and win seats in regularly scheduled elections, but they could not draw on conflicts between ruling elites and external parties to extract substantial electoral resources. This electoral strength and stability for Congress meant that they could behave in fashions more like an authoritarian state than would be the case in a highly competitive electoral environment.

This second claim is relevant because it serves as the foil to the first part of my argument. India's ruling elites had the power, through relationships with both sides of the Cold War, to draw on substantial external resources to support both industrial development and domestic adjustment. But, at the same time, low levels of electoral competition, in part also enabled by these relationships, meant that leaders could, if need be, push policy in directions that might not be broadly popular. Thus, the government had the flexibility to enact policies deemed necessary to promote development but also had the resources to balance any extreme negative outcomes from these efforts. This combination of resources made the pursuit of economic development in a democratic context a more viable option than was the case in most other post-colonial states, all else equal.

Conclusion

The discussion in this chapter offers a view on the relevance of India's foreign policy to domestic institutions and the practice of democracy. I have highlighted the role of prime minister Nehru in particular, because the strategy of non-alignment is fundamental to the benefits India received domestically from its strategic position internationally. In this sense, Nehru as an individual was perhaps fundamental to foreign policy outcomes described here.

At the same time, the Congress Party's emphasis on democratic practice throughout the Independence movement implied that a democratic government

64 Hardgrave and Kochanek, India, 507.

was an almost definite outcome of independence and this expectation was codified in India's Constitution. Consequently, with regard to the domestic political system, democracy was the expectation of the majority of parties involved, and the approval of the Constitution for the most part tied the Prime Minister's hands in terms of initial electoral practice. While this was not sufficient for democratic consolidation in many other post-colonial states, the previous democratic experience of state leaders helped to increase the likelihood of success.

Thus, this analysis does not depend on a purely executive or institutional explanation for the ways in which foreign policy contributed to democratic consolidation. Rather, I argue that Nehru was able to take advantage of the foreign policy that he largely designed, in order to facilitate broader domestic goals within a particular set of established institutions and societal dynamics. Like the established explanations for India's democratic success that this chapter complements, I highlight the ways in which local state-society relations, and in particular the power of agricultural interests within India's democracy, shaped the decisions of state leaders. It was this context that made measured industrial development, enabled by foreign technical assistance and balanced by foreign aid for broader social development, the most viable economic development strategy. Yet, it was India's foreign policy strategy that in many ways made this domestic outcome, and the stable democracy it promoted, possible.

On the Periphery of a Global Conflict: India and the Cold War, 1947-1991

Robert J. McMahon

Indians celebrated their freedom from British colonial rule at the very moment that the Cold War had become the dominant factor in international affairs. Indeed, Jawaharlal Nehru's eloquent "tryst with destiny" speech came right on the heels of another famous speech: U.S. Secretary of State George Marshall's offer to underwrite the economic reconstruction of war-torn Europe. The Marshall Plan, as it came to be called, solidified the division of Europe – and soon much of the world as a whole – into two hostile camps. Try as it might over the next four decades, India could never fully escape the powerful gravitational pull exerted by the Soviet-American struggle for ideological and geostrategic supremacy.

This chapter explores the evolution of Indian foreign policy during the Cold War era. It analyzes the roots and logic of the non-aligned strategy articulated and implemented by Nehru and his successors, seeing it as India's answer to the multiple challenges that the bipolar structure of international politics posed to its independence and security. Non-alignment gave overall shape and coherence to Indian diplomacy throughout this period of great power strife. Yet India's leaders also adapted it to changing conditions, particularly the American alliance with regional rival Pakistan, the growing hostility of China, and the Sino-Soviet split. As early as the 1960s, Indian non-alignment had metamorphosed from a policy of equidistance from the great powers to one that made partnership with Moscow the guiding lodestar of Indian foreign policy.

Nehru's determination to prevent newly independent India from being seduced into joining one or the other of the Cold War camps established the pattern that all Indian governments would follow throughout the Cold War era. Indeed, long before India threw off the fetters of British colonial control, Nehru had declared regularly – and to great public acclaim – that independent India would carefully guard its hard-won freedom by steering its own diplomatic path. An active and positive stance of non-alignment, Nehru had promised his countrymen and proclaimed to the world, would be the guiding principle of independent India's foreign policy. On September 7, 1946, the Gandhian disciple articulated the core element of his foreign policy philosophy in a nationwide radio address. "We propose so far as possible," he explained, "to keep away from the power politics of groups aligned against each other, which have led in the past to world wars and which may again lead to disasters on an even vaster scale."[1] At a press conference several weeks later, the man who was then serving as both vice-president and minister for external affairs in the interim Indian government was even more explicit. "In the sphere of foreign affairs," Nehru stated, "India will follow an independent policy, keeping away from the power politics of groups aligned one against another."[2]

The staunchly nationalistic Indian statesman was adamant that his nation would never again tolerate a position of subservience to another country. "For too long we of Asia have been petitioners in Western courts and chancelleries," Nehru complained in one pre-independence speech. "That story must now belong to the past. We intend to stand on our own legs. We do not intend to be the playthings of others." Insisting that India and other newly emergent Asian countries would follow their own counsel and pursue external policies consistent with their own values and interests, he said that Asian peoples would never again allow themselves to be treated as "pawns."[3]

A strictly non-aligned foreign policy, in Nehru's formulation, would strengthen his young nation's freedom and independence while simultaneously advancing the cause of world peace. Foreign relations constituted "the test of independence" for him. "Once foreign relations go out of your hand into the charge of somebody else," he cautioned, "to that extent and in that measure you are not independent." Nehru was convinced, furthermore, that alliances and alignments just aggravated international tensions, sowing the seeds of future conflicts. By standing apart from each of the Cold War blocs, the Indian leader was hopeful that India could avoid being sucked into an intrinsically asymmetrical relationship; it could at the same time model a more fruitful path for other postcolonial states to follow while contributing to the forging of a more peaceful and just postwar order.[4]

From the outset, Nehru's concept of non-alignment commanded wide and deep support from nearly all sectors of India's extraordinarily diverse society. The ethical-moralistic approach to world affairs reflected in Nehru's soaring rhetoric appealed to Indians' burgeoning sense of national pride. Many practical-minded Congress Party elites also considered non-alignment an intelligent strategy for maximizing India's international stature and influence. Plainly, a posture of Cold War neutrality put India in a position where it could draw much needed economic development support from both West and East. "Even in ac-

1 Nehru, Selected works, Second Series, I, 405.
2 Nehru, Selected works, Second Series, I, 492.
3 Merrill, Bread and the Ballot, 15; Nehru, An Anthology, 362.
4 Nehru, An Antology, 367.

cepting economic help," a realistic Nehru confided to one top adviser, "it is not a wise policy to put all our eggs in one basket."[5] Non-alignment also made good sense politically; an all-out embrace of the West – or of the East – would inevitably have alienated certain powerful forces within Indian society, thereby generating unwanted domestic divisions at the very moment when India was trying to construct a viable state. Nehru's dynamic, independent approach thus served multiple functions for the young nation, ingeniously marrying principle with pragmatism in a manner fully consistent with Indian values, traditions, and perceived national interests.

During his first visit to the United States, in October 1949, the Indian prime minister – a man who exerted virtually complete control over his country's foreign policy – placed strong emphasis on the idealistic dimensions of India's preferred diplomatic stance. "The preservation of peace forms the central aim of India's foreign policy," he proclaimed. "It is in the pursuit of this policy that we have chosen the path of nonalignment." This, he hastened to add, was neither a passive policy nor a "submission to what we consider evil." Rather, Nehru framed non-alignment as "a positive and dynamic approach" to the problems facing India and the world. He told his American audiences that newly independent India stood for "peaceful coexistence," the tolerance of different social systems, anti-colonialism, and unwavering support for the fundamental principles of non-aggression and non-interference in the affairs of other countries.[6]

To American ears, however, Nehru's words dripped with a supercilious sanctimony that they found grating. The problem was compounded by what the Harry S. Truman administration considered a gross underestimation of the communist menace that was emblematic of the Indian leader's naïveté. Washington had hoped that New Delhi would cooperate with the West in seeking to contain communist advances on the Asian mainland, a hope that gained especial urgency with Mao Zedong's proclamation of the People's Republic of China just weeks before the Indian leader's arrival in Washington. His visit dashed such wishful thinking. Wary that U.S. policy makers would try to lure India into a firm commitment to the West in exchange for much needed economic aid, Nehru avoided discussion of India's economic needs. Instead, he stressed at every opportunity that his country's commitment to non-alignment was unalterable. "I want to make no commitments which come in the way of our basic policy," the prime minister had assured his chief ministers before his departure for the United States. Indians were not "going as beggars to the U.S. or to any other country," he wrote them. "It is better to starve than to beg and become dependent on

5 Quoted in Bandayopadhyaya, Nehru and Non-alignment, 173.
6 Quoted in Brands, India and the United States, 35.

others."[7] As Indian Foreign Secretary K. P. S. Menon put it in a speech in mid-1949: "We do not want to be a supplicant at the door of the United States... If we have to fight Communism, we would like to do so out of our own free choice and not at the dictation of the United States."[8]

From Nehru's perspective, his first trip to the United States achieved an essential objective by crystallizing India's chosen foreign policy orientation for his American hosts. As Sir Oliver Franks, the British Ambassador in Washington, astutely observed in a report to his government: "At all events, it was made abundantly clear to the American public that they could not look to India as a ready-made replacement for China [in] the cold war against Communism."[9] Indeed, Nehru told his interlocutors that New Delhi intended to recognize the new communist regime in Beijing at the earliest opportune moment, and advised – however gratuitously – that the Americans should follow suit. He also informed them with characteristic self-assurance that colonialism, not communism, represented the gravest threat to world peace.[10]

For its part, the Truman administration quickly grew frustrated with what it considered an uncooperative and shortsighted policy – and one that was proclaimed, to make matters worse, in irritatingly self-righteous tones. Secretary of State Dean Acheson characterized Nehru, in his memoirs, as "one of the most difficult men with whom I have ever had to deal."[11] The crusty U.S. Ambassador in New Delhi, dyed-in-the-wool cold warrior Loy W. Henderson, described the Indian prime minister as "vain and immature." In a cool appraisal of Nehru's visit, Henderson wrote that "the general impression was left in America that India was making no contribution to [the solution of] world problems, was unlikely to do so as long as the present policy persisted and that Nehru displayed little sense of the practical realms."[12] Sir Archibald Nye, the U.K. High Commissioner in India, found himself largely in agreement with his American counterpart, decrying to his own government the Indians' "unrealistic approach to

7 Nehru, Letters to Chief Ministers, October 2, 1949. Quoted in Nehru, Letters to Chief Ministers 1947-1964, Vol. I (LCM), 471.

8 K.P.S. Menon speech, Wellington, Nehru Memorial Museum and Library (NMML), K.P.S. Menon Papers, File No. 35.

9 Franks to the Foreign Office, November 3, 1949, UK National Archives (UKNA), FO 371/76097.

10 Memorandum of conversations between Nehru and Acheson, October 12, 1949, U.S. National Archives (USNA), Department of State Records (DSR), Record Group 59, 845.021/10-1249; Memorandum of conversation between Acheson and Nehru, October 13, 1949, Harry S. Truman Library, Dean Acheson Papers.

11 Acheson, Present at the Creation, 439-440.

12 Nye to the Commonwealth Relations Office, December 9, 1949, UKNA, FO 371/760097.

world problems" and their penchant "for lecturing other people on the highest moral plane."[13]

In the aftermath of Nehru's American tour, a distinct chill pervaded Indo-American relations. Political differences, ideological cleavages, and cultural misperceptions proved powerful impediments to a constructive bilateral relationship. The genuine partnership between the world's two biggest democracies that pro-Indian sympathizers in the U.S. State Department and their pro-American counterparts in India's Ministry of External Affairs desired suddenly seemed a fanciful dream. Sir Girja Shankar Bajpai, the senior civil servant in the External Affairs Ministry and a leading advocate of closer Indo-American ties, admitted to an American colleague that he worried about Nehru's bitterness toward the United States. Bajpai added that, on a personal level, he was deeply disturbed to see Washington and New Delhi drifting apart so rapidly.[14]

The outbreak of war on the Korean peninsula, on June 25, 1950, appeared at first to offer a fortuitous opportunity for an easing of tensions. Nehru promptly condemned North Korea's "full scale and well laid-out invasion," much to Washington's delight. "Aggression has taken place by North Korea over South Korea," he declared in a forceful statement before the Lok Sabha. "That is a wrong act that has to be condemned, that has to be resisted."[15] But the prime minister refused to countenance Indian participation in the United Nations-sanctioned force dispatched to defend South Korea. "Our moral help is a big enough thing," he commented privately, "which out-balances the petty military help of some other countries."[16] Nehru, moreover, remained skeptical about U.S. intentions and strongly criticized the Truman administration's decision to send the U.S. 7th Fleet to the Taiwan Strait as well as its commitment of increased military aid to French forces battling the Viet Minh insurgency in Vietnam. Each of those moves, made as a riposte to the Soviet-backed North Korean attack and the wider communist challenge U.S. analysts were sure it heralded, reflected what Nehru and most Indian elites judged to be the abject failure by the United States to accommodate itself to the irresistible nationalist currents sweeping across postcolonial Asia.

In the months that followed the inception of hostilities in Korea, Indian and American worldviews clashed repeatedly over the most efficacious response to the conflict. On July 12, Nehru took it upon himself to write personal letters to Acheson and Soviet leader Josef Stalin, suggesting a grand bargain: that the

---

13 Nye to Syers, April 6, 1950, UKNA, DO 35/2932.

14 Henderson to the State Department, August 7, 1950, USNA, DSR, 611.91/8-750.

15 India, Parliamentary Debates: Official Record, 1950, 223, 236.

16 Quoted in Gopal, Nehru, 101.

People's Republic of China be admitted to the UN; that the Soviet Union cease its boycott of that body; and that peace talks immediately commence to ensure that the Korean conflict remain a local one. Although the Soviets accepted Nehru's peace offer, the Americans demurred; privately, they expressed intense aggravation with Nehru's meddlesome and naïve appeals. The breach between the two countries widened when the Indian leader remonstrated publicly against the U.S. and UN decision to cross the 38th parallel, and then against General Douglas MacArthur's subsequent move toward the Chinese border. The entry of massive numbers of Chinese forces into the conflict in November 1950 just validated for Nehru his assessment of Americans as rash warmongers who posed a greater threat to world peace than the Soviets or the Chinese.[17] The Central Intelligence Agency concluded that India's determination to maintain its independence "at virtually any cost… has of late resulted in a tendency to appease world Communism and in [a] failure to support the West in its program of combating world Communist aggression."[18]

Even a positive American response, in mid-1951, to India's request for food aid in order to offset the potentially dire consequences of a bad harvest wound up generating ill will between the two countries. Nehru grew irritated by the U.S. Congress's dithering, and especially by the efforts of some undiplomatic legislators to extract concessions from India in return for American wheat. "India is not so down and out," he stormed in a public speech, "as to accept any conditions dictated by any foreign country in the matter of importing food that sullies our honor." India's gratitude for the dispatch of American wheat was thus vitiated by the manner in which the legislative debate played out, giving added weight to a popular Indian narrative that depicted the United States as a heavy-handed bully unsympathetic to India's needs and aspirations and intent on making the young nation march to an American drumbeat.[19]

America's cultivation of Pakistan as a Cold War ally drove an even deeper wedge between New Delhi and Washington. Suspicion, enmity, and mistrust beset Indo-Pakistani relations from the very moment of partition. Rivalry over the contested accession of the state of Kashmir to India triggered open hostilities between the two infant nations in 1947-1948. The UN Security Council helped negotiate a tenuous cease-fire in 1948, but the unsettled Kashmir question continued to be a running sore – as it remains to this day. When rumors of an impending security pact between Karachi and Washington reached Nehru in early 1953,

17 McMahon, Cold War on the Preiphery, 82-88; Stueck, Korean War, 50-52, 139-140.

18 National Intelligence Estimate, India's Position in the East-West conflict, in Foreign Relations of the United Stated (FRUS), 1956, Vol. 6, 2, 2174-79.

19 Nehru quoted in Henderson to the State Department, April 30, 1951, USNA, DSR, 891.03/4-3051; McMahon, "Food as a Diplomatic Weapon."

he responded with barely controlled fury. The Indian statesman described the prospective U.S.-Pakistani alliance as a repetition of "the history of colonial domination gradually creeping in," and complained that if the United States supplied any military aid to Pakistan that decision would bring the Cold War "to India's borders." In his vigorous efforts to preempt a Pakistani-American alliance, Nehru almost certainly overplayed his hand. His public criticisms made it difficult for the Dwight D. Eisenhower administration to back away from a tentative agreement – especially one that it thought enhanced U.S. security interests in the Middle East and South Asia – without appearing to yield in the face of Indian pressure. Nehru also sought, without success, to impress upon Pakistani Prime Minister Mohammed Ali the adverse regional effects of alignment with the United States. Acceptance of U.S. arms would thrust Pakistan "into the region of the Cold War," he warned, thereby jeopardizing India's security and placing South Asia in the forefront of the superpower conflict. "This is a matter of serious consequence to us," he cautioned. "All our problems will have to be seen in a new light."[20]

Despite those entreaties, in April 1954 the United States and Pakistan concluded a mutual security agreement that transformed the latter into a formal American ally. Shortly thereafter, Pakistan acceded to two multilateral, anti-communist groupings: the Southeast Asia Treaty Organization and the Baghdad Pact. Virtually overnight, it had become, as one top Pakistani military figure boasted, "America's most allied ally."[21] The Pakistani-American alliance undercut a core assumption within India's governing circles that their nation's vastly superior size, population, resources, and economic base would long guarantee Indian regional hegemony. The alliance also destroyed Nehru's hope that South Asia could remain outside the Cold War vortex. Most leading sectors of Indian opinion took it as a given that the American commitment to Pakistan was specifically directed against India – largely as a punishment for New Delhi's proudly independent diplomatic path – even though that factor actually played no significant role in U.S. decision-making. In a private letter to one of his ministers, Nehru speculated that the United States wanted a strengthened Pakistan in order to check India's power within the region. "In effect Pakistan becomes practically a colony of the United States. . . . The United States imagine that by this policy they have completely outflanked India's so-called neutralism and will thus bring India to her knees," he wrote. "Whatever the future may hold,

20 Brands, India and the United States, 75-76.

21 Ayub Khan, The Pakistan-American Alliance: Stresses and Strains, 200.

this is not going to happen. The first result of all this will be an extreme dislike of the United States in India."[22]

Nehru's non-alignment strategy was rooted in the conviction that India's external and internal needs would best be served by maintaining a position of equipoise vis-à-vis the superpowers. The U.S.-Pakistani mutual security agreement, however, called that conviction into question. With its chief adversary now fortified by American arms and entrenched in the Western alliance system, India vied to rebalance the geopolitical scales by tilting toward China and the Soviet Union.

As a first step in that direction, India moved quickly to resolve its earlier differences with China over the tangled and emotionally charged Tibet question. In the four decades between the fall of the Qing dynasty and the establishment of a communist government in Beijing, Tibet had enjoyed the *de facto* status of an independent polity. Determined to assert his new government's sovereign control there, Mao dispatched People's Liberation Army (PLA) forces to Tibet in October 1950. When India registered concern about China's show of force in neighboring Tibet, an area in which New Delhi claimed special rights inherited from the British Raj, Mao testily instructed the Chinese Foreign Ministry to inform the Indian Government that "Tibet is China's internal issue, and no foreign country has the right to interfere."[23] Bajpai captured the fears of many in New Delhi's national security establishment when he warned that India would now have on its northern frontiers "a militaristic and aggressive nation." Eager to forge a positive relationship with the new China, Nehru chose not to contest China's occupation of Tibet – and, as always, he had the last word on Indian foreign policy. Nehru recorded his conviction, at the time, that "the real protection we should seek is some kind of understanding with China."[24]

To that end, in the immediate aftermath of the U.S.-Pakistani mutual security agreement, the two Asian powers signed a treaty by which India officially relinquished its special privileges in the Himalayan kingdom while formally recognizing Tibet as a "region of China." The Sino-Indian accord of April 29, 1954, acknowledged the reality of *de facto* Chinese Communist control over Tibet. According to Hugh Richardson, the former British (and Indian) representative in Lhasa, it also amounted to a "countersignature by India of the death warrant of Tibetan independence."[25]

---

22 Gopal, Nehru 2, 185.

23 Chen Jian, "Tibetan Rebellion of 1959," 81.

24 Raghavan, War and Peace, 233-234.

25 Knaus, Orphans of the Cold War, 51-53.

New Delhi took more than a little solace from the fact that, while it made significant concessions to Beijing, it gained in return China's acceptance of the five principles of *Panchsheel*. Those precepts, which at India's request were inscribed in the treaty, included: mutual respect for sovereignty and territorial integrity; non-aggression; non-interference in the affairs of another country; relations based on equal and mutual benefit; and peaceful coexistence. It was one of Nehru's fondest ambitions to have those principles accepted not just as the cornerstone of Sino-Indian relations, but as the cornerstone of a more peaceful international order. In June, Chinese Premier Zhou Enlai visited New Delhi and, during the course of his discussions with Nehru, sought to ease the Indian ruler's disquiet about China's forward policy in Tibet. Significantly, neither man brought up the unsettled Chinese-Indian border. Nehru was consciously striving to emphasize common ground between the two countries; accordingly, he shoved the potentially divisive border question onto a backburner.[26]

Belying later criticisms of his overly trusting attitude toward the Chinese, Nehru remarked at the time that "no country has any deep faith in the policies of another country, more especially with regard to a country which tends to expand."[27] However foolishly, he was assuming that India and China could construct a bilateral relationship rooted in good faith and mutual self-interest, thereby creating a favorable climate in which a subsequent resolution of the conflicting border claims between the two states could be amicably reached. In November, Nehru traveled to China where his hosts arranged a lavish reception. Once again, the Chinese labored during private discussions to ease his concerns about developments in Tibet. Once again, neither side devoted significant attention to border issues, with Zhou casually alluding to these as small matters. Nehru evidently hoped that these warm meetings, together with the April 1954 treaty, heralded a long period of friendly relations between New Delhi and Beijing. The famous "Hindi-Chini bhai bhai" slogan captured what seemed to be an unprecedented spirit of amity and respect among Asia's two largest nations – and the seeming success of Nehru's conciliatory strategy.[28]

India simultaneously strove to strengthen its ties with the Soviet Union. The death of Stalin in March 1953 served as an essential precondition for moving relations between Moscow and New Delhi out of cold storage. The long-serving Russian dictator had disparaged India as a bourgeois state that functioned as a tool of Anglo-American imperialism; for Stalin, the only Asian country that truly counted in world affairs was Mao's China. The collective Kremlin leader-

---

26 Raghavan, War and Peace, 240-242.

27 Raghavan, War and Peace, 241.

28 Chen Jian, "Tibetan Rebellion of 1959," 82-83.

ship that followed Stalin reversed the strongman's policies toward the Third World by nearly 180 degrees. Beginning in 1954, Communist Party Secretary Nikita Khrushchev and his colleagues began avidly courting uncommitted countries such as India, eyeing them as potentially valuable partners in a broader, anti-imperial strategy aimed at weakening the Western camp. Keenly attuned to Moscow's changing philosophy, India's Ambassador K. P. S. Menon forwarded a memorandum to New Delhi, in April 1954, which alerted his superiors to these "extremely favorable" new currents. India could benefit, he forecast presciently, from the likely dispensation of Stalin's successors to provide material support and lend developmental expertise in return for Indian goodwill. That goodwill would help the Soviet Union offset the disquieting pattern of the United States "picking off one weak or compliant Asian State after another and hitching it to its wagon." The flow of Soviet aid would plainly redound to India's advantage, as Nehru, Menon, and others had long contemplated, because it would lessen Indian dependence on the West for needed developmental support.[29]

The mid- and late-1950s witnessed a flowering of Indo-Soviet relations. In November 1954, the Russians offered to help construct and finance a large steel mill at Bhilai, an industrial showcase project long desired by the Indian government. Much to New Delhi's satisfaction, Moscow's post-Stalinist leadership was clearly eager to assume a major role in India's industrialization drive. Nehru's high-profile trip to Moscow, in June 1955, offered unmistakable testimony to the dramatic turnaround in the Soviet Union's diplomatic priorities. The much-ballyhooed buildup of the Indian prime minister in the Soviet press and the huge crowds that turned out for Nehru's public appearances spoke volumes about India's suddenly heightened value to the Kremlin's rulers. Then, in December, Soviet leaders Khrushchev and Nikolai Bulganin paid an equally high-profile return visit to India, spending three weeks traveling throughout the country. They offered Nehru's government generous economic assistance, held out the prospect of increased Indo-Soviet trade, renewed their commitment to help construct the steel mill at Bhilai, expressed a willingness to sell India advanced military aircraft, and came out in vigorous support of India's claims to Kashmir. Nehru referred approvingly to the "feast of friendliness" that now obtained between the two countries.[30]

---

29 Hilger, "The Soviet Union and India: The Years of Late Stalinism"; Hilger, "The Soviet Union and India: The Khrushchev Era"; Mastny, "Soviet Union's Partnership," 52-53.

30 Mansingh, "Indo-Soviet Relations in the Nehru Years"; Hilger, "The Soviet Union and India: The Khrushchev Era"; Record of a talk between Nehru, Bulganin and Khrushchev, November 21, 1955, NMML, Subimal Dutt Papers, Subject File 17.

Less than two years after the conclusion of the worrisome Pakistani-American arms agreement, India had successfully pulled off a series of shrewd counter-moves. Those had simultaneously tightened New Delhi's relations with both Beijing and Moscow – without inflicting any lasting damage on its relations with Washington. Nehru and his top advisers were convinced that India's pro-active diplomacy had significantly enhanced its overall strategic position.

At the landmark Bandung conference of the Asian and African nations, in April 1955, the Indian ruler stood at the peak of his international stature. He reveled in the accolades he received from so many quarters of the Third World as the champion of a principled policy of independence and non-alignment. Nehru's India served, moreover, as an inspiration for and prime mover behind what would soon become a concerted effort on the part of a determined group of non-aligned states to constitute an independent, third force in world politics. Together with Josef Broz Tito of Yugoslavia and Gamal Abdel Nasser of Egypt, each of whom he formed warm personal bonds with, Nehru emerged as a pivotal figure in that movement. His uncommon eloquence, his international prestige, and his country's position as the largest and most populous of the non-aligned nations won Nehru a leadership role in what the Belgrade Conference of 1961 officially proclaimed as the Non-Aligned Movement (NAM).[31]

Even the Americans, for all their anxieties about India's developing ties with China and the Soviet Union, scrambled to assuage Nehru and to recover lost ground with India. The Eisenhower administration invited the Indian leader to undertake what became a surprisingly amicable state visit to the United States in December 1956, replete with a personal invitation to meet with President Eisenhower at his rustic farm in Gettysburg, Pennsylvania. Shortly thereafter, Washington responded positively to India's request for American assistance in meeting looming shortfalls in the financing for its second Five-Year Plan. By 1958, India had become a leading recipient of U.S. economic assistance, even as it maintained its friendly relations with America's two communist adversaries.[32]

Yet, below the surface, simmering tensions roiled Sino-Indian relations. Those were fed by deep ideological differences between the two states, still-unresolved border issues, and Chinese suspicions about Indian meddling in Tibet. In March 1959, a rebellion erupted in Tibet that the PLA brutally suppressed. Nehru, with near unanimous support from the Indian parliament and populace, granted asylum to the Dalai Lama, Tibet's spiritual leader, and about 7,000 of his followers. The Indian prime minister's decision to provide asylum to the fleeing Tibetans enraged Mao and his inner circle, setting in motion what

---

31 Lawrence, The Rise and Fall of Non-Alignment.

32 McMahon, Cold War on the Periphery, 221-239.

a leading historian has called "one of the most dramatic turns in state-to-state relations during the Cold War era."[33] Chinese authorities had long suspected the Indians of covertly encouraging and aiding the Tibetan rebels so as to maintain a semi-autonomous buffer zone along their common border. Now, sure that Nehru's actions supplied proof of India's perfidy, they labeled the Indians as "expansionists" and publicly denounced their blatant interference in the internal affairs of China.[34]

In the summer and autumn of 1959, bloody clashes broke out between Chinese and Indian forces garrisoned along the contested border. Chinese propaganda mounted a relentless attack on Nehru for his presumed provocations. For his part, the Indian leader bemoaned the duplicity and open hostility of his once-friendly neighbor. He wrote his chief ministers, in October 1959, that India now had to face "a powerful country bent on spreading out to what they consider their old frontiers and possibly beyond."[35] Nehru and Zhou held a series of face-to-face meetings in April 1960 in a failed effort to reach an accord on the contest border, with neither man displaying any inclination to compromise on what each saw as fundamental matters of principle.[36]

The conjoined Tibet and border crises impaled the Soviet Union on the horns of a painful dilemma, underscoring the uncertain international repercussions of the ongoing Sino-Indian dispute. Relations between Moscow and Beijing had grown increasingly testy in the post-Stalin era. The Soviets certainly did not want to alienate their erstwhile Chinese communist comrades further by siding with India in the border conflict. Yet, at the same time, Khrushchev and his associates counted India as one of the most pro-Soviet states in the Third World; they thus judged it imperative to avoid any words or actions that might open a fissure in the carefully nurtured Indo-Soviet relationship. In an attempt to find a middle ground, Moscow issued a public statement proclaiming neutrality in what it called a dispute between friends. A disappointed and aggrieved Mao nevertheless blasted his ally's pose of impartiality as an abject betrayal. He concluded that China could no longer depend on the Soviet Union, accusing it of "accommodation and compromise on important matters of principle."[37]

The Sino-Soviet rift thus deepened along with – and in some measure *because of* – the Sino-Indian rift. At a time when most observers and statesmen

---

33 Chen Jian, "Tibetan Rebellion of 1959," 80.

34 Chen Jian, "Tibetan Rebellion of 1959," 84-88.

35 Nehru, October 26, 1959, LMC, 303-313.

36 Raghavan, War and Peace, 256-266. See also the essay by Manjeet Pardesi in this volume.

37 Hilger, "The Soviet Union and India: The Khrushchev Era"; Mastny, "Soviet Union's Partnership," 57.

alike still viewed the Cold War as a bipolar conflict between the Eastern and Western blocs, Nehru had come to recognize that it was, in reality, becoming a much more complicated affair. The Cold War, he grasped, was fast becoming a three dimensional, rather than just a bipolar, conflict – one in which the United States, the Soviet Union, and China were each competing against the other two, on both ideological and geostrategic grounds. Unfortunately for India, geography seemed to have conspired to thrust it into the middle of that emerging three-sided struggle much sooner and more perilously than in the case of any other peripheral nation.

The emerging tripolar character of the Cold War rivalry offered both challenges and opportunities to India. On the one hand, China's growing hostility punctured a core assumption of India's non-alignment strategy: namely, the belief that a combination of good will, adept diplomacy, and the absence of any aggressive intentions would enable New Delhi to maintain friendly relations simultaneously with Moscow, Washington, and Beijing. On the other hand, Nehru was buoyed by Soviet support, which did not falter even in the face of a steady drumbeat of Chinese invective. Much to his gratification, the Soviets confirmed their commitment to India in the midst of the bloody Sino-Indian border clashes by extending a $375 million line of credit for nonmilitary purposes. That reassurance fortified Nehru's conviction that the relationship with Moscow now comprised an irreplaceable cornerstone of Indian security policy in a fast changing international environment. He and his chief military and civilian advisers persuaded themselves that China would not dare a military strike against India because the Soviet Union, solicitous of its Indian partner, would act to discourage or deter any open Chinese aggression. Consequently, the Indian leader pursued an aggressive, if risky, forward strategy in Aksai Chin and other disputed areas, moving troops into contested territory and refusing to cede any of India's claims.[38]

On October 20, 1962, the unthinkable happened. Chinese forces launched major attacks against Indian positions in the rugged terrain of both Ladakh, in Indian-occupied Kashmir, and the Northeast Frontier Agency. The attacks not only drove Indian defenders into inglorious retreat; they also shattered Indian complacency and rendered obsolete a guiding premise of Indian foreign policy. Over the next several days, India suffered stunning reverses, leading to alarm, anguish, and much soul-searching among elites and ordinary citizens alike. On October 25, a visibly shaken Nehru made an astonishing admission in a nationwide address. "We were getting out of touch with reality in the modern world, and we were living in an artificial atmosphere of our own creation," he con-

38 Mastny, "Soviet Union's Partnership," 56-58.

fessed. "We have been out of it, all of us, whether it is the government or the people."[39]

The Soviet Union yanked another leg out from under India's security stool when it quickly jumped to China's side. In the immediate aftermath of the Chinese attacks, Khrushchev chided Nehru in a sharply worded personal letter for his failure to show "a due urge for reconciliation." The Soviet ruler urged Nehru to accept Chinese terms for a border settlement. An aggrieved Nehru countered that the victimized Indians adamantly opposed making any concessions under duress to the Chinese aggressors. The official newspaper *Pravda* chose this highly fraught moment to reaffirm the strength of Sino-Soviet friendship as "based on an identity of aims" and the "joint ideology" of Marxism-Leninism. Preoccupied with the simultaneous crisis triggered by the clandestine emplacement of Soviet nuclear missiles in Cuba, Kremlin leaders considered it imperative to close ranks with China. They could not afford to risk forfeiting China's ideological sympathy and solidarity at so unusually perilous a moment in the broader Cold War.[40]

Seemingly abandoned by the Soviet partner he had become so heavily dependent on, Nehru turned in desperation to the United States. The combination of the Chinese onslaught, the failure of Indian defenses, and the slap in the face from Moscow had left Indian security policies in tatters – and placed the continuation of India's non-aligned foreign policy in grave jeopardy. A humbled and panicked Nehru turned to the United States for support. President John F. Kennedy, eager to compete for what he saw as the potentially huge Cold War prize that India could become if it moved openly toward the West, leaped at the opportunity. In a personal letter to Nehru of October 28, Kennedy wrote: "I want to give you support as well as sympathy."[41] Then, before New Delhi and Washington could agree on the details of a specific military assistance package, the Indian position suddenly deteriorated further – and in alarming fashion – after the rout of Indian forces that followed a disastrous counter-attack in the Aksai Chin region. On November 19, Nehru appealed to the United States once again, this time with especial urgency. In two letters that he sent to Kennedy on that day, the Indian prime minister requested the immediate dispatch of twelve squadrons of all-weather U.S. fighter aircraft and the prompt installation by the United States of a sophisticated radar network on Indian soil. He even asked for U.S. personnel to pilot the fighter jets and to operate the requested radar sta-

---

39 Gopal, Nehru 3, 233.

40 Raghavan, War and Peace, 306-307; Mastny, "Soviet Union's Partnership," 61-62.

41 Kennedy to Nehru, October 28, 1962, John F. Kennedy Library, President's Office File, India.

tions. Nehru appeared willing, in effect, to swap non-alignment for a U.S. commitment to the defense of India. As his leading biographer has observed: "Certainly if India was to be defended by massive American aid, non-alignment, if it survived, would require a fresh definition; and perhaps not many in India, apart from Nehru, believed any longer in its reality."[42]

Facing what probably stands as the pivotal moment in India's Cold War foreign policy, Nehru managed to salvage the essence of Indian non-alignment due to a fortuitous mix of circumstances. Had Chinese forces chosen to go on the offensive against an increasingly vulnerable Indian military, and had the Soviets persisted in their pro-Chinese policy, Nehru would have had little choice but to embrace U.S. defense support – even if that meant jettisoning non-alignment. On November 20, however, China unexpectedly declared a unilateral cease-fire and began pulling its troops back from their forward positions. That this development transpired *before* Kennedy had even responded formally to Nehru's extraordinary request for U.S. help meant that India could regain some precious space and time for diplomatic maneuvering. In addition, the Soviet Union had already adopted a more accommodating stance toward India following the denouement of the Cuban crisis. On November 8, Khrushchev assured India's ambassador that New Delhi had no greater and more sincere friend than Moscow. The communist party chief promised further that the Soviets would honor all existing contracts with India, including those governing the training of pilots and the supply of transport aircraft and spare parts.[43]

The Kennedy administration's delays and half-measures also influenced Nehru's decision to cling to non-alignment. U.S. policy makers dragged their feet on emergency military support for India, tried to extract more concessions than Nehru was willing to make, and then, after a protracted bureaucratic process, offered substantially less aid than the Indian military had hoped to receive. In the end, the U.S. alliance with Pakistan, which yielded intelligence facilities that the American government prized, set limits on the amount and extent of the military assistance that Kennedy and his successor, Lyndon B. Johnson, were willing to extend. Pakistan's fury at the prospect of a U.S.-Indian military supply relationship, coupled with the breakdown by mid-1963 of a new round of Indo-Pakistani talks on the Kashmir dispute that the Americans had insisted upon, factored heavily in U.S. decision making.[44]

Thus, once the dust cleared from the military debacle of 1962, India's prewar non-aligned policy essentially remained intact. But it was a neutralist stance

---

42 Gopal, Nehru, 228-329.

43 Raghavan, War and Peace, 308-309.

44 McMahon, Cold War on the Periphery, 292-318.

with an even more pronounced tilt toward the Soviet Union than before, establishing a pattern that would, in fact, obtain for the duration of the Cold War. Diplomatic and defense officials in India were agreed that China constituted their nation's chief enemy, an assessment resoundingly confirmed by the government's extensive strategic review of 1963. The Soviets similarly viewed China as *their* enemy number one by that time. The strategic convergence between India and the Soviet Union was rooted, consequently, in a shared fear of a common enemy.[45] Ironically, India's strategic position actually improved in crucial respects after the humiliating military confrontation with China. Drawing military assistance both from the Soviet Union and from the West, India moved quickly to enhance its overall defense capabilities. U.S. military aid proved remarkably short-lived, of course; the Johnson administration terminated it with the onset of the Indo-Pakistani War of 1965. Soviet military aid, on the other hand, remained a *sine qua non* of Indian foreign and defense policy for Nehru and for his successors throughout the 1960s, 1970s, and 1980s.

Nehru himself, broken in spirit and health, suffered a fatal heart attack in May 1964. He was replaced by the lackluster Lal Bahador Shastri, who retained the fundamental elements of Nehruvian foreign policy during his brief tenure. Most importantly, Shastri affirmed non-alignment as a stratagem for avoiding any formal security commitments. Non-alignment no longer connoted a stance of equidistance from the great powers, though, and his government continued to tilt toward Moscow. The Indo-Pakistani war of 1965 did nothing to alter that basic policy orientation.

Pakistan initiated the conflict, largely in a vain effort to resolve the Kashmir stalemate by force of arms. India's military acquitted itself well during the fighting, helping to ease some of the lingering embarrassment of the Sino-Indian war three years earlier. Indicative of the growing stature of the Soviet Union on the subcontinent – and the corresponding decline in America's influence – Indian and Pakistani leaders accepted an offer of Soviet mediation, agreeing to a cease-fire during negotiations held at Tashkent, in Soviet central Asia. One scholar goes so far as to label the Tashkent agreement "the most constructive accomplishment in the history of Soviet-Indian relations."[46] Certainly it confirmed New Delhi's growing trust of and dependence on Moscow – one of the enduring legacies of Nehru's foreign policy. The war also substantially deepened Indian resentment of the United States. Reflecting a view commonly held among Indians, the *Times of India* placed "direct responsibility" for the war on Washing-

---

45 Mastny, "Soviet Union's Partnership," 63.
46 Mastny, "Soviet Union's Partnership," 64.

ton's shoulders, singling out the "incredible folly" of U.S. arms supplies to Pakistan as the ultimate cause of the conflict.[47]

When Prime Minister Shastri died suddenly, following a heart attack at Tashkent, the ruling Congress Party turned to Indira Gandhi, Nehru's daughter, to replace him as prime minister. Many scholars have drawn stark contrasts between the lofty idealism of Nehru and the unsentimental realism of his presumably more pragmatic daughter. Yet, in terms of the fundamentals of Indian foreign policy, striking continuities obtain between the closing years of the Jawaharlal Nehru era and the entirety of the Indira Gandhi era (1966-1977 and 1980-1984). Gandhi shared with her father an affinity for the Soviet Union (albeit a considerably stronger one) and a deep distrust of China. Likewise, she too possessed an instinctive unease with the West, a disdain for American materialism, and contradictory feelings of attraction and repulsion toward Western culture. Throughout her tenure as prime minister, Gandhi harbored a strong revulsion toward what she saw as American self-righteousness and hypocrisy – again mirroring her father's deep-seated prejudices. She proved especially suspicious of the Central Intelligence Agency: the prime minister regularly accused the U.S. Government of meddling in Indian internal affairs through its spy agency.[48]

Indian national interests, Gandhi was convinced, demanded a foreign policy of closeness toward the Soviet Union, distance from the United States, and wariness toward China. She rejected her father's pre-1962 policy of conciliation and compromise with Beijing in favor of the strategy that he adopted in the aftermath of the Sino-Indian War: reliance on a powerful, modern military force, ever-vigilant defense, and close cooperation with Moscow. The bitterness and depth of the Sino-Soviet split meant that the Soviet Union, like India, sought the containment of China. Gandhi's identification of the Soviet Union as India's most valuable strategic partner flowed from that common interest and stands as perhaps the central, defining feature of her foreign policy. Her careful cultivation of Moscow rested neither on sentiment nor on illusions about the communist state's beneficent intentions: rather, it sprouted from the hardheaded realism that lay behind all of her diplomatic and strategic decisions. All nations, Gandhi believed, "were guided only by their own interest and had no obligations to other countries which did not conform to those interests."[49]

At the same time, she continued to pay obeisance to the fundamental precepts of non-alignment, however compromised her semi-alignment with the Soviet Union had rendered her father's original vision of that diplomatic philoso-

---

47 Editorial, Times of India, November 12, 1965.

48 Tharoor, Reasons of State, 62-64, 78-81.

49 Mastny, "Soviet Union's Partnership," 64.

phy. On July 7, 1966, shortly after her ascendance to the prime ministership, Gandhi delivered a nationwide broadcast in which she emphasized that India's "adherence to the guiding principle of non-alignment" remained at the heart of Indian foreign policy. Despite "the breakdown of old alignments and the emergence of newer patterns of polycentric power," she stressed, non-alignment remained a positive and vital force in world affairs. "Non-alignment can harmonize the tensions which grow out of changing alignments," Gandhi declared. "Its existence eases and permits departures from the conformity of ideological power-groups... Its practice is consistent with friendship for all."[50]

Two issues, in particular, exacerbated Gandhi's mistrust of the United States early in her tenure. They drove a fresh wedge between New Delhi and Washington while fostering, as if by default, even stronger bonds between New Delhi and Moscow. The first of those issues was the nagging food shortfall that was already approaching crisis proportions when Gandhi assumed power. India's new ruler recognized her country's dependence on the United States, especially through its Public Law 480 program, for essential wheat shipments; yet she chafed at the subordination to the American colossus created by that need. To compound the problem, President Lyndon B. Johnson chose to use U.S. food aid as a crude weapon of influence. He put U.S. wheat shipments to drought-plagued India on a short leash, forcing New Delhi to shift its development priorities toward the agricultural sector so as to make it less reliant on American commodity assistance. Becoming less reliant on the United States, of course, served India's interests as well. But Johnson's heavy-handedness imposed needless additional strains on a relationship already reeling from the 1965 war and the suspension of U.S. military aid that followed. LBJ's willingness to withhold available American food reserves when millions of desperate Indians were facing possible starvation, engendered an angry Indian backlash against American bullying and insensitivity.[51]

The second issue was U.S. military involvement in Vietnam, which had escalated dramatically under President Johnson and which Gandhi instinctively viewed as emblematic of U.S. imperialism. She took a measured and moderate approach to the Vietnam War at first, even offering a peace proposal in summer 1966 that the Johnson administration found not entirely unhelpful. Shortly thereafter, however, the prime minister traveled to Moscow for talks with Soviet leaders and joined with them in issuing a communiqué that blasted U.S. policy in no uncertain terms. The statement warned about the increasing risks of general war "as a result of aggressive actions of imperialists and other reactionary

50 Ministry of External Affairs of India, Foreign Affairs Record (July 1967), 172-173.

51 McMahon, "Toward Disillusionment and Disengagement," 166-169.

forces." Even Ambassador Chester Bowles, the most pro-Indian American diplomat of the Cold War era, labeled the Soviet-Indian communiqué "a shocking document." The less forgiving Johnson was infuriated by what he considered Gandhi's slap in the face, and the U.S. Government issued a vigorous protest.[52]

The prime minister's increasing hostility to U.S. actions in Vietnam coincided with her pronounced shift to the left, a move dictated by domestic political calculations. In March 1967, she sent a fawning birthday greeting to aging North Vietnamese leader Ho Chi Minh, once again provoking an angry American response. "If she feels she must slant her 'non-alignment' in favor of the Communist world in order to keep her credentials clear with Moscow," exclaimed Secretary of State Dean Rusk, "she cannot maintain her credentials with the US. The general mood in this country does not permit us to act like an old cow which continues to give milk, however often one kicks her in the flanks."[53]

During the presidency of Richard M. Nixon, Indo-American relations reached a new low. One of the original backers of the U.S.-Pakistan alliance as Eisenhower's vice president, Nixon entered the White House with a set of deeply held pro-Pakistani and anti-Indian biases. Those attitudes, together with his pursuit of rapprochement with China, ensured an exceptionally rocky phase in Indo-American relations, culminating with the infamous dispatch of the *U.S.S. Enterprise* to Indian waters at the height of the 1971 Indo-Pakistani war over Bangladesh.[54]

In March 1971, Pakistani General Mohammed Yahya Khan initiated a brutal crackdown on a popular, peaceful, and democratically-sanctioned autonomy movement within his nation's eastern half. Millions of refugees fled across the border to Indian West Bengal, imposing a crippling burden on the Gandhi government. Nixon and his top foreign policy hand, National Security Adviser Henry A. Kissinger, coddled the Yahya Kahn regime rather than condemn its wholesale assault on democracy and human rights, as many observers in the United States and abroad urged, in large part because Pakistan was then serving as a secret intermediary between the United States and China. The two men feared that Gandhi, who they saw as a coldly calculating Machiavellian figure, might use the refugee influx as a pretext for deploying military force to break up Pakistan. The result of such an action could wreak havoc with their broader geopolitical vision for a revamped American security policy. It could lead, they believed, to the dismemberment of Pakistan, a humiliating defeat for an ally of the United States and China, a severe blow to the budding Sino-American rap-

52 Lawrence, "Limits of Peacemaking," 248-251.

53 Rusk to Bowles, May 18, 1967, FRUS 1964-1968, Vol. 25, 859-860.

54 McMahon, "Danger of Geopolitical Fantasies."

prochement, and a political and strategic triumph for both India and the Soviet Union.[55]

On August 9, 1971, Gandhi signed a friendship treaty with the Soviet Union. Although less than a formal bilateral alliance, the agreement did pledge that the two nations would consult during crises and that neither would support a third party against the other. This diplomatic move represented Gandhi's protective response to what struck her and many Indians as the sudden emergence of a destabilizing U.S.-Pakistani-Chinese entente. The Soviet Union, for its part, valued the treaty as a formal confirmation of its special partnership with India as well as a useful counter-weight to the budding Sino-American relationship.[56] Nixon and Kissinger fumed about the agreement, erroneously depicting India in its wake as a Soviet "stalking horse" or client state – a grievous misreading of the fiercely independent-minded Gandhi. The Indo-Soviet pact thus played into the inveterate Nixon-Kissinger penchant for viewing regional events through the distorting lens of superpower geopolitics. "If there is a continued heavy outflow of refugees," Kissinger predicted, "India will use it as a pretext to go to war. This will blow our China policy." Consequently, he insisted upon the need for the administration to remain firm since "the Indians are playing an absolutely ruthless game."[57]

By late October, with an estimated nine million East Bengalis having crossed the border into India, Gandhi and her cabinet were inching closer to a decision to use force against Pakistan. Only military action, the prime minister concluded, could relieve the intolerable burden created by the Pakistani Government's obstinate refusal to end its reign of terror and compel it to accept the inevitability of an independent East Pakistan. On November 4, with talk of war in the air, the Indian prime minister visited Washington. But her talks with Nixon resembled a "dialogue of the deaf," in the apt characterization of one State Department observer. The American president and his national security adviser found the Indian head-of-government unusually prickly and condescending – alternatively referring to her in private conversations as a "bitch" and "the old witch"; for her part, Gandhi found her American hosts to be obtuse about the grave refugee crisis confronting India.[58]

---

55 Memorandum for the record of a Senior Review Group meeting, August 1, 1971, FRUS 1969-1976, Vol. 11, 323-329.

56 Mastny, "Soviet Union's Partnership," 68-69.

57 Minutes of a Washington Strategic Action Group meeting, September 26, 1971, 1969-1976, Vol. 11, 398.

58 Kissinger, White House Years, 878-889; Kux, India and the United States, 297-302; Memorandum for the President's Files, November 4, 1971, FRUS 1969-1976, Vol. 11, 493-499.

On December 3, to everyone's great surprise, Pakistan made the first military move, launching air attacks against Indian territory from West Pakistan. Gandhi ordered an immediate attack in the east – an assault that had originally been planned for December 4 – while authorizing a more limited military action in the west. By December 5, the Indians had easily established their military superiority in the field. Nixon and Kissinger, who had centralized decision making in the White House during this crisis to an unprecedented extent, fretted that a quick Indian victory would represent a major blow to their geostrategic ambitions. "What we are seeing here," Kissinger told Nixon, "is a Soviet-Indian power play to humiliate the Chinese and also somewhat us." Pakistan's defeat, he feared, would leave the Chinese "despising us" and the Russians thinking that "they backed us down."[59]

Kissinger, accordingly, persuaded Nixon to order the *U.S.S. Enterprise* carrier task force to head immediately to the Indian Ocean to demonstrate American resolve and, presumably, dissuade Gandhi from attacking West Pakistan. At the same time, the president instructed Kissinger to approach China's UN representative, Huang Hua, about the possibility of moving Chinese troops to the Indian border. Beijing, which had no interest in initiating troop movements, no less threatening actual intervention, demurred. The war soon ended, at any rate, with India's military commander accepting the surrender of his Pakistani counterpart in the east on December 16. That night, a triumphant Gandhi proposed a cease fire in West Pakistan.[60]

India had served as midwife to the birth of an independent Bangladesh, severely weakening its now-dismembered regional rival. In the process, India dealt an embarrassing setback to both China and the United States, each of whom had aligned itself with Pakistan. With India's great military and diplomatic victory, Gandhi stood as the pinnacle of her power. Fellow Indians hailed her as Durga, the invincible goddess of Hindu lore; the *Economist* dubbed her the "Empress of India."[61] Yet the Bangladesh conflict actually did little to alter New Delhi's overall foreign policy strategy in the Cold War; rather, it just served to confirm among Indian elites the wisdom of Gandhi's prewar course of leaning toward Moscow while keeping Washington at arm's length. "The main consequences" of the war, in the keen observation of a former U.S. diplomat, "were severe and long-lasting damage to US relations with India and enhanced Soviet influence with New Delhi." Indian anger and resentment over the U.S. tilt

59 Telephone conversations between Nixon and Kissinger, December 5, 1971, FRUS 1969-1976, Vol. 11, 632-647.

60 McMahon, "Danger of Geopolitical Fantasies," 263-266.

61 Malhotra, Indira Gandhi, 141.

toward Pakistan, and the *Enterprise* episode in particular, would linger for the remainder of the Cold War, casting a dark shadow over Indo-American relations. Similarly, the image of the Soviet Union "as India's friend in times of need" took firm root among leaders and populace alike.[62]

On May 18, 1974, India exploded an underground nuclear device at Pokharan in the Rajastan desert, becoming the world's sixth nuclear power. Although almost everything about the Gandhi government's decision to join the nuclear club remains highly classified, many scholars have speculated that it was justified in part by Indian determination to avoid another Nixon-style effort to intervene in Indian affairs. Americans expressed outrage with India's successful nuclear detonation, the most serious blow to the non-proliferation regime in a decade. The next year, not coincidentally, the Gerald R. Ford administration resumed arms sales to Pakistan. India protested the latest U.S. affront in vociferous terms. Its defense minister charged that the U.S. commitment would "retard the process of normalization of relations in the subcontinent," while Gandhi likened the renewed arms shipments to a "reopening of old wounds."[63] Relations between New Delhi and Washington sustained yet another blow when Gandhi proclaimed a national emergency, in June 1975, imposing *de facto* martial law. In a much repeated quip, Daniel Patrick Moynihan, a former ambassador to India, bluntly told an interviewer: "When India ceased to be a democracy, our actual interest there just plummeted. I mean, what does it export but communicable disease?"[64]

The surprise victory of the Janata Front in India's national elections of 1977, which elevated Morarji Desai to the prime ministership, brought a temporary improvement to Indo-American relations. The Jimmy Carter administration hailed the return of democracy to India. Desai, for his part, sought to move India's international posture closer to true non-alignment and hence less open hostility to the United States, and President Carter was greeted warmly during a 1978 visit to India. But the collapse of the Janata coalition, the return of Indira Gandhi to power following Indian elections in January 1980, and, most significantly, the Soviet invasion of Afghanistan in December 1979, led to an abrupt reversal in the short-lived warming trend.[65]

India's refusal to condemn unequivocally the aggression of its Soviet ally, together with Prime Minister Gandhi's denunciation of U.S. military aid to Pakistan, produced a predictable anti-Indian backlash in the United States. Late in

---

62 Kux, India and the United States, 307, 318.

63 Brands, India and the United States, 153.

64 Quoted in Kux, India and the United States, 337.

65 Kux, India and the United States, 347-356.

1980, partly in gratitude for India's "realistic and balanced response" to its conflict in Afghanistan, the Soviet Union extended a $1.6 billion, 15-year credit to India for military purchases. By that point, India was importing fully eight-five percent of its arms from Moscow.[66]

Throughout the 1980s, relations between Washington and New Delhi remained chilly, much as relations between Moscow and New Delhi continued to be exceptionally warm. Massive U.S. support for Pakistan, a reward for its critical role in funneling arms to the anti-Soviet insurgents in Afghanistan, proved a near-insuperable obstacle to closer ties. Although the diplomatic and political atmospherics improved following the replacement of Indira Gandhi by her son Rajiv, following the former's assassination in October 1984, core differences in interests and perspective continued to plague the bilateral relationship right up to the end of the decade. Only with the sudden end to the Cold War in 1989-1990 and the subsequent collapse of the Soviet Union would Indian elites begin to question the foreign policy shibboleths inculcated by three generations of the indomitable Nehru dynasty.

Conclusion

From 1947 to 1991, Indian foreign policy was shaped and constrained by the structure of an international system dominated by the Cold War. The decision of Nehru and his successors to opt for a policy of non-alignment, eschewing any formal security commitments to either of the blocs, made eminent sense given India's economic needs, geostrategic location, and political aspirations. Its non-aligned posture also proved consistent with Indian ideals and values. That policy stance paid handsome dividends: it enabled the young nation to draw economic and, for a time, military aid from both the Soviet Union and the United States; to develop enduring bonds with many fellow post-colonial states; and to assume global stature and prestige disproportionate to its actual power as a leader of the nascent Non-Aligned Movement.

Yet India's leaders also demonstrated nimbleness in adapting non-alignment to changing international and regional circumstances. In that regard, the souring of Sino-Indian relations and the onset of the shattering border war with China in 1962 proved a watershed in India's Cold War foreign policy. To counter Chinese hostility, India developed an especially close relationship with the Soviet Union, a partnership that placed a powerful stamp on India's foreign relations from the early 1960s until the end of the Cold War. New Delhi and Moscow each saw the other as a necessary counterweight to Beijing, their common adversary. That choice compromised the initial Nehruvian conception of non-

66 Mastny, "Soviet Union's Partnership," 75.

alignment as a policy of equidistance from East and West; it also left India adrift following the implosion of the Soviet Union in 1991. *Realpolitik*, more than principled aloofness from great power politics, thus came to characterize India's approach to the Cold War during that conflict's final three decades.

Divided Nations: India and Germany

Amit Das Gupta

Introduction

Would anyone consider India a divided nation? While we are used to speaking of two Chinas, two Germanies, two Koreas and two Vietnams, not a word has ever been heard of two Indias. Nevertheless the term "Partition," used in India to describe the creation of two independent states – Pakistan and the Indian Union – at the end of British colonial rule in South Asia in 1947 indicates that an entity broke into pieces. Yet although many South Asians considered the partition problematic and suffered from the consequences, there were few efforts to revise it. In the early years of independence, some hopes formulated for a merger of the two states, but the lasting existence of Pakistan was accepted relatively quickly. No Indian government ever pursued a reunification policy, and even when Pakistan fell apart in 1971 there was no debate about "bringing back" East Bengal into the Indian Union.

Still, certain parallels between South Asia and Germany are evident. As with the Federal Republic of Germany (FRG) and the German Democratic Republic (GDR), before the rise of Hindu nationalism hardly anyone doubted the common heritage of India and Pakistan, which made the two more twins than neighboring (if hostile) states. In both cases the legitimacy of the antagonist was challenged: West Germans spoke of a communist dictatorship, East Germans of a rule of monopoly capitalism and Nazism. India saw Pakistan's founding logic based on the alleged incompatibility of different religions; Pakistan doubted that a secular state could manage the multitude of religions. The term "puppet regime" (of the Soviets or the United States, respectively) was common in Germany from 1949 onwards. In South Asia it was used with reference to Pakistan after military cooperation with the United States had begun in 1954, followed by a military takeover in 1958. In the context of partition, all sides had territorial claims, be it the East German territories under Polish and Soviet administration or Kashmir.

Obviously the comparative metaphor has limits. India immediately recognized Pakistan, whereas the FRG until 1990 never treated the GDR as a fully legitimate state. Whilst the German question throughout the Cold War had top priority in both Bonn and East Berlin, India's difficult relationship with Pakistan ranked high but never became the focal point of its foreign affairs. Still, it can be useful to hint at those parallels in the beginning of the analysis: First, they provided the background for a specific Indian understanding of the German problems. Second, the Indian attitude towards questions like the popular claim for plebiscites to guarantee self-determination was inevitably influenced by India's experience of partition, the relationship with Pakistan, and its Kashmir policy.

There are more cases of India interacting with divided nations. With respect to Korea and Vietnam, New Delhi recognized neither side. The fact that India had full diplomatic relations with only one German state, the FRG, until 1972, and only then recognized the GDR did not present an exception, unlike many authors argue.[1] Having established diplomatic relations with Nationalist China in 1948, New Delhi, on December 30, 1949, recognized the People's Republic of China and supported its claims towards a reintegration of Taiwan into the Chinese homeland.[2] This policy did not follow principles but political realities. That is true to some extent for the two Germanies, too, as will be shown below.

Indo-West German relations: A slow start based on a fateful decision

Three completely new states, a world war, a large geographic distance and a very short history of prewar interaction:[3] Against this background, one might expect a zero hour in Indo-German relations in the late 1940s. In fact, though, several continuities exercised a strong influence on postwar relations between India and Germany. It is well known that a number of leading Indian politicians had studied in Germany before Hitler came to power and returned to India with a positive impression of Germany and German nationalism. Among them were the later Presidents Sarvepalli Radhakrishnan and Zakir Hussain. Then there were the diplomats who provided continuity in Indo-German relations: Wilhelm Melchers, head of the Orient Department at the Foreign Office during the Nazi period, had shortly after the war returned to the West German diplomatic service and became the FRG's second ambassador in New Delhi in 1957, unconcernedly using his established contacts with the Bose family and others. Herbert Richter, counselor at the embassy from 1952 to 1958, had served at the consulates general in Bombay and Calcutta in the 1930s. On the Indian side, A.C.N. Nambiar had been head of the Indian office in Berlin from 1928 onwards and had served as Subhas Chandra Bose's closest aid in Germany during World War II. Girija Mookherjee, who had worked with him at the time, came to Bonn as press attaché in the 1950s as well.

The journalist and *SS-Hauptsturmführer* Giselher Wirsing had played a role during the Bose interlude in Nazi Germany. He taught Bose German[4] and, from

1 Misra, India's Policy; Tripathi, India's Foreign Policy.
2 Heimsath and Mansingh, Diplomatic History, 186.
3 Barooah, India; Hauner, India; Kuhlmann, Subhas Chandra Bose.
4 Kuhlmann, Bose, 158.

1961 onwards, strongly influenced the West German view on India with his articles in newspapers like *Christ und Welt* and as editor of the journal *IndoAsia*.[5] The GDR had its own expert, Herbert Fischer, who had spent several years in the Gandhi Ashram in the 1930s.[6] After his return to India in 1958, his Indian contacts[7] gave the GDR considerably more weight in India than it would have had otherwise.

Similar personnel continuities existed in the economic sphere: The offices of Siemens India had been closed down in 1939 and put under custody.[8] Whereas the German nationals were detained until 1945, Siemens employees of other nationalities continued their work under the roof of the newly founded Protos Engineering Bombay. Thus Siemens India *de facto* did not cease to exist, and when Siemens Germany sent old India hands to India for survey missions in the late 1940s they met former colleagues who, under the name of Protos, had established themselves on independent India's market. Chief engineers like Wilhelm, the former head of the Siemens Bombay office, and Haskell and Kloss as representatives of the commercial side guaranteed a continuation of Siemens's India business. Also, former partners like Tata Iron & Steel were keen to renew the prewar cooperation.[9]

In 1951 India established full diplomatic relations with the FRG. For the GDR it would take until October 1972 to achieve this recognition. The unequal treatment of the two Germanies negatively impacted relations between New Delhi and East Berlin, and occasionally relations with Moscow, and its continuation would be a permanent point of discussion with Bonn in the years to come. New Delhi's official explanation for not recognizing the GDR was that it did not want to present an obstacle to German reunification; this claim was maintained up until as late 1968.[10] The actual reasons were threefold: First, independent India inherited the decision of the government of British India to open a military mission in the Western sectors of Berlin in October 1945 on invitation of the Allied Powers. For the important contribution it had made to the wartime efforts, India was supposed to benefit from German reparations. When India gained independence two years later, an Indian, Khub Chand, became

5 Frei and Schmitz, Journalismus, 173-180.

6 Fischer, DDR – Indien, 9-12.

7 Voigt, Indienpolitik, 71-74.

8 Letter from engineer E. Rottenbücher, Siemens Belgrade, July 5, 1940, to Siemens Halske AG, Auslandsabteilung. Siemens Aktenarchiv München (SAA), 68 Li 156.

9 Letter from director Plettner to director Bauer, August 15, 1949. SAA, 11 Bauer Lc 107.

10 "The Question of the German Democratic Republic," April 11, 1968, NMML, P.N. Haksar Papers, I and II Installments, Subject Files 36.

head of the mission. In 1949, when the FRG was founded with Bonn as its seat of government and the Allied High Commission also based there, the Nehru government decided to be represented by Khub Chand in both Berlin and Bonn, and thus came to be present in the FRG exclusively.

Khub Chand and others did suggest that India should treat the Soviet sector (and later the GDR) similar to the FRG.[11] The constellation of the early Cold War, however, constituted the second factor for India's decision to recognize West Germany only, although no Indian government would ever have admitted this because the principles of non-alignment allowed a partisan stand neither towards the two Germanies nor towards the two blocs. The Western powers, including the United Kingdom, exercised strong influence to prevent recognition of the GDR.[12] Stalin considered Nehru a lackey of imperialism.[13] East Berlin, following in the wake of Moscow, did not respond to New Delhi's overtures. An Indian trade mission did not receive a favorable response in summer 1948,[14] and Vice President Radhakrishnan, when secretly meeting East German President Wilhelm Pieck on October 7, 1952, was given a cool welcome. Whether Pieck mentioned the question of diplomatic recognition at all is uncertain.[15]

Exploratory talks between the embassies of India and the GDR in Beijing in late 1951 revealed the third factor that made recognition difficult: India's national interests, specifically the economic relations with West Germany.[16] On July 28, 1948, a trade agreement with the combined British and US occupation zones (*Bizone*) had been signed, and New Delhi was keen to expand economic relations. India was pursuing a rapid industrialization strategy and tried to avoid dependencies on other countries; in this context, cooperation with a politically weak but economically strong West Germany appeared as a perfect solution. There were of course political strings attached to favorable trade conditions, namely the non-recognition of the GDR. In the early 1950s, Bonn's political demand must have appeared as a *quantité negligible* to India, even more so as

---

11 Voigt, India's Road, 30-32.

12 Gray, Germany's Cold War, 14.

13 Nihal Singh, The Yogi, 3-4.

14 Voigt, Indienpolitik, 7-8.

15 The protocol of the GDR Foreign Ministry does not mention the question of recognition, see Note from October 8, 1952, Winzer, Political Archive German Ministry of Foreign Affairs, Berlin (PA AA, MfAA, A 13873), and Ambassador Dutt in his memoirs (p. 316) supports that view. Radhakrishnan's son and biographer Sarvepalli Gopal, however, mentions a telegram of Dutt from October 8, 1952 telling the opposite (Gopal, Radhakrishnan, 274, footnote 53).

16 Das Gupta, Handel, 69-71.

Khub Chand[17] and Nehru himself[18] in 1948 and 1950 told West German counterparts that they considered the partition of Germany unnatural, thereby signaling sympathies with the democratic FRG. The latter rapidly became a *de facto* sovereign and internationally influential state, whereas the GDR until 1955, when it became a member of the Warsaw Pact, remained a Soviet marionette; even thereafter it remained relatively weak internationally, financially and economically.

India, willing to play a role in world affairs and to promote a more peaceful style of diplomacy, was the first country to end the state of war with West Germany on January 1, 1950. Between 1953 and 1955, Indo-West German economic cooperation began to intensify. A consortium led by the Krupp, DEMAG and Gutehoffnungshütte companies won the contract to build the steel plant at Rourkela in 1953. Daimler Benz and Tata formed the joint venture TELCO for the construction of trucks. For the strategically important construction of the Banihal tunnel, India's first all-season road connection to Jammu and Kashmir, Baresel & Kunz from Stuttgart were invited.[19] From 1948 onwards India tried to recruit German experts to support its industrialization efforts. The development of political relations, however, lagged behind. Nehru had turned down American offers to enter into a military alliance. When Pakistan jumped in to close the South Asian gap in the Northern Tier, Nehru blamed the Eisenhower Administration for bringing the Cold War to the subcontinent. Americans and Indians also viewed the situation in fundamentally different terms. Against this background, closer contacts with the leading non-aligned country might have harmed West German attempts to achieve full and equal integration into the Western block. India's first ambassador to the FRG, Subimal Dutt, believed this to be the main reason why Bonn kept a distance from New Delhi and why he was never received by Chancellor Adenauer. Vice President Radhakrishnan, visiting Bonn in October 1952 without an official invitation, was treated with the minimum of protocol. Neither his modesty nor his attempts to create understanding for Stalin's fears of Germany were received well.[20] The choice of Indian and West German ambassadors deepened the impression of a contrast between strong Indian interest vis-à-vis the FRG and West German reservations vis-à-vis India: Nehru sent one of his top diplomats, Dutt, who would become India's Foreign Secretary soon after his time in Bonn, whereas Adenauer chose Ernst Wilhelm Meyer, an outsider in the Foreign Service who had quit his position in protest

17 Friedensburg, Es ging um Deutschlands Einheit, 252–253.
18 Das Gupta, Handel, 51.
19 Das Gupta, Handel, 81-84.
20 Dutt, With Nehru, 310-311.

against Hitler. Meyer made many friends in India. His reports, often enthusiastic about Nehru and the chances of cooperation, were not received with much interest in Bonn, however.[21] When Nehru came to Europe in 1953 and 1955, the FRG did not extend an invitation to him.

India's willingness to cooperate with the FRG had its limits, however. New Delhi had praised a proposed trade agreement in 1952 as a foremost political document symbolizing the good relationship between the two countries. Yet in early 1953 it surprisingly refused to sign the agreement, arguing that it could be understood as a preliminary peace treaty. Radhakrishnan's encounter with the GDR's President, Pieck, demonstrated that India was generally open towards the second German state. Whether Radhakrishnan intended to mediate between the two Germanies – which is what his East German counterparts believed – remains open to debate. However, by meeting Pieck, Radhakrishnan violated Bonn's basic assumption that the GDR could not be understood as a state. In the context of a United Nations debate on free elections in Germany in November 1951, the Indian delegate suggested that direct negotiations between the two German states might be desirable. Finally, Deputy Foreign Minister Anil Kumar Chanda declared on November 13, 1952, that the Indian embassy in Bonn was installed merely to maintain economic contacts with the Western occupation zones.[22] India refused to fully embrace the West German standpoint on the 'German Question' because it did not want to expose itself in a sensitive debate in which it did not have much to gain. Also, there were reservations towards the Adenauer administration: Radhakrishnan considered Bonn's revisionist claim of Germany's former Eastern territories unacceptable.[23] Nehru went even further when he speculated that Adenauer wanted to reestablish Germany in the borders of 1914.[24] Similarly, many Indians considered the FRG's attempts to join NATO part of an effort to promote reunification, seeing that they ignored Soviet security interests.

India's publicly displayed distrust vis-à-vis West Germany stood in contrast to New Delhi's willingness to cooperate in secret. When Nehru was approached by Adenauer's aides in 1953 to support the Chancellor's attempts to release the German prisoners of war from the Soviet Union, he declared his willingness to help solve a humanitarian question behind closed curtains. The course of action he chose is unknown.[25] The Indian ambassador A.C.N. Nambiar indicated that

---

21 Das Gupta, Handel, 62-64.

22 Das Gupta, Handel, 69-73.

23 Voigt, Indienpolitik, 13.

24 Report no. 1056 of the embassy in Cairo, Pawelke, PA AA, Files of the embassy New Delhi, vol. 17.

25 Das Gupta, Handel, 75-76.

talks had been held during Nehru's visit to the Soviet Union in summer 1955, and an aide of the prime minister – without explicitly mentioning the prisoners of war or the German Question – encouraged the Chancellor to follow a self-confident strategy in negations during the latter's forthcoming visit to Moscow, which in effect led to the release of the prisoners.[26] Another delicate secret co-operation developed around India's attempts to modernize its armed forces. When Daimler Benz was invited to build trucks in India, a secret part of the contract included the construction of a tank, though most parts would have to be produced in West Germany, where arms production was not allowed yet. In the end, the scheme was not realized; in 1955 India decided to buy British Centurion tanks. Nehru did succeed in recruiting former Focke-Wulf chief engineer Kurt Tank to build India's first supersonic fighter jet, however.[27]

Getting to know each other, 1954-1958

The date of October 18, 1954 marked a breakthrough in New Delhi's German policy: Several non-socialist countries had signed trade agreements with the GDR's Chamber of Commerce, but India was the first country to sign an agreement with the East Berlin government. The latter had taken the initiative by offering India the delivery of industrial plants and know-how in return for the establishment of trade missions. The GDR's Politbureau members believed that India had entered negotiations because of its dire economic situation, the effort to keep equal distance to both blocks, and Chinese influence in favor of East Germany.[28] Krishna Behari Lall, Joint Secretary in the Ministry of Economic Affairs, claimed to have acted independently.[29] The Indian government, however, was at strife. After a GDR delegation had been waiting in an Indian hotel for two days without knowing when and with whom to negotiate, the Soviet embassy intervened. Thereafter Nehru, who received the delegation, and H.V.R. Iengar, General Secretary in the Ministry of Economic Affairs, offered a warm welcome. Lall, on the contrary, wanted to avoid "German Democratic Republic" and see it replaced by "East Germany" in the agreement. Though finally the official term ("German Democratic Republic") was accepted, Lall succeeded in granting the agreement the lowest possible status: Formally it was no intergovernmental agreement but merely an exchange of letters.[30] While trade missions were to be opened in Bombay and Calcutta, there was none admitted in Delhi

26 Das Gupta, Handel, 116-119.
27 Das Gupta, Handel, 83-84.
28 Voigt, Indienpolitik, 40-43.
29 Interview with the author in New Delhi, October 3, 1996.
30 Voigt, Indienpolitik, 46-47.

and recognition remained a taboo for the moment. Yet East Berlin had gotten a foot on the ground and was keen to intensify the contacts. In April 1955 prime minister Otto Grotewohl sent a first letter to Nehru via the Bombay trade mission. In the following year a confidential exchange of letters took place between the two.[31]

Bonn's surprisingly calm reaction was among the factors that encouraged India to further modify its stand. Only five days after the conclusion of the East German-Indian trade agreement, Bonn signed the Paris Agreements, which made the FRG a NATO member in May 1955. Consequently, German reunification had become highly unlikely in the foreseeable future. In June and July Nehru traveled to Europe and was received warmly in Moscow and other capitals of the Warsaw Pact. Though he felt appalled by the socialist leaders and dictatorships, he felt that their fear of Germany was authentic. A visit to Auschwitz deepened this impression. Public statements that the two Germanies should negotiate directly further indicated a change of mind. Since Nehru was known for allowing others to influence his opinion in direct exchanges, Adenauer should have used the chance, many believed. Seemingly carelessly, however, the Chancellor signaled his disinterest in Nehru. Neither he nor a member of the cabinet met the prime minister during a stopover in Düsseldorf, whereas opposition leader Erich Ollenhauer, who had established contacts with Nehru in London in February 1955, paid his respects. When Nehru spent a few days in Switzerland, he was once again contacted by a confidant of the Chancellor who explained the Chancellor's position.[32] Adenauer's reluctance must be seen in the light of skepticism of the Western allies against his proposed visit to Moscow in September. Direct interaction with the leading politician of the non-aligned nations would have made his mission even more difficult.

The FRG's establishment of diplomatic relations with the USSR was a clever move that gave Bonn much more room to maneuver in international affairs. On the other hand, with regard to the neutral and non-aligned countries, it presented a Pandora's Box. If there was only one Germany, as the FRG had been claiming since 1949, why did Adenauer accept the existence of two German embassies in Moscow? And why then should New Delhi, Cairo and Belgrade not permit an East German embassy? Prior to Adenauer's journey to Moscow, Nehru had signaled that he would avoid everything that might hinder successful West German-Soviet talks. Asked about his stand towards the GDR after the Chancellor's return from Moscow, Nehru stated that the question of recognition had not been raised in Delhi; India, however, was not willing to formally

31 Das Gupta, Handel, 112-114, 122.
32 Das Gupta, Handel, 116-117.

guarantee the permanent non-recognition of the GDR and insisted on maintaining informal and formal contacts with East Berlin. Hence, Nehru seemed to consider allowing a GDR embassy in India later.[33] Obviously, he was not convinced by Bonn's argument that the USSR's responsibility for Berlin and Germany allowed the unique presence of two German embassies in Moscow, whereas no other country had reason to follow the Soviet example. Aware of the weakness of its argument, Bonn in December 1955 formulated the Hallstein Doctrine, which confirmed the FRG's claim of being the sole representative of the German people. If a foreign nation recognized the GDR, this would be seen as an unfriendly act, which would be answered with measures including the possible termination of relations.

For India the Hallstein Doctrine came almost too late. The GDR hit the mark at an industrial fair in New Delhi in October and November by displaying a statue of a man made of glass speaking six languages, among them Hindi. Nehru had told Trade Minister Heinrich Rau in advance that he was willing to meet if Rau avoided any publicity and traveled as a private citizen. Apparently the prime minister intended to agree to the opening of a GDR trade mission in the capital to allow direct communication. The GDR's success at the fair brought Rau a place in the government guest house and high-ranking meetings. Soon thereafter, West German Ambassador Meyer was informed by now Foreign Secretary Dutt that India's Germany policy had changed: The GDR would not be recognized. However, Germany's partition had turned out to be permanent and the legitimacy of the Ulbricht administration was no less doubtable than that of the many dictatorships whose United Nations membership was supported by the West. Therefore India would vote for GDR membership in United Nations commissions with mostly humanitarian mandates.[34] The state visit of Soviet leaders Nikolai Alexandrovich Bulganin and Nikita Sergeyevich Khrushchev a short time later, during which they declared support for India's standpoints towards Kashmir and Goa, deepened the impression that Nehru finally had established balanced relations with both blocks and permanent contacts with both Germanies. The latter also meant the beginning of permanent quarrels about the status of the GDR.

While the FRG still received preferential treatment from India, many observers in Bonn feared that full recognition of the GDR was imminent. It took five years of diplomatic relations and the visit of a GDR minister until the Federal Government sent a member of the cabinet to India. Vice Chancellor Heinrich Blücher in January 1956 was welcomed more warmly than his socialist

33 Das Gupta, Handel, 121.
34 Das Gupta, Handel, 121-123.

counterparts, especially as he displayed a true interest in bilateral political and economic cooperation. The prime minister explained that the recognition of the GDR was not intended for the moment, and that German reunification was in India's interest. The Hallstein Doctrine had passed its first test.

Nehru's talks with Adenauer during his state visit in July 1956 did not lead to closer cooperation; instead, the antipathies between the two political leaders grew deeper. Adenauer found Nehru naïve at best and accused him of not understanding the communist threat. The prime minister in reverse diagnosed a crusade mentality in Adenauer. Nevertheless he seemed to have found the Chancellor authentic and his arguments partially convincing.[35] When he met Yugoslavia's Tito and Egypt's Nasser immediately after Adenauer's visit, he disapproved of a communiqué mentioning the existence of two German states, arguing that the GDR was a dictatorship. From there on he repeatedly prevented joint statements of leading non-aligned countries in favor of East Berlin. For a period of two years he also terminated the exchange with Grotewohl.[36]

Besides the personal exchange with West German politicians, India's economic problems played a role in preventing a further upgrade of the GDR by New Delhi. Already before Nehru arrived in Bonn, it had become known that India's second Five-Year-Plan had run into serious troubles and foreign loans on a large scale would be needed. The FRG inevitably had to play a prominent role in this process because it possessed the largest trade surplus of all Western countries doing trade with India. Hence, Bonn became an important member of the Aid India Consortium, which was established in August 1957. The Federal Government, aware of India's importance as an overseas market, never tied economic aid to the non-recognition of the GDR. India would never have accepted direct pressure or blackmail but realized that accepting aid did not allow for attacks on the main pillar of West German foreign policy. Whether New Delhi ever had the chance to trigger the recognition of the GDR among the non-aligned and neutral countries cannot be said. Yet Bonn feared precisely such a domino effect. Hence, aid was to deepen and stabilize the bilateral relationship. The visit of Minister of Commerce Ludwig Erhard in India in October 1958 underlined this position: Having identified India as a market and an economic partner comparable to the industrialized European countries as early as 1953,[37] Erhard's advice to promote private business in a country with a large state sector fell on fruitful ground.

35 Note on the Prime Minister's tour abroad June-July 1956, secret, August 15, 1956, NMML, Subimal Dutt Papers, Subject Files 89.

36 Das Gupta, Handel, 133-150.

37 Erhard (ed.), Deutschlands Rückkehr zum Weltmarkt, 139.

Parallel crises: Berlin and the Indo-Chinese border conflict, 1958

The combination of a vivid political relationship with the FRG and mere trade relations with the GDR characterized India's Germany policy for years. East Germany, besides sending congratulatory telegrams and promoting a modest economic exchange, had not much to offer New Delhi. India's political leadership had no illusions about the situation in the GDR.[38] Contrastingly, Bonn ranked high among the trade partners and donors. It did not pursue any specific interests in Asia, but had general influence in world affairs, which could be used in favor of India's economic interests, for example in the context of the Aid India Consortium or the European Economic Community. Two crises and a regime change, however, ended the relatively quiet period of Indo-German relations. On November 27, 1958, Khrushchev posed an ultimatum to demilitarize West Berlin and establish it as an independent political entity. The ultimatum triggered the second Berlin Crisis. While Bonn struggled to maintain its influence in the Western part of the city, the GDR was keen to close the last loophole in the Iron Curtain and to reach a separate peace treaty. The Berlin Crisis became a global conflict, partly because it had the potential to result in a massive confrontation of the two blocks, and partly because the two German states unleashed propaganda campaigns of formerly unknown intensity. Both Bonn and East Berlin considered India a key country in their struggle: Expecting support of their respective allies, the non-aligned states were the ones to be convinced, should it be in United Nations debates or with regard to public opinion in general. No one had more influence in this heterogeneous conglomerate than Nehru. Tito's recognition of the GDR in 1957 had remained an isolated step, and Nasser was too deeply involved in the Middle Eastern quarrels. The Indian Prime Minister figured as a moral institution. Hence, from late 1958 to late 1962, New Delhi was the site of a long line of German visitors, consultations with and protests of the German representations, and media campaigns to win the support of the public. In this respect, India had become the most important battlefield of the intra-German Cold War outside of Europe.

India, meanwhile, began to encounter troubles and became entangled ever deeply into the Cold War. After the Chinese occupation of Tibet in 1951, the two Asian giants had not been able to find a compromise about their new common border. Maximum claims from both sides and Beijing's increasingly aggressive conduct of negotiations had led to a stalemate. After the Indians in September 1958 had learned about a Chinese road through what was considered a part of Kashmir, they felt Beijing was trying to establish a *fait accompli* and ready to use force if necessary. When, in 1959, the Tibetans rebelled and the

38 Dutt, With Nehru, 314-316.

Dalai Lama was granted asylum in India, the Chinese in turn came to believe in an Indian conspiracy, and August 1959 saw the first military skirmishes in the Himalayas. The Indian Army was not fit to win a massive confrontation. Nehru therefore turned his hopes towards the Soviet Union to influence Beijing and to exercise pressure. Urgently needing Western aid, the Soviet benevolence could hardly be won with a general foreign policy turn. Gestures towards the GDR, however, might annoy the FRG, which was keen to protect its export interests. Against this background, the Berlin Crisis became an additional burden for India and later on a tool in New Delhi's policy towards the USSR.

Another factor influencing India's Germany policy was Ayub Khan's coup in Pakistan in October 1958. The Commander-in-Chief took over power and until 1965 succeeded in promoting internal stability and economic growth. A member of the Baghdad Pact and SEATO, Pakistan's chances of becoming a valuable partner of the West seemed to grow. Being much more pro-Western than India, Pakistan received backing in the South Asian quarrels and could increase its share of aid, specifically in the form of the Aid Pakistan Consortium of 1960. The FRG actively supported this strategy, which was conceived in Washington. Though West German business interests in Pakistan were as minimal as the latter's influence on the non-aligned world's stand towards the GDR, many observers in Bonn developed a feeling of solidarity toward Pakistan: For one, the straight-forward Ayub Khan was more of their liking than the enigmatic Nehru. Second, Pakistan's claim for Kashmir in the name of self-determination seemed to parallel the demand for free elections in East Germany. Finally, both countries felt deprived of their legitimate rights by history. Bonn's tilt towards Islamabad under the late Adenauer and the Erhard administrations became more and more visible, which inevitably had repercussions on India's German policy. New Delhi soon wanted to free itself from permanent involvement in the German quarrels and focus on its own priorities. Up to summer 1960 there were strong indicators that Nehru as well as Foreign Secretary Dutt, who had become the key figure in India's Germany policy, planned to fully recognize the GDR.[39]

A GDR document[40] claims that India once again used a visit by Vice President Radhakrishnan to Bonn in November 1959 to mediate the German question. According to a GDR correspondent and a member of the Communist Party of India, Nehru encouraged Federal President Theodor Heuss and Adenauer to neutralize Germany for a period of twenty years. The proposal allegedly found

39 Letter from Ambassador Melchers to Assistant Secretary von Bargen from March 21, 1959, PA AA, Department 411, vol. 127.

40 Report from journalist Max Kahane, December 15, 1958, attached to a letter of the newspaper "Neues Deutschland" to Walter Ulbricht from August 22, 1958, Georg Krausz, BArch-SAPMO, Ulbricht papers, vol. 1324.

sympathies with Heuss but not with Adenauer.[41] It seems unlikely that the scenario took place as reported because Nehru knew that Adenauer would never accept such a suggestion. Also, the prime minister had always turned down previous requests to take any initiative in trying to solve the German Question, arguing that India lacked the necessary influence. Adenauer, who had hoped to win over the prime minister for an initiative in the United Nations in late 1957, had received a blunt rebuff: Within the United Nations all problems would be eternalized.[42] India, after the outbreak of the second Berlin Crisis, was willing to provide East Germany with an upgrade in relations, which took shape when Grotewohl and Foreign Minister Lothar Bolz visited India for four days in January 1959. Formally this was just a stopover. *De facto* the Indian government had welcomed the opportunity to hold talks with East Berlin. Nehru was keen to receive information from the number two in the GDR hierarchy and took the time for two long meetings. The result, however, was not to the visitors' liking. The plump demands for recognition were not only turned down but answered in a comparatively rude manner. The prime minister made it clear he had no intent to mediate, and that he considered the wave of refugees from the GDR as a clear sign of a lack of confidence in the Ulbricht administration. Indian Defense Minister Krishna Menon, Nehru's closest confidant, declared his disinterest in visiting the GDR. Even worse, Tito, visiting India at the same time, refused to meet Grotewohl, regretted East Berlin's recognition by Yugoslavia,[43] and advised Nehru to keep a distance.[44] Nevertheless, East Berlin could claim a symbolic upgrade: It was the first time the Indian and the East German prime ministers had talked in person. Bonn launched a countermove and in February sent Berlin Mayor Willy Brandt to Delhi. Nehru and Brandt developed a cordial relationship, and the Prime Minister in public confirmed that his Germany policy would not be changed. Privately, however, he sought the demilitarization of Central Europe, and he refused to bring up the Berlin question in the United Nations. He also made it known that he saw no more chances for German reunification.

In the late 1950s, the Indian government had a change of minds: The continuing existence of the GDR was beyond doubt, the Hallstein Doctrine was believed to be outdated, Germany's former Eastern territories lost for good. Adenauer was seen as a hindrance for a compromise, while his devotion to reunification was considered questionable.[45] As a result, on December 3, 1959, Nehru

41 Das Gupta, Handel, 177.

42 Das Gupta, Handel, 152-154.

43 Das Gupta, Handel, 216-217.

44 Report of Ambassador Melchers from April 13, 1959, No. 429/59, PA AA, Melchers Papers, vol. 44.

45 Das Gupta, Handel, 218-221.

stated that nobody, including the government in Bonn, wanted reunification: "When I say not want it obviously means that everybody wants a solution on his own lines, while realizing a hundred percent that it won't arrive on one's own line, therefore we do not want that solution."[46] Dutt informed West German news correspondent Thilo Bode that the recognition of the GDR was no immediate question. India, however, would decide following its own national interests exclusively. The Hallstein Doctrine never had been put to the test and the West German explanation for the coexistence of two German embassies in Moscow did not convince New Delhi. The USSR might have a special status for the FRG but not for New Delhi. Dutt's public statement was an open attack on Bonn, which caused a number of statements of solidarity for the FRG's stand from other states, making an isolated recognition of the GDR – if intended at all – even more unlikely. Still there was logic behind that move, namely the attempt to squeeze out more West German aid by applying political pressure. More relevant were India's troubles with China, in which the two Germanies had started playing a role: Whereas the Federal Government had declared the disputed Ladakh region to be within Indian borders, Grotewohl alleged that the Indian Army had invaded Chinese territory. Neither statement was welcome: Nehru needed the Soviet Union to contain the People's Republic of China and might have been hoping to create more support by publicly accepting some of the realities of the German question.[47]

Having exposed themselves unnecessarily, Nehru and Dutt hoped that the Four Power conference scheduled for May 1960 would clarify the situation. It was expected that the United States and the United Kingdom would accept compromises with the USSR, which would make the non-recognition policy obsolete. Until then New Delhi proclaimed stability: East Berlin's Vice Foreign Minister Otto Wintzer in February was told that it would take fifty years before diplomatic relations could be established. Talking with FRG Foreign Minister Heinrich von Brentano the same month, Nehru massively criticized the GDR visitor and the aggressive policy of Khrushchev. Assurances about India's Germany policy, however, were lukewarm at best. Dutt informally let it be known that a termination of aid in the case of GDR recognition against the background of West German export interests seemed highly unlikely. After all, there were already five states with two German embassies. The Western powers would not wage a war over West Berlin and would give in if Moscow signed a separate

46 Record of Foreign Secretary van Scherpenberg, December 4, 1959, PA AA, Department 709, vol. 1263.

47 Das Gupta, Handel, 223-229.

peace treaty with the GDR.[48] Khrushchev's cancellation of the conference ended Indian hopes for a solution of the crisis by a third party. Preoccupied with the Chinese border conflict, Delhi was not interested in any more initiatives concerning Germany. In September Nehru stated that India would not recognize the GDR, a message eagerly awaited in Bonn. A short meeting with Adenauer in Düsseldorf a month later, however, disclosed ongoing differences about Berlin.[49]

During the days around the construction of the Berlin Wall on August 13, 1961, those differences became relevant. Throughout the summer, the government of India refused to make any statement about the German Question. A newspaper article published just two days ahead of the final division of Berlin revealed Nehru's point of view: The right to self-determination was relevant, but even more relevant was the right to security for Germany's neighbors. The FRG should not possess nuclear weapons and accept the Oder-Neisse border with Poland as final. Parts of the Rapacki Plan, which suggested Central Europe's demilitarization, were found acceptable. When the Berlin Wall began to take shape, Nehru, on August 16, demanded free access to West Berlin and called the GDR a mere geographic fact. As driving forces for the crisis, however, he made out mutual anxieties and fears of a revival of German militarism. The next day he declined a motion by the Communist Party of India to recognize the GDR, though he found some logic in the demand: "We have trade relations with the East German Government. De facto we recognize it. They have got a Consul here and we are dealing with them in many ways; this is not that we boycott them."[50] On August 23, he stated that India would treat the GDR *de facto* "as a sovereign, independent country which we recognize". Only a war could reverse the German-Polish border, and free access to West Berlin was not based on any treaty but on "a concession from the Soviet authorities".[51] Two days later Nehru corrected this last, incorrect statement. To the disappointment of the West Germans, he did not mention the humanitarian and moral aspects of the Wall with a single word. He also refused to help Adenauer with a belated attempt to overcome the deadlock because he did not want to get involved in German-German relations as a matter of principle: The Globke Plan proposed liberalization measures within the GDR, followed by a West German recognition, separate free elections and separate plebiscites about reunification. An all-German government would decide about membership in international alliances. The Chan-

48 Das Gupta, Handel, 229-231.

49 Das Gupta, Handel, 238.

50 Report No. 2146/61 of Counsellor von Heyden, New Delhi, from December 12, 1961, PA AA, Department 709, vol. 1343.

51 Jawaharlal Nehru's Speeches, Vol. IV, 352-354.

cellor had hoped that the presentation of the plan by a leading non-aligned politician in Moscow would improve its chances of acceptance.

Once the partition of Germany and Berlin seemed to have been settled for good, Nehru treated the GDR increasingly coolly. Emissaries sent right after the Wall had come into being faced demonstrative disinterest. By pure coincidence, the first conference of the non-aligned nations in Belgrade was scheduled two weeks later, from September 1 to 6, 1961. Naturally the German Question ranked high on the agenda. Some of the political leaders present in Belgrade pushed for a joint recognition of the GDR, which would have made the Hallstein Doctrine obsolete. Notwithstanding the cessation of diplomatic relations with Bonn in 1957, the economic exchange had continued, Tito argued. Nkrumah hinted at the consensus that there were two German states – a breakthrough in itself. Why not take both steps right now? Nasser, however, opposed such a move because the political and, even more importantly, the economic assistance of the FRG seemed indispensable.[52] Nehru had come to Belgrade to promote a moderate position and prevent overly partisan positions. In talks behind the scenes, he supported Nasser and opposed a passage in the joint communiqué demanding recognition of the GDR.[53] In his view, the Wall had ended the flux of refugees and affirmed the existence of the second German state. Thus an explosive constellation was overcome. Now the moment had come to redirect the attention from Central Europe to the developing world and the Indo-Chinese border conflict. Visiting Moscow right after the conference, Nehru criticized Khrushchev for blaming Adenauer and Charles de Gaulle for the international tensions: "Nehru's impression was that the basic factor influencing Soviet policy was the growing fear of the German Federal Republic. Khrushchev would welcome negotiations but would insist on the recognition of East Germany." Whether Sarvepalli Gopal's assessment that "this did not seem to Nehru an insuperable obstacle"[54] is correct seems questionable. After all, the GDR's status in India had not changed, and the cautious joint communiqué of September 11, 1961 was to become the blueprint for the coming years. Nehru agreed "that the facts of the existence of the German states at present could not be ignored and that any attempt to change the frontiers will have dangerous consequences. He stressed the imperative need for finding a peaceful solution to the German problem through negotiations among the parties concerned."[55] Compared to earlier statements this was an affront to the Federal Government. In August and Sep-

52 Gray, Germany's Cold War, 127-130.

53 Das Gupta, Handel, 247-248.

54 Gopal, Nehru, vol. III, 186-187.

55 Report of Ambassador von Mirbach, No. 1456/66, August 29, 1966, PA AA, B 37, vol. 230.

tember 1961 Nehru had said not more than what the majority of the world, including Bonn's Western allies, were thinking. Still, India's relations with both German states cooled down until late 1962. The GDR, after Grotewohl's comments about the border conflict and the Wall, found no more sympathies in New Delhi. The FRG was kept at a distance, too: Radhakrishnan refused to visit West Berlin in November 1961, and Indian politicians and officials avoided any further statements about the German question. Nehru's pragmatic approach towards the Berlin Crisis upset many West Germans who had believed that the Indian leader should at least have found words of compassion. The Indian occupation of Goa in December 1961 deepened the alienation: The Indian press wrongfully reported that large amounts of West German arms had been found and that Adenauer had criticized the resort to force.[56] The Chancellor exploded when talking with Pakistan's Minister for Energy, Zulfikar Ali Bhutto soon thereafter: He did not understand why the United Nations had tolerated India's unwillingness to consider resolutions concerning Kashmir. He had never shared the great sympathies for India and felt that Pakistan deserved much more.[57]

Even if India had considered a new approach to its Germany policy, the border war with China led to a commitment in favor of the FRG, which would last until Bonn was willing to recognize the GDR a decade later. The Chinese attack on India on October 20, 1962, disclosed the military and political unpreparedness of India. Because of the Cuban Missile Crisis, both superpowers were preoccupied. Panicking, Nehru asked Western governments for support, including arms. The Western media portrayed the conflict as an assault by an aggressive socialist dictatorship on a peaceful democracy, and politicians followed suit. For Moscow and its satellites the situation was complicated: The Kremlin needed Chinese support in the Cuban Missile Crisis and kept quiet. A GDR newspaper was unwise enough to support the Chinese version of the border conflict. The contrast to the West German media and Bonn's political statements could not have been sharper. The Adenauer administration quickly understood that it would be one of the winners of the war: Nehru had to offer something in return for Bonn's support, which was, of course, an Indian Germany policy in favor of the FRG. Once East Berlin once again had sided with Beijing, supporting the FRG became an easy decision for New Delhi. The messenger was Nehru's sister Vijayalakshmi Pandit, who visited Bonn in late October 1962: She stated that India had always supported the FRG, even if the policy of non-alignment had not always allowed clear statements. New Delhi knew this had

56 Das Gupta, Handel, 255-256.

57 Protocols of September 6, 1961 to February 24, 1962. Protocol from December 21, 1961, Weber, Stiftung Bundeskanzler-Adenauer-Haus, Adenauer Papers, vol. 60.

led to misunderstandings. However, Indians shared the West German idea of freedom, but not the interpretation of the Eastern block. Federal President Heinrich Lübke, the first high-ranking visitor to arrive in India after the war in late November 1962, made Nehru promise to give no further statements about the existence of two German states. In return, the Federal Government agreed to finance the extension of the Rourkela steel plant, which was meant in part to be used for the arms industries. A year later, Bonn decided to pay for a plant and the know-how to produce hardened armor plates. Immediate help, however, was extremely modest: Apart from four tons of winter uniforms for mountain warfare, Indian hopes for a generous extension of aid were mostly disappointed. Nevertheless Nehru kept his word.

West German angst, Indian reliability, 1962 to 1971

After 13 years of pursuing an active (if sometimes drifting) Germany policy, Indian governments were not willing to take any more initiatives with regard to the German Question. From 1962 to 1972, the country was absorbed by struggles with hostile neighbors: After China had humiliated its rival, Pakistan tried to solve the Kashmir dispute by force as well. The Indian Army reached a stalemate; the peace negotiations in Tashkent merely resulted in a return to the *status quo ante*. Only in 1972, when Pakistan's Eastern Wing (Bangladesh) revolted, was New Delhi able to overthrow the archenemy and break it into two pieces. Three wars together with massive economic problems and changes in government led to India withdrawing from international affairs.[58] While Nehru had been a towering figure of world politics, his successors Lal Bahadur Shastri and Indira Gandhi did not win much recognition abroad. The second reason for New Delhi ending its active Germany policy was that after the Wall had come into being the German question had been settled for the time being. The FRG's Western allies believed that it was time for Bonn to adapt to the new situation and come to terms with the existence of the GDR.

This adaption process, however, proved to be painful, and India was at times affected by futile attempts to turn back the clock. With Adenauer stepping down in 1963 and a weak Chancellor Erhard in charge, until late 1966 the decisive figure in foreign affairs was Foreign Secretary Karl Carstens. Especially after the rather pro-western and seemingly weak Shastri had become Indian Prime Minister, Bonn tried to regain lost territory. When Radhakrishnan, now President, in Moscow in September 1964 literally repeated Nehru's formula about the existence of two German states and the support for a peaceful reunification via negotiations of all parties concerned, it triggered massive West German protests.

58 Das Gupta, "Indiens sicherheitspolitische Wende."

Naturally, Bonn saw the dam erected by Nehru torn down only four months after his death. Bonn bluntly threatened India with a reduction of aid and even hinted at the possibility of Bonn offering support for Pakistan's claims regarding Kashmir. Those threats prevented India from making similar statements, yet they also poisoned relations: Bonn ignored that India's national interests categorically demanded good relations with both the FRG and the USSR. The Soviets made their claims just like the West Germans did. The permanent protests from Bonn had quickly tired the Nehru administration in the 1950s. In the 1960s the ongoing complaints and threats were understood as a sign of general distrust in New Delhi's commitment to Bonn.

In fact, besides repeating the formula of 1961, India, in the face of Soviet pressure, did much to help the Hallstein Doctrine survive. At the conference of the non-aligned nations in Cairo in 1964, Shastri helped to avoid any resolution mentioning the existence of two German states. The GDR itself faced consequent denial: Earlier that year, East Berlin had offered a loan of 200 million DM, a large sum for both countries, which showed the desperate mood of the Ulbricht administration. Bruno Leuschner, an economic expert who submitted the offer, had to undergo painful questioning about the Wall by Indian Foreign Secretary Gundevia.[59] The latter even mentioned that India did not regret recognizing the FRG and that it did not see any attempts from East Berlin to work toward reunification. Vice Foreign Ministers Lakshmi Menon and Wolfgang Kiesewetter ran into a hefty dispute about the Wall. The visit turned out to be a complete failure: New Delhi refused the loan and allowed neither an embassy nor a consulate general. The proposal for a cultural agreement was turned down, too.[60] The GDR's attempts to impress India with political successes in Ceylon proved futile as well. In fact, the experiences of Prime Minister Sirimavo Bandaranaike were to confirm the wisdom of staying away from East German machinations: The GDR had convinced the ambitious Bandaranaike that a consulate general would not provoke harsh reactions by the FRG. If such a move nevertheless would lead to a cessation of aid, East Berlin would step in. When Bonn – with a side glance to India – terminated aid, Ceylon had to realize that the GDR was not able to raise adequate loans.[61]

So while India behaved loyally vis-à-vis the FRG, Bonn's sympathies with Pakistan endangered the Indian non-recognition of the GDR. West German support initially had been rather uncontroversial. The arms industries had been supported by license production of infantry rifles and ammunition only, hardly a

59 Voigt, Indienpolitik, 402-404.
60 Das Gupta, Handel, 305-306.
61 Gray, Germany's Cold War, 154-158.

threat to India. With Ayub Khan in charge, disappointments around the Berlin Crisis and the Goa invasion, a tilt towards Pakistan manifested itself in ever changing proportions of aid towards the two South Asian rivals. The license manufacturing of the anti-tank missile COBRA, which was used in the Kashmir war of 1965, received even more attention. The war marked a threshold in West German involvement in subcontinental hostilities: When the Pakistani military failure became apparent West Germany promised fighter jets and tanks. The intelligence service and some circles within the Foreign Office and the Ministry of Defense naively believed that the delivery of highly visible weapons systems could be camouflaged (although the scandal around secret arms transfers to Israel in 1965 should have told the contrary).[62] Taking such a risk was even more surprising as a weakened Pakistan could not have much value for the continuation of Bonn's Germany policy, whereas a morally strengthened India was even more useful than before. The FRG was never able to substitute for the United States as the dominating outside power in South Asia. When the first of 90 jets appeared at Pakistani airports, the FRG received heavy Indian criticism.[63] When in 1968 plans for the delivery of 200 tanks became known,[64] Prime Minister Gandhi told ambassador von Mirbach that the GDR would be recognized immediately if a single German tank was discovered in Pakistan.[65]

West Germany's ill-conceived South Asia policy of the mid-1960s came to an end with the coalition government led by Christian Democrat Chancellor Kurt Georg Kiesinger and Social Democrat Foreign Minister Willy Brandt in late 1966, both proven friends of India. The most relevant change was one of tone. When Kiesinger, as the first Federal Chancellor ever, visited New Delhi in November 1967, the talks were characterized by mutual understanding. The strategy of trying to find a consensus instead of exercising pressure paid off. Kiesinger courteously asked how the Indians would respond in case the FRG was to reestablish diplomatic relations with Yugoslavia, notwithstanding the GDR embassy in Belgrade. Gandhi replied that such a decision would have no repercussions on India's German policy, but that the Indian Trade Mission in East Berlin might have to be upgraded due to an understanding with the GDR. Such a step would inevitably lead to an upgrade of GDR trade missions in India. Kiesinger only asked to avoid anything that might trigger a domino reaction.[66]

62 Mohr, Waffen für Israel.

63 Das Gupta, Handel, 429-437.

64 Das Gupta, Handel, 457.

65 Note from June 20, 1968, Harkort, in: Akten zur Auswärtigen Politik der Bundesrepublik, 1968, vol. I, document 101, footnote 15.

66 Akten zur Auswärtigen Politik der Bundesrepublik, 1967, vol. II, document 399.

This display of confidence improved relations markedly. New Delhi was ready to await the green light from Bonn before it would upgrade the GDR diplomatically.[67] Even when Kiesinger told Ambassador Khub Chand in March 1969 that there was a wide range of options between the current situation and full recognition, the Gandhi administration did not take this as an invitation to admit consulates general. With the election of Brandt as West German Chancellor on September 19, 1969, and the establishment of a coalition between the Social Democrats and the Liberals, expectations grew high for a turnaround in Bonn's Germany policy. Accordingly, the new Chancellor in his first State of the Nation Address spoke of two German states, indicating that the FRG had accepted reality. Furthermore, the Hallstein Doctrine was modified: Governments were to recognize the GDR only once the two Germanies had come to terms with each other. Gandhi in early 1970 confirmed she would not come in the way of Brandt's new position toward Eastern Europe (*Neue Ostpolitik*). The Brandt administration, however, knew that India, in order to underline its claim of being a leading Third World power, could hardly be expected to be the very last to recognize the GDR. Bonn kept New Delhi well-informed about its negotiations with the Eastern governments. The conclusion of the treaties between Bonn and the USSR and Poland in late 1970 was welcomed with enthusiasm in India. In the Indian press the assertive Brandt was portrayed in bright colors, whereas Ulbricht appeared as an obstacle to détente. Though the German-German and the West German-Czech talks ran into problems, Gandhi seemed willing to practice restraint at least for a while.

A major crisis in Pakistan, however, made the continuation of New Delhi's pro-West German policy doubtful for almost a year. After the Awami League under Mujibur Rahman had won a landslide victory in Pakistan's first general elections, a new government seemed likely to implement the Bengali claims for far-reaching autonomy. The prospect of being ruled by Bengalis was not acceptable to West Pakistani elites. On March 25, 1971, the military took over power in the Eastern wing of Pakistan. Leading politicians were taken into custody, and the armed forces attempted to decapitate the Bengali intellectual, administrative and military elites. After ten million refugees had fled to India in late April, a government-in-exile of Bangladesh came into being, which was tolerated but not recognized by India. Soon it became clear the military was not able to control the situation. The first entity to make use of the foreseeable birth of the new state was the GDR: In May 1971, Abdus Samad Ahmad, the foreign minister of the government-in-exile, was received in East Berlin like a representative of a sovereign country. Over the following months the GDR succeeded in

67 For the following see Das Gupta, "India and Ostpolitik."

convincing the government-in-exile to agree on mutual recognition as soon as Bangladesh became independent. The calculation behind this strategy was that New Delhi had to follow suit as its new client received such full-hearted support from East Berlin, while the FRG was not expected to act against the United States backing Pakistan. An Indian recognition of the GDR might have had an international domino effect. This again would have fundamentally altered the basis of the German-German negotiations, where the FRG's trump card was to admit international recognition of East Germany.

India waited calmly until the Sino-American détente and the Indo-Soviet treaty in the summer provided the background for the foreseeable Indo-Pakistani war: Gandhi wanted to use the chance to divide India's arch enemy and support self-determination in what was to become Bangladesh. She also feared that the continuing influx of refugees into the fragile Northeastern part of India could become a source of instability. Though the Soviets informed India that they did not approve the assertive GDR policy, the new constellation was not to the latter's detriment. However, the West German-Indian cooperation proved much stronger. Nobel Prize winner Brandt appealed to the Pakistani authorities to release Mujibur Rahman. Behind closed doors he showed much understanding for India's difficulties. When the Prime Minister visited Bonn on November 11, 1971, Brandt and Gandhi had a mutually beneficial conversation between friends. Gandhi declared full support for the *Neue Ostpolitik* by providing a remarkable explanation: "For the first time since the Weimar Republic there was a government in Germany led by the Social Democrats, and therefore India would avoid everything that might create problems for this government."[68] In reverse, Brandt and Scheel overruled regulations forbidding the export of arms into areas of tension and allowed the resumption of deliveries of chemicals for the Indian ammunition industries and motors for armored carrier prototypes.

In the weeks between late 1971 and early 1972, a window of opportunity seemed to open up for East Berlin. After the war had ended on December 17, the GDR hoped to receive recognition from an internationally isolated India through the establishment of diplomatic relations with Bangladesh. The plan failed, however, for several reasons. First, the USSR did not consider East German interests and recognized the new state on January 24, thereby ending India's isolation. Second, Bonn effectively organized a countermove: Acting together with the United Kingdom and keeping the Indians informed, from mid-January onwards the FRG convinced West European governments to recognize Bangladesh jointly in early February in order to limit Soviet influence. Third, the new state acted different than expected. Mujibur Rahman, when released from prison,

68 Akten zur Auswärtigen Politik der Bundesrepublik, 1971, vol. 3, Doc. 389.

found the earlier agreement with the GDR concerning the mutual recognition not to be in the interest of Bangladesh. After the war the country needed large amounts of aid, which only the West could provide. Therefore Dacca tried to win time and urged the FRG to send its ambassador first. Together, those three factors had the effect that New Delhi escaped East German pressure once again. Only when the German-German negotiations reached a breakthrough would the recognition of the GDR help India earn goodwill in East Berlin and Moscow. In this situation, Gandhi acted in a typically shrewd manner: The press conference at which the recognition of the GDR was made public took place in the very early hours of October 8, 1972. Due to the time difference, the GDR could claim India had done so on its national holiday, October 7, whereas the FRG took October 8, a day like any other.

Benign neglect and German unification

Indo-German relations from 1972 onwards were characterized by what West German ambassador Dirk Oncken in 1978 called "benign neglect."[69] The German Question seemed to be settled, and India, busy with domestic issues, became less and less visible in international affairs. There were hardly any conflicting interests between New Delhi and Bonn, but also hardly any other contact points. Even the economic relations had lost intensity with Gandhi's nationalization politics and the far-reaching sealing of the Indian market. The GDR's irrelevance in international affairs became apparent: Marginal economic cooperation was accompanied by the well-known congratulatory telegrams. In the field of cultural cooperation, the West German Max Müller Bhavans were highly popular, whereas the GDR only infrequently gained the Indian public's attention.

Rajiv Gandhi's attempts to modernize India resulted in a re-launch of Indo-West German relations. Visiting Bonn in 1988, Gandhi wanted to stimulate the economic exchange and political contacts with the FRG; hence, he declared the FRG India's most important partner in Europe. Bonn was also supposed to function as a door opener for the European Market. Domestic turbulence in India interrupted his efforts, however. In the fall of 1989, just when the GDR was collapsing and the Wall was torn down, an intensive election campaign and allegations of corruption tied to the Bofors scandal took India's attention away from Europe. On November 29, 1989 V.P. Singh formed a new government, whose members – with the exception of Foreign Minister Inder Kumar Gujral – had not much experience in international affairs. The Singh administration, free from

69 Report of Ambassador Oncken from September 27, 1978, No. 1740, in: Akten zur Auswärtigen Politik der Bundesrepublik, 1978, vol. II, Doc. 284.

historical ballast, quickly sided with the FRG. The predecessor government had been irritated when Chancellor Helmut Kohl had not discussed his program for German and European unification with the FRG's allies, however, the response of the new Indian government was overall positive.[70] The new GDR administration under Hans Modrow, on February 1, 1990 tried to regain the initiative by proposing a German confederation and neutrality, but the effort was in vain. Raja C. Menon, an influential political advisor from the Institute for Defence Studies and Analyses, told the First Secretary of the East German embassy only four days later that the plan was outdated.[71] After the first free elections to the GDR People's Chamber on March 18 had made clear that unification would take place in the foreseeable future, Principle Secretary Deskmukh on April 9 declared India's full and warmhearted support. Vis-à-vis Foreign Secretary Lautenschlager he reiterated hopes that a united Germany would support Indian economic interests in Europe.[72] New Delhi of course did not have a say in German affairs but let it be known that its sympathies were with unification if its economic contracts with the GDR were honored. This was the message when Foreign Ministers Hans-Dietrich Genscher and Inder Kumar Gujral met on June 21 and 22, 1990. Unification was celebrated in India with great enthusiasm. Prime Minister Singh confirmed that India saw German "as its 'window to Europe'."[73] India's attitude towards the developments of 1989/90 was influenced by three considerations: With regard to the Indian economic reforms, the FRG was the preferred partner. Second, unification would result in a new world order in which Germany would play a leading role and India would enjoy more leeway. Third, curiosity and empathy with the humanitarian side of unification played a major role. In fact, these three factors had shaped India's Germany policy in the postwar years. Global politics had long hindered the development of Indo-German relations. Notwithstanding irritations and distrust during the difficult years from 1954 to 1966, different governments in New Delhi had pursued a remarkably constant Germany policy.

70 Telegram no. 1606 from ambassador Seitz, December 4, 1989, PA AA, Zwischenarchiv, vol. 140724E.

71 Note from First Secretary Kupfer, GDR embassy New Delhi, February 7, 1990, PA AA, MfAA, ZR904/03E.

72 Telegram from Elias for the embassy New Delhi from April 11, 1990, PA AA, Zwischenarchiv, vol. 140724E.

73 Telegram no. 1444 from ambassador Seitz, October 5, 1990, PA/AA, Zwischenarchiv, vol. 140724E.

Conclusion

Coming back to the parallels of the German-German and the Indo-Pakistani cases in the early post-war years, one can ask if any parallel developments took place later, too. For example, South Korea understood Germany's unification as an encouragement for the prospects of a Korean unification. Many people inside and outside South Asia believe that close Indo-Pakistani cooperation is a realistic perspective. An optimist might argue that certain preconditions for German unification exist in South Asia nowadays: India has learned to accept territorial realities *de facto* just like the FRG did in the early 1970s. At the time, Chancellor Brand believed that the acceptance of post-war borders for the time being and the renunciation of violent means would lead to a new peaceful order in Europe with a united Germany. One might compare that approach with the Gujral Doctrine, according to which New Delhi is willing to cooperate more closely with its smaller neighbors even if the benefits are asymmetrical. On the economic level, India has developed into a powerhouse, which attracts the attention of many Pakistanis. Similarly, relations between East and West Germany were influenced by unequal economic development, and many observers believed that the FRG's economic strength would sooner or later lead to the collapse of the GDR. There were also important strategic developments: Since the mid-1980s both Pakistan and India have possessed nuclear weapons. This constellation allowed for more fruitful negotiations and general rapprochement, because warfare had *de facto* become impossible. Finally, Bollywood is as fascinating for Pakistanis as West German television used to be for East Germans. Here, however, the similarities end, as every realist must admit: There is the heritage of the bloodshed and mass-migration in the context of Partition, which has made reconciliation difficult right from the beginning. Whereas the Germans were divided against their will, the Indo-Pakistani border was agreed by Indian and Pakistani politicians, and at least theoretically the people had the choice to opt for one of the two countries. Moreover, while comparisons between India and the FRG might make sense in some aspects, Pakistan does not have anything in common with the GDR besides being the smaller and weaker of the two entities. East Germany disappeared as soon as the Soviet Union gave it up, not only due to its weak international standing and its economic problems but also because it had no support from its own people. Pakistan, notwithstanding shortcomings, is nobody's puppet. It may not have developed a positive identity, but being "non-India" always was, still is, and most likely will continue to be the smallest common denominator of its heterogeneous population. While millions of West Germans visiting the GDR every year kept family ties and friendships alive, those born in South Asia after Partition have had very little first-hand experience with their neighbors. Apart from diplomats and politicians, traveling has been almost impossible for decades. There is no island like Berlin within India or Pakistan that would make permanent cooperation necessary. The South Asian rivals have not reached more agreement than the Indus Water Treaty from 1960, which took place under massive pressure from Western donors. Even today regional cooperation in the framework of the South Asian Association for Regional Cooperation [SAARC], direct trade and direct travel for average citizens is difficult. Whereas many Germans kept their common cultural identity over decades and thereby laid the basis for peaceful unification in a European context, in South Asia divides have further deepened over time, with no end in sight.

Between Regional and Global Interests: The Indo-Soviet Treaty of 1971

Srinath Raghavan

I.

On 9 August 1971, the foreign ministers of India and the Soviet Union signed a treaty of "Peace, Friendship and Cooperation". The treaty was aimed at "expanding and consolidating the existing relationship of sincere friendship" between the two countries. It was valid for twenty years. Both the context in which the treaty was concluded and the provisions of the document occasioned considerable commentary and speculation. After all, the treaty was signed at the height of the crisis in South Asia, which was sparked off by Pakistan's crackdown on Bengali nationalists in its eastern wing and resulted in a massive exodus of Bengali refugees into the adjoining states of India. The fact that Bengali rebels were operating against the Pakistani Army from sanctuaries in eastern India was an open secret. The treaty itself seemed to be designed to backstop India's approach to the crisis. Article IX of the treaty stated that

> "In the event of either Party being subjected to an attack or a threat thereof, the High Contracting Parties shall immediately enter into mutual consultations in order to remove threat and to take appropriate effective measures to ensure peace and the security of their countries."[1]

Unsurprisingly, many contemporary observers saw the treaty as setting the stage for an armed intervention by India. US National Security Advisor Henry Kissinger, for instance, believed that the Soviet Union had "seized a strategic opportunity" by not only assuring India of its continued support but also providing a hedge against Chinese intervention in support of Pakistan. "With the treaty," Kissinger wrote later, "Moscow threw a lighted match into a powder keg."[2] Interestingly, most Indian analysts and scholars tend to see the treaty in a similar, if more positive, vein. Writing on the fortieth anniversary of the signing of the treaty, an advisor to then Prime Minister Indira Gandhi claimed that it was "difficult to exaggerate the importance" of the treaty. "Armed with the treaty", Mrs.

---

1 Treaty of Peace, Friendship and Cooperation between the Republic of India and the Union of Soviet Socialist Republics, 9 August 1971 in Jain (ed.), Soviet South Asian Relations 1947-1978, vol. 1, 113-16.

2 Kissinger, The White House Years, 866-67.

Gandhi moved decisively to tackle the crisis in a manner of her choosing.[3] Historians down the years have echoed these assessments.

Such interpretations err in inferring causes from consequences. The treaty was not the product of a strategic consensus between India and the Soviet Union on the crisis in South Asia. Drawing on hitherto untapped archival sources from India, this essay argues that India and the Soviet Union sought rather different objectives in concluding the treaty. These divergent interests were being pursued well before the Bangladesh crisis erupted in March 1971, but with limited success on both sides. The crisis, however, enabled the two countries to muffle their differences and find common ground. But these differences persisted even after the treaty was inked.

This essay also contests another influential interpretation of the Indo-Soviet treaty. In this reading, the treaty represented an irrevocable break with India's stance of non-alignment. Kissinger, for instance, held that "Nehru's daughter was deliberately steering nonaligned India toward a de facto alliance with the Soviet Union."[4] Other scholars have echoed this view. Nayantara Sahgal argues that the treaty was "in essence a security based alliance" and that it "represented a complete reversal in foreign policy."[5] Indira Gandhi's most recent biographer, Katherine Frank, holds that the treaty "served to bury this Nehruvian principle once and for all."[6] Dennis Kux argues that "it was hard to assert—as India did—that New Delhi remained true to the cardinal principle of nonalignment".[7] Contrary to these claims, this essay argues that whilst the treaty did mark an attenuation of India's non-alignment, it was done with considerable reluctance. The Indians were acutely aware of the fact that they could be seen as a Soviet ally and tried hard to ensure that this was not the case.[8]

II.

At 11.30 p.m. on 25 March 1971, the Pakistani Army launched Operation Searchlight. The military junta led by General Yahya Khan had decided to use force to rein in the incipient nationalist movement in East Pakistan. The operation was not only aimed at the leadership of the Awami League, which spearheaded the movement, but also at its bases of support amongst the populace. In

3 Parthasarathi, "Forty Years of the Indo-Soviet Treaty: A Historic Landmark at the Global Level."

4 Kissinger, White House Years, 866-67.

5 Sahgal, Indira Gandhi: Her Road to Power, 84.

6 Frank, Indira: The Life of Indira Nehru Gandhi, 334.

7 Kux, India and the United States: Estranged Democracies, 295.

8 See the contribution by Robert McMahon in this volume.

the ensuing ruthless "pacification campaign", hundreds of thousands fled their homes and crossed the border into India. In a couple of months' time, the number of refugees would be counted in millions. The Bengali units of the Pakistan Army and paramilitary forces were sought to be "disarmed". Many of them put up a staunch resistance and soon looked across the border for help from India. Even as India struggled to evolve a coherent and workable approach to managing the crisis, it was surprised that the Soviet Union took the lead in criticising the Pakistani military action.

On 2 April 1971 the Soviet President, Nikolai Podgorny, made a public appeal to Yahya Khan expressing "great alarm" at the turn of events in East Pakistan, urging Yahya to take "the most urgent measures to stop the blood-shed and repression" and to move towards a "peaceful political settlement." This would at once be in the interest of Pakistan and in "the interest of preserving peace in the area". Podgorny's letter reiterated an earlier message to Yahya from the Chairman of the Council of Ministers, Alexei Kosygin. In his message of 28 March, Kosygin had warned, in a thinly-veiled reference to the US and China, that "imperialist circles" and "forces in Asia" could use the situation in detriment to the "integrity of Pakistan". This was entirely in keeping with earlier assurances from the Soviet foreign ministry that Moscow stood for a peaceful resolution of the East Pakistan problem on the basis of a united Pakistan.[9]

From the outset the Soviet Union emphasised the need for peace and stability within Pakistan and in the subcontinent. The Soviets were averse to the fracturing of Pakistan on strategic and ideological grounds. On the former, they believed that a break-away East Pakistan would be vulnerable to the influence and domination of China. Similarly they held that if the crisis turned into an India-Pakistan conflict, the resulting instability would redound to the advantage of China. From an ideological standpoint, the Soviets regarded the leader of the Awami League, Sheikh Mujibur Rahman, as a "bankrupt bourgeois". The Communist Party of the Soviet Union (CPSU) also quickly made it clear to the Communist Party of India (CPI) that it stood for a speedy settlement on the basis of regional autonomy for East Pakistan. As a senior member of the CPI would later note, the Soviet Union "was against the redrawing of boundaries and would, if it came to that, have condemned but condoned Pakistan's repression of the people of East Pakistan to keep its state identity intact."[10]

9 Text of Nikolai Podgorny's letter to Yahya Khan, 2 April 1971, Bangladesh Documents, vol. 1, 510-11; Kosygin's message cited in Marker, Quiet Diplomacy: Memoirs of an Ambassador of Pakistan.

10 "Guidelines for Consultation with the Communist Party of East Pakistan during the 9th Congress of the Communist Party of India", 30 September 1971, Archive of Parties and Mass Organizations of the Former German Democratic Republic in the Federal

Moscow adopted a two-pronged approach to the crisis. On the one hand, it sought to dissuade India from a military intervention in East Pakistan. The Soviet leadership were particularly concerned that the public clamour in India to support the Bengalis might force the hand of India's prime minister, Indira Gandhi. On the other hand, Moscow tried to push the regime in Pakistan to move towards a peaceful, political resolution of the problem.

The Indian government was naturally pleased with Podgorny's public message. Kosygin had, in fact, consulted the Indian ambassador in Moscow, D.P. Dhar, about the message. Both in Moscow and in New Delhi, the Indians had been urging the Russians to take a tough stand on East Pakistan. On publication of Podgorny's message, Dhar wrote to the prime minister's secretary and most influential advisor, P.N. Haksar, that "we have got every reason to feel satisfied about this unique diplomatic achievement". He claimed that the Soviet leadership had "overcome their inhibitions about so-called principles of national integrity etc., which controlled their policy regarding similar situation in Biafra". India "should fully take advantage of this unusual development" to bring to bear international pressure on the Yahya regime.[11]

The Indian ambassador considerably over-estimated both the extent to which the Soviet Union would turn the screws on Pakistan and the willingness of the Soviet leadership to support a secessionist movement. The first indication of the former came even as Dhar was penning his letters to Haksar. The Soviet Charge d'Affaires in New Delhi called on the Indian foreign minister, Swaran Singh, to convey a message from his government for Mrs. Gandhi. The message relayed a complaint lodged by the Pakistanis with the Soviet ambassador in Islamabad that "small armed groups" from Indian territory were "infiltrating into East Pakistan to help the freedom fighters". The Soviet government "thought that it was their duty to bring this to the notice of their Indian friends and particularly of the Prime Minister. It would be highly appreciated in Moscow if P.M. [Prime Minister Gandhi] could share her views."[12] Moscow evidently wanted to ensure that New Delhi was not worsening the situation in East Pakistan.

This did not go down well with the Indian Foreign Minister. Swaran Singh patiently but firmly responded that "India had no intention of intervening militarily in the matter" The allegation of Indian infiltration into East Pakistan was

---

Archives Berlin (BArch-SAPMO), DY 30/IV A 2/20, no. 642; Sen, A Traveller and the Road: The Journey of an Indian Communist, 314.

11 Two letters from D.P. Dhar to Haksar, 4 April 1971, Nehru Memorial Museum and Library, New Delhi (NMML), P. N. Haksar Papers, III Instalment, Subject File 227.

12 Record of Foreign Minister's conversation with USSR Charge d'Affaires at 6 p.m. on 4 April 1971, 5 April 1971, NMML, P.N. Haksar Papers, III, Subject File 276.

"entirely incorrect". If anything India was worried about people pouring in from East Pakistan. "We were not keen on having refuge-seekers coming in large numbers." The Soviet official, however, requested that the message should be conveyed to the Indian Prime Minister and her reply obtained. The prime minister read the record of the conversation the next day and directed that a reply to the Soviet leadership be drafted stating India's position.[13]

Meantime, Moscow also conveyed its thinking through party channels, mainly during the 24th Congress of the CPSU held from 31 March to 10 April. The leader of the CPI delegation, Rajeshwar Rao, had a meeting with Ambassador Dhar on 2 April. Dhar asked Rao to circulate material on the developments in East Pakistan to the other party delegations and to seek permission for the East Pakistani delegation to make a statement at the Congress. Rao spoke to Boris Ponomarev, the head of the International Department of the CPSU Central Committee. Ponomarev made it clear that while he had some sympathy for the Bengalis' struggle, he was certainly not in favour of rushing to their aid. On the contrary, he told Rao "to use his influence with Indira Gandhi to work for a negotiated settlement." The Soviets were reluctant even to allow Rao to circulate the resume on East Pakistan. When asked why it had not been circulated, the representative in charge of the India Desk blandly replied that his cyclostyling machine was out of order. Rao himself had to get the material cyclostyled and practically push the CPSU apparatchik to distribute it. But the party leadership was not willing to go any further. They again urged Rao and other CPI delegates "to persuade Indira Gandhi not to precipitate matters".[14]

In the following weeks, Moscow sought to adopt a careful equipoise between India and Pakistan, urging restraint on the former while prodding the latter towards a political settlement in East Pakistan. It ended up displeasing both. The Soviet leadership's response to the letter from Mrs. Gandhi was rather circumspect. Not only did it fail to offer any positive promise of action, it also asked India to exercise restraint and keep the Soviet Union fully informed of its thinking. The Soviet leadership also conveyed their concern over the pitch of the public response in India to the happenings in East Pakistan. The only crumb of support held out by Moscow was the promise of another appeal to Pakistan.

Even the ebullient D.P. Dhar found the message quite "bleak" and "unhappy". But he quickly got over the grey spell and put the most positive gloss on the Soviet Union's stance. "What more really can we expect of a major power in

---

13 Record of Foreign Minister's conversation with USSR Charge d'Affaires at 6 p.m. on 4 April 1971; Prime Minister's comment on the same, 5 April 1971, NMML, P. N. Haksar Papers III, Subject File 276.

14 Top secret and personal letter from Dhar to Haksar, 4 April 1971, NMML, P. N. Haksar Papers III, Subject File 227; Sen, A Traveller and the Road, 314, 319-20.

such circumstances?" he wrote to Haksar. "They really cannot commit themselves to any concrete offer of aid and endorsement of an aggressive policy of intervention at this stage. These are matters which they would like to be understood than recorded and perhaps this could explain their reticence to be explicit." It was important, he urged, "to read between the lines" and not to read too much into their request that India should "carry on the present policy of restraint and caution". Dhar was sharp enough to realise that this amounted to clutching at straws. "I hope I do not sound too optimistic", he wrote.[15] But it was clear that the ambassador and his government had their work cut out for them.

The Soviet leadership was simultaneously in touch with the Pakistanis. Director of the South Asia department in the foreign ministry, A.A. Fomin met Dhar and gave him a summary of the discussion with the Pakistanis. Dhar made it clear that India could not remain content with anodyne messages from the Soviet leadership. The principal concern for New Delhi was the inflow of refugees from East Pakistan. In a matter of four weeks, "from a mere trickle it has become a deluge and reached the six hundred thousand mark." Judging by the tempo of military operations in East Pakistan, this was expected to swell further. "[T]his was too high a price to pay for one's restraint", Dhar observed. Emphasising the mounting magnitude of the refugee problem, he told Fomin that "a few tins of milk powder or a few blankets would not be enough." He emphasised that there should be some "international scrutiny ... to discover the main cause of which this human exodus was only an effect".[16]

Dhar's remarks underlined the Indian government's stand on the developing refugee crisis. Whilst India would canvass for international aid and assistance for the refugees, it would insist that the refugee influx could only be stemmed and reversed if the fundamental political problem in East Pakistan was addressed to the satisfaction of the Bengalis. Herein lay the gulf between Moscow and New Delhi's views on the crisis. The Indian envoy took it upon himself to narrow these differences.

In two long letters to Haksar, Dhar laid out his assessment of the situation and the way forward. The Soviet leadership, he argued, would "slowly, in spite of their native and sometimes irritating conservatism, bring their policies on the same grid as ours. I will, however, repeat that this will be a gradual process." Dhar, however, knew full well that persisting with the current approach to Moscow might not result in a concordance of views about the crisis, or at least within a time-frame acceptable to India. He, therefore, drew attention to the

15 D.P. Dhar to Haksar, 18 April 1971, NMML, P. N. Haksar Papers III, Subject File 89.

16 Indian Embassy Moscow to Foreign Ministry, 28 April 1971, NMML, P. N. Haksar Papers III, Subject File 227.

wider dimensions of the crisis. The "blatant and aggressive statements emanating from China" against India were a matter of concern. He was personally inclined, "without being reckless", to the view that these amounted to "nothing more than an empty threat". Yet the possibility of a Chinese military intervention in support of Pakistan brought into focus the "poignant fact that in case such an eventuality materialises, we shall have to go it alone." Dhar reminded Haksar that it was

> "in the context of such situations and with a view to dealing with them specifically and with greater self-confidence that we had mooted the desirability of drawing up the 'Document' between us and the Soviet Union. How about signing this 'Document' now?"[17]

III.

The 'Document' that Dhar was referring to was the draft of a treaty of friendship and cooperation between India and Soviet Union. The idea of such a treaty had first been mooted by Moscow in early 1969. From the outset, the two sides sought to pursue different objectives in working towards such a treaty. From Moscow's standpoint the primary aim of the treaty was to secure a special relationship with India and ensure that India stood with the Soviet Union in the latter's escalating rivalry with China. After a trip to India in early March 1969—coinciding with the clash between Soviet and Chinese troops on the Ussuri—the Soviet Defence Minister, Marshal Andrei Grechko, assured Dhar that "the Soviet Union would come to India's assistance in case of aggression from China or Pakistan" and suggested "some kind of a Treaty of Friendship and Cooperation between India and USSR". It was evident to Dhar that the Russians' suggestion was driven by "the increasing tension in their relations with China which posed a threat to them as well as us." On a visit to India the next month, Dhar told Foreign Secretary T.N. Kaul that India should explore "the possibility of cashing in on this offer and if the Soviet Union was forthcoming and made certain commitments, then we might agree to enter into a Treaty of Friendship and Cooperation with them."[18]

The Indian government shared the Soviet assessment about the potential threat from China. The Soviet assurance of support in the event of an attack by China was welcomed in New Delhi. Kaul had been ambassador in Moscow dur-

---

17 Two letters from D.P. Dhar to Haksar, 29 April 1971, NMML, P. N. Haksar Papers III, Subject File 227.

18 Extracts from Romesh Bhandari to D.P. Dhar, 27 March 1969; Note by T.N. Kaul, 7 April 1969, NMML, P. N. Haksar Papers III, Subject File 203. On Grechko's visit to India also see, Noorani, Brezhnev Plan for Asian Security: Russia in Asia, 60-61.

ing the Sino-Indian war of 1962 and had seen the unwillingness of Nikita Khrushchev to take sides between the Chinese "brother" and the Indian "friend". Haksar, too, was enthusiastic about the idea of a treaty. "My own reaction", he informed the Prime Minister, "is entirely favourable as such a treaty will reflect coincidence of our interests at present."[19] But in "cashing in" on the Soviet offer, the Indians' objective was rather different. Their main concern was Moscow's attitude to India-Pakistan relations and its relationship with Islamabad.

Following the successful mediation between India and Pakistan at Tashkent in early 1966, the Russians basked in the warmth of their new-found influence in South Asia. Indeed, they began to take their role as peace-broker between India and Pakistan rather seriously. In July 1968, Kosygin wrote to Indira Gandhi expressing hope that the two neighbours would be able to make significant progress in normalising their relations. He suggested that the Indus Water Treaty of 1960 could provide a framework for the solution of the problems over sharing the waters of the Ganges. Mrs. Gandhi gently but firmly, replied that there was no scope for third-party mediation on the core problems between India and Pakistan. She asked Kosygin to "exercise your growing influence with Pakistan and persuade them to start direct discussions with us with the object of normalising our relations."[20]

Around the same time, Moscow dropped yet another bomb-shell by announcing military sales to Pakistan. The quantum of arms sold to Pakistan was small in comparison to what India had got, but the reaction in India was decisively negative. Opposition parties on the Right had a field day castigating the government's foreign policy and particularly its relations with the Soviet Union. The Jana Sangh organised a huge demonstration outside the Soviet embassy—a gathering that eventually had to be dispersed by the police using tear gas and batons. Moscow's move underscored the need not only to shore up ties with the Russians but also the domestic political implications of the Indo-Soviet relationship. Haksar told the prime minister that the Soviet decision was undoubtedly "erroneous and misguided". India should convey to them "both our feelings and reasons for our assessment." But he emphasised the importance of not overreacting to this development. The Indians conveyed their displeasure to the So-

---

19 Haksar's minutes for the Prime Minister, 31 March 1969, on D.P. Dhar to Kewal Singh (Secretary, Ministry of External Affairs), 31 March 1969, NMML, P. N. Haksar Papers III, Subject File 203. On the Soviet Union's role in the Sino-Indian conflict, see Raghavan, War and Peace in Modern India: A Strategic History of the Nehru Years, 299-309.

20 Indira Gandhi to Kosygin, 20 July 1968, NMML, P. N. Haksar Papers III, Subject File 135.

viet leadership during President Zakir Husain's visit to Moscow in July 1968 and subsequently in meetings with officials.[21]

Thus, when the Russians proposed a treaty in March 1969, India's central aim was to restore the exclusivity in its political and strategic relationship with Moscow and to ensure that the flow of arms to Pakistan was stanched. Dhar's immediate reaction was that if India agreed to consider this proposal, "the Soviet Union would perhaps be inclined to supply us the more sophisticated weapons, bombers, etc. which we badly needed."[22] Mrs. Gandhi agreed with Dhar, Kaul and Haksar that the treaty would help in bolstering ties with Moscow. But she was more concerned about the potential implications of such a treaty and wanted to move gingerly.

For one thing, she was worried about the domestic political fall-out of a treaty. Whilst some sections on the Left—especially the pro-Soviet CPI—might welcome it, the rest of the political spectrum was likely to react negatively. The main opposition parties on the Right—the Jana Sangh and Swatantra—would mount a political offensive accusing her of locking India into an embrace with Moscow and alienating it further from the West. More importantly, she was engaged in a tussle with an influential group of senior members of her own party. Many of her opponents in the Congress Party were politically conservative and distrusted, not to say disliked, the Soviet Union. A treaty with Moscow would give them a solid handle to take on the prime minister.

Indira Gandhi was also concerned about international reaction to a treaty. Relations with the US were already on a low-ebb, owing to India's vocal criticism of the American war in Vietnam. Washington had done nothing to remove the arms embargo imposed during the 1965 India-Pakistan war. But the US was providing much-needed food aid and was closely involved in launching the Green Revolution to spur India's food production. Indira Gandhi was also mindful of the fact that a treaty might further strain India's relations with China.

Underlying both sets of concerns, domestic and international, was Mrs. Gandhi's unwillingness to abandon the central tenet of non-alignment: the need to avoid being ensnared into military alliances. She was clear, therefore, that the treaty should be carefully drafted to avoid the impression that India had become a Soviet ally. Her key advisors insisted that this was easily done. Haksar, for instance, claimed that "if we enter into arrangements with the USSR, we can offer

21 Indira Gandhi to A.B. Vajpayee, n.d. (c. 15 July 1968); Haksar's note for Prime Minister, 13 July 1968, NMML, P. N. Haksar Papers III, Subject File 135; NMML, Oral History Transcript (OHT) A.K. Damodaran.

22 Note by T.N. Kaul, 7 April 1969, NMML, P. N. Haksar Papers III, Subject File 203.

the same to the rest of the world, including the USA."[23] But the prime minister was not entirely convinced.

In a meeting with Kosygin in May 1969, Mrs. Gandhi tartly summarised India's objection to this turn in Soviet policy. "Nothing should be done", she said, "from which it could be inferred that the Soviet Union treated India at par with Pakistan … an equidistance between India and Pakistan tended to cause irritation in India". Further, they were "specially [*sic*] worried with regard to Soviet [military] help [to Pakistan], as such help might neutralise what we have obtained from the Soviet Union."[24] Kosygin heard her out and went on to suggest that Indira Gandhi should arrange a summit meeting with Yahya Khan. Mrs. Gandhi made it clear that she did not share this assessment.

Kosygin also sought her views on the idea of a treaty. Mrs. Gandhi's reply indicated her cautious attitude: "she would not say that it was a wrong step to take, but she did think that the matter had to be considered very carefully and specially the reaction both within the country or in China [*sic*]. One had also to carefully consider in what way such a Treaty should be formulated." Kosygin graciously conceded that the matter "required earnest and careful thinking". Mrs. Gandhi agreed that they "could go on with exploratory talks in Moscow".[25]

Mrs. Gandhi referred to the draft of the treaty recently handed over by the Soviets. The points raised by her underscored her concerns about such a treaty. "Firstly," she told Kosygin, "it would not be appropriate to have any phraseology in the Treaty which might be misunderstood and construed as a shift from our stand of non-alignment." Second, "the Treaty should not contain anything which might be construed—even though we may not mean it that way—by others as directed against a third party. Such a thing would not be appropriate." Kosygin agreed with both the points. But it was obvious to both the leaders that China was a common cause for concern. When the prime minister raised the possibility of a Chinese attack on India, Kosygin said that the "Soviet Union was ready to incorporate in the Treaty something on 'mutual assistance'." Mrs. Gandhi noted that "such a clause would then become a military agreement." "It would be so provided India wants to solve her military affairs", replied Kosygin. He added that he was "sure India would probably resort to such consultations"

23 Haksar's note to Prime Minister, 10 September 1969, NMML, P. N. Haksar Papers III, Subject File 203.

24 Record of conversation between Indira Gandhi and Kosygin, 6 May 1969, NMML, P. N. Haksar Papers III, Subject File 140.

25 Record of conversation between Indira Gandhi and Kosygin, 6 May 1969, NMML, P. N. Haksar Papers III, Subject File 140.

regardless of whether the clause existed or not. The Soviet Union would not insist on it either way.[26]

The first revised draft of the treaty prepared by the Indian government had no reference to 'mutual assistance' or to military and security matters. Besides, the treaty was valid initially for five years and was extendable for another five. Following Mrs. Gandhi's meeting with Kosygin, the draft was further revised. It now included a clause on mutual consultations in the event of a threat to either party.[27] Discussions on the draft were initially carried on at the level of officials—by Dhar in Moscow and Kaul in New Delhi.

These discussions were soon overtaken by political developments in India. From June 1969 onwards, it was increasingly clear that Mrs. Gandhi was headed for a showdown with the Congress Party bosses. The point of no return was reached in August, when Mrs. Gandhi opposed the party's nominee for election as president of India and ensured that her own candidate prevailed. Although a formal split in the Congress Party did not occur until November 1969, it was evident that Mrs. Gandhi would soon be heading a minority government. It was increasingly clear, too, that she would have to go for mid-term polls. In this context, Mrs. Gandhi's concerns about the domestic fall-out of the treaty were sharply accentuated.

The Indian foreign minister, Dinesh Singh, visited Moscow in September 1969. He handed over to his Russian counterpart, Andrei Gromyko, a more or less finalised draft of the treaty from the Indian side. He also conveyed to Gromyko that India could not sign the treaty at this point. Gromyko assured him that they understood Mrs. Gandhi's difficulties at this juncture. The Soviet politburo had approved of the treaty including the clause on mutual consultations.[28] And there the matter rested.

Meanwhile, the Indians continued to harp on their concerns vis-à-vis Pakistan. These efforts paid off when the Russians decided to stop military sales to Pakistan in early 1970. However, the Soviet decision was prompted not by their concurrence with India's assessment regarding arms for Pakistan, but by their desire to buttress the domestic standing of Indira Gandhi, who was heading a minority government and had swerved sharply to the left in domestic politics

---

26 Record of conversation between Indira Gandhi and Kosygin, 6 May 1969, NMML, P. N. Haksar Papers III, Subject File 140; 'Soviet assessment of China and Chinese policies', note sent by Kaul to Haksar, n.d. (c. June 1971), NMML, P. N. Haksar Papers III, Subject File 258.

27 Model Draft of Treaty, n.d., NMML, P. N. Haksar Papers III, Subject File 203.

28 D.P. Dhar to Kaul, 9 October 1969, NMML, T.N. Kaul Papers (I-III Installment); NMML, OHT A.K. Damodaran; 'Soviet assessment of China and Chinese policies', note sent by Kaul to Haksar, n.d. (c. June 1971), NMML, P. N. Haksar Papers III.

and economics. Furthermore, the shutting of the arms pipeline to Pakistan did not mean that the Soviets had abandoned their efforts to ensure stability in South Asia. Kosygin was particularly keen to promote "a trade and transit agreement" between India, Pakistan and Afghanistan, which would be "beneficial for the whole region." He also kept insisting on "the relevance of [the] Tashkent [declaration]". The Indians, in the meantime, persisted with their request for advanced military equipment and technology—often in the context of Soviet attempts to drag their feet, if not demur.[29]

The Soviets, for their part, patiently awaited the resumption of discussions on the treaty. Fomin told Dhar that "after the elections if the Indian Government was of the view that the time was opportune and propitious for resuming a discussion on the 'Document', we would not find the Soviet Government wanting in their desire to reciprocate fully."[30] In the elections of March 1971, Indira Gandhi won a decisive majority. Soon after, the crisis in East Pakistan flared up.

IV.

When Dhar broached with Haksar the idea of signing the treaty towards the end of April 1971, he revisited the factors that had previously given pause to the prime minister. He argued that the context had dramatically changed owing to the East Pakistan crisis. If the treaty was signed now, "we shall give a counter blow to the Pakistani morale and they may succumb to the continuing pressures of the East Bengal situation." From the domestic perspective, too, this was "the psychological moment to have this Document as a new weapon in our armoury." Of course, the reaction of China and the US had to be considered. But these, he felt, could be managed. The real question was whether the Russians would be agreeable to signing the treaty at this juncture. "I am not sure about their willingness or otherwise ... But their mind can be probed."[31]

The prime minister, however, remained ambivalent about the treaty. Dhar grew anxious at New Delhi's refusal to make a positive move. He was aware that the ball was in India's court and that the Soviet leadership were unlikely to raise the matter. Unless India took the lead on the treaty, it would not be able to ensure a concordance of interests with the Soviet Union regarding the ongoing

---

29 Record of conversation between Kaul and Kosygin, 25 May 1970; Record of conversation between D.P. Dhar and Kosygin, 23 March 1971; Record of conversation between D.P. Dhar and Colonel General D.S. Sidorovich, 22 March 1971; D.P. Dhar to Kaul, 25 March 1971, NMML, P. N. Haksar Papers III, Subject File 276.

30 D.P. Dhar to Kaul, 3 March 1971, NMML, P. N. Haksar Papers III, Subject File 203.

31 D.P. Dhar to Haksar, 29 April 1971, NMML, P. N. Haksar Papers III, Subject File 227.

crisis. Dhar was also troubled by the fact that his time in Moscow was running out. Mrs. Gandhi wanted him back in New Delhi to help manage the crisis. Dhar launched a valiant effort to highlight the key point of convergence of Indian and Soviet interests: the threat from China. By so doing, he hoped to rekindle Moscow's interest in the treaty and perhaps even convince the Russians to take the first step in reviving the draft.

During his farewell call on Marshal Grechko, Dhar observed that India was "passing through a very difficult phase" owing to refugees and the threats from Pakistan. To add to India's woes, "our friend from the North" had also assumed a threatening posture. Grechko took the bait. He said that India should "not be worried by Pakistan". But it should "take into account the unpredictable enemy from the North." After making some observations on the sources of Chinese animosity to the Soviet Union, he assured Dhar that if China started "to use aggression, the USSR would not hesitate to use its strength and force in repelling it." Grechko said that it would be of "vital importance" to India and the USSR if their relationship was "fixed" in a "treaty of mutual help". For "such a document would deter any one from embarking on an adventure against India."[32]

Dhar responded that "an agreement had been reached in principle" at the level of officials on the treaty. The "meal was ready on the plate". Grechko said that this was "his personal view", that the time was "opportune and appropriate", and that the treaty should "contain some reference to military cooperation also." Dhar undertook, with satisfaction, to convey the Marshal's views to his government.[33]

Reporting on his meeting with Grechko to Kaul and Haksar, Dhar made a strong pitch for signing the treaty. He wondered if India was "being wise in reacting in a lukewarm manner to the Soviet offer of unequivocal help to us."[34] Dhar was, of course, exaggerating the Soviet willingness to support India in the unfolding crisis. Grechko, in fact, had said twice that he saw the treaty as a deterrent against aggression from Pakistan and China.[35] The Russians regarded the treaty as a chance to stabilise the situation in the subcontinent by reassuring India and hopefully forestalling it from precipitating a war.

32 Record of Conversation between D.P. Dhar and Marshal Grechko, 5 June 1971, NMML, P. N. Haksar Papers III, Subject File 258.

33 Record of Conversation between D.P. Dhar and Marshal Grechko, 5 June 1971, NMML, P. N. Haksar Papers III, Subject File 258.

34 D.P. Dhar to Kaul (copy to Haksar), 5 June 1971, NMML, P. N. Haksar Papers III, Subject File 258.

35 Record of Conversation between D.P. Dhar and Marshal Grechko, 5 June 1971, NMML, P. N. Haksar Papers III, Subject File 258.

The day after Dhar's meeting with Grechko, Foreign Minister Swaran Singh reached Moscow for consultations with the Soviet leadership. The visit was part of his trip to several countries to drum up support for India's stance on the crisis. In Moscow, he had an additional objective: to secure Soviet support for India against the possibility of Chinese intervention. Swaran Singh's discussions with the Soviet leaders made it clear that there was a convergence views regarding China. But on the crisis itself, the two countries continued to hold different positions.

In a long meeting with Kosygin, Swaran Singh observed that two steps had to be taken without delay. First, "the military regime must stop all its activities so that an end is put to the daily influx of refugees." Second, "conditions must be created in East Bengal, conditions of normalcy, so that these refugees can return with some sense of safety." This was possible only if negotiations were commenced with the leadership of the Awami League: "I mean the genuine Awami League, so that the party which was chosen by the people installed in power." India had "shown a great deal of restraint but there is a limit to this restraint. Unless there is a rapport [*sic*] and a solution which is brought about quickly, we fear that a situation, though we wish to avoid it all costs, may develop which may endanger peace."[36]

While India saw the two parts of the problem—refugees on Indian soil and a political solution in East Pakistan—as inextricably intertwined, the Soviet Union preferred to treat them separately. From Moscow's standpoint, addressing the refugee problem would remove the potential *casus belli* for India and so ensure stability in the subcontinent.

Thus Kosygin insisted that "these events could be divided into two separate parts". The first was "absolutely clear, lawful and just". "Refugees must go back, all of them, every one of them", he stated. He suggested that "we should concentrate, in the first instance, on this issue of refugees." On the second question Kosygin was guarded: "technically speaking … it can be resisted on the grounds of being a matter which relates to a domestic jurisdiction." If India linked the second question to the first, Pakistan would claim that India was only interested in meddling in its internal affairs. In dealing with the second issue India should act to ensure the Bengalis' struggle "continues, so that it succeeds after the return of the refugees." The Chairman suggested "in strict confidence" that India could continue to support the Bengali guerrillas as well as the mass struggle. "Therefore, let us not bundle the two [issues] together, but give all pos-

---

36 Record of conversation between Swaran Singh and Kosygin, 8 June 1971, NMML, P. N. Haksar Papers III, Subject File 203.

sible help to the democratic forces ... You are a politician, you know what I am implying."[37]

In his meeting with Gromyko, Swaran Singh raised the potential threat from China and urged Moscow "even now ... to consider some appropriate steps". Gromyko recalled the earlier discussions on the treaty. "What do you think about the feasibility or otherwise of resuming this exchange of views and ideas regarding their Draft Document?" he asked. It was Swaran Singh's turn to be cautious: "we may be too late, events may over-take us. Can we think of something quickly?" When Gromyko stressed the idea of a treaty, Singh tentatively said that "We could resume the threads of discussion."[38] That evening, Swaran Singh was asked by New Delhi to convey India's willingness to resume negotiations on the treaty. He told Gromyko the next day that India was ready and that "such an agreement will ... act as a deterrent to China and Pakistan against embarking on any military adventure."[39] The ball was set rolling again.

V.

Back in New Delhi, Foreign Secretary Kaul began revisiting the draft treaty drawn up two years earlier. Grechko had specifically told Dhar that the Indo-Soviet treaty should include some reference to military cooperation. Kaul demurred. "I do not think a specific reference to military cooperation is necessary in our draft as it might give the impression of entering into a military alliance." Instead, Article IX of the Indian draft, which called for "mutual consultations" should be strengthened by adding words to the effect "...with a view to removing the threat". This would be incorporated in the final text of the treaty. Another subsequent modification to Article IX was the inclusion of the sentence that each side undertook "to abstain from providing any assistance to any third party that engages in armed conflict with the other Party." In so doing, India sought to foreclose the possibility of Soviet political assistance or military sales to Pakistan in the event of active hostilities.[40]

---

37 Record of conversation between Swaran Singh and Kosygin, 8 June 1971, NMML, P. N. Haksar Papers III, Subject File 203.

38 Record of conversation between Swaran Singh and Gromyko, 7 June 1971, NMML, P. N. Haksar Papers III, Subject File 203.

39 Record of conversation between Swaran Singh and Gromyko, 8 June 1971, NMML, P. N. Haksar Papers III, Subject File 203. For the joint statement issued during the visit, see Jain (ed.), Soviet South Asian Relations, 111-12.

40 Note to Prime Minister and Foreign Minister by Kaul, 15 June 1971, NMML, P. N. Haksar Papers III, Subject File 89.

Kaul told the prime minister and foreign minister that it was best go for a formal treaty which could be published "without any secret clauses in it". This would be in keeping with India's policy of non-alignment. To reaffirm India's adherence to this policy, "we could offer a similar Treaty to USA and some of our neighbouring countries like Afghanistan".[41]

In the wake of Swaran Singh's visit, the Russians began to step up their diplomatic efforts. In a long meeting with the Pakistani ambassador on 22 June, Kosygin said "with all sincerity that Pakistan and India should resolve their differences without resorting to a conflict. We say it to you and we say it to India." More importantly, he added, "We do not want to interfere in your internal affairs. This is for you alone to decide. We think a democratic government should find its legitimate rights. It will find it, sooner or later."[42] Clearly, the Soviet Union was adopting a similar line, albeit with different emphases, in its dealings with India and Pakistan. Their ability to maintain this would come under increasing strain owing to the Yahya regime's unwillingness to take positive steps towards creating conditions for the refugees to return.

The Russians simultaneously encouraged India to conclude the treaty expeditiously. Ambassador Nikolai Pegov met Haksar and sought to allay India's misgivings. "The loudest and most vociferous opponents would be the Chinese", but the treaty would put an end to their "tactics of blackmail". At the same time, though, Moscow wanted to ensure that India would not bring matters to a head vis-à-vis Pakistan. As Haksar noted, Pegov "was very keen to know whether we were making any offensive preparations against Pakistan."[43]

Ironically, the impetus to finally sign the treaty came not from the Russians but from developments with the United States. Henry Kissinger visited Delhi in early July 1971. From there he went to Islamabad, whence he undertook his celebrated secret trip to Beijing. On 15 July, President Richard Nixon announced the breakthrough with the People's Republic and his own forthcoming trip to China. Two days later, Kissinger met the Indian ambassador, L.K. Jha, and told him that if China intervened in an India-Pakistan war, the US would be unable to help India. It was at this point that Mrs. Gandhi overcame her lingering doubts about the treaty and moved forward speedily to conclude it.

Noting Kissinger's message to Jha, Foreign Secretary Kaul told the prime minister that it "changed the whole perspective in which the Soviet proposal has to be considered." If the Sino-American détente succeeded, "there is no alterna-

41 Note to Prime Minister and Foreign Minister by Kaul, 15 June 1971, NMML, P. N. Haksar Papers III, Subject File 89.

42 Marker, Quiet Diplomacy, 123-30.

43 Handwritten note by Haksar on his meeting with Pegov, n.d. (c. 25 June 1971), NMML, P. N. Haksar Papers III, Subject File 229.

tive left to us but to have a reliable friend in case of necessity." The treaty "will safeguard us against the supply of any Soviet military support to Pakistan if she engages in a conflict with us." It would also "act as deterrent" to both Pakistan and China. Kaul emphasised the point that the treaty "does not conflict with our conception of non-alignment". Non-alignment did "not mean if our security and territorial integrity are threatened we cannot enter into any arrangements we may consider necessary to meet and avert such a threat." The treaty, he insisted, "did not put us in the Soviet camp". On the contrary India may be able to sign similar treaties with a host of other countries: "Afghanistan, Ceylon, Iraq, and possibly Burma, Malaysia and Indonesia." But, as earlier, the Indians overestimated the Soviet Union's willingness to support their stance on the crisis. Thus Kaul believed that "with the signing of this treaty we can be assured of Soviet support ... regarding our stand on Bangla Desh".[44] It would soon transpire that things were not as simple as that.

On 3 August, D.P. Dhar returned to Moscow for final negotiations on the treaty. Over two long meetings with Gromyko, Dhar ironed out the draft text of the treaty. However, when it came to discussing the crisis, the Russians stuck to their earlier stance. In the second meeting, Dhar conveyed a message from Mrs. Gandhi to the Soviet leadership. India, he stressed, "did not want a war." Mrs. Gandhi wished to impress upon the Soviet leaders that "it was absolutely necessary to put our heads together to prevent a war, to take steps so that adventurers did not unleash it." He added, however, that if "a war was forced on India", the two countries "should jointly assess how best the situation could be met. They had to "determine the means and methods of cooperating with each other in the economic, political and defence fields so as to meet the situation effectively."

Gromyko's response was non-committal. Soviet policy on the crisis "was well-known to the Indian leaders." Moscow shared New Delhi's "concern at the military clique's repression in East Pakistan." But so far as India-Pakistan relations were concerned, "the Soviet Union firmly believed that peace between the two was in the interest of both the peoples of India and Pakistan and all people in the whole of South Asia." Gromyko assured Dhar that they "felt very strongly" about the situation and were "doing everything possible to prevent aggravation." He promised to convey Mrs. Gandhi's message to Kosygin, Podgorny and Brezhnev.[45]

---

44 Note to Prime Minister and Foreign Minister by T.N. Kaul, 3 August 1971, NMML, P. N. Haksar Papers III, Subject File 49.

45 Records of conversations between D.P. Dhar and Gromyko, 3 & 4 August 1971, NMML, P.N. Haksar Papers III, Subject File 280.

Meeting Kosygin the next day, Dhar went over the same ground and laid out India's assessment of the crisis. Mrs. Gandhi, he told Kosygin, "has asked me to convey to you her assurances that we will do everything to preserve peace. She will do her best to avoid a war with Pakistan." But India also had "to take into account the possibility of a conflict also." How should India and the USSR "confer with each other to act to meet such a contingency?" he asked. Kosygin conceded that "the situation is complicated and becoming more complicated everyday." Kosygin would make it "absolutely clear" to Pakistan that Moscow will not provide any military equipment or spares. They would also "apply economic pressure to moderate the bellicose policy of the Pakistan Government".[46]

However, Kosygin was emphatic that "war is not in the interests of India." He observed that Pakistan and the US were fully aware of the support being given by India to the Bengali rebels. "It is my advice that you should be more careful ... otherwise you will face many difficulties and many dangers." The Russians were evidently pulling back from their earlier approach of a wink-and-nod towards India's assistance for the insurgency. India, said Kosygin, should ensure that "Pakistan and her friends ... know that you have the strength to counter-act all their nefarious designs." That fact "alone will enable you to avert war."[47] In short, the Russians continued to have a very different view on tackling the crisis and saw the treaty as increasing India's deterrent capability and so preserving peace in the subcontinent.

Gromyko flew to New Delhi and signed the treaty on 9 August. In his meeting with Mrs. Gandhi the next day, the Soviet foreign minister reiterated his government's view on dealing with the crisis. Moscow's assessment was that "the Pak [*sic*] military will not succeed in keeping down the people of East Pakistan for long and the rule is doomed." But, he added, "it is not for us to prejudge whether East Pakistan should be separate from West Pakistan or one with it". "You may rest assured", said Gromyko choosing his words carefully, "that in regard to the refugees we shall always support your position." He added that "it would be very good if your Government continues the restraint and regards the situation in a cold blooded way".[48]

Mrs. Gandhi said that "situation is not static". Refugees were continuing to pour in. "I do not know what we can do unless some solution is found. I am posing the question to you what can we do?" Gromyko evasively replied that "it is

46 Record of conversation between D.P. Dhar and Kosygin, 5 August 1971, NMML, P.N. Haksar Papers III, Subject File 280.

47 Record of conversation between D.P. Dhar and Kosygin, 5 August 1971, NMML, P.N. Haksar Papers III, Subject File 280.

48 Record of conversation between Prime Minister and Gromyko, 10 August 1971, NMML, T. N. Kaul Papers, Subject File 19.

not an easy problem and there is no easy solution." He assured Mrs. Gandhi they would apply "considerable pressure" on Yahya Khan. "Pakistan government must give guarantees of security to those people who left because of unbearable conditions."[49] As earlier, the Russians refused to commit themselves to addressing the political problem in East Pakistan. The gulf between the two sides had not been bridged despite signing the treaty of friendship.

VI.

The subsequent developments in Indian and Soviet attitudes on the crisis cannot be dealt with in detail here. Suffice it to say that if the Soviet Union eventually came down on India's side in the unfolding crisis, it was not simply because of the Indo-Soviet treaty. Rather, it was the Yahya regime's unwillingness to make any credible moves either to draw the refugees back to East Pakistan or to create a stable political situation. It was only after Mrs. Gandhi's visit to Moscow in late October 1971—when she made it clear that India could not tolerate the status quo for much longer—that the Russians reluctantly decided to put their eggs in the Indian basket. Then too, their support to India was not entirely unconditional.

As this account suggests, Moscow's support for India was not a foregone conclusion. The Soviet Union and India pursued rather different objectives in concluding the treaty. Whilst the threat from China was an important commonality in their outlooks, their approaches to the crisis diverged. The Soviet Union sought to promote stability in South Asia and was not in favour of splitting Pakistan, especially by the use of force. Thus Moscow supported India's demand for the return of refugees and tacitly approved of its support to the Bengali rebels. But it refused to go along with the Indian assessment that this required a political settlement in East Pakistan with the Awami League. By signing the treaty, it hoped to enhance India's ability to deter Pakistan and China and so forestall the chances of war.

India, for its part, believed that Pakistan was doomed as a single entity, and that the independence of Bangladesh had to be brought about within a relatively short span of time. The Soviet Union's careful balancing act was problematic from a political standpoint. Of equal concern to India was the possibility that Moscow might resume its military supplies to Pakistan. It was to deal with these, as well as the threat from China, that New Delhi went ahead to conclude the agreement. But to India's chagrin, the Russians were unwilling to go with India even after the treaty was signed. The assumption of historians as well as

---

49 Record of conversation between Prime Minister and Gromyko, 10 August 1971, NMML, T. N. Kaul Papers, Subject File 19.

contemporaries that the Indo-Soviet treaty mid-wifed the birth of Bangladesh does not hold up.

This essay also shows that the treaty was not tantamount to a wholesale abandonment of non-alignment by India. Indeed, Prime Minister Indira Gandhi had had her reservations on this count ever since the treaty was first mooted in 1969. It was at her insistence that the draft treaty was carefully worded to remove any notion that India was entering into an alliance with the Soviet Union. Even when the idea of the treaty was resuscitated in mid-1971, she did not move as quickly as many of her advisors wished her to. She eventually did so only when it became clear that the Sino-American rapprochement could impinge upon the crisis in South Asia to India's detriment. It was when India found itself at the crossroads of regional and global interests that the treaty with the Soviet Union left the drawing board and came into existence.

Bibliography

Abercrombie, Patrick. *Greater London Plan 1944: a report prepared on behalf of the Standing Conference on London Regional Planning* (London: His Majesty's Stationery Office, 1945).

Abraham, I.: *The Making of the India Atomic Bomb: Science, Secrecy and the Postcolonial State* (New York: Zed Books, 1998).

Acheson, Dean. *Present at the Creation: My Years at the State Department* (New York: Norton, 1969).

Adeney, Katherine. *Federalism and Ethnic Conflict Regulation in India and Pakistan* (London: Macmillan, 2006).

Adserà, Alicia and Boix, Carles. "Constitutions and Democratic Breakdowns," in *Controlling Governments: Voters, Institutions, and Accountability*, eds. José María Maravall and Ignacio Sánchez-Cuenca (Cambridge: Cambridge University Press, 2008), 247-301.

Agrama, Hussein Ali. "Secularism, Sovereignty, Indeterminacy: Is Egypt a Secular or a Religious State?" in *Comparative Studies in Society and History*, 52.3, (2010): 495-523.

Agrawal, P.: *India's Nuclear Development: Plans and Policies. A Critical Analysis* (New Delhi: Northern Book Centre, 1996).

Agrawal, Sushila. *Press, Public Opinion and Government in India* (Jaipur: Asha Publications House, 1970).

Agrawal, Vivek. "Privatizing the Public: A Strategy for Transit oriented Development in Chandigarh," in *Celebrating Chandigarh. 50 Years of the Idea*, ed. Jaspreet Takhar (Chandigarh: Chandigarh Perspectives, 2002), 263-293.

Ahmed, Samina. "Pakistan's Nuclear Weapons Program: Turning Points and Nuclear Choices," in *International Security* 23.4 (Spring 1999).

Aiyar, Mani Shankar. *Confessions of a Secular Fundamentalist* (New Delhi: Viking, 2004).

Aiyar, Sana. "Fazlul Huq, Region and Religion in Bengal: The Forgotten Alternative of 1940-43," in *Modern Asian Studies*, 42.6 (2008), 1213-49.

Akten zur Auswärtigen Politik der Bundesrepublik Deutschland, Vol. 1- (München: Oldenbourg, 1989-).

Anderson, R. S. *Building Scientific Institutions in India: Saha and Bhabha* (Montreal: McGill Univ. Press, 1975).

Ang, Ien. "Globalisierung der Medien, kultureller Imperialismus und der Aufstieg Asiens," in *Grundlagentexte zur transkulturellen Kommunikation*, eds. Andreas Hepp and Martin Löffelholz (Konstanz: UVK, 2002), 561-585.

Ansari, Jamal H. "A Strategy for the Development of the National Capital," in *Delhi: The Deepening Urban Crisis*, eds. Patwant Singh and Ram Dhamija (Delhi: Sterling Publishers Private Limited, 1989), 136-42.

Anthias, Floya. "Evaluating 'Diaspora': Beyond ethnicity?" in *Sociology*, 32.3, (1998a): 557-580.

Anthias, Floya. "Rethinking Social Divisions: Some Notes Towards a Theoretical Framework," in *Sociological Review*, 46.3 (1998b): 505-535.

Appadorai, Arjun "The Asian Relations Conference in Perspective," in *International Studies* 18.3 (1979): 275-285.

Appadurai, Arjun. *Modernity at Large: Cultural Dimensions of Globalization* (Minneapolis: University of Minnesota Press, 1996).

Arendt, Lijphart, "The Puzzle of Indian Democracy: A Consociational Interpretation," in *American Political Science Review* 90: 2 (1996).

Arun, Prakash, "India's Quest for an Indigenous Aircraft Carrier," in *RUSI Defense Systems* (Summer 2006): 50-52.

Ashutosh, Varshney. "Why Democracy Survives," in *Journal of Democracy* 9.3 (1998): 36-50.

Athique, Adiran M. "The Global Dispersal of Media: Locating Non-Resident Audiences for Indian Films," in *Medi@sia: Global Media/tion In and Out of Context*, eds. Todd Joseph Miles Holden, and Timothy J. Scrase (London, New York: Routledge, 2006), 188-206.

Austin, Granville. "Language and the Constitution: The Half-Hearted Compromise," in *The Indian Constitution: Cornerstone of a Nation* (Delhi: Oxford University Press, 1966).

Austin, Granville. *Working a Democratic Constitution: The Indian Experience* (New Delhi: Oxford University Press, 1999).

Austin, H. *Anatomy of the Kerala Coup* (New Delhi: People's Publication House, 1959).

Ayoob, Mohammed. *India and Southeast Asia: Indian Perceptions and Policies* (London: Routledge, 1990).

Ayub Khan, Mohammed. "The Pakistan-American Alliance: Stresses and Strains," in *Foreign Affairs* 44:1 (1964): 200.

Bahrdt, Hans Paul. *Die moderne Großstadt* (Reinbek bei Hamburg: Rowohlt, 1961).

Baldev, Raj Nayar and T.V Paul. *India in the World Order: Searching for Major Power Status* (New Delhi: Cambridge University Press, 2004).

Bandyopadhyaya, J. "Nehru and Non-alignment," in *Indian Foreign Policy: The Nehru Years*, ed. B. R. Nanda (Honolulu: University of Hawaii Press, 1976), 170-184.

Banerjea, Benoyendra Nath, and M. N Roy. *People's Plan for Economic Development of India* (Delhi: A. K. Mukerjee, 1944).

Bangladesh Documents, Volume 1 (Madras: BNK Press, n.d.).

Banham, Reyner. *Die Revolution der Architektur* (Reinbek bei Hamburg: Rowohlt, 1964).

Barnds, William J. *India, Pakistan, and the Great Powers* (New York: Praeger, 1972).

Barnett, Marguerite. *The Politics of Cultural Nationalism in South India* (Princeton: Princeton University Press, 1976).

Barooah, Nirode Kumar. *India and the Official Germany 1886-1914* (Frankfurt/Main: Lang, 1977).

Barrier, N.G. (ed.), *The Roots of Communal Politics* (Columbia, Mo.: South Asia Books, 1976).

Barrington Moore. *Social Origins of Dictatorship and Democracy: Lord and Peasant in the Making of the Modern World* (Boston: Beacon Press, 1966).

Basu, Kaushik (ed.), *The Oxford Companion to Economics in India* (New Delhi: Oxford University Press, 2007).

Bauer, Peter. "B.R. Shenoy: Stature and Impact" in *Cato Journal* 18.1 (1998a/b): 1-10.

Baumann, Martin. "Diaspora: Genealogies of Semantics and Transcultural Comparison," in *Sociology of Diaspora: A Reader, Vol. 1* ed. Ajaya K. Sahoo, and Brij Maharaj (Jaipur, India: Rawat Publication, 2007), 63-83.

Bayly, Susan. *Caste, Society and Politics in India: from the Eighteenth Century to the Modern Age* (Cambridge: Cambridge University Press, 1999).

Beaton, L. and J. Maddox. *The Spread of Nuclear Weapons* (Westport: Greenwood Press, 1976).

Berghahn, Volker Rolf. *America and the Intellectual Cold Wars in Europe: Shepard Stone between Philanthropy, Academy, and Diplomacy* (Princeton, N.J: Princeton University Press, 2001).

Bernier, Justin. "Asia's Shifting Strategic Landscape: China's Strategic Proxies," in *Orbis* 47.4 (Autumn 2003): 629-643.

Besancon, Marie. "Relative Resources: Inequality in Ethnic Wars, Revolutions, and Genocides," in *Journal of Peace Research* 42 (2005).

Bhargava, Rajeev. "What is Secularism For?" in *Secularism and its Critics,* ed. Rajeev Bhargava, (New Delhi: Oxford University Press, 1998).

Bhatia, S. *India's Nuclear Bomb* (Ghaziabad: Vikas, 1979).

Bhatia, Sunil. *American Karma: Race, Culture, and Identity in the Indian Diaspora (*New York: New York University Press, 2007).

Bhatia, Sunil. "Interpreting the Meanings of Schooling, Hybridity, and Multicultural Citizenship in Diaspora Communities," in *Learning Research in Human Science,* ed. William Penuel, and Kevin O'Connor. (National Study for the Society of Education, 2010), 66-81.

Bhatia, Sunil. "9/11 and the Indian Diaspora," in *Journal of Intercultural Studies* 29 (2008b): 21-39.

Bhatia, Sunil. "Rethinking Culture And Identity in Psychology: Towards a Transnational Cultural Psychology," in *Journal of Theoretical and Philosophical Psychology* 28 (2008a): 301-321.
Bhatia, Sunil and Anjali Ram. "Rethinking "Acculturation" in Relation to Diasporic Cultures, and Postcolonial Identities," in *Human Development* 44 (2001): 1-17.
Bhatia, Sunil, and Anjali Ram. "Theorizing Identity in Transnational and Diaspora: A Critical Approach to Acculturation," in *International Journal for Intercultural Research* 33 (2009): 14-149.
Bhatnagar, K.P. et al., *Transport in Modern India* (Kanpur: Kishore Publishing House 1961).
Bhatt, S.C. "New Trends in the Press," in *Mass Media in India 1998-99*, ed. Joel Bara and Veena Dixit (New Delhi: Ministry of Information and Broadcasting, 1999), 2-10.
Bhatt, Vikram and Peter Scriver. *After the Masters: Contemporary Indian Architecture* (Ahmedabad : Mapin Publishers Pvt. Ltd, 1990).
Bhattacharya Mehta, Rini. "Bollywood, Nation, Globalization: An Incomplete Introduction," in *Bollywood and Globalization: Indian Popular Cinema, Nation, and Diaspora* ed. Rini Bhattacharya Mehta and Rajeshwari Pandharipande (London: Anthem Press, 2010), 1-14.
Bhowmik, Sharit, "Street Vendors" in *Oxford Companion*, ed. Dirk Bronger (Gotha: Justus Perthes, 1996).
Bieber, Hans-Joachim, "Die Atombombe als Statussymbol. Anmerkungen zur indischen Nuklearpolitik," in: *Eliten im Wandel*, ed. Karl Christian Führer et al. (Münster: Westfälisches Dampfboot, 2004), 388-427.
Bieber, Hans-Joachim, "Kernwaffen als nationales Statussymbol", in *Die singuläre Waffe. Was bleibt vom Atomzeitalter*, ed. Constanze Eisenbart, forthcoming.
Bieber, Hans-Joachim: "Zur Frühgeschichte der indischen Nuklearpolitik," in *Geschichte und Gesellschaft* 31 (2005): 373-414.
Blackmer, Donald L.M. *The MIT Center for International Studies: The Founding Years, 1951-1969* (Cambridge: MIT CENIS, 2002).
Bockman, Johanna, and Gil Eyal. "Eastern Europe as a Laboratory for Economic Knowledge: The Transnational Roots of Neoliberalism" in *The American Journal of Sociology* 108.2 (2002): 310-352.
Bockman, Johanna, and Michael A. Bernstein. "Scientific Community in a Divided World: Economists, Planning, and Research Priority During the Cold War," in *Comparative Studies in Society and History* 50.03 (2008): 581-613.
Brah, Avtar. *Cartographies of Diaspora: Contesting Identities* (New York: Routledge, 1996).

Brands, H. W. *India and the United States: The Cold Peace* (Boston: Twayne, 1990).

Brass, Paul, *The Politics of India since Independence,* Second Edition (Cambridge: Cambridge University Press, 2008).

Brass, Paul. "Elite Interest, Popular Passions, and Social Power in the Language Politics of India", in *Ethnic and Racial Studies* 27:3 (2004).

Brass, Paul. *Language, Religion, and Politics in North India* (Cambridge: Cambridge University Press, 1974).

Bratton, Michael and Nicolas van de Walle. *Democratic Experiments in Africa: Regime Transitions in Comparative Perspective* (Cambridge, UK: Cambridge University Press, 1997).

Brosius, Christiane. *India's Middle Class: New Forms of Urban Leisure, Consumption and Prosperity* (New Delhi, London: Routledge, 2010).

Brown, L. M. et al. (eds.). *20th Century Physics* (Bristol: Institute of Physic, 1995).

Buszynski, Les. "Vietnam Confronts China," in *Asian Survey* 20.8 (August 1980): 829-843.

Cassidy, D. C. *Werner Heisenberg* (Heidelberg: Spektrum Akademie Verl., 1995).

Census of India 1961 – Delhi, Census Atlas, ed. S.R. Gotra, Vol. 19.9 (Delhi: Government of India Press, 1965).

Census of India 1971 – Supplement. Provisional Population Totals, ed. A. Chandra Sekhar (New Delhi: Government of India Press, 1971).

Cetinyan, Rupen. "Ethnic bargaining in the shadow of third-party intervention," in *International Organization* 56.3 (2002).

Chadda, Maya. "Integration through Internal Reorganization: Containing Ethnic Conflict in India", in *The Global Review of Ethnopolitics* 2:1 (2002).

Chakraborty, Phani Bhusan and Brojen Bhattacharya. *News behind Newspapers: A Study of the Indian Press* (Calcutta: Minerva Associates Publications, 1989).

Chakravarty, Ranjan and Nandini Gooptu. "Imagi-nation: the media, nation and politics in contemporary India," in *Cultural Encounters. Representing 'otherness'*, ed. Elizabeth Hallam and Brian Street (London, New York: Routledge, 2000), 89-107.

Chakravarty, Sukhamoy. *Development Planning: The Indian Experience* (Oxford: Clarendon Press, 1987).

Chkravartty, Gargi. *P. C. Joshi: A Biography* (New Delhi: National Book Trust, 2007).

Chandra, Bipan; Mukherjee, Mridula and Aditya Mukherjee. *India after Independence: 1947-2000* (New Delhi: Penguin Books, 1999).

Chandra, Pankaj, "Textile and Apparel Industry," in *Oxford Companion*, ed. Basu (London: Oxford University Press, 2007).

Chandrasekhar, B.S. "Analysing Indian Language Newspaper Readership", in *The Hoot,* October 16, 2002. Accessed March 31, 2011. http://www.thehoot.org/web/home/searchdetail.php?sid=572&bg=1.

Chari, Sharad, *Fraternal Capital. Peasant Workers, Self-Made Men and Globalization in Provincial India* (Stanford: Stanford University Press, 2004).

Chatterji, Joya. *The Spoils of Partition: Bengal and India, 1947-1967* (Cambridge: Cambridge University Press, 2007).

Chattopadhyay, Raghabendra. "Indian Business and Economic Planning, 1930-56," in *Business and Politics in India: A Historical Perspective* (New Delhi: Manohar, 1991), 308-350.

Chattopadhyay, Swati. *Representing Calcutta. Modernity, Nationalism, and the Colonial Uncanny* (London and New York: Routledge, 2005).

Chaudhary, Devbrat R. "Mind the Gap between the Metro and the Rest," *India Today*, January 29, 2011. http://indiatoday.indiatoday.in/site/articlePrint.jsp?aid=128059 (Accessed March 1, 2011).

Chaudhuri, Sukanta (ed.), *Calcutta. The Living City* Vol. 1: *The Past*, Vol. 2: *The Present* (Delhi: Oxford University Press, 1990).

Cheape, Charles W. *Moving the Masses. Urban Public Transport in New York, Boston and Philadelphia, 1880 - 1912* (Cambridge: Harvard University Press, 1980).

Cheng, Tun-jen. "Democratizing the Quasi-Leninist Regime in Taiwan," in *World Politics* 41 (July 1989).

Cherry, Gordon E. *The Evolution of British Town Planning. A History of Town Planning in the United Kingdom During the 20th Century And of the Royal Town Planning Institute, 1914-74* (Leighton Buzzard, Beds.: Hill, 1974).

Chima, Jugdgep S. *The Sikh Separatist Insurgency in India: Political Leadership and Ethnonationalist Movements,* (New Delhi: Sage Publications, 2010).

Chou, Rosiland and Joe R. Feagin. The Myth of the Model Minority: Asian Americans Facing Racism (Boulder, CO: Paradigm Publishers, 2008).

Chowdhry, K. *Change-in-Organizations* (Bombay: Somaiya Publ., 1973).

Chowdhry, K. and V. Sarabhai. "Organization for Developmental Tasks: Atomic Energy Commission of India," in *The Indian Journal of Public Administration* 14 (1968): 3 ff.

Clark, Colin. "Development Economics: The Early Years," in *Pioneers in Development*, ed. Gerald M. Meier and Dudley Seers. (Oxford: Oxford University Press, 1984).

Clarkson, Stephen. *The Soviet Theory of Development: India and the Third World in Marxist-Leninist Scholarship* (Toronto: University of Toronto Press), 1978.

Clifford, James. "Introduction: Partial Truths," in *Writing Culture: The Poetics of Ethnography,* ed. James Clifford and George E. Marcus (California: University of California Press, 1986), 1-26.

Clissold, Stephen (ed.), *Yugoslavia and the Soviet Union 1939-1973. A Documentary Survey* (London: The Royal Institute of International Affairs, 1975).

Cohen, R. "Rethinking 'Babylon': Iconoclastic Conceptions of the Diasporic Experience," in *Journal of Oxford* 21.1 (1995): 5-18.

Cohen, Stephen P. *India: Emerging Power* (Washington, D.C.: Brookings Institution Press, 2001).

Collier, Paul and Anke Hoeffler, "Greed and Grievance in Civil War," in *Oxford Economic Papers* 56 (2004).

The Communist Party in Kerala: Six Decades of Struggle and Advance (New Delhi: National Book Centre, 1994).

Condit, Carl W. *The Chicago School of Architecture: A History of Commercial and Public Building in the Chicago Area, 1875-1925* (Chicago: University Press, 1964).

Cornell, Svante. "Autonomy as a Source of Conflict: Caucasian Conflicts in Theoretical Perspective," in *World Politics* 54 (2002).

Correa, Charles. "Chandigarh: The View from Benares," in *Le Corbusier: The Garland Essays,* ed. H. Allen Brooks (New York: Garland 1987), 197-202.

Cunningham, David; Kristian Skrede Gleditsch, and Idean Salehyan, "It takes two: A dyadic analysis of civil war duration and outcome," in *Journal of Conflict Resolution* 53 (2009).

Dahl, Robert. *Democracy and Its Critics* (New Haven, CT: Yale University Press, 1989).

Das Gupta, Amit: *Handel, Hilfe, Hallstein-Doktrin: die bundesdeutsche Südasienpolitik unter Adenauer und Erhard 1949 bis 1966* (Husum: Matthiesen, 2004).

Das Gupta, Amit. "India and Ostpolitik," in Carola Fink and Bernd Schaefer (eds.), *Ostpolitik, 1969-1974: European and Global Responses* (Cambridge: Cambridge Univ. Press, 2009), 163-181.

Das Gupta, Amit. "Indiens sicherheitspolitische Wende zwischen 1962 und 1974," in Sebastian Buciak and Rüdiger von Dehn (eds.), *Indien und Pakistan – Atommächte im Spannungsfeld regionaler und globaler Veränderungen. Beiträge zur Außen- und Sicherheitspolitik Südasiens* (Berlin: Köster, 2010), 93-118.

Das Gupta, Jyotirindra. *Language Conflict and National Development: Group Politics and National Language Policy in India* (Berkeley: University of California Press, 1970).

Das, Suranjan. "The 1992 Calcutta Riot in Historical Continuum: A Relapse into Communal Fury?" in *Modern Asian Studies* 34.2 (2000): 287-91.

Davenport, Christian. "State Repression and Political Order," in *Annual Review of Political Science* 10.1 (2007).

Dayal, Anuj. *A Dream Revisited. An Archival Journey into the Making of the Delhi Metro Rail* (New Delhi: Delhi Metro Rail Corporation Ltd, 2003).

"Dekolonizatsii Teorii," in Ekonomicheskaya Entsiklopedia Politicheskaya Ekonomia, Tom I (Moscow: Izdatel'stvo "Sovetskaya Entsiklopedia", 1972), 374.

Delhi 1999: A Fact Sheet (New Delhi: National Capital Region Planning Board. Ministry of Urban Development. Government of India, 1999).

Delhi Gazetteer. Published by the Government of India (New Delhi: Government of India Press, 1976).

Desai, Radhika. "Die Ausbürgerung Einheimischer und die Einbürgerung von Ausländern: Der Hindu-Nationalismus und das Revival des Hindi-Kinos in den 1990er Jahren," in *Südasien* 4, (December 2007): 43-45.

Deshmukh, Chintaman Dwarkanath. *Economic Developments in India - 1946-1956. A Personal Retrospec*. (Bombay: Asia Publishers House, 1957).

Dipoyudo, Kirdi. "Indonesia-India Bilateral Relations," in *Indonesian Quarterly* 13.4 (October 1985): 509-523.

"The Discussions of S.A. Dange with the C.P.S.U. (b)," in *Revolutionary Democracy* 7.1 (2001).

Dissanyake, Wimal. "Globalization and the Experience of Culture: The Resilience of Nationhood," in *Globalization, Cultural Identities, and Media Representations,* ed. Natascha Gentz, and Stephan Kramer (Albany, NY: State University of New York Press, 2006): 25-44.

Dixit, J N. *Makers of India's Foreign Policy: Raja Ram Mohun Roy to Yashwant Sinha* (New Delhi: HarperCollins and The India Today Group, 2004).

Dobell, W M. "Ramifications of the China-Pakistan Border Treaty," in *Pacific Affairs* 37.3 (Autumn 1964): 283-295.

Dörner, Andreas. *Politainment: Politik in der medialen Erlebnisgesellschaft* (Frankfurt a.M.: Suhrkamp, 2001).

Domar, Evsey D. *Essays in the Theory of Economic Growth* (New York: Oxford University Press, 1957).

Doshi, B. V. et al. "In Search of India's Future Cities," in *Celebrating Chandigarh: 50 Years of the Idea,* ed. Jaspreet Takhar (Chandigarh: Chandigarh Perspectives, 2002), 247-260.

Dossal, Miriam. *Imperial Designs and Indian Realities. The Planning of Bombay City 1845-1875* (Delhi: Oxford University Press, 1991).

Drieberg, Trevor and Sarala Jag Mohan. *Emergency in India* (New Delhi: Manas Publishers, 1975).

Dunning, Thad. "Conditioning the Effects of Aid: Cold War Politics, Donor credibility, and Democracy in Africa," in *International Organization* 58.2 (2004): 409-423.

Durth, Werner and Gutschow, Niels. *Träume in Trümmern. Planungen zum Wiederaufbau zerstörter Städte im Westen Deutschlands 1940-1950. Band I: Konzepte* (Braunschweig et al.: Vieweg, 1988).

Dutt, Subimal. *With Nehru in the Foreign Office* (Calcutta: Minerva, 1977).

Dutt, V P. *India's Foreign Policy* (New Delhi: Vani Educational Books, 1984).

Dyakov, A. M. *Crisis of British Rule in India and the New Stage in the Liberation Struggles of Her Peoples* (Bombay: PPH, 1950).

Eisinger, Angelus. *Die Stadt der Architekten: Anatomie einer Selbstdemontage* (Gütersloh et al.: Bauverl. et al., 2005).

Ekbladh, David. *The Great American Mission: Modernization and the Construction of an American World Order* (Princeton: Princeton University Press, 2010).

Ekonomicheskaya Entsiklopediya Politicheskoy Ekonomiki, Vol. 1 (Moscow: Izd. Sovetskaya Entsiklopediya, 1972).

Engerman, David C. "West Meets East: The Centre for International Studies and Indian Economic Development," in *Staging Growth: Modernization, Development, and the Cold War*, ed. David C. Engerman, Nils Gilman, Mark H. Haefele, and Michael E. Latham (Amherst, MA: University of Massachusetts Press, 2003).

Engerman, David C. et al. (ed.), *Staging Growth: Modernization, Development, and the Global Cold War* (Amherst: University of Massachusetts Press, 2003).

Engerman, David C. and Unger, Corinna R. "Towards a Global History of Modernization," in *Diplomatic History* 33.3 (2009): 375–385.

Engineer, Asghar Ali. "Behind the Communal Fury," in *Economic and Political Weekly*, 17.10 (Mar 6, 1982): 356-7.

Engineer, Asghar Ali. "Communal Riots in Godhra: A Report," in *Economic and Political Weekly*, 16.41 (10 October 1981): 1638-1640.

Erhard, Ludwig (ed.). *Deutschlands Rückkehr zum Weltmarkt* (Düsseldorf: E-con, 1953).

Escobar, Arturo. *Encountering Development: The Making and Unmaking of the Third World* (Princeton, N.J: Princeton University Press, 1995).

Evenson, Norma. *Chandigarh* (Berkeley: University of California Press, 1966).

Evenson, Norma. *The Indian Metropolis: A View toward the West* (New Haven et al.: Yale University Press, 1989).

Fearon, James. "Commitment problems and the spread of ethnic conflict," in *The International Spread of Ethnic Conflict,* ed. Donald Lake and David Rothchild, (Princeton: Princeton University Press, 1998).

Fearon, James. “Rationalist Explanations for War,” in *International Organization* 49:3 (1995).
Fearon, James. “Why Do Some Civil Wars Last So Much Longer Than Others?” in *Journal of Peace Research* 41, (2004).
Feldbauer, Peter, et al. (ed.), *Mega-Cities. Die Metropolen des Südens zwischen Globalisierung und Fragmentierung* (Frankfurt am Main: Brandes & Apsel, 1997).
Fic, Victor M. *Kerala: Yenan of India: 1937-1969* (Bombay: Nachiketa Publications, 1970).
Fischer, David. *History of the International Atomic Energy Agency. The First Forty Years* (Wien: IAEA, 1997).
Fischer, Herbert. *DDR – Indien. Ein Diplomat berichtet* (Berlin: Staatsverlag der Deutschen Demokratischen Republik, 1984).
Fischer-Tiné, Harald, and Michael Mann (eds.), *Colonialism as Civilizing Mission. Cultural ideology in British India* (London: Anthem Press, 2004).
Fishman, Robert. *Urban Utopias in the Twentieth Century: Ebenezer Howard, Frank Lloyd Wright, Le Corbusier* (New York: Basic Books, 1977).
Forrester, Duncan. “The Madras Anti-Hindi Agistation, 1965: Political Protest and its Effect on Language Policy in India”, in *Pacific Affairs* (1966).
Foster, William Z. “People’s Front and People’s Democracy,” in *For a Lasting Peace, for a People’s Democracy* 11.32 (1950).
Frankel, Francine R. *India's Political Economy, 1947-1977: The Gradual Revolution* (Princeton, N.J: Princeton University Press, 1978).
Fravel, M Taylor. *Strong Borders, Secure Nation: Cooperation and Conflict in China’s Territorial Disputes* (Princeton: Princeton University Press, 2008).
Frei, Norbert and Johannes Schmitz. *Journalismus im Dritten Reich* (München: Beck, 1989).
Friedensburg, Ferdinand. *Es ging um Deutschlands Einheit: Rückschau eines Berliners auf die Jahre nach 1945* (Berlin: Haude & Spener, 1971).
Friedman, Milton, and Rose D Friedman. *Two Lucky People: Memoirs* (Chicago: The University of Chicago Press, 1998).
Fry, Maxwell. “Le Corbusier at Chandigarh”, in *The Open Hand. Essays on Le Corbusier,* ed. Russel Walden (Cambridge: MIT Press, 1977), 350-363.
Galbraith, John Kenneth. *Ambassador's Journal; a Personal Account of the Kennedy Years* (Boston: Houghton Mifflin, 1969).
Galbraith, John Kenneth. *A Life in Our Times: Memoirs* (Boston: Houghton Mifflin, 1981).
Gallanter, Marc. “Hinduism, Secularism, and the Indian Judiciary,” in ed. Rajeev Bhargava, *Secularism and its Critics* (New Delhi: Oxford University Press, 1998).

Ganchovski, Nedelcho. *The Days of Dimitrov As I Witnessed and Recorded Them* (Sofia: Sofia Press, 1979).

Gandhi, Sahil, *Affordability of Housing in Mumbai* (Working Paper VSU WP 37, Vibhuti Shukla Centre, Department of Economics, University of Mumbai, 2010).

Ganguly, Keya. "Migrant Identities: Personal Memory and the Construction of Selfhood," in *Cultural Studies* 6.1 (1992): 27-49.

Ganguly, Sumit. *Conflict Unending: India-Pakistan Tensions since 1947* (New York: Columbia University Press, 2001).

Ganguly, Sumit. *The Crisis in Kashmir: Portents of War, Hopes of Peace* (Cambridge: Cambridge University Press, 1997).

Ganguly, Sumit. "India and China: Border Issues, Domestic Integration, and International Security," in *The India-China Relationship: What the United States Needs to Know*, ed. Francine R Frankel and Harry Harding (New York: Columbia University Press, 2004), 103-133.

Ganguly, Sumit. "The Sino-Indian Border Talks, 1981-1989: A View from New Delhi," in *Asian Survey* 29.12 (December 1989).

Ganguly, Sumit. "Six Decades of Democracy," in *Journal of Democracy* 18.2 (2007): 30-40.

Ganguly, Sumit. "Why India Joined the Nuclear Club," *The Bulletin of Atomic Scientists* (April 1983): 30-3.

Garnier, Tony. *Die ideale Industriestadt. Une Cité industrielle. Eine städtebauliche Studie* (Tübingen: Wasmuth,1989).

Garver, John W. "China's Decision for War with India in 1962," in *New Directions in the Study of China's Foreign Policy* ed. Alastair I Johnston and Robert S Ross, (Stanford: Stanford University Press, 2006), 86-130.

Garver, John W. "China's Kashmir Policies," in *India Review* 3.1 (January 2004): 1-24.

Garver, John W. "The Indian Factor in Recent Sino-Soviet Relations," in *The China Quarterly* no. 125 (1991).

Geddes, Patrick. *Cities in Evolution* (London: Benn, 1968).

Gellner, Ernest. *Nations and Nationalism* (Ithaca: Cornell University Press, 1983).

Ghani, Ejaz, *The Poor Half Billion in South Asia. What is Holding Back Lagging Regions?* (New Delhi: Oxford University Press, 2010).

Ghosh, Abhijit. "Dynamics of India-China Normalisation," in *China Report* 31.2 (May 1995): 251-270.

Ghosh, Amitav. "The Diaspora in Indian Culture," in *Public Culture* 2.1 (1989): 73-78.

Ghosh, Partha S. "Bangladesh at the Crossroads: Religion and Politics," in *Asian Survey,* 33.7 (July 1993), 697-710.

Ghosh, Shohini. "Media and the Aftermath: One or two things I know after 9/11," in *The little magazine: via media* 4.2, ed. Antara Dev Sen, (2003): 11-17.

Ghoshal, Baladas, "India and Southeast Asia: Prospects and Problems," in *India and Southeast Asia: Challenges and Opportunities*, ed. Baladas Ghoshal (New Delhi: Konark Publishers, 1996).

Giddens, Anthony. *Modernity and Self-Identity: Self and Society in the Late Modern Age* (Palo Alto, CA: Stanford University Press, 1991).

Giedion, Siegfried. *Raum, Zeit, Architektur* (Ravensburg: Maier, 1965).

Girling, J L S. "The Guam Doctrine," in *International Affairs* 46.1 (January 1970): 48-62.

Glick-Schiller, Nina, Linda Basch, and Cristina Szanton-Blanc. "From Immigrant to Transmigrant: Theorizing Transnational Migration," in *Anthropological Quarterly* 68 (1995): 48-63.

Goel, Tripta, "Urban Bus Transit System in Delhi-An Assessment of the Quality of Service", in *Indian Journal of Transport Management*, (2000).

Goh, Evelyn. *Constructing the US Rapprochement with China, 1961-1974: From 'Red Menace' to 'Tacit Ally'* (Cambridge: Cambridge University Press, 2005).

Goldman, Marshall I. "A Balance Sheet of Soviet Foreign Aid," in *Foreign Affairs* 43.2 (1965): 349-360.

Goldstein, Judith. "International Institutions and Domestic Politics: GATT, WTO, and the Liberalization of International Trade," in *The WTO as an International Organization*, ed. Anne O. Krueger (Chicago: University of Chicago Press, 1998), 133– 60.

Goldstein, Judith. "International Law and Domestic Institutions: Reconciling North American 'Unfair' Trade Laws," in *International Organization* 50.4 (1996): 541-564.

Goldstein, Melvyn C. *A History of Modern Tibet, Volume 2 - The Calm before the Storm, 1951-1955* (Berkeley: University of California Press, 2007).

Gollan, John. *People's Democracy for Britain. Report to the 22nd National Congress of the Communist Party* (London: Easter, 1952).

Gooptu, Nandini. *The Politics of the Urban Poor in Early Twentieth Century* (Cambridge: Cambridge University Press, 2001).

Gopal, Sarvepalli. *Jawaharlal Nehru: An Anthology* (New Delhi: Oxford University Press, 1980).

Gopal, Sarvepalli. *Jawaharlal Nehru: A Biography*, 3 Vol. (Cambridge: Harvard University Press, 1975-1984).

Gopal, Sarvepalli. *Radhakrishnan: A Biography* (Delhi: Oxford Univ. Press, 1989).

Gordon, Sandy. *India's Rise to Power in the Twentieth Century and Beyond* (London: St. Martin's Press, 1995).

Gould, William. *Bureaucracy, Community and Influence in India: Society and the State, 1930s-1960s* (London: Routledge, 2011).

Gould, William. "Contesting 'Secularism' in colonial and postcolonial north India between 1930 and 1950s," in *Contemporary South Asia* 14.4, (2005): 481-494.

Gould, William. *Hindu Nationalism and the Language of Politics in Late Colonial India* (Cambridge: Cambridge University Press, 2004).

Gourevitch, Peter. "The Second Image Reversed: the international sources of domestic politics," in *International Organization* 32.4 (1978): 881-912.

Government of India, Department of Atomic Energy. *Ten Years of Atomic Energy in India, 1954-1964* (Bombay: GoI, 1964).

Government of the United States. *Statistical Abstract of the United States* (Washington, D.C.: U.S. Government, 1970).

Gray, William Glenn. *Germany's Cold War: the Global Campaign to Isolate East Germany, 1949-1969* (Chapel Hill: Univ. of North Carolina Press, 2003).

Grewal, Reeta, "Urban Morphology under Colonial Rule," in *The City in Indian History*, ed. Indu Banga (Delhi: Manohar Publishers, 1994), 173-90.

Gruliow, L. (ed.), *Soviet Views on the Post-War World Economy* (Washington: Public Affairs Press, 1948).

Guillien, Mauro F. *The Taylorized Beauty of the Mechanical. Scientific Management and the Rise of Modernist Architecture* (Princeton: Princeton University Press, 2006).

Gupta, Narayani, *Delhi Between Two Empires 1803-1931. Society, Government and Urban Growth* (Delhi: Oxford University Press, 1981).

Gupta, Shishir. "Army passes intel to Govt: PLA men at pass linking PoK to China," in *Indian Express* 31 August 2010.

Gurr, Ted. "Peoples against States: Ethnopolitical Conflict and the Changing World System," in *International Studies Quarterly* 38 (1994): 347-377.

Gurr, Ted. *People Versus States: Minorities at Risk in the New Century* (Washington, D.C.: United States Institute of Peace Press, 2000).

Hagerty, Devin T. "India's Regional Security Doctrine," in *Asian Survey* 31.4 (1991): 351-363.

Halder, Dilip, *Urban Transport in India. Crisis and Cure* (New Delhi: Bookwell, 2006).

Hale, Henry. "The Parade of Sovereignties: Testing Theories of Secession in the Soviet Setting," in *British Journal of Political Science* 30 (2000): 31-56.

Hall, Peter. *Cities of Tomorrow. An Intellectual History of Urban Planning and Design in the Twentieth Century* (Oxford et al.: Blackwell, 1988).

Hall, Peter D. *The Political Power of Economic Ideas: Keynesianism across Nations* (Princeton, N.J: Princeton University Press, 1989).

Hanson, A. H. *The Process of Planning: a Study of India's Five-Year Plans, 1950-1964* (London: Oxford U.P, 1966).

Hardgrave Jr., Robert L. and Stanley A. Kochanek. *India: Government and Politics in a Developing Nation* (Boston: Thomson Wadsworth, 2000).

Hardgrave, Richard L. "The Riots in Tamilnad: Problems and Prospects of India's Language Crisis," in *Asia Survey* 5 (1965): 399-407.

Harper, Kristine C. and Ronald E. Doel, "Environmental Diplomacy in the Cold War: Weather Control, the United States, and India, 1966-1967," in *Environmental Histories of the Cold War,* ed. J. R. McNeill and Corinna R. Unger, (New York: Cambridge University Press and The German Historical Institute, 2010), 115-138.

Harrison, Selig S. "China's Discreet Hold on Pakistan's Northern Borderlands," in *The New York Times*, 26 August 2010.

Harrison, Selig S. *India and the United States*. (New York: Macmillan, 1961).

Harrison, Selig. *The Most Dangerous Decades: An Introduction to the Comparative Study of Language Policy in Multi-Lingual States* (New York: Columbia University Press, 1957).

Hart, D. *Nuclear Power in India: A comparative Analysis* (London: Allen & Unwin, 1983).

Hasan, Mushirul. "Indian Muslims since Independence: In Search of Integration and Identity", in *Third World Quarterly,* 10.2 (1988), 818-842.

Hasan, Mushirul. *Legacy of a Divided Nation: India's Muslims since Independence* (London: Hurst and Co., 1997).

Hasan, Mushirul. "The Muslim Mass Contacts Campaign: An Attempt at Political Mobilisation," in *Economic and Political Weekly* 21.27 (December 1986): 2273-80.

Hasan, Zoya. "Changing Orientation of the State and the Emergence of Majoritarianism in the 1980s," in *Social Scientist* 18.8/9 (Aug-Sept. 1990): 27-37.

Hauner, Milan. *India in Axis Strategy: German, Japan, and Indian Nationalists in the Second World War* (Stuttgart: Klett-Cotta, 1981).

Hazarika, Sanjoy. "India and China cite each other for massing troops in the Himalayas," in *The New York Times*, 8 May 1987.

Heimsath, Charles H. *India's Role in the Korean War* (PhD dissertation, Yale University, 1956).

Heimsath, Charles H. and Surjit Mansingh. *A Diplomatic History of Modern India* (Calcutta: Allied Publishers, 1971).

Helweg, Arthur W. and Usha Helweg. *An Immigrant Success Story: East Indians in America* (Philadelphia: University of Pennsylvania Press, 1990).

Hilger, Andreas. "Revolutionsideologie, Systemkonkurrenz oder Entwicklungspolitik? Sowjetisch-indische Wirtschaftsbeziehungen in Chruschtschows Kaltem Krieg," in *Archiv für Sozialgeschichte* 48 (2008): 389-410.

Hilger, Andreas. "The Soviet Union and India: The Years of Late Stalinism," www.php.isn.ethz.ch/collections/coll_india/intro_stalin.cfm?

Hilger, Andreas. "The Soviet Union and India: The Khrushchev Era and its Aftermath until 1966," www.php.isn.ethz.ch/collections/coll_india/intro_khrushchev.cfm?

Hilpert, Thilo. *Le Corbusiers "Charta von Athen". Texte und Dokumente* (Braunschweig: Vieweg, 1984).

Historical and Polemical Documents of the Communist Movement of India, Vol. 1: 1943-1972 (Vijayawada: Tarimela Nagireddy Memorial Trust, 2007).

Hodgson, "The Ideological Origins of the Population Association of America," in Population and Development Review, 17 ().

Home Department, *Report of the States Reorganisation Commission, 1955* (New Delhi: Government of India Press, 1955).

Horowitz, Donald. *Ethnic Groups in Conflict* (Berkeley: University of California Press, 1985).

Huntington, Samuel P. *Political Order in Changing Societies* (New Haven: Yale University Press, 1968).

Hussain, T Karki. "India's China Policy: Putting Politics in Command" in Satish Kumar, ed. *Yearbook on India's Foreign Policy, 1989* (New Delhi: Sage, 1990).

Huxley, Tim. *Defending the Lion City: The Armed Forces of Singapore* (St. Leonards, Australia: Allen & Unwin, 2000).

Ian, Anthony. *The Arms Trade and Medium Powers: Case Studies of India and Pakistan 1947-90* (Hertfordshire: Harvester Wheatsheaf, 1992).

Inda, Jonathan. X. and Renato Rosaldo. "Introduction: A World in Motion." in *The Anthropology of Globalization: A Reader*, ed. by Jonathan X. Inda, and Renato Rosaldo (Malden, MA: Blackwell Publishing 2002), 1-35.

India Planning Commission. *Papers Relating to the Formulation of the Second Five Year Plan* (Delhi: Govt. of India Planning Commission, 1955).

Indian Committee for Cultural Freedom. *Studies on the Plan Frame: Papers Considered by a Study Group Set up by the Indian Committee for Cultural Freedom* (Bombay: Published by V.B. Karnik for the Indian Committee for Cultural Freedom, 1955).

Indian Statistical Institute. *History and Activities, 1931-1959* (Calcutta: Indian Statistical Institute, 1959).

Isphani, Mahnaz Z. *Roads and Rivals: The Political Uses of Access in the Borderlands of Asia* (Ithaca: Cornell University Press, 1989).

Iyer, V.R. Krishna. "Foreign Print Media Incarnating as Indian Fourth Estate?" in *Economic and Policital Weekly* 29.49 (December 1994): 3082-3085.

Jacob, T. G. (ed.). *National Question in India. CPI Documents 1942-47* (New Delhi: Odyssey Press, 1988).

Jacobs, Jane. *Tod und Leben großer amerikanischer Städte* (Braunschweig: Bertelsmann, 1963).

Jagmohan, *Island of Truth* (New Delhi: Vikas Publishing House, 1978).

Jain, B. M. Nuclear Politics in South Asia. In Search of an Alternative Paradigm (Jaipur, 1994).

Jain, R. K. (ed.). Soviet South Asian Relations 1947-1978, 2 Vols. (New Delhi: Radiant Publishers, 1978).

Jalal, Ayesha. *The Sole Spokesman: Jinnah, the Muslim League and the Demand for Pakistan* (Cambridge: Cambridge University Press, 1985).

Jawaharlal Nehru's Speeches, Vol. 4 (Delhi: GoI, 1983).

Jeffrey, Robin. "Breaking News," in *The little magazine: via media* 4.2, ed. Antara Dev Sen, (2003): 6-10.

Jeffrey, Robin. *India's Newspaper Revolution: Capitalism, Politics and Indian-Language Press, 1977-99* (New Delhi: Palgrave Mac Millan, 2000).

Jenne, Erin K. *Ethnic Bargaining: The Paradox of Minority Empowerment,* (Ithaca, NY: Cornell University Press, 2007).

Jensen, Joan. M. *Passage from India: Asian Indian Immigrants in North America* (New Haven, CT: Yale University Press, 1988).

Jian, Chen. "The Tibetan Rebellion of 1959 and China's Changing Relations with India and the Soviet Union," in *Journal of Cold War Studies* 8.3 (2006): 54-101.

Joglekar, K.G. "The Print Media: 'The Cat must Bell Itself'," in *Mass Media in India 1998-99*, ed. Joel Bara and Veena Dixit (New Delhi: Ministry of Information and Broadcasting, 1999), 7-12.

Johnson, William Arthur. *The Steel Industry of India*. (Cambridge: Harvard University Press, 1966).

Jones, Justin. "The Shi'a Muslims of the United Provinces of India, c. 1890-1940," PhD Dissertation, University of Cambridge, (2007).

Joshi, Chitra. "Bonds of community, ties of religion: Kanpur textile workers in the early twentieth century," in *The Indian Economic and Social History Review* 22.3 (1985), 251-80.

Joshi, Kiran. *Documenting Chandigarh. The Indian Architecture of Pierre Jeanneret,* ed. Edwin Maxwell Fry and Jane Beverley Drew (Ahmedabad: Mapin Publishing, 1999).

Joshi, Subhash R. and B.S. Bhatia. "Medien in Indien." in *Internationales Handbuch Medien*, ed. Hans-Bredow-Institut für Medienforschung an der Universität Hamburg, (Baden-Baden: Nomos, 2004), 871-881.

Juergensmeyer, Mark. *The New Cold War? Religious Nationalism Confronts the State* (Berkeley: University of California Press, 1994).

Kalecki, Michał. *Developing Economies*. Ed. Jerzy Osiatyński (Oxford: Clarendon Press, 1993).

Kalia, Ravi. *Chandigarh: The Making of a City* (Delhi: Oxford University Press, 1987).

Kapur, Rajiv. *Sikh Separatism: The Politics of Faith* (New Delhi: World Book Centre, 1988).

Kaul, Man Mohini. "ASEAN-India Relations during the Cold War," in *India and ASEAN: The Politics of India's Look East Policy,* ed. Frédéric Grare and Amitabh Mattoo (New Delhi: Manohar and Centre de Sciences Humaines, 2002).

Kaur, Ravinder, "Planning Urban Chaos: State and Refugees in Post-Partition India," in *Urbanization and Governance in India*, ed. Evelin Hust and Michael Mann (Delhi: Manohar Publishers, 2005), 229-50.

Kautsky, John H. *Moscow and the Communist Party of India* (New York: MIT Press, 1956).

Kavic, Lorne J. *India's Quest for Security: Defense Policies, 1947-1965* (Berkeley: University of California Press, 1967).

Keddie, Nikki. "Pakistan's Movement against Islamization," in *MERIP Middle East Report,* (Sept-Oct 1987): 148.

Kennedy, John F. *The Strategy of Peace*. 1st ed. (New York: Harper, 1960).

Keohane Robert O. and Helen V. Milner. *Internationalization and Domestic Politics* (Cambridge: Cambridge University Press, 1996).

Kerala's Answer to KPCC Charges (New Delhi: CP Publication, 1959).

Khan, Yasmin. "Performing Peace: Gandhi's Assassination as a Critical Moment in the Consolidation of the Nehruvian State," in *Modern Asian Studies,* 45.1 (2011): 57-80.

Khandelwal, Madhulika. S. *Becoming American, Being Indian: An Immigrant Community in New York City* (Ithaca, NY: Cornell University Press, 2002).

Khilnani, Sunil. *The Idea of India* (New York: Farar, Straus and Giroux, 1997).

Kibria, Nazli. *Becoming Asian American* (Baltimore: The John Hopkins University Press, 2002).

Kidambi, Prashant. *The Making of an Indian Metropolis. Colonial Governance and Public Culture in Bombay, 1890-1920* (Aldershot and Burlington, VT: Ashgate, 2007).

Kidwai, Sabina. "Images of Muslim Women in Indian Television Serials," in *Behind the Veil: Representation of Muslim Women in Indian Writings in English 1950-2000*, ed. A.R. Kidwai (New Delhi: APH Publishing, 2007), 148-166.

King, Robert. *Nehru and the Language Politics of India* (Delhi: Oxford University Press, 1999).

Kissinger, Henry A. *White House Years.* (Boston: Little, Brown, 1979).

Kivimäki, Timo. "'Reason' and 'Power' in Territorial Disputes: The South China Sea," in *Asian Journal of Social Science* 30.3 (2002): 525-546.

Klaehn, Jeffrey. "A Critical Review and Assessment of Herman and Chomsky's Propaganda Model," in *European Journal of Communication* 17.2 (June 2002): 147-182.

Klein, Christina. *Cold War Orientalism: Asia in the Middlebrow Imagination, 1945-1961* (Berkeley: University of California Press, 2003).

Knaus, John Kenneth. *Orphans of the Cold War: America and the Tibetan Struggle for Survival* (New York: Public Affairs, 1999).

Kohli, Atul. "Can Democracies Accommodate Ethnic Nationalism? Rise and Decline of Self-Determination Movements in India," in *The Journal of Asian Studies* 56:2 (1997): 325-344.

Kohli, Atul. *The Success of India's Democracy* (Cambridge: Cambridge University Press, 2001).

Kohli, M S. and Kenneth Conboy, *Spies in the Himalayas: Secret Missions and Perilous Climbs* (Lawrence: University Press of Kansas, 2002).

Koshy, Susan. "Category Crisis: South Asian Americans and Questions of Race and Ethnicity," in *Diaspora*, 7.3 (1998): 285-319.

Kragh, Helge S.: Dirac. *A Scientific Biography* (New York: Cambridge Univ. Press, 1990).

Kuhlmann, Jan: *Subhas Chandra Bose und die Indienpolitik der Achsenmächte* (Berlin: Schiler, 2003).

Kulke, Hermann and Rothermund, Dietmar. *Geschichte Indiens* (Stuttgart: Kohlhammer, 1982).

Kumar, Keval. *Mass Communication in India* (Bombay: Jaico Publishing House, 1987).

Kun, Bela (ed.). *Kommunisticheskii internatsional v dokumentakh, 1919-1932* (Moscow, 1933).

Kundu, Amitabh. "Changing Agrarian System and Urban-Rural Linkages," in *Handbook of Agriculture in India* ed. Shovan Ray (New Delhi: Oxford University Press, 2007), 183-206.

Kux, Dennis, *India and the United States: Estranged Democracies*. (Washington: National Defense University Press, 1993).

Laitin, David. *Language Repertoires and State Construction in Africa* (Cambridge: Cambridge University Press, 1992).

Lajpat Rai, Lala. *The Evolution of Japan and other Papers* (Calcutta: R. Chatterjee, 1918).

Latham, Michael E. *Modernization as Ideology: American Social Science and "Nation Building" in the Kennedy Era* (Chapel Hill: University of North Carolina Press, 2000).

Latham, Michael E. *The Right Kind of Revolution: Modernization, Development, and U.S. Foreign Policy from the Cold War to the Present* (Ithaca: Cornell University Press, 2011).

Lawrence, Mark A. "The Limits of Peacemaking: India and the Vietnam War, 1962-1968," in *The Search for Peace in Vietnam, 1964-1968*, ed. Lloyd C. Gardner and Ted Gittinger (College Station: Texas A&M University Press, 2004), 231-259.

Lawrence, Mark A. "The Rise and Fall of Non-Alignment," in *The Cold War in the Third World*, ed. Robert J. McMahon, (New York: Oxford University Press, forthcoming).

Le Corbusier. *The Radiant City* (London: Faber and Faber, 1967).

Leifer, Michael. "Conflict and Regional Order in Southeast Asia," in *Adelphi Papers* (London: International Institute of Strategic Studies, 1980).

Lelyveld, David. "Disenchantment at Aligarh: Islam and the Realm of the Secular in Late Nineteenth Century India," in *Die Welt des Islams*, New Series, 22.1/4 (1982): 85-102.

Lemin, I. M. *Obostrenie krizisa Britanskoi imperii posle Vtoroi Mirovoi Vojny* (Moscow: Akademiya Nauk, 1951).

Leonard, David K. and Scott Straus. *Africa's Stalled Development: International Causes and Cures* (Boulder: Lynne Reiner Publishers, 2003).

Leonard, Karen. *Making Ethnic Choices: California's Punjabi Mexican Americans* (Philadelphia: Temple University Press, 1992).

"Letter of C. Rajagopalachari to J. Nehru on the advice of R.P. Dutt to Indian Communists (4th March 1951)," in *Revolutionary Democracy* 14.2 (2008).

Lewis, John and Litai Xue. *China Builds the Bomb* (Stanford: Stanford University Press, 1991).

Lichbach, Mark. "Deterrence or Escalation?: The Puzzle of Aggregate Studies of Repression and Dissent," in *Journal of Conflict Resolution* 31 (1987): 266-297.

Little, Ian Malcolm David. *Economic Development: Theory, Policy, and International Relations*. (New York: Basic Books, 1982).

Lloyd, I. Rudolph, ''Urban Life and Populist Radicalism: Dravidian Politics in Madras," in *Journal of Asian Studies* 20.3 (1961): 283-297.

Lok Sabha Secretariat. *Lok Sabha Debates on the Report of the States Reorganisation Commission* (Delhi: Lok Sabha Secretariat, 1956).

Ludden, David. *Geschichte Indiens* (Essen: Magnus, 2006).

Lüthi, Lorenz M. *The Sino-Soviet Split, 1956-1966: Cold War in the Communist World* (Princeton: Princeton University Press, 2008).

Madan, T.N. "Secularism in its Place," in *Journal of Asian Studies* 46.4 (1987): 747-59.

Mahalanobis, P. C. *The Approach of Operational Research to Planning in India*. (New York: Asia Pub. House, 1963).

Mahalanobis, P. C. "Some Observations on the Process of Growth of National Income," in *Sankhyā: The Indian Journal of Statistics (1933-1960)* 12.4 (1953): 307-312.

Mahalanobis, P. C. *Talks on Planning* (New York: Asia Pub. House, 1961).

Malaviya, H. D. *Kerala: A Report to the Nation* (Bombay: PPH, 1958).

Malenbaum, Wilfred. "Who Does the Planning?" In *Leadership and Political Institutions in India* (1959): 301-313.

Malhotra, Inder. *Indira Gandhi: A Personal and Political Biography* (Boston: Northeastern University Press, 1989).

Malik, Mohan. "Nuclear Proliferation in Asia: The China Factor," in *Australian Journal of International Affairs* 53.1 (1999): 31-41.

Manjapra, Kris and Sugata Bose (ed.), *Cosmopolitan Thought Zones: South Asia and the Global Circulation of Ideas* (Hampshire: Palgrave Macmillan, 2010).

Mankekar, Purnima. *Screening Culture, Viewing Politics: An Ethnography of Television, Womanhood, and Nation in Postcolonial India* (Durham, London: Duke University Press, 1999).

Mann, Michael. *Geschichte Indiens. Vom 18. bis ins 21. Jahrhundert* (Paderborn etc.: utb, 2005).

Mann, Michael. "Town Planning and Urban Resistance in the Old City of Delhi, 1937-77," in *Urbanization and Governance in India*, ed. Evelin Hust and Michael Mann (Delhi: Manohar Publishers, 2005), 251-78.

Mann, Michael and Samiksha Sehrawat. "A City With a View: The Afforestation of the Delhi Ridge 1883–1913," in *Modern Asian Studies* 43.2 (2009): 543-70.

Mann, Michael and Samiksha Sehrawat. "Delhi's Belly: The Management of Water, Sewerage and Excreta in a Changing Urban Environment during the Nineteenth Century," in *Studies in History* 23.1 (2007), 1-31.

Mann, Michael and Samiksha Sehrawat. "Vision und Realität einer werdenden Mega-City," in *Megastädte im 20. Jahrhundert*, ed. Wolfgang Schwentker (Göttingen: Vandenhoeck und Ruprecht, 2006), 185-211.

Mansingh, Surjit. "India-China Relations in the Post-Cold War Era," in *Asian Survey* 34.3 (March 1994): 289-293.

Mansingh, Surjit. "Indo-Soviet Relations in the Nehru Years" Accessed March 1, 2011.
www.php.isn.ethz.ch/collections/coll_india/NehruYearsIntroduction.cfm?

Mansingh, Surjit and Steven I. Levine, "China and India: Moving Beyond Confrontation," in *Problems of Communism* 38.2-3 (1989): 30-49.

Marker, Jamsheed. *Quiet Diplomacy: Memoirs of an Ambassador of Pakistan* (Karachi: Oxford University Press, 2010).

Marriott, John. *The Other Empire. Metropolis, India and Progress in the Colonial Imagination* (Manchester and New York: Manchester University Press, 2003, 2009).

Maslennikov, V. M. "On the Leading Role of the Working Class in the National Liberation Movement of the Colonial Peoples," in *Reports to the Institute of Economics and Pacific Institute of the Academy of Sciences. Colonial Peoples' Struggle for Liberation* (Bombay: PPH, 1950).

Mastny, Vojtech. "The Soviet Union's Partnership with India," in *Journal of Cold War Studies* 12.3 (2010): 50-90.

Mazzarella, William. *Shoveling Smoke: Advertising and Globalization in Contemporary India* (Durham, London: Duke University Press, 2003).

Mazzarella, William. "Very 'Bombay': Contending with the Global in an Indian Advertising Agency," in *Cultural Anthropology* 18.1 (2003b): 33-71.

McAdam, Doug; Sidney Tarrow, and Charles Tilly, *Dynamics of Contention* (Cambridge: Cambridge University Press , 2003).

McGowan, Patrick J. "Africa and Non-Alignment: A Comparative Study of Foreign Policy," in *International Studies Quarterly* 12.3 (1968): 262-295.

McGranahan, Carole. "Tibet's Cold War: The CIA and the Chushi Gangdrug Resistance, 1956-1974," in *Journal of Cold War Studies* 8.3 (2006a).

McMahon, Robert J. *The Cold War on the Periphery: The United States, India, and Pakistan* (New York: Columbia University Press, 1994).

McMahon, Robert J. "The Danger of Geopolitical Fantasies: Nixon, Kissinger, and the South Asia Crisis of 1971," in *Nixon in the World: American Foreign Relations, 1969-1977*, ed. Fredrik Logevall and Andrew Preston (New York: Oxford University Press, 2008), 249-268.

McMahon, Robert J. "Food as a Diplomatic Weapon: The Indian Wheat Loan of 1951," in *Pacific Historical Review* 56.3 (1987): 349-377.

McMahon, Robert J. "Toward Disillusionment and Disengagement in South Asia," in *Lyndon Johnson Confronts the World: American Foreign Policy, 1963-1968*, ed. Warren I. Cohen and Nancy Bernkopf Tucker (New York: Cambridge University Press, 1994), 135-171.

Mehrotra, Santosh. *India and the Soviet Union: Trade and Technology Transfer* (Cambridge: Cambridge University Press, 1990).

Meller, Hellen E. "Urbanization and the Introduction of Modern Town Planning Ideas in India, 1900-1925," in *Economy and Society. Essays in Indian Economic and Social History*, ed. Kirti N. Chaudhuri and C. J. Dewey (Delhi: Oxford University Press, 1979), 330-50.

Meller, Hellen E. *Patrick Geddes. Social Evolutionist and City Planner* (London etc.: Routledge, 1990).

Menon, C. Achutha. *The Kerala Agrarian Relations Bill* (New Delhi: Communist Party Publ., 1958).

Menon, C. Achutha. *Three Years in Office* (Trivandrum: Government of Kerala, 1973).

Menon, M. G. K. "Homi J. Bhabha, 1909-1966," in *Royal Institution of Great Britain. Proceedings* 41 (1967): 426.

Merrill, Dennis. *Bread and the Ballot: The United States and India's Economic Development, 1947-1963* (Chapel Hill: University of North Carolina Press, 1990).

Metcalf, Thomas R. *An Imperial Vision: Indian Architecture and the British Raj* (Delhi etc: Oxford University Press, 2002).

"Mighty Advance of the National Liberation Movement in the Colonial and Dependent Countries," in *For a Lasting Peace, For a People's Democracy*, (1950), January 27.

Mishra, Surjya Kanta. "On Agrarian Transition in West Bengal," in *The Marxist* 23.2 (2007): 1-22.

Misra, Kashir Prasad. *India's Policy of Recognition of States and Governments* (Bombay: Allied Pubs, 1966).

Mitscherlich, Alexander. *Die Unwirtlichkeit unserer Städte. Anstiftung zum Unfrieden* (Frankfurt am Main: Suhrkamp, 1965).

Mohr, Marcus. *Waffen für Israel: westdeutsche Rüstungshilfe vor dem Sechstagekrieg* (Berlin: Köster, 2003).

Monshipouri, Mahmoud. "Backlash to the Destruction at Ayodhya: A View from Pakistan," in *Asian Survey* 33.7 (1993a), 711-721.

Morehouse, W. "Nehru and Science: The Vision of New India," in *Indian Journal of Public Administration* 15 (1969): 48 ff.

Morehouse, W. *Science in India. Institution Building and the Organizational System for Research and Development* (Bombay: Popular Prakashan, 1971).

Morris, Morris D. "The Growth of Large-Scale Industry to 1947," in *The Cambridge Economic History of India*, Vol, II (Cambridge: Cambridge University Press, 1983), 553-676.

Mountbatten Award and After. Political Resolution of the Central Committee of the Communist Party of India (Bombay: Peoples Publication House, 1947).

Mukherji, Rahul. "Appraising the Legacy of Bandung: A View from India," in eds. Seng Tan and Amitav Acharya *Bandung Revisited: The Legacy of the 1955 Asian-African Conference for International Order* (Singapore: NUS Press, 2008), 160-179.

Mumford, Eric. *The CIAM Discourse on Urbanism, 1928-1960* (Cambridge and London: MIT Press, 2000).

Munro, Ross H. "India: The Awakening of an Asian Power," in *Time*, 3 April 1989.

Munshi, Shoma. *Prime Time Soap Operas on Indian Television* (New Delhi: Routledge, 2010).

Murti, M.N. et al., *Social Cost-Benefit Analysis of Delhi Metro* (Delhi: Institute of Economic Growth, 2006).

Naidu, G.V.C. "The Indian Navy and Southeast Asia," in *Contemporary Southeast Asia* 13.1 (June 1991): 72-85.

Nair, Tara S. "Growth and Structural Transformation of Newspaper Industry in India: An Empirical Investigation," in *Economic and Political Weekly* 38.39 (27 Sep 2003): 4182-4189.

Najjar, Fauzi M. "The Debate on Islam and Secularism in Egypt," in *Arab Studies Quarterly (ASQ)* 18 (1996): 1-25.

Namboodiripad, E. M. S.: *Agrarian Reforms. A Study of the Congress and Communist Approach* (Bombay: CP Publication, 1956).

Namboodripad, E. M. S. *The Communist Party in Kerala* (New Delhi: National Book Centre, 1994).

Namboodripad, E. M. S. *On the Agrarian Question in India* (Bombay: PPH, 1952).

Namboodiripad, E. M. S.: *A Short History of the Peasant Movement in Kerala* (Bombay: Peoples Publication House, 1943).

Nanda, B. R. (ed.). *Science and Technology in India* (New Delhi: Vikas, 1977).

Naregal, Veena. "Cable Communications in Mumbai: integrating corporate interests with local and media networks," in *Contemporary South Asia* 9.3 (2000): 289-314.

Naregal, Veena. *Language, Politics, Elites, and the Public Sphere: Western India under Colonialism* (New Delhi: Permanent Black, 2001).

Nayar, Baldev Raj: "Nationalist Planning for Autarchy and State Hegemony. Development Strategy under Nehru," in *Globalization and Politics in India*, ed. by idem (New Delhi: Oxford University Press, 2007), 161-195.

Needell, Allan A. ""Truth Is Our Weapon: Project TROY, Political Warfare, and Government-Academic Relations in the National Security State," in *Diplomatic History* 17.3 (July 1993): 399-420.

Nehru, Jawaharlal. *Letters to Chief Ministers*, Vol. 1-5 (London: Oxford Univ. Press, 1985).

Nehru, Jawaharlal. *Selected Works of Jawaharlal Nehru*, Second Series, (New Delhi: Oxford University Press, 1985 ff.).

Nehru, Jawaharlal. *The Official Languages: Jawaharlal Nehru's Speeches 1949-1968* (New Delhi: Publications Division, Ministry of Information and Broadcasting, Government of India, 1963).

Neyazi, Taberez Ahmed. "Cultural imperialism or vernacular modernity? Hindi newspapers in a globalizing India," in *Media Culture Society* 32.6 (2010): 907-924.

Nihal Singh, Surendra: *The Yogi and the Bear: Story of Indo-Soviet Relations* (New Delhi: Allied Publ., 1986).

Nilekani, Nandan, *Imagining India. Ideas for the New Century* (London: Penguin 2010).

Ninan, Sevanti. *Headlines from the Heartland: Reinventing the Hindi Public Sphere* (New Delhi: Sage, 2007).

Ninan, Sevanti. *Through the Magic Window: Television and Change in India* (New Delhi: Penguin Books, 1995).

Noorani, A. G. "India's Quest for a Nuclear Guarantee," in *Asian Survey* 7.7 (July 1967): 490-502.

Nossiter, T. J. *Communism in Kerala* (New Delhi: OUP, 1982).

Özden, Caglar and Mirvat Sewadeh, "How Important is Migration?" in *The Poor Half Billion*, ed. Ghani.

Oswald, Hans. *Die überschätzte Stadt: Ein Beitr. d. Gemeindesoziologie zum Städtebau* (Freiburg i. B.: Phil. Fak. Diss., 1965).

Overstreet, Gene D. and Marshal Windmiller. *Communism in India* (Berkeley: University of California Press, 1959).

Padhi, Kulamani, "Agricultural Labour in India – A Close Look," in *Orissa Review*, (2007): 23-28.

Pandey, Gyanendra. *The Ascendancy of the Congress in Uttar Pradesh: A Study in Imperfect Mobilization* (Delhi: Oxford University Press, 1978).

Panikkar, K M. *In Two Chinas: Memoirs of a Diplomat* (London: George Allen & Unwin, 1955).

Papanek, Gustav. "Foreign Advisors and Planning Agencies," in *The Crisis in Planning: The Issues*, edited by Mike Faber and Dudley Seers (London: Chatto and Windus, 1972), 172-187.

Pardesi, Manjeet S. "Instability in Tibet and the Sino-Indian Strategic Rivalry: Do Domestic Politics Matter?" in *Asian Rivalries: Conflict, Escalation, and Limitations on Two-level Games*, ed. Sumit Ganguly and William R Thompson (Stanford: Stanford University Press, 2011).

Pardesi, Manjeet S. "Southeast Asia in Indian Foreign Policy: Positioning India as a Major Power in Asia," in *India's Foreign Policy: Retrospect and Prospect*, ed. Sumit Ganguly (New Delhi: Oxford University Press, 2010).

Patel, Sujata and Alice Thorner (eds.), *Bombay: Metaphor for Modern India* (Delhi etc: Oxford University Press, 1996).

Paul, T. V. "The Enduring Sino-Pakistani Nuclear/Missile Relationship and the Balance of Power Logic," in *Nonproliferation Review* 10 (Summer 2003).

Penney, Lord. Homi Jehangir Bhabha, 1909-1967," in *Biographical Memoirs of Fellows of the Royal Society* 13 (1967): 39 ff.

Perkovich, George. *India's Nuclear Bomb: The Impact on Global Proliferation* (Berkeley: University of California Press, 1999).

Pevehouse, Jon C. "Democracy from the Outside-In? International Organizations and Democratization," in *International Organization* 56.3 (2002): 515-549.

Polanyi, Karl. *The Great Transformation* (New York: Farrar & Rinehart, Inc., 1944).

Posen, Barry. "The Security Dilemma and Ethnic Conflict," in *Survival* 35:1, (1993): 27-47.

Prakash, Gyan. *Another Reason: Science and the Imagination of Modern India* (Princeton, N.J: Princeton University Press, 1999).

Prashad, Vijay. *Everybody was Kung Fu Fighting: Afro-Asian Connections and the Myth of Cultural Purity* (Boston: Beacon Press, 2001).

Prashad, Vijay. *The Karma of Brown Folk* (Minneapolis, MN: University of Minnesota Press, 2000).

Prakash, Vikramaditya. *Chandigarh's Le Corbusier. The struggle for Modernity in Postcolonial India* (Seattle, Washington: University of Washington Press, 2002).

Priya, Ritu, "Town Planning, Public Health and Delhi's Urban Poor," in *Urban Studies*, ed. Sujata Patel and Kushal Deb (Delhi: Oxford University Press, 2006), 223-48.

Pucher, John, et al. "Urban Transport Crisis in India," in *Transport Policy* 12 (2005), 185-98.

Punathambekar, Aswin. "Bollywood in the Indian-American Diaspora: Mediating a Transitive Logic of Cultural Citizenship," in *International Journal of Cultural Studies*, 8.2 (2005): 151-173.

Puri, Balraj. "Indian Muslims since Partition," in *Economic and Political Weekly* 28.40 (2 October 1993), 2143-4.

Quraishi, Zaheer Masood. "Electoral Strategy of a Minority Pressure Group: The Muslim-E-Mushawarat," in *Asian Survey* 8.12 (December 1968): 976-987.

Quraishi, Zaheer Masood. "Emergence and Eclipse of Muslim Majlis-e-Mushawarat," in *Economic and Political Weekly* 6.25 (1971), 1229-1234.

Racioppi, Linda. *Soviet Policy towards South Asia since 1970* (Cambridge: Cambridge University Press, 1994).

Raghavan, G.N.S. *The Press in India: A New History* (New Delhi: Gyan Publishing House, 1994).

Raghavan, Srinath. *War and Peace in Modern India* (London: Palgrave Macmillan, 2010).

Raghavan, V. R. *Conflict without End* (New Delhi: Viking, 2002).

Raghuram, Parvati and Ajaya J. Sahoo. "Thinking "Indian Diaspora" for our Time," in *Tracing the Indian Diaspora: Contexts, Memories and Representations,* ed. Parvati Raghuram, Ajaya J. Sahoo, Brij Maharaj, and Dave Sangha (New Delhi: Sage Publications, 2008): 1-20.

Rahman, A. and K. D. Sharma (eds.). *Science Policy Studies* (Bombay: Somaiya Publ., 1974).

Raj Nayar, Baldev. *Minority Politics in the Punjab* (Princeton: Princeton University Press, 1966).

Rajagopal, Arvind. "Consumer Identity and Image-Based Politics," in *Economic and Political Weekly* 29.27 (2 July 1994): 1659-1668.

Rajagopal, Arvind. *Politics After Television: Hindu Nationalism and the Reshaping of the India Public* (Cambridge: Cambridge University Press, 2001).

Rajimwale, Anil: *Life and Works of P. C. Joshi* (New Delhi: PPH, 2007).

Ram, Anjali. "Framing the Feminine: Diasporic Readings of Gender in Popular Indian Cinema," in *Women's Studies in Communication* 25.1 (2002): 28–39.

Ram, Anjali. *Gender, Diaspora and Bollywood: Readings Out of Place (*New York: Peter Lang, forthcoming).

Ramachandran, K N. "India-Indonesia Relations: 1947-1975," in *Self-Reliance and National Reliance,* ed. K. Subrahmanyam (New Delhi: Abhinav Publications, 1975), 147-158.

Ramadorai, Tarun and Sanjoy Bhattacharya. "India: State Censorship and the Indian 'Emergency' of 1975-77," in *Censorship: A World Encyclopedia*, ed. Derek Jones, Vol. 2, E-K, (London, Chicago: Fitzroy Dearborn Publ., 2001), 1173-1176.

Ramanna, R. "Development of Nuclear Energy in India," in T. T. Poulose (ed.), *Perspectives of India's Nuclear Policy* (New Delhi: Young Asia Publ., 1978), 1 ff.

Ranadive, B. T. "Lessons of Kerala," in *New Age*, September, 1959.

Rangaswamy, Padma. *Namaste America: Indian Immigrants in an American Metropolis* (Pennsylvania: Pennsylvania State University Press, 2000).

Ravindran, K.T. "A Stage of Siege. How Four Decades of Official Apathy, Corruption and Distorted Plan Implementation Have Resulted in a Royal Mess in Delhi," *Frontline* 17,25, http://www.frontlineonnet.com/fl1725/17251160.htm.

Rawat, Vidya Bhusan. *Press & Prejudice: An Insightful Analysis of Hindi Media* (New Delhi: Institute of Objective Studies, 2003).

"Record of the Discussions of J.V. Stalin with the Representatives of the C.C. of the Communist Party of India, Comrades Rao, Dange, Ghosh and Punnaiah, on 9th February, 1951," in *Revolutionary Democracy* 12.2 (2006).

"Record of the Discussions of Rajani Palme Dutt with M.K. Gandhi, Sardar Patel and Jawaharlal Nehru, (1946)," in *Revolutionary Democracy*, 11.2 (2005).

Reeves, Peter, Graham B.D. and Goodman J.M. *A Handbook to Elections in Uttar Pradesh 1920-1951* (Delhi: Manohar, 1975).

Reichow, Hans Bernhard. *Die autogerechte Stadt* (Ravensburg: Maier, 1959).

Reichow, Hans Bernhard. *Organische Baukunst* (Braunschweig: Westermann, 1949).

Richards, N. *Sir Shanti Swarup Bhatnagar: A Biographical Study of India's Eminent Scientist* (Devnagar: New Book Society, 1948).

Roeder, Philip. "Power-Dividing as an Alternative to Ethnic Power-Sharing," in *Sustainable Peace: Democracy and Power-Sharing Institutions after Civil Wars* ed. Philip Roeder and Donald Rothchild (Ithaca: Cornell University Press, 2005).

Rosen, George. *Western Economists and Eastern Societies: Agents of Change in South Asia, 1950-1970* (Baltimore: Johns Hopkins University Press, 1985).

Rosenberg, Göran. "Das Journalisten-Ich," in *Lettre* (German edition) 62.3 (Autumn 2003): 110-112.

Rostow, W. W. *Eisenhower, Kennedy, and Foreign Aid* (Austin: University of Texas Press, 1985).

Rothermund, Dietmar, *India in the Great Depression, 1929-1939* (New Delhi: Manohar, 1992).

Rothermund, Dietmar, *India: The Rise of an Asian Giant* (New Haven and London: Yale University Press, 2008).

Rothermund, Dietmar, "The Industrialization of India: Technology and Production," in *Economic History of India from Eighteenth to Twentieth Century*, ed. Binay Bhushan Chaudhuri (New Delhi: Centre for Studies in Civilization, 2005), 437-524.

Rothermund, Dietmar (ed.), *Liberalising India. Progress and Problems* (New Delhi: Manohar, 1996).

Rowe, Colin and Koetter, Fred. *Collage City* (Cambridge, Massachusetts: MIT Press, 1978).

Roy-Chaudhury, Rahul. *Sea Power and Indian Security* (London: Brassey's, 1995).

Rudolph, Lloyd I, and Susanne Hoeber Rudolph. *In Pursuit of Lakshmi: The Political Economy of the Indian State* (Chicago: University of Chicago Press, 1987).

Rudra, Ashok. *Prasanta Chandra Mahalanobis: A Biography* (Delhi: Oxford University Press, 1996).

Rudra, Nita. "Globalization and the Strengthening of Democracy in the Developing World," in *American Journal of Political Science* 49.4 (2005): 704-730.

Rudurappa, Sharmilla. *Ethnic Routes to Becoming American: Indian Immigrants and the Culture of Citizenship* (New Brunswick, NJ: Rutgers University Press, 2004).

Rushdie, Salman. *The Satanic Verses* (Dover, Delaware: The Consortium, 1992).

Saavala, Meena, *Middle-Class Moralities. Everyday Struggle over Belonging and Prestige in India* (Hyderabad: Orient Black Swan 2010).

Sachs, Wolfgang, ed. *The Development Dictionary: A Guide to Knowledge as Power*. 2nd ed. (London: Zed Books, 2010).

Safran, William. "Diaspora in Modern Societies: Myths of Homeland and Return," in *Diaspora* 1.1 (1991): 83-99.

Saha, Meghnad, "Technological Revolution in Industry - How the Russians did it," in *Science and Culture* 8 (1943): 398.

Sambanis, Nicholas and Annalisa Zinn, "From Protest to Violence: Conflict Escalation in Self-Determination Movements," (unpublished paper, 2006).

Sangal, O. P. *Telengana and the Rajeshwar Rao Leadership* (Allahabad, 1951).

Sankhdher, M.M. *Secularism in India: Dilemmas and Challenges* (New Delhi: Deep & Deep Publ., 1995).

Sardesai, D R. *Indian Foreign Policy in Cambodia, Laos, and Vietnam* (Berkeley, CA: University of California Press, 1968).

Sarin, Madhu, "Chandigarh as a Place to Live in," in *The Open Hand. Essays on LeCorbusier* ed. Russel Walden (Cambridge and London: MIT Press 1977), 374-411.

Sarin, Madhu. *Urban Planning in the Third World. The Chandigarh Experience* (Oxford: Mansell Publishers 1982).

Sartori, Andrew. *Bengal in Global Concept History: Culturalism in the Age of Capital* (Chicago: University of Chicago Press, 2008).

Sathyamurthy, T. V. *Industry and Agriculture in India since Independence. Social Change and Political Discourse in India* (Delhi: Oxford University Press, 1995).

Schneider, Nadja-Christina. "Media culture, advertising and consumerism in India," in *Rising India – Europe's Partner?* ed. Klaus Voll and Doreen Beierlein (Berlin: Weissensee, 2006), 819-833.

Schneider, Nadja-Christina. *Zur Darstellung von 'Kultur' und 'kultureller Differenz' im indischen Mediensystem. Die indische Presse und die Repräsentation des Islams im Rahmen der Zivilrechtsdebatte, 1985-87 und 2003* (Berlin: Logos, 2005).

Schwartzberg, Joseph. "Factors in the Linguistic Reorganization of Indian States," in *Region and Nation in India*, ed. Paul Wallace (New Delhi: Oxford University Press, 1985).

Scott, James C. *Seeing like a State. How Certain Schemes to Improve the Human Condition Have Failed* (New Haven, London: Yale University Press, 1998).

Seers, Dudley. "Why Visiting Economists Fail," in *The Journal of Political Economy* 70.4 (1962): 325-338.

Sen, Mohit (ed.), *Documents of the History of the Communist Party of India, Vol. VIII: 1951-1956* (New Delhi: PPH, 1977).

Sen Gupta, Bhabani. "Waiting for India: India's Role as a Regional Power," *Journal of International Affairs* 29.2 (1975): 171-184.

Sengupta, Ranjana, *Delhi Metropolitan. The Making of an Unlikely City* (New Delhi: Penguin Books India, 2007).

Sert, Jose Luis. *Can our Cities Survive? An ABC of Urban Problems, their Analysis, their Solutions* (Nendeln: Kraus, 1979).

Shah, K. T. *National Planning, Principles & Administration* (Bombay: Vora, 1948).

Shaikh, Farzana. *Community and Consensus in Islam: Muslim Representation in Colonial India, 1860-1947* (Cambridge: Cambridge University Press, 1989).

Shakya, Tsering. *The Dragon in the Land of the Snows: A History of Modern Tibet since 1947* (New York: Penguin, 1999).

Sharan, Awadhandra, "Claims on Cleanliness. Environment and Justice in Contemporary Delhi," in *Sarai Reader 02: The Cities of Everyday Life* (Delhi/Amsterdam: Sarai Media Lab, 2002), 31-7.

Sharma, Andrew. "India and Its Media: Commercialization, Liberalization and Democratization," in *Global Media Economics: Commercialization, Concentration and Integration of World Media Markets*, ed. Alan B. Albarran and Sylvia M. Chan-Olmsted (Iowa: Iowa State University Press, 1998), 255-265.

Sharma, D. *India's Nuclear Estate* (New Dehli: Lancers Intern., 1983).

Sharma, Shri Ram. *India-China Relations, 1972-1991, Part II* (New Delhi: Discovery Publishing House, 2003).

Sharpe, J. "Gender, Nation, and Globalization in *Monsoon Wedding* and *Dilwale Dulhania Le Jayenge*," in *Meridians: Feminism, Race, Transnationalism*, 6.1 (2005): 58-81.

Sharpe, Jenny. "Is the United States Postcolonial? Transnationalism, Immigration, and Race," in *Diaspora*, 4.2 (1995): 181-197.

Shuval, Judith. "Diaspora migration: Definitional Ambiguities and a Theoretical Paradigm" in *Sociology of Diaspora: A Reader Vol. 1* ed. Ajaya K. Sahoo and Brij Maharaj (Jaipur, India: Rawat Publication, 2007), 28-42.

Siedler, Wolf Jobst et al. *Die gemordete Stadt. Abgesang auf Putte und Straße, Platz und Baum* (Berlin: Herbig,1964).

Siemiatycki, Matti, "Message in a Metro: Building Urban Rail Infrastructure and Image in Delhi, India," in *International Journal of Urban and Regional Research* 30.2 (2006): 277-92.

Singh, A.I. *The Origins of the Partition of India* (Oxford: Oxford University Press, 1987).

Singh, B. (ed.). *Jawaharlal Nehru on Science and Society: A Collection of his Writings and Speeches* (New Delhi, 1988).

Singh, Brijeshwar. "Memories," in *D School: Reflections on the Delhi School of Economics*. Ed. Dharma Kumar and Dilip Mukherjee. (Delhi: Oxford University Press, 1995).

Singh, Gurpahal. *Ethnic Conflict in India: A Case-Study of Punjab* (London: Macmillan, 2000).

Singh, J. (ed.). *Management of Scientific Research* (Bombay: Popular Prakashan, 1973).

Singh, J.: *Some Eminent Indian Scientists* (Delhi: GoI, 1991).

Singh, Sanjay K., "Review of Urban Transportation in India," in *Journal of Public Transport* 8.1 (2005), 79-97.

Singh, T. *Indian Parliament: Authentic, Comprehensive and Illustrated Biographical Dictionary of Members of the two Houses of Parliament* (New Delhi: GoI, ca. 1957).

Singhal, Arvind and Everett M. Rogers. *India's Communication Revolution: From Bullock Carts to Cyber Marts* (New Delhi: Sage, 2001).

Smith, C.: *India's ad hoc Arsenal: Direction or Drift in Defence Policy?* (Oxford: Oxford Univ. Press, 1994).

Sobolev, A. I. *People's Democracy, a New Form of Political Organization of Society* (Moscow: Foreign Languages Publ. House, 1954).

Sobolev, A. I. et al. (eds.), *Outline History of the Communist International* (Moscow: Progress Publishers, 1971).

Som, Reba. "Jawaharlal Nehru and the Hindu Code: A Victory of Symbol over Substance?" in *Modern Asian Studies,* 28.1 (1994), 165-194.

Sonwalkar, Prasun. "India: Makings of Little Cultural/Media Imperialism?" in *Gazette* 63.6 (2001b): 505-519.

Sonwalkar, Prasun. "'Murdochization' of the Indian press: From by-line to bottom-line," in *Media, Culture and Society* 24.6 (2002): 821-834.

Sonwalkar, Prasun. "Opposition to the Entry of the Foreign Press in India, 1991-1995: The Hidden Agenda," in *Modern Asian Studies* 35.3 (2001a): 743-763.

Sridharan, Kripa. *The ASEAN Region in India's Foreign Policy* (Aldershot: Dartmouth Publishing Company, 1996).

Ståhlberg, Per. *Lucknow Daily: How a Hindi Newspaper Constructs society* (Stockholm: Almqvist & Wiksell, 2002).

Stalin, I. V. *Sochinenia*, Vol. 16, 1 (Moscow: Izd. ITRK, 2011).

Stargardt, A. W. "The Emergence of the Asian System of Powers," in Modern Asian Studies 23.3 (1989): 561-595.

„Stenographic Record of the Discussion of the Members of the Committee of the CC VKP (B) with the Representatives of the CC Communist Party of

India on 4th and 6th February 1951", in *Revolutionary Democracy*, 12.2 (2006).

Stepan, Alfred. "Federalism, Multi-National Societies, and 'State Nation", in *Democracy and Diversity: India and the American Experience*, ed. K. Shankar Bajpai, (Delhi: Oxford University Press, 2007), 225-261.

Stepan, Alfred; Linz, Juan and Yogendra Yadav. *Crafting State-Nations: India and Other Multinational Democracies* (Baltimore: The Johns Hopkins University Press, 2011).

The Struggle for Full Independence and People's Democracy. Communist Party Statement of Policy (Bombay: People's Publishing House, 1947).

"The Struggle for People's Democracy and Socialism – Some Questions of Strategy and Tactics," in *Communist*, 2 (1949).

Stueck, William. *The Korean War: An International History* (Princeton: Princeton University Press, 1995).

Subrahmanyam, K. *India and the Nuclear Challenge* (New Delhi: Lancer Intern., 1986).

Subramanian, Narendra. *Ethnicity and Populist Mobilization: Political Parties, Citizens, and Democracy in South India* (Oxford: Oxford University Press, 1999).

Sunaina, Maira and M. *Desis in the House: Indian American Youth Culture in New York City* (Philadelphia: Temple University Press, 2002).

Sundaram, Ravi. *Pirate Modernity. Delhi's Media Urbanism* (London and New York: Routledge, 2010).

Sundarayya, Putchalapalla. *An Autobiography*, ed. by Atlury Murali (New Delhi: National Book Trust, 2009).

Sundarayya, Putchalapalla. *My Resignation* (New Delhi: India Publishers & Distributors, 1991).

Suryanarayan, V. "Looking Ahead: India and Southeast Asia in the 1990s, New Perspectives, New Challenges," in *India and Southeast Asia,* ed. Ghoshal (New Delhi: Konark Publishers in association with India International Centre, 1996).

Tan Eng Bok, Georges. "How Does the PLA Cope with 'Regional Conflict' and 'Local War'?" in *China's Military: The PLA in 1990/91* ed. Richard H Yang, (Kaohsiung: National Sun Yat-sen University, 1991).

Tarlo, Emma, *Unsettling Memories. Narratives of the Emergency in Delhi* (London: Hurst & Company, 2003).

Tarrow, Sydney. *Power in Movement: Social Movements and Contentious Politics* (Cambridge: Cambridge University Press, 1998).

Thakur, Ramesh. "India's Vietnam Policy, 1946-1979," in *Asian Survey* 19.10 (October 1979): 957-976.

Thakur, Ramesh. *The Politics and Economics of India's Foreign Policy* (London: Hurst, 1994).

Thakurdas, Purshotamdas. *A Brief Memorandum Outlining a Plan of Economic Development for India* (Harmondsworth: Penguin books, 1944).

Tharoor, Sashi. *Reasons of State: Political Development and India's Foreign Policy under Indira Gandhi, 1966-1977* (New Delhi: Vikas, 1982).

That Thien, Ton. *India and South East Asia, 1947-1960* (Genève: Librairie Droz, 1963).

Theoharis, Athan G, ed. *The Central Intelligence Agency: Security under Scrutiny* (Westport, Conn: Greenwood Press, 2006).

Thomas, Amos Owen and Keval Kumar. "Copied from without and cloned from within: India in the global television format business," in *Television across Asia: Television industries, programme formats and globalization*, ed. Albert Moran and Michael Keane (London, New York: Routledge, 2004), 122-137.

Thomas, Raju G C. "Energy Politics and Indian Security," in *Pacific Affairs* 55.1 (Spring 1982): 32-53.

Thomas, Raju G C. "The Indian Navy in the Seventies," in *Pacific Affairs* 48.4 (Winter 1975-1976): 500-518.

Thomas, Raju G C. "Nonalignment and Indian Security: Nehru's Rationale and Legacy," in *Journal of* Strategic Studies 2.2 (1979): 153-171.

"Three Letters from the CPI to J.V. Stalin with the Handwritten Comments of the Soviet Leader, February 14, 1951," in *Revolutionary Democracy* 16.1 (2010).

Toft, Monica. The Geograp*hy of Ethnic Violence*: *Identity, Interests, and the Indivisibility of Territory* (Princeton: Princeton University Press, 2003).

Tölöyan, Kachig. "Rethinking Diaspora(s): Stateless Power in the Transnational Moment," in *Diaspora 5* (1996): 3-35.

Tomlinson, John. "Internationalismus, Globalisierung und kultureller Imperialismus," in Grundlagentexte zur transkulturellen Kommunikation, ed. Andreas Hepp and Martin Löffelholz (Konstanz: UVK, 2002), 140-163.

Tripathi, Manjul Rani. *India's Foreign Policy on Diplomatic Recognition of States and Governments* (Delhi: B. R. Publ., 1990).

Tse-tung, Mao. *Agrarian Reform and People's Victory in China* (Bombay: PPH, 1948).

Unger, Corinna R. "Rourkela, ein 'Stahlwerk im Dschungel' Industrialisierung, Modernisierung, und Entwicklungshilfe im Kontext von Dekolonisation und Kaltem Krieg (1950-1970)" *Archiv für Sozialgeschichte* 48 (2008): 367-388.

Valdés, Juan Gabriel. *Pinochet's Economists: The Chicago School of Economics in Chile* (Cambridge: Cambridge Univesity Press, 1995).

Van Der Veer, Peter. *Religious Nationalism: Hindus and Muslims in India* (Berkeley: University of California Press, 1994).

Vardhe, Ashwini. "Clash of Titans," in *Society* (Oct 2003): 108-110.

Varga, E. *Izmeneniya v ekonomike kapitalizma v itoge vtoroi mirovoi voiny* (Moscow: Goz. Izd. Politicheskoi Literatury, 1946).

Varshney, Ashutosh, and Sidiq Ahmed. *Battles Half Won: The Political Economy of India's Growth and Economic Policy since Independence* (Washington: Commission on Growth and Development, 2008).

Verma, Ajay. "Chandigar cleanest of all," in *Rediff News,* July 29, 2011.

Vertovec, Steven. "Conceiving and Researching Transnationalism," in *Ethnic and Racial Studies*, 22.2 (1999): 447-462.

Viva, Ona Bartkus, *The Dynamic of Secession* (Cambridge: Cambridge University Press, 1999).

Voigt, Johannes H. *Die Indienpolitik der DDR. Von den Anfängen bis zur Anerkennung (1952-1972)* (Köln: Böhlau, 2008).

Waheguru, Pal Singh Sidhu and Jing-dong Yuan, *China and India: Cooperation or Conflict?* (Boulder, CO: Lynne Rienner Publishers, 2003).

Walker, Connor, *Ethnonationalism: The Quest for Understanding* (Princeton: Princeton University Press, 1993).

Walter, Barbara. "Information, uncertainty, and the decision to secede." *International Organization* 60:1 (2006): 105-135.

Walter, Barbara. *Reputation and Civil War: Why Separatist Conflicts Are So Violent* (Cambridge: Cambridge University Press, 2009).

Walton-Roberts, Margaret. "Globalization, national autonomy and non-resident Indians," in *Contemporary South Asia* 13.1 (March 2004): 53-69.

Ward, Michael. *Quantifying the World: UN Ideas and Statistics* (Bloomington: Indiana University Press, 2004).

Watt, Carey A. and Michael Mann (ed.), *Civilizing Missions in Colonial and Postcolonial South Asia: From Improvement to Development* (London: Anthem Press, 2011).

Weber, Eugene. *Peasants into Frenchmen: The Modernization of Rural France 1870-1914* (Stanford: Stanford University Press, 1976).

Weber, Max. *Economy and Society* (Berkeley: University of California Press, 1968).

Webster, Neil. "Panchayati Raj in West Bengal: Popular Participation for the People or the Party?" in *Development and Change* 23.4 (1992): 129-163.

Weiner, Myron. *Party Building in a New Nation: The Indian National Congress* (Chicago: University of Chicago Press, 1967).

Weiss, Anita M. "Women's Position in Pakistan: Socio-Cultural Effects of Islamization," in *Pacific Affairs* 25.8 (August 1985): 863-80.

Werbner, Pnina. "The Place which is Diaspora: Citizenship Religion, and Gender in the Making of Chaordic Transnationalism," in *Sociology of Diaspora: A Reader*, *Vol. 2*, ed. Ajaya K. Sahoo, and Brij Maharaj (Jaipur, India: Rawat Publication, 2007), 643-662.

White, Peter, *Public Transport. Its Planning, Management and Operation* (London: University College London Press, 1995).

Widmalm, Sven. *Kashmir In Comparative Perspective: Democracy And Violent Separatism In India* (New York: Routledge, 2002).

Wilkinson, Steven. "India, Consociational Theory and Ethnic Violence," in *Asian Survey,* 40.5 (2000): 767-91.

Wilkinson, Steven I. *Votes and Violence: Electoral Competition and Ethnic Riots in India* (Cambridge: Cambridge University Press, 2006).

Wittner, L. S. *One World or None. A History of the World Nuclear Disarmament Movement through 1953*, Vol. 1 (Stanford: Stanford Univ. Press, 1993).

Wolfrum, Sophie. "Funktionale Stadt: Patchwork City," in *Multiple City. Stadtkonzepte 1908-2008* ed. idem and Winfried Nerdinger, (Berlin: Jovis, 2008).

Wolpert, Stanley. *Jinnah of Pakistan* (New York: Oxford University Press, 1984).

Xiaoming Zhang, "China's 1979 War with Vietnam: A Reassessment," in *The China Quarterly* 184 (2005): 851-874.

XX. S"ezd Kommunisticheskoi Partii Sovetskogo Soyuz (Moscow: Gosudarstvennoi izdatel'stvo politicheskoi literatury, 1956).

Zachariah, Benjamin. *Developing India: An Intellectual and Social History, C. 1930-50.* (New Delhi: Oxford University Press, 2005).

Zachariah, Benjamin. *Nehru.* (London; New York: Routledge, 2004).

Zelizer, Barbie. "Reading the Past Against the Grain: The Shape of Memory Studies," in *Critical Studies of Mass Communication* 12.2 (1995): 214-239.

Zimmermann, Clemens. *Die Zeit der Metropolen. Urbanisierung und Großstadtentwicklung* (Frankfurt am Mail: Fischer Verlag, 1996).

Zinkin, T. *Challenges in India* (London: Chatto & Windus 1966).

About the authors

Sunil Bhatia is an associate professor of human development. His research examines how globalization and transnational migration have redefined the meaning of culture, identity, and acculturation in the field of cultural psychology. He has published over 25 articles and book chapters on issues related to self, immigrant identity, and cultural psychology. His publications include a book, *American Karma: Race, Culture and Identity in the Indian Diaspora* (2007, New York University Press) and other articles, such as "Strategic subversions of the sacred: The cultural psychology of religious identities" (in press, *Culture and Psychology*) and "Darwin on race, gender, and culture" (2009, *American Psychologist*).

Hans-Joachim Bieber is Professor Emeritus for Modern History at the University of Kassel, Germany. Prior to his professorship, he was head of the planning department of the University of Kassel and worked for the German Science Council. His research focuses on German social history, including the history of German Jews; history of globalization; history of the 'nuclear age'; and the history of German-Japanese cultural relations.

Nicolas Blarel is a PhD student in the Department of Political Science at Indiana University, Bloomington. His main areas of interest are International Relations and Comparative Politics, and he is particularly interested in security issues in South Asia.

Jennifer Bussell is an Assistant Professor in the Lyndon B. Johnson School of Public Affairs at the University of Texas at Austin. Her research explores the political economy of corruption and reform in India. She received her Ph.D. in Political Science from the University of California, Berkeley.

Amit Das Gupta received his PhD in history with a dissertation on West Germany's South Asia policy (1949 to 1966) from the University of Erlangen-Nürnberg. He was a special lecturer in contemporary history at the Germany Institute of the University of Amsterdam, and he worked as a senior research fellow at the Institute of Contemporary History in Berlin. He is currently working on a biography of Subimal Dutt, a high-ranking civil servant and diplomat in colonial and postcolonial India.

David C. Engerman is Professor of History at Brandeis University. He is the author of two books on American views of Russia/USSR: *Modernization from the Other Shore* (Harvard, 2003) and *Know Your Enemy* (Oxford, 2009). He has also edited two works on modernization theory: *Staging Growth* (Massachusetts, 2003) and "Modernization as a Global Project" (*Diplomatic History*, June 2009). His essay for this volume is a part of his new research on *The Global Politics of the Modern: India and the Three Worlds of the Cold War.*

William Gould is Senior Lecturer in Indian History at the University of Leeds, UK. He is the author of *Hindu Nationalism and the Language of Politics in Late Colonial India* (Cambridge, 2004), and recently worked on a collaborative AHRC funded research project with Royal Holloway, London, entitled "From Subjects to Citizens: Society and the Everyday State in India and Pakistan, 1947-1964". In connection with the latter he published *Bureaucracy, Community and Influence: Society and the State in North India, 1930-1967* (London, 2011) and *Religion and Conflict in South Asia, 1860-2000* (Cambridge, 2012).

Andreas Hilger specializes in the history of 20th-Century International Relations and on Soviet History and is working on a book about the Soviet Union's relations with South Asia since 1941. He lectures at Hamburg University and is currently working for the Independent Commission on the History of the German Intelligence Service. He is editor of *Die Sowjetunion und die Dritte Welt* (München: Oldenbourg, 2009) and co-editor of *Indo-Soviet relations: New Russian and German evidence* (Zurich: PHP 2008-2011).

Michael Mann is Professor of History and Society of South Asia at Humboldt University Berlin. He is the author of *Bengalen im Umbruch: Die Herausbildung des britischen Kolonialstaates, 1754-1793* (Stuttgart: Franz Steiner Verlag, 2000); *Geschichte Indiens: Vom 18. bis zum 21. Jahrhundert* (Paderborn: Schöningh-utb, 2005); *Sinnvolle Geschichte*: Historische Repräsentationen im neuzeitlichen Südasien (Heidelberg: Draupadi Verlag, 2009), *Geschichte Südasiens 1500 bis heute* (Darmstadt: Wissenschaftliche Buchgesellschaft, 2010) and, most recently, *Sahibs, Sklaven und Soldaten. Geschichte des* Menschenhandels *rund um den Indischen Ozean* (Darmstadt: Wissenschaftliche Buchgesellschaft/Verlag Philipp von Zabern, 2012).

Robert J. McMahon is the Ralph D. Mershon Distinguished Professor of History at Ohio State University. A specialist in the international politics of the Cold War, he is the author of several books. Those include: *Cold War on the Pe-*

riphery: The United States, India, and Pakistan (New York: Columbia University Press, 1994); *The Cold War: A Very Short Introduction* (Oxford: Oxford University Press, 2003); and *Dean Acheson and the Creation of an American World Order* (Dulles, VA: Potomac Books, 2009).

Boris Niclas-Tölle is a PhD student in history at the School of Humanities and Social Sciences of Jacobs University Bremen. His work focuses on development planning and socialist policies in South Asia in a modern global history context.

Manjeet S. Pardesi is a PhD student in the Department of Political Science at India University-Bloomington.

Srinath Raghavan is Senior Fellow at Centre for Policy Research, New Delhi. He is the author of War and Peace in Modern India: A Strategic History of the Nehru Years (Basingstoke: Palgrave Macmillan, 2010).

Anjali Ram is an Associate Professor of Global Communication at Roger Williams University, Bristol, RI. Her research examines gendered identity in the context of popular culture, migrant identity and globalization. Her publications have appeared in journals such as *International Journal of Intercultural Relations, Women's Studies in Communication, Human Development, Mind, Culture and Activity, Culture and Psychology* and in edited books such as *Mediated Women, Communicating Ethnic and Cultural Identity,* and *Sociology of the Diaspora: A Reader.* She is currently working on a book that examines how Bollywood related media practices and representations circumscribe and facilitate a re-imagining of gendered identities, cultural selves, and national belonging among first and second-gereration women and girls of the Indian diaspora.

Mohan Rao is Professor at the Centre of Social Medicine and Community Health (CSMCH), School of Social Sciences, Jawaharlal Nehru University, New Delhi. A medical doctor specialised in public health, he has written extensively on health and population policy, and on the history and politics of health and family planning. He is the author of *From Population Control to Reproductive Health: Malthusian Arithmetic* (Sage, New Delhi, 2004) and has edited *Disinvesting in Health: The World Bank's Health Prescriptions* (Sage, New Delhi, 1999) and *The Unheard Scream: Reproductive Health and Women's Lives in India* (Zubaan/Kali for Women, New Delhi, 2004). With Sarah Sexton, he is editor of *Markets and Malthus: Gender, Health and Population in Neoliberal Times* (Sage, New Delhi, 2010).

Dietmar Rothermund is Professor Emeritus of South Asian History at the South Asian Institute, University of Heidelberg. Among his major works are *India: The Rise of an Asian Giant* (2008), *The Routledge Companion to Decolonization* (2006), and *An Economic History of India* (2nd ed. 1993).

Nadja-Christina Schneider is Junior Professor for Mediality and Intermediality in Asian and African Societies at Humboldt University, Berlin. Her areas of interest include processes of medialisation and social change (focus on South Asia, especially India) and debates on gender, media and Islam.

Vijay Singh is an Associate Professor with the history department of Satyawati College at the University of Delhi. He has published on Soviet and Communist history (with contributions to *The Collapse of the Soviet Union*; *Revolutionary Democracy*). Singh is currently writing a book on Soviet economic policies between 1941 and 1961.

Corinna R. Unger is Associate Professor of Modern European History at Jacobs University Bremen, Germany. She has published on the history of development aid and modernization, philanthropy and exile, on the history of science and on the Cold War. She is currently writing a book on Indian, American and West German development approaches and practices in the post-1947 era.